Blacktino

MW00399129

Blacktino Queer Performance

E. Patrick Johnson and Ramón H. Rivera-Servera, editors

Duke University Press • Durham and London • 2016

© 2016 Duke University Press
All rights reserved
Printed in the United States of
America on acid-free paper ∞
Designed by Amy Ruth Buchanan
Typeset in Caecilia by Tseng
Information Systems, Inc.

Library of Congress Cataloging-in-Publication Data
Names: Johnson, E. Patrick, [date] editor. | Rivera-
Servera, Ramón H., [date] editor.
Title: Blacktino queer performance / E. Patrick Johnson
and Ramón H. Rivera-Servera, editors
Description: Durham : Duke University Press, 2016.
Includes bibliographical references and index.
Identifiers: LCCN 2015040884
ISBN 9780822360506 (hardcover : alk. paper)
ISBN 9780822360650 (pbk. : alk. paper)
ISBN 9780822374657 (e-book)
Subjects: LCSH: Gays and the performing arts—United States. |
Homosexuality in the theater—United States. | Gay theater—
United States. | Hispanic American theater—United States. |
African American theater—United States. | Performance. | Critical
pedagogy.
Classification: LCC PN1590.G39 B533 2016 | DDC 791.086/64—dc23
LC record available at http://lccn.loc.gov/2015040884

Cover art: Marsha P. Johnson (left) and Sylvia Rivera (right)
at the Christopher Street Liberation Day Gay Pride Parade,
New York City, June 24, 1973. Photo by Leonard Fink, courtesy
of the LGBT Community Center National History Archive.

To the foremothers,

Marsha P. Johnson and **Sylvia Rivera**

And to our companions,

Joel Valentín-Martinez and **Stephen J. Lewis**

Contents

Acknowledgments

An anthology such as this has lots of moving parts and therefore takes a collective to bring to fruition. This was particularly true with *Blacktino Queer Performance*. We would first like to thank the artists—Pamela Booker, Sharon Bridgforth, Cedric Brown, Javier Cardona, Jeffrey Q. McCune Jr., Paul Outlaw, Coya Paz, and Charles Rice-González, whose work inspired this project and some of whom performed at our Blacktino Queer Performance festival in 2008 at Northwestern University. We also say thank you to our colleagues who interviewed the artists and who critically engaged their work through the essays collected here.

We would be remiss if we did not thank our research assistants, Eddie Gamboa, Andreea Micu, Didier Morelli, and Shoniqua Roach, without whom we could not have prepared the volume for publication.

To our partners, Stephen J. Lewis and Joel Valentín-Martinez, we say thanks for putting up with us turning our vacations into research trips! We love you both!

Finally, we say thank you to our editor, Courtney Berger, who has been nothing but encouraging and excited about this project from start to finish. We hope it's the first of many collaborations with you!

Introduction

ETHNORACIAL INTIMACIES IN BLACKTINO QUEER PERFORMANCE

E. Patrick Johnson and Ramón H. Rivera-Servera

We thought we were the first Rivera/Johnson blacktino queer duo, but we are not. Long before we premiered, paraded, and pumped up our blacktino drag in the ivory tower and down the hallowed halls of Northwestern University, transgender and drag queen militants Sylvia Rivera and Marsha P. Johnson were painting the streets of New York red with their fierce self-presentation and activism, which includes participation in the Stonewall Riots of 1969. Both Rivera and Johnson serve as our blacktino drag mothers, and their friendship and commitment to social justice for queers of color reflect the "sisterhood" and political commitments shared by the editors of this volume. Born in 1951 in New York to a Puerto Rican father and Venezuelan mother, at age eleven Sylvia Rivera became homeless and lived on the streets, where she found refuge among drag queens. Despite her social class, she always served high femme face and chic shawl couture. Her coactivist friend, black drag queen Marsha P. Johnson, who was born in neighboring New Jersey in 1944, preferred a more kitsch, but nonetheless fierce look, for as she says in the film *Pay It No Mind: The Life and Times of Marsha P. Johnson*, she "never, ever, ever [did] drag seriously" because "she didn't have the money to do serious drag." Grounded by their experiences of growing up as poor, queer, outcasts, in the early 1970s Rivera and Johnson cofounded Street Transvestite Action Revolutionaries (STAR), an organization they created to support homeless young drag queens and transgender people. Queer, Latina/o, black, poor—and fierce—these two drag foremothers' stories align with the editors' personal histories, politics, collaborative spirit, and sartorial signifying.

Two nappy-headed queens—one reared in a shotgun apartment in an all-black neighborhood in the U.S. South and the other in a roomier home but no less black neighborhood in the countryside of Puerto Rico—E. Patrick and Ramón were destined to cross paths in the way that queer migrations and diasporas traffic in the uncanny and the serendipitous. One would think that E. Patrick's bad Spanish, taught to him in high school by a teacher with a severe southern drawl (e.g., she pronounced "dígame la verdad" as "DEE-go-may law-BER-dawd"), and Ramon's ignorance of black American vernacular (e.g., he did not know that a "hoopty" is an expensive car such as a Cadillac that is visually in disrepair) would prohibit them from crossing linguistic and physical borders to collaborate. And yet, it was the confluence of queer fate, orishas, and a penchant for racial drag that brought these two misfits together to initiate the blacktino bristerhood modeled by mothers Sylvia and Marsha.

When we met in the fall of 2006 during Ramón's campus visit for a job in the Department of Performance Studies at Northwestern where E. Patrick was the chair, we did not know we were kin, except through our queerness. Ramón did not know of E. Patrick's mother's ignorance about Latina/o culture when she made the occasional racist comment about "a thousand" of those "foreigners" living in the same house and "smelling bad," referring to the new population of Mexican immigrants who had moved into the family's once all-black neighborhood of public housing, despite the fact that E. Patrick's mother and her seven children all lived in a one-bedroom apartment just thirty years prior. E. Patrick did not know of Ramón's grandmother's fear of Ramón being thought of as black and her causing him to have a deviated septum because of the clothespin she clamped on his nose to keep it pointed. Ironically, this same grandmother would travel with Ramón in 2013 to North Carolina, E. Patrick's state of birth, to the North Carolina Museum of History for the annual African American Culture Celebration during the 150th anniversary of the Emancipation Proclamation.

These family "outings" to each other about race and class undergird the ways in which we are both implicated in the fictions we inherited from biological and chosen kin. Our "nappy headed" epistemologies led us to different interpretations of race and class due to the cultural contexts in which we were reared, but do not undo the persistent promiscuity with which our queerness seeks pleasure "inside" the other. Part of the pleasure is the intellectual incest that keeps us primed and ready to pursue coalitions across what might seem to be impenetrable gaps. As queer, black, and Latino performance scholars, we wanted to find a way to cull the richness of our multiple subjectivities that would allow for the confluences, comparisons, and contradictions therein. Rather than sashay away, we desired to stay and shantay our way into the troubled erotic waters of black and brown conjugal elaborations. It was through our dedication to the labor of queer production that *Blacktino Queer Performance* was born.

This collection brings together the performance scripts of black and Latina/o queer playwrights and performance artists working in the United States, along with critical essays and interviews conducted or written by leading scholars of black, Latina/o, and queer expressive practices. The volume seeks to stage a conversation between queer black and brown performance works and critical traditions. That is, we want to propose with this anthology that there is much to be gained from the particular comparative interarticulation of black and Latina/o queer expressive practices that the very term "blacktino" introduces.

From the outset it is important that we engage the three terms that compose the title of the anthology: "blacktino," "queer," and "performance." We see as productive the interanimation of these terms as they coalesce, collide, and converge variably along the promiscuous borders of race, ethnicity, gender, sexuality, and class. These terms allow us not only a way to contextualize the artists' and scholars' works that are contained between the anthology's covers but also a way to engage our interdisciplinary "homes" of black studies, Latina/o studies, queer studies, and performance studies. Indeed, each of these areas has had its share of stubborn elisions of gender, sexuality, and performance in the case of black and Latina/o studies, and race in the case of queer and performance studies. There is also evidence of ethnoracial silos in black studies around issues of *latinidad* and in Latina/o studies around issues of blackness. Concomitantly, we wish to move beyond the bourgeois academic ivory tower and engage the material conditions of the projects, barrios, dance floors, and other sites where quotidian forms of racialized queerness manifest through performance. We believe, therefore, this titular triumvirate of *Blacktino Queer Performance* provides us an opportunity to mine the discursive and material terrain that these terms always already engage—on the streets and in the sheets.

Variously spelled as "blacktino," "blaktino," or "blatino," the term accounts for both interracial subjectivities and social relations. In popular mainstream media, "blacktino" generally describes children of African American and Latino mixed heritage as well as black Latinos or Afro-Latinos with Afro-diasporic ancestry outside the U.S. national boundaries. In this sense, the term can address the historical legacy of Afro-descendant Latin American migrants to the United States as well as slightly more contemporaneous social and cultural exchanges between U.S. African American and U.S. Latina/o communities. Nonetheless, while the United States is the "common ground" upon which these black and brown artists produce their work, they also gesture well beyond U.S. borders into Cuba, Dominican Republic, Mexico, Haiti, Puerto Rico, and West Africa.

But "blacktino" has also been animated in myriad ways to point to other forms of exchange of intimacy between black and brown. The example of Marsha P. Johnson and Sylvia Rivera is one of many instances where queer leisure and queer politics converge. An important antecedent to blacktino is to be found in the Third World and women-of-color feminisms of the 1980s, which sought to develop alliances among feminists invested in critical race and postcolonial frameworks for understanding and enacting the politics of gender and sexuality and which still exists through organizations like the Audre Lorde Project and Salsa Soul Sisters in New York and Allgo in Texas. Of primary relevance to our project is the currency the term "blatino" gained in the 1990s onward as a designation for black and brown queer relations; from dance clubs like Blatino Bronx Factory, Escuelita, and Krash in New York City, Bench and Bar in Oakland, and Traxx in Atlanta; to the artistic collaborations like that of the BlakTino Festival at the Bronx Academy of Arts and Dance. "Blatino" also emerged during this period as a significant subgenre of gay porn that featured sex between Latino and African American performers. Harlem Boys, Latino Fan Club, and Enrique Cruz's Lamancha Videos are perhaps three of the best-known production companies to develop under this rubric in New York City, but the trend has developed into a more formalized network of nightlife spots, websites, blogs, porn awards, and much more. It has also extended geographically beyond New York, Philadelphia, and the rest of the northeast United States to projects as varied as the annual Blatino Oasis Retreat in Palm Springs (begun in 2006), gay escort services in Texas, and Miami's Cock Boys porn flicks featuring black and Latino performers getting jiggy with it.

Blacktino as a designation recognizes a history of cohabitation between African American and Latina/o communities, animates black and brown sexual and social intimacies in the present, and centers cultural and political desires that might yield more solidary futures. Colonization and subjugation, as well as resistance to and perseverance in the face of these structural forms of domination, mark these histories and futures of intimacy. While the black Atlantic slave trade inaugurated a nonvoluntary diaspora, one by-product of that event was not only the syncretic process of African and Latina/o American cultures, but also the queering of the Atlantic itself, as Omi'seke Natasha Tinsley has so beautifully argued.[1] It also produced various religious forms where black and brown bodies imbibe gender/queer orishas, as the work of Sharon Bridgforth captures.[2]

We are also aware of the ways in which blacktino, or the more common usage of blatino, may inaugurate a troublesome collapse of difference in the eyes of a consuming homonormative public that simply homogenizes racial otherness as fetishistic ahistorical object.[3] This is perhaps much more present in the pornography industry, but also in circulation in much of the nightclub scene, whereby blatino can run the risk of making a problematically amalgamated "colored object" available to white patrons. And it is precisely because the term "blacktino" allows us to look at all of these things at the same time—queer subjects who configure their identities as both black and brown; queer social exchanges, intimacies, and conflicts between African Americans and Latinas/os; and the historical and contemporary relationships between black and Latina/o queer communities with homonormative whiteness—that we think the term proves both adequate and generative for our collection.

It does not come as news that queer theory, from its early inception, has had some "race" trouble. The inattention to or downright hostility toward race as a category of analysis in queer studies was met with a backlash that continues.[4] Nonetheless, the capaciousness of the term "queer" was too productive to throw the baby out with the bath water—even if we wanted to kill our little darling! We agree with Jafari Sinclaire Allen's assessment that "queer does . . . uniquely capture the sense of the nonnormative status of men, women, and others who identify with or are identified as homosexual or bisexual, and those whose gender self-identification is not resonant with the sex assigned to them at birth."[5] What black and Latina/o scholars have done, then, is to make queer work by throwing shadings of meaning on it such as E. Patrick Johnson's rearticulation of "queer" as "quare" or developing new theoretical frameworks altogether. Two such examples are José Esteban Muñoz and Roderick Ferguson, who, building off of the intersectional advocacy of women-of-color feminism and performance, asked us to regard seriously the variables of race, ethnicity, and class when venturing into the focused analysis of gender and sexuality that so shaped the formation of queer theory and queer studies in the American academy. Muñoz proposed the notion of "disidentification" to explain the complicated process through which queer artists of color work on and against a system in which they are always already entrenched, while Ferguson's "queer of color critique" brings to bear an indictment of canonical sociology's incessant reinforcement of heteropatriarchy and patholo-

gizing of bodies of color as perverse.[6] Undergirding both theoretical formations is the argument that queer ethno-racial minorities, especially
when working class and/or the working poor, converge at the margins
of homonormative white culture.

No less through theory than through performance did 1970s and 1980s
feminists of color forge the physical and metaphorical "bridge" that in-
stantiated the interconnectedness of race, gender, class, and sexuality.
Nonetheless, performance studies has also had its moments of racial
amnesia, casting to the side the contributions of black and brown artists who have, arguably, been at the forefront of creative scholarly production.[7] As with queer studies, however, performance as method, object, and trope has proved useful in enunciating identity as a complex
and contested site. More germane to our project here, however, is the
fact that performance is a site at which brown and black queer cultures
share what Allen, following Marshall Sahlins, Sherry Ortner, and Stuart
Hall, calls "conjunctural moments." According to Allen, "conjunctural
moments . . . index the temporal space in which the articulation . . . of
sometimes related and other times opposing or unrelated discourses,
practices, or trajectories reshape, reimagine, or alter our view of the
present" (214). Performance as a key transcendent temporal and spatial
trope symbolizes nicely the promiscuous and frisky relations between
black and brown.

Before we delve into the contents of this collection, let us consider briefly, as foundational examples, the powerful and widely cir-
culated works of Ntozake Shange, Cherríe Moraga, and Djola Branner,
all pieces that render black and Latina/o intersections and offer us an
entry point into the theorization of blacktino as a performance ana-
lytic. In Ntozake Shange's now canonical choreopoem/play *for colored
girls who have considered suicide/when the rainbow is enuf*, the character
"Lady in Blue" announces: "my papa thot he was puerto rican & we
wda have been/cept we waz just reglar niggahs wit hints of Spanish."[8]
And the speaker in Cherríe Moraga's poem "MeXicana Blues" says: "I
am/that much/American/a colored woman cryin'/in black English/a
song that won't hurt/nobody with my bitterness."[9] Lady in Blue is
on her way to hear Nuyorican musician Willie Colón play in Spanish
Harlem, fusing black vernacular with Spanglish on and off the salsa
dance floor, while Moraga's speaker employs the trope of the downtrod-
den "colored woman" (i.e., black) to speak to the history of exploitation
of Chicana labor. In both instances the blues motif sutures black and
brown through linguistic, psychic, emotional, and physical geographies
of intimacy.

Intimacy is highlighted through religion in Djola Branner's play *oranges & honey*, in which Rafael, a young queer Cuban, makes an offering of oranges and honey to the orisha Oshun, the goddess of the river, where he seeks healing from the memory of being raped by his stepbrother. In one scene, Rafael and Oshun dance to house music as Rafael remembers the passion he feels toward a man he meets on the dance floor, initiated by the music: "his eyes las manos his thighs/como una flor the heat rose/his pinga full and/throbbing against mine, y con las manos grandes/he touched my nipple y como un volcan i exploded/right there on the dance floor."[10] As a black queer writer and performer, Branner is familiar with black queer nightlife and the role the dance floor plays where house music is a generative force of spiritual and sexual ecstasy.[11] In this scene, he combines the ritual of black queer club life with that of Afro-Latino religious ritual as Rafael "dances" with Oshun, who is neither male nor female, "making connections between diasporic blackness, gender fluidity, house music, religion, sexuality, spirituality and how they are intertwined to create a site of healing."[12]

In their works, Shange, Moraga, and Branner demonstrate the dynamic role blacktino may play as an optic for understanding engagements with black and Latina/o experience, aesthetics, and erotics in performance. They also evidence the history of blacktino in feminist and queer performance. It is between their playing up and feeling up— that is, erotically and indulgently touching—blackness and latinidad where we find blacktino similarly manifests in the works included in this collection.

This "unholy" trinity (some might say perverse trinity) of blacktino, queer, and performance, then, proves generative to make the multiple moves we wish to make to frame this gathering of black and Latina/o queer work. We suggest that "blacktino" as a framing device or critical optic allows us to maintain the goals of queer-of-color critique and to ground it in the specificities of black and brown intergroup relations. We privilege "queer" to recoup its radical potentiality and futurity. Performance makes material the discursive conditions of life at the margins. And we are serious about what performance makes possible! From Marsha P. Johnson's generous poor drag to Sylvia Rivera's passionately angry banter, it is performance that sustains blacktino and queer not simply as an assumed continuum of identity but, perhaps more significantly, as purposeful practice.

Our approach is then to engage with the history and contemporary manifestations of black and brown queer intimacies in contemporary queer performance in the United States and the diaspora. Accordingly, we wish to chart a way of understanding convergences and divergences of black and Latina/o queer experience that assume these intimate relations as critical, even formative. To put it simply, we are as interested in works that address the intersection of black and Latina/o queer communities as we are in assuming those intersections when critically looking at works by black and Latina/o queer artists next to each other. *Blacktino* is then a sociologically specific as well as a critically comparative project. But remaining true to the performance paradigm, blacktino is also the thing we wish to both imagine and make real in the very practice of criticism. We invite our reader to adopt a blacktino queer approach to analysis by not assuming the units of this collection to be discrete or impermeable.

In this volume, we bring together nine black and Latina/o queer artists' work. The diversity of these artists registers not only along the lines of ethno-racial affinity, but also generationally, from well-established artists to newcomers, and from artists working within traditional theater forms to those who work outside them. For us, such a broad array of artists and art making that nonetheless reflects the sensibilities and politics of black and Latina/o queer aesthetics and cultures, speaks to the multiple ways in which social relations recur to discursive as well as material ways of performing race and sexuality.

The materials collected here—script, essay, interview—accentuate further blacktino as a reading strategy as it highlights the relationships among playwrights, performers, designers, and critics. For example, the scripts on their own avail themselves to close readings, but information about the playwright's process and the critic's assessment of the work provides a multiplicity of voices in the act of meaning making. In a few instances, the scholar also functions as artistic collaborator, as in the case of Tamara Roberts, Matt Richardson, and Marlon Bailey. Their insightful ruminations about the performance process offer a metacritical frame rarely available to audiences and readers who seldom have access to such a perspective. Moreover, the critics and interviewers do more than advocate and champion the works collected here; some of them, such as D. Soyini Madison and Lisa B. Thompson, also challenge the writers on their artistic and political choices. Indeed, the process of assembling this collection instituted blacktino queer performance as critical collaborative practice, as we staged a conversation among artists and scholars. In introducing the contents below we map out some of these conversations, not to delimit but to open up the myriad connections across texts, critical arguments, and conversations on process. It is our hope that these will produce even more conversations about these artists, their techniques, and the intellectual labor that their work, in collaboration with scholars, makes possible.

We open the collection with poet, playwright, and director Sharon Bridgforth. She has been pushing the boundaries of conventional artistic forms for many years—and her show *The love conjure/blues Text Installation* is no exception. Based on her book *love conjure/blues*, which she defines as a "performance novel," the text installation project draws on multimedia, including video and sound, to tell the story of gender-variant and queer rural black southerners—those living, dead, and unborn. Though the story is told from the vantage of one performer, a griot, the various media—poetry, narrative, film, sound—register a cacophony of voices that speak multiple truths and temporal and spatial realities. The video projection of the ensemble performing parts of the text, along with images of the bayou and flowing rivers, engulfs the audience and the actor, submerging both in the queer cosmology of the rural South and its "other worldly" inhabitants.

Matt Richardson's essay, "Reinventing the Black Southern Community in Sharon Bridgforth's *The love conjure/blues Text Installation*," attributes the effectiveness of such representations to Bridgforth's employment of the theatrical jazz aesthetic, a non-Western theatrical form that "acknowledges multiple states of reality." Drawing on his own participation as a performer in the filmed components of the text installation, interviews with Bridgforth, and his work with her as member of the Austin Project, a women-of-color-focused artists' group, Richardson employs an ethnographic perspective to analyze Bridgforth's work. He suggests that the act of performance vis-à-vis the theatrical jazz aesthetic allows Bridgforth to bring disparate realities together—realities based on rural southern queer life—inaugurating reconciliation and healing between and among the South's queer and nonqueer black communities. Ultimately, Richardson believes that it is indeed the overlap of text, image, and sound that unhinges gender from static representations and that enables Bridgforth to conjure the voices of black queer elders and ancestors to tell their stories.

In her interview with Sandra L. Richards, Bridgforth talks through some of the challenges of creating a piece that brings together the dead, the living, and the unborn. Key to tackling that challenge is her own process of workshopping her work so that she may learn from actors what should and should not stay in the piece. Tone and rhythm that emanate from the musicality of southern speech are the primary sources of Bridgforth's writing process that she then "gives" to her performers and says, "What do you think?" It is the collaborative component of her work, she says, that is in keeping with jazz—a rigid structure with room for improvisation. Because of this Bridgforth thinks of her text as a "musical score."

The collaborative spirit of Bridgforth's jazz aesthetic resonates with the ensemble methodologies of Teatro Luna, the only all-Latina feminist theater ensemble currently active in the United States. Since its inception in 2000, the company has been devoted to the development of theater about the Latina experience and has done so through an ethnographic performance methodology that collects the stories of women, including those of the performers, as primary source material for script development. *Machos*, which is included in this collection, represents a new application of this method as the stories collected through the interview process were those of men, Latinos and non-Latinos alike, interviewed about their experiences with the privileges and pressures of racialized masculinity. In this eclectic collection of thematically arranged skits, with some musical numbers as interludes, the Teatro Luna women perform in male drag scenes that range from serious explorations of gender propriety and heterosexual relationships to hilariously comic renditions of homosocial intimacy and homophobic anxieties.

In her essay, "Voicing Masculinity," Tamara Roberts attends to the development of the script in rehearsal and focuses on three key elements of *Machos* as a performance: the juxtaposition of multiperspectival group scenes with single-story emphasis, the use of female performers in male drag, and the incorporation of camp within a primarily realist aesthetic platform. Written from the insider perspective of the sound designer, Roberts's close and incisive analysis demonstrates the various ways in which Teatro Luna approached the study of masculinity through performance to question the inner workings of heteropatriarchy and its reliance on quotidian dramaturgies to rehearse its naturalized force. But she also offers a poignant critique of the inherent biologism of the company's approach, concluding that the difference "between macho as a state of being, and being macho as a performance, is made but ultimately reinscribed" in *Machos*.

Roberts's observations are further illuminated in Patricia Ybarra's interview with *Machos* director and Teatro Luna cofounder Coya Paz. Paz describes her collaboration with the Teatro Luna ensemble as defined by varying investments in, and sometimes rejections of, feminism among company members. These differences result in frictive but nonetheless productive engagements with masculinity. Especially significant is Paz's discussion of the company's exploration of the ways machismo exerts very specific kinds of pressure on men who in turn develop survival practices in response. Notably, she also discusses her ongoing concern throughout the process with not erasing or excusing the potential injurious consequences of these "survival" masculinities to women. These consequences extend as well to queer men, whom Paz discusses as similarly encountering the violence of masculinity during the gender workshops that led to the performance.

E. Patrick Johnson's *Strange Fruit* picks up on the position of queer men, black queer men to be precise, and their experiences of gender and sexuality in a heteronormative and racist world. If Teatro Luna's *Machos* launches the feminist theater collective into an exploration of masculinity, in his solo performance, Johnson honors the debt of his black queer gay male self-understanding and self-assertion to the politics of black feminism and the vernacular knowledge modeled and imparted by the black southern women in his family. Assuming a fragmentary structure to traverse a kaleidoscopic journey into black queer experience, Johnson moves quickly from scene to scene, playing not only himself but others in his story, both to present an assemblage of the pictorial, literary, and sonic black archives of queer life and to theorize the experiences it evidences.

As Johnson explains in his interview with Bernadette Marie Calafell, there is an intentional investment in juxtaposing the framed actions of the performer to a wealth of projected images to create a sensorial overload for the audience. This excess of intertextual references, anchored onto the materiality of the live labor of the performer before us, prompts Jennifer DeVere Brody in her essay, "Passing Strange: E. Patrick Johnson's *Strange Fruit*," to engage with Johnson's "doing" of black gay art without falling into the pitfalls of essentialism. This results in a "documentary performance that draws on actual events in Johnson's life while highlighting their performative dimensions and also contextualizing them in a critical genealogy of black gay image making," the autobiographical and autoethnographic concerns Johnson points to in his interview.

Javier Cardona's highly physical performance piece *Ah mén* is similarly concerned with exploring queer navigations of racialized heteromasculinity. Best known for his solo work, Cardona works with an ensemble of six performers, including himself, to explore the interrelation between Puerto Rican religious tradition and disciplines and queerings of race, gender, and sexuality. *Ah mén* achieves this through a flirtatious engagement with innuendo, a staple of Catholic discretion, and its suggested undoings in the slippages of queer gesture or the anxious same-sex intimacies of Puerto Rican male homosociality. As Celiany Rivera-Velázquez and Beliza Torres Narváez suggest in their analysis of the piece, *Ah mén* "parodies Caribbean and Latin American moralistic discourses that thrive in their condemnation and exclusion of those who do not conform to normative gender expressions." At the same time, they note, the piece seems to ritualistically install its alternatives; choreographing ways of being together, queerly. And it is precisely this tension between the examination, even mocking, of structural oppression and the less announced assertion of queer possibility that Cardona seems to balance in his work and in his engagement with "queer" as a generative designator. As he discusses in his interview with Jossianna Arroyo, his interest or potential investment in queer has less to do with formally assumed political narratives than with the difference, even alterity, it may introduce to constructions of the norm, both social and aesthetic.

One of the many themes that emerges across several of these works, Cardona's among them, is the disavowal of sexuality as an identity. In black and Latina/o communities alike one's sexual practices do not always align with a sexual identity. This tension might have something to do with the complex history of black and brown people's bodies being seen as abject and their sexuality pathological, and the response to that abjection and pathologizing discourse being one of social conservative views of sexuality in general and nonnormative sexuality in particular. In Jeffrey Q. McCune Jr.'s *Dancin' the Down Low*, for example, he takes up the question of whether black men who have sex with men, but who do not identify as gay, are actually self-loathing or if their "down low" status suggests a more nuanced sexual expression that resists compulsory homonormative notions of "coming out." Based on ethnographic research in bars, online, and in phone chat rooms that black and Latino men frequent, *Dancin' the Down Low* highlights the paradox of "down low" nomenclature: sexual behavior that is purportedly clandestine is quite often performed in public spaces. The play suggests that by engaging in down-low behavior these men (and some women) must "dance" around a host of discursive and material traps that either pressures them to claim a sexual identity or that positions them as vectors of contagion.

Lisa B. Thompson's essay on the play, "Queering Black Identity and Desire: Jeffrey Q. McCune Jr.'s *Dancin' the Down Low*," analyzes the play on its own terms by calling attention to the way in which it queers and troubles traditional notions of black male sexuality. Thompson argues that the dancing metaphor in the piece operates on many registers: it indexes the way the men "pivot between identities and worlds," creatively refusing to be "fixed in place," and the way they "dance around the truth—a strategy to avoid an answer or commitment." Thompson also commends McCune's inclusion of black women's voices, but suggests that the play could offer equally complicated depictions of black women as it does of black down-low (DL) men.

In his interview with John Keene, McCune suggests that DL men being blamed for the rise of new cases of HIV/AIDS among heterosexual black women motivated him to write a play that would counter that discourse. McCune tells Keene that writing the play was his way "to perform activism while also at the same time producing theater" and as "a corrective to the media's discussions of down-low men, particularly concerning the demonizing narratives around just plain-old cheaters without explanation, with no gesture towards the social, economical or sociopolitical issues black men are facing."

In Cedric Brown's *Cuban Hustle*, Cuban and American relations remain at the center, but the play homes in on the question of power relations vis-à-vis desire. The play is told from the perspective of a black gay American tourist, who meets Félix, a young Afro-Cuban, on a trip to Cuba. The Narrator and Félix have an intense fling, leading to the American agreeing to have Félix come to the United States to live with him. After the Narrator sends him the money, however, Félix disappears abruptly, leaving the Narrator questioning, "Was it love or money?" This rhetorical question is not one only posed to Félix, but to the Narrator himself.

Marlon M. Bailey's essay, "Love and Money: Performing Black Queer Diasporic Desire in *Cuban Hustle*," echoes this question, but mostly engages the play from the perspective of how its thematics highlight the limited erotic possibilities and marginalization of black gay men in the United States and Cuba and, alternatively, the potential of erotic desirability in the black queer diaspora. Having performed in a production of the play, Bailey, like Richardson writing about *The love conjure/blues Text Installation*, has the benefit of an insider's perspective. As such, he argues that it is performance that most effectively demonstrates black queer diasporic desire as it manifests in the play. Ultimately, Bailey suggests that the play demonstrates "the transcendent possibilities of alternative sexual and sociocultural geographies and imaginaries."

In her interview with Brown, D. Soyini Madison raises questions regarding the play's seemingly unsympathetic politics toward Cuba as inferred by the title and presented through the portrayal of the character Félix. While Brown resists the suggestion that the play portrays Cuba in a unilaterally unsympathetic light, he does admit that the play is a "metaphor for the relationship between the U.S. and Cuba" and undergirded by what Madison refers to as a "political economy of love," which speaks to the "politics of poverty in the so-called Third World." Brown suggests, however, that despite the power differential in the relationship between the Narrator and Félix, both men are in search of something that neither can fully provide.

Pamela Booker's *Seens from the Unexpectedness of Love* brings the focus back to a North American context, but nonetheless transgresses borders and boundaries. Specifically, the play unmoors gender to any specific body while also being very committed to telling the story of lesbian lovers. Like Bridgforth and so many of the other artists in the volume, Booker riffs on Western theatrical conventions to both comment on their restrictions and demonstrate how one might exploit those very conventions to subvert them. Indeed, the entire play seems to provide a metacommentary on theater itself in its employment of Brechtian alienation effects, a Greek chorus, masks, and the occupations of the protagonists as theater artists, as a way to call into question what the audience and the two protagonists are seeing through their "rose-colored glasses." Is it really love for the other? The theater? Neither?

Omi Osun Joni L. Jones's essay, "'Public Intimacy': Women-Loving-Women as Dramaturgical Transgressions," takes up the question of theatrical conventions in the play to suggest that Booker uses the trope of love and experiments with dramatic form in order to offer a "resistive" strategy against oppressive forms. Those oppressive forms, according to Jones, are the homophobic black community in which the two characters live and the traditional conventions and themes of black theater. She suggests that Booker's play, while about two black women, does not make race the central theme, but rather their queerness. Coupled with their queerness is their middle-class status, which, according to Jones, positions the protagonists as outside "normative" representations of middle-class blackness. Jones argues that "it is the *visible* fact of Queerness, of public sexual intimacy between [the two characters]—both the scene it makes as display of queerness, and the act of queerness being *seen* by a policing public—that must be immediately punished by society."

In Tavia Nyong'o's interview with Booker, the playwright discusses her engagement with theater as a form through these characters, but with the aim of highlighting the ways in which love is staged—not only in our romantic relationships but in our relationships in the theater itself, leading her to ask, "And what does it say about who these people really are when they go home at the end of the day from the theater and remove their masks?" Nyong'o also engages Booker about the characters' resistance to gender specificity, noting that from the outset of the play it is difficult to discern their gender. In her response, Booker explains what is perhaps the point of the play: "There are some larger global features or universal themes that are necessarily implicit in how people love regardless of gender."

Paul Outlaw's show *Berserker* ramps up the ante in both its themes and performance conventions. The central characters of the play are nineteenth-century slave-rebellion leader Nat Turner and the 1980s white serial killer Jeffrey Dahmer, whose victims were African American and Asian American men. Beyond representing diametrically opposed motivations for their actions, Turner and Dahmer are brought together in this play through Outlaw's association of both with the European mythological figures, berserkers, who, when on the battlefield, could slip "into a state of uncontrolled psychic fury" in which they would "exhibit the most inexplicable and gratuitous cruelty." Outlaw's performance choices reflect this "psychic fury," as he appears naked at the outset of the play and variously bursts bags filled with the entrails of murdered bodies and a number of highly stylized "gruesome" acts to represent the violence that each man has enacted. The audience is challenged to make sense of this provocative coupling while also attending to Outlaw's own personal story of family tension around colorism that seems to hover above the play as metaphor for all kinds of social relations.

Charles I. Nero does not shy away from the question that readers and audiences of this play undoubtedly ask by making it the title of his essay: "What's Nat Turner Doing Up in Here with All These Queers? Paul Outlaw's *Berserker*; A Black Gay Meditation on Interracial Desire and Disappearing Blackness." Nero is not being facetious and fervently engages the question as to why Outlaw would juxtapose a figure like Nat Turner, who murdered whites in order to escape chattel slavery, with Jeffrey Dahmer, a person who murdered African American and Asian-descended men for sport. In wrestling with this question, Nero conjectures that the pairing is Outlaw's commentary on American masculinity and interracial desire. Nero argues that by creating a symbolic "battlefield" onstage, Outlaw works through the complexity of desire for the racial other.

In his interview with Vershawn Ashanti Young, Outlaw inevitably answers Nero's question about Turner's presence among the queers when he says that "gay men seem to have a thing with Nat Turner" because they "relate to violence—going off on somebody—as a fantasy, from the place of 'I have been put down.'" This seems to corroborate

Nero's reading of the play as being about desire for the other. Outlaw also comments on the various registers of the stories he wants to tell in general. They involve American history, personal history, race, sex, gender, and sexuality, but ultimately he is compelled to tell the history of blacks and whites in this country because, according to him, there has been no real discussion of race since 1865. Surprisingly, when Young asks Outlaw about the politics of his play, he responds, "It has no politics. I don't think that a piece of art can have politics." Undoubtedly, Outlaw's audiences disagree.

We close the collection with the work of Charles Rice-González. In *I Just Love Andy Gibb*, Rice-González brings us back into the experience of black gay Latinos, Puerto Ricans to be exact, and their navigation of racial economies that render them problematically between or beyond black and white. Rice-González presents the parallel and intersecting stories of two black queer Puerto Rican men, or perhaps, the adult and adolescent version of the same character, coming to recognize their/his racialized self-hatred and move toward an appreciation and love of their/his blackness. Set in the Bronx, much like his acclaimed novel for young audiences, *Chulito*, the piece focuses on the interaction between the two characters, both dark-skinned Puerto Ricans, similarly oriented toward light-skinned objects of desire: a teenage infatuation with white Australian disco sensation Andy Gibb in the case of Roy and a more adult obsession with his light-skinned roommate in the case of Carlos.

In his essay, "Learning to Unlove Andy Gibb: Race, Beauty, and the Erotics of Puerto Rican Black Queer Pedagogy," Lawrence La Fountain-Stokes characterizes the piece as a "therapeutic dream play." Framing his argument through Marlon Riggs's proposition that black men loving each other constitutes a revolutionary act, La Fountain-Stokes explores the politics of racial visibility and invisibility within the homoerotic frameworks of the play. In his interview with Ramón H. Rivera-Servera, Rice-González further discusses his own politics of art production as a queer and black Puerto Rican writer and also explains his investments in *I Just Love Andy Gibb* to argue for a more affirmative assumption of blacktino and queer as identitarian and political ways of being in the world.

These scripts, interviews, and essays showcase blacktino in ways that we hope announce the always already erotic terrain of ethnoracial encounters. Whether through forced contact from structural and institutional racism and homophobia, ancestral blood, or cross-racial desire, queer black and Latina/o bodies cannot escape the touch of the past, present, or future. What become clear over these pages, then, are the inevitable flirtations, seductions, and even cuckolds that mark the contours of any ethnoracial love affair. Paying homage to elders Johnson and Rivera, we, the queer progeny of that blacktino coupling, offer this collection as a continuation of the legacy for which they fought and fucked.

Notes

1 See Omi'seke Natasha Tinsley, *Thiefing Sugar: Eroticism between Women in Caribbean Literature* (Durham, NC: Duke University Press, 2010).

2 For more on gender/queer orishas, see Yvonne Daniels, *Dancing Wisdom: Embodied Knowledge in Haitian Vodou, Cuban Yoruba, and Bahian Candomble* (Urbana: University of Illinois Press, 2005).

3 For a fuller discussion on this topic, see Dwight A. McBride, *Why I Hate Abercrombie and Fitch: Essays on Race and Sexuality* (New York: New York University Press, 2005), especially his chapter "It's a White Man's World: Race in the Gay Marketplace of Desire."

4 See, for example, Juana María Rodríguez, *Queer Latinidad: Identity Practices, Discursive Spaces* (New York: New York University Press, 2003); Roderick A. Ferguson, *Aberrations in Black: Toward a Queer of Color Critique* (Minneapolis: University of Minnesota Press, 2003); E. Patrick Johnson and Mae G. Henderson, eds., *Black Queer Studies: A Critical Anthology* (Durham, NC: Duke University Press, 2005); José Esteban Muñoz, *Cruising Utopia: The Then and There of Queer Futurity* (New York: New York University Press, 2009); Michael Hames-García and Ernesto Javier Martínez, eds., *Gay Latino Studies: A Critical Reader* (Durham, NC: Duke University Press, 2011); and Sharon Patricia Holland, *The Erotic Life of Racism* (Durham, NC: Duke University Press, 2012).

5 Jafari S. Allen, "Black/Queer/Diaspora at the Current Conjuncture," GLQ: A Journal of Lesbian and Gay Studies 18, nos. 2–3 (2012): 222.

6 José Esteban Muñoz, *Disidentifications: Queers of Color and the Performance of Politics* (Minneapolis: University of Minnesota Press, 1999); Ferguson, *Aberrations in Black*.

7 For a discussion of this elision, see E. Patrick Johnson, "Black Performance Studies: Genealogies, Politics, Futures," in *The Sage Handbook of Performance Studies*, ed. D. Soyini Madison and Judith Hamera (Thousand Oaks, CA: Sage, 2006), 446–63.

8 Ntozake Shange, *for colored girls who have considered suicide/when the rainbow is enuf* (New York: Scribner Poetry, 1975), 11.

9 Cherríe L. Moraga, "MeXicana Blues," in *A Xicana Codex of Changing Consciousness* (Durham, NC: Duke University Press, 2011), 51–53.

10 Djola Branner, *oranges & honey*, in *sash & trim and other plays* (Washington, DC: RedBone Press, 2013), 58.

11 For more on the blurring of the secular and the sacred in the black gay club,

see E. Patrick Johnson, "Feeling the Spirit in the Dark: Expanding Notions of the Sacred in the African American Gay Community," *Callaloo* 21, no. 2 (Winter/Spring 1998): 399–416.

12 E. Patrick Johnson, foreword to *sash & trim and other plays*, by Djola Branner (Washington, DC: RedBone Press, 2013), xiii.

Part I

The love conjure/blues Text Installation

Sharon Bridgforth

HISTORY

The love conjure/blues Text Installation was created from a series of experiments based on the *love conjure/blues* performance/novel
Written by Sharon Bridgforth
Published by RedBone Press. Pub. Date: October 2004

WORKSHOP PRODUCTION

The John L. Warfield Center for African and African American Studies, University of Texas at Austin. 3/2004. Writer Sharon Bridgforth. Featuring: Director/Composer, Helga Davis; Performers: Helga Davis, Florinda Bryant, Daniel Dodd-Ellis, Daniel Alexander Jones, Omi Osun Joni L. Jones, Sonja Perryman, Marlah Fulgham, Sean Tate, and Carsey Walker, Jr.

WORKSHOP PRODUCTION

The John L. Warfield Center for African and African American Studies, University of Texas at Austin. 9/2004. Writer Sharon Bridgforth. Director/Composer, Helga Davis. Musicians Fred Cash, Jr. & Greg Rickard. Performers: Helga Davis, Florinda Bryant, Daniel Dodd-Ellis, Gina Houston, Daniel Alexander Jones, Omi Osun Joni L. Jones, Sonja Perryman, and Sean Tate.

ALTER FILM

Producer/Writer Sharon Bridgforth. Producer/Filmmaker/Editor Krissy Mahan. Art Direction, Wura Ogunji. Featuring: Laurie Carlos, Omi Osun Joni L. Jones, Annelize Machado.

INSTALLATION FILM

Executive Producer/Writer/Director, Sharon Bridgforth. Producer/Director of Photography/Editor/Projection Composer, Jen Simmons. Composer, Helga Davis. Cast: Jafari Sinclaire Allen, Phillip Alexander, Florinda Bryant, Wesley Bryant, Alix Andrew Chapman, Helga Davis, Firesong, Jeffery "Da'Shade" Johnson, Daniel Alexander Jones, Omi Osun Joni L. Jones, Renita Martin, Lady Red McGlotten, Courtney Morris, Sonja Perryman, Matt Richardson, Sheree Ross, Damon Stith, Dorcas Sowunmi, 3Jazz Collective (Joao Costa Vargas, Philippe Vieux & Kevin Witt), Rick Glascock—Vibraphone, Tonya Lyles—Drums, Martin Perna—Shakere.

THE LOVE CONJURE/BLUES TEXT INSTALLATION PRODUCTIONS
(WITH INSTALLATION FILM)

Performer: Sharon Bridgforth Off Center, in Austin, Texas 6/2007.

Performers: Sharon Bridgforth and Florinda Bryant. South Dallas Cultural Center 3/2008.

Performer: Omi Osun Joni L. Jones. Department of Performance Studies, Northwestern University, BlakTino Queer Performance Festival 4/2008.

The love conjure/blues Text Installation considers a range of possibilities of gender expression and sexuality within a rural, Black working class context. It articulates African-American sensibilities, history and oral traditions. Exploring the ways that we have survived; knowing the middle passage, slavery, jim crow and lynching. The piece is a reflection of the ways that Black people have used artistic expression to transmit stories of survival. *The love conjure/blues Text Installation* re-imagines the traditional role of the Griot. Asserts queer as sacred. Claims the blues as ritual—in concert with Ancient practices and new creations. In *The love conjure/blues Text Installation*, the past-the present-the future-the living–and the dead co-exist together weaving dreams/Prayers/Love expressed.

Set: The room is a living Altar. The audience is installed in the room. In the round. Three video projectors, three media screens needed. Three STATIONS: Sturdy rocking chair, Small platform for performer to stand on (2′ × 2′-ish), The Lady-Cloth hanging of Our Lady Of Guadalupe that the performer stands in front of.

Running Time: 90 Minutes.

Cast: 1W: GRIOT. (Larger cast/live band optional.)

FILM. (THE OCEAN & CIVIL RIGHTS ERA / LAYERED.)
ENTER DANCING
DANCE AT CURTAIN FOR A FEW BEATS

DANCE TO CENTER (COVER THE ROOM / YOU ARE SAGING IT)

DANCE TO THE LADY   FREEZE (HOLD IT)
STAND (HOLD IT / WATCH FILM)
WALK SLOWLY! BEHIND CURTAIN (YOU ARE SAGING AGAIN)
DANCE OUT
DANCE TO ROCKER
WALK SLOWLY BEHIND ROCKER/CURTAIN
DANCE OUT (YOU ARE SAGING)

DANCE TO DRUM   FREEZE (HOLD IT)
STAND (HOLD IT / WATCH FILM)
STAND ON DRUM

(Take time Be a Blessing. Do the Blessing. Be in Ceremony.
The stage is an Altar. Be Intentional. Be Mindful. BE PRESENT.
Celebrate Engage with film/family and the audience.
be in it. Enjoy. take your time. Remember this is The Prayer . . .)

GRIOT. FROM DRUM
they took his drum.
he make another.
they took his drum
he make another / cut and carve and stretch and lace a little late late
till it new
then drum.
you could hear it cross town and town
which scare ole marsa who send they to take that drum and that one
then
beat him and take drum and beat him and take drum and
beat him.
still / he make another and another
then drum.
then ole marsa send they to take he thumb   toss in jar
like for pickling.
still he drum
like he daddy he grand and grand and grand before now / before crossing

Fig. I.1. Omi Osun Joni L. Jones rehearses *The love conjure/blues Text Installation*.
Photo by Sharon Bridgforth.

he still drum so marsa send they take other thumb he still drum they
take he
finger he finger he finger every time still drum
till none left.
they seal jar place on kitchen table where many have to pass
remember   stay in place.

then all wee hours he sit and rocking back and forth cry soft close eyes
rocking and rocking till some full moons pass / one night
he run to dirt trail between back of the big house and field
jump center
with feet
make sound
with him mouth
make sound
low to the ground legs bend feet

he spin
fast fast stir dirt make dust
loud and loud
overseer come but can't get close
dust and wind raise hit face
ole marsa run scared
ole marsa with gun and whip and more overseers
run through house run in kitchen
trying to run out the back door to stop that drum
but can't get out the door / in kitchen by table ole marsa he gun and whip and
more overseers stuck   legs won't move past the table / holding the jar
very still no smile
isadora the conjuration woman / head unwrapped
let thick gray braids stand round face and black eyes on black black skin
she stand there hold jar no smile
let ole marsa can't move
not even curse can't raise fist whip gun
overseers can't beat
can't drop draws and act the animal they has been
can't make no tie and cut and burn and starve and sell and kill like usual
isadora stand there watch ole marsa eyes get big when he notice she holding
that jar which is empty. she move her eyes to the table where his scraps
from lunch still scraps and him eyes get big at the plate now empty
cause he know they done fed him them fingers.
him eyes roll back in head
drummer feet too fast to see dust whirl raise the wind wind knock kitchen
door open lift ole marsa up high in the air
drop him down flat on the floor
overseers been knocked down
wind lift marsa high up drop him down
isodora   still
watch
lift bam lift bam
ten times this go on ole marsa been pass out
overseers too. till
ole marsa's spirit float around the room
slam down into his body on the ground
then ole marsa open his eyes

he ain't ole marsa no more
he just john harrison
overseers dead   dead   dead.
isadora say they gone *come back slaves next time.*
we leave.
every one of us we leave that night. john don't say a thing.
we just walk off
ain't no plantation no more never since that time / not on these grounds.
us
we come here.
this been our home
free
for a long time now.

WALK BEHIND SCREENS TO ROCKER. WATCH FILM FROM ROCKER

FILM (MR. FIGURMAN & FRIENDS)
slim figurman
handed a stranger a card what read
figure's flavors.   the world's finest.
come get a taste.
slim like to press them
hand writ cards
to folk coming through for the first time.
he be all dressed lik a fancymann
talking so many cirlces / till don't nobody know what the hell
he talking about.
the new to it / always stand for it
nodd here and there
throw in a word when slim take a breath.
probably is all slim really want after all
somebody to listen
talk for a bit.

anyway

we all know
slim call heself running a ho house
but slim ain't running nothing or nobody.
so the place he call figure's flavors / we calls it
bettye's.

yessuh/cause slim's sister bettye be the one running that jernt.
and what it is is the best blues inn in the country.
first off bettye know how to keep a clean room
so the stop overs always be happy/feel rested and cared for
but more important/bettye can cook so gotdamngood
make you want to kick your own ass. i trying to watch
see if bettye been throwed some powders off in them pots/make
the cooking so much excitement
for the tastes.

anyway

chile/musicians from states away haul they music over to bettye's just
to be up in there   get a taste. don't even charge bettye to play/course
na
some of them tasting more than good cooking from bettye.
look like her favorites   be extra fed. but they all of them gets tips
meals
and a room/long as they willing to work/and play hard.

and do the jernt be packed!
mens womens some that is both some that is neither/be rolling all up
and
between the sounds/laying up in them rent rooms/and dancing off all
bettye's home cooking.

anyway

it was a hot night after a hot day.
the peoples was in they finest/fresh pressed and set for whatever
bettye's
was about to bring. it was rib night   the start of the week-end. folk was
still eyes bright hearts light pockets packed full of laughter/and on the
ready.
that night was a wo'mn named big bill what rose up out of bettye's room.
big bill had on the finest suit i have seen to this day.
come in with she suit black/hat low/glasses dark/and shoes so
shinning make
your head hurt. big bill walk through
the crowd part/as she make way to the piano in the corner of the room.
big bill's long legs reach strong

one powerful in front the other/her unbuttoned jacket open close open
close
as she walk/pants pull here here
here
material ripple across she crotch   which appear packing a large and
heavy
surprise   i glance over to bettye/see she seeing too/smiling down
where big bill pants pull and ripple large/and not so suttle in the crotch.
bettye fanning still   sweat run all around her face.
i ain't got time be looking at bettye/look back
big bill taking she jacket off/take she hat off/slowly roll up one crisp
sleeve/then the other/loosen she tie/turn her big broad back to the
room/sit down/and ever so slightly nod she nappy head.
at that guitar sam pull up take a chair next to she. big bill nod
again even more slight/and a big ole
powerful sample of wo'mness stroll center the room. sway step smile
sway
step smile sway sway she went till she in place standing center inside a
moment of stillness.   then suddenly/the three of them hit a note
all at the same time/*aaaaaaawwwwwwwhhhhhh*
went the sound   and i declare some kind of hunger-spirit swept through
the
room. took everybody's mind in one swoop.
after that
wasn't nothing but bodies feeding the feeling till sunday sunrise just before
first service. shiiit. we still rest broken from all that business. big mama
sway/singing

i gots geechee lips
i gots geechee hips
i gots a geechee kiss
that'll you'll never forget
but you got to
show me that you want it
show me that you need/so
if you can't show me that you want it
go on/pack your thangs and go.

chile
what a time.

something about they sound almost stop my heart.
i knew it weren't the liquor
    cause wasn't nothing in my cup but that strong ass coffee bettye
    serve/which could been over work my heart/but i don't think so.
see/bettye don't allow no drinking in she jernt.
not since she lost her first love lushy boudreax to the gussle.
naw/lushy ain't dead
that's her yonder holding up the back of the jernt.
bettye lost lushy from she bed   when she kicked that drunk ass out
one last time.
been upset about that ever since. mostly at herself/say she got so
caught up
loving what lushy could have been/she wouldn't see what lushy really
was.

anyway

lushy don't drink no more/bettye don't like the smell of the
drink/reminding
her of the hard times/so we all forced stay in our right minds
when we come to bettye's
    well not all of us/cause you know any fool can find a way to tilt they
    cup if they want to. but bettye's no liquor rule do cut down on the
    free flowingness of it
which is a relief really
because usually with the drinking come the looking and the looking
bring
the knives/cause folk can't just look at they own peoples they gots to
always
cast a looking at somebody's somebody else/and the knives bring the
cussing and the cussing bring the swoll chest and the swoll chest
always
interrupt the good time.

but the good time don't hardly get stopped at bettye's
so i been happy as a greedy cat in a rat shack.
yessuh/i been happy/yeah.

(END OF FILM)

STAY IN ROCKER WATCH FILM FROM ROCKER.

GRIOT TELL PARTS OF THE STORY WITH FILM.
FILM (ANCESTOR)

aaawwwhhh aaawwwhhhaaawwwhhh
aaawwwhhh aaawwwhhhaaawwwhhh
aaawwwhhh aaawwwhhhaaawwwhhh
aaawwwhhh aaawwwhhhaaawwwhhh

dey used ta hang niggas by dey thumbs aaawwwhhh yessuh if'n a nigga had
da nerve ta tink dey life wuz worf mo den a dog or cat dey'd strang dat
nigga up. aaawwwhhh. yessuh dey tookn my own daddy data way saw dey
take he my own daddy dey kilt he cause he a smart man too smart to be able
to hide it so dey took he cause he weren't able to mask him brightness and
aaawwwhhh yessuh

my life it ain't never been de same since dat day i saw dey stringed

my daddy i saw he hanging from de tree by he thumbs.

aaawwwhhhh when certain kinda things happen sometimes you jes
aaawwwhhhh

GRIOT
thats my gran-gran-daddy/big paw/my father's father's father. every
day
they say he tell that story at sunrise/he tell it like he praying/like he not
really in the room/like somebody else speaking it for him. they say each
morning when he tell it/it's as if you just happen to walk into a conversation
he having   cept ain't nobody there but him.

WALK TO CENTER WALK IN A CIRCLE
(you are making ceremony/shifting the mood)

FILM (ANCESTOR)
**this is home. the place that earthed you. it's a sore/a wound/this
ground/the place i grew up in.**

that's uncle daddy/he my father's father. i think he done heard big
paw's story once too many times/is now a little touched by it
or something.

WALK TO THE LADY

FILM (ANCESTOR)
i am the cry that won't come out i am the pain stuck i am the me that never
was sorry now i am for the moments i choked away for the lost touches
diminished faded like yellow against the sun.
i was born too early to be allowed to exist i was drowned the day i was born
of heartache and loss i am

GRIOT. STAY WITH THE LADY
that's big paw's sister ma-dear. they all lives here/big paw uncle daddy
and ma-dear live here at the home house with my mama the wife of my
daddy/who dead for some time now. one day my mama called me in the
city/said **chile come home/the ole folk want you.** not knowing what
that mean/but being used to doing what mama say/i got quick down
to the home house. there i found mama standing on the porch with she
bag packed. she
said **bye gurl   i be back.** i thought/well i guess/mama need a time
off from the home house big paw uncle daddy and ma-dear. *bye mama* i
said/from
the porch waving waving waving till she disappear in the road.

i turn to go in the house and there they were big paw uncle daddy and
ma-dear/standing around me   justa staring/smiling big ole toothless
love. i hug them each tight tight. go in the house unpack in mama's
little room/what
used to be her and daddy's.

FILM (ANCESTOR)
we peoples got made in de way south. i hab been made new papers ova and
ova forta git em prayers jes right/lay em prayers south of de water and
dirt/jes under de light of de candle. na. what i needn be a real shoutn so dat
we bringn plenty wittness from de way south place to guide'n de babies safe
home.

tell only God and the preacher yo prayers write what you wish on

parchment paper / then hide it from yourself for one year. go back to it / and know the power of God.

with broken teeth and bodies that have gone unchecked for years
we've been living here through careless times and danger

gurl you better listen good. *we telling you something / you hear.*

GRIOT. WITH THE LADY
big paw uncle daddy and ma-dear started talking to me. problem is they talking to me in my dreams. in wake time / they just smile they big toothless
smiles hold my hands / taking turns for long walks in the evening / work the garden early morning / clean house mid-day. they be sweeping / brushing the floor with flower water and powder every morn-ing early i wake to one of them staring down at me smiling smiling. till finally i don't know what day
it is no more and i can't separate my thoughts from words words from dreams dreams from prayers said out loud / and lately i'm thinking i'm visiting them in they dreams too.

is you done emptied de water from under de bed / shreded da paper / dumped de dirt / blow'd out de candle / make room for de new dream'n? yes i have done all that / and i cleaned with smoke and powder / placed my prayers on parchment paper surrounded by water / hidden **good. now set the candles in the east window / circle earth around the bed**

DANCE TO DRUM
FREEZE AT DRUM HOLD IT
STRAIGHTEN HOLD IT
GET ON DRUM DANCE WITH FILM / WITH HEELS / STAY LOW

FILM (ANCESTOR)
i am he that was king / captured sold and shipped for selling i am **she whose tongue they took so as not to tell** i am he made to walk chained next to a wagon cross state lines i am **she who lived in the woods / leader of the ones that fought** i am he that scouted getaway time i am the run-ner through the corn i *am the seer in the night* i am the crawler in the light i *am the one that got away i am elizabeth daughter of cora the child of sarah* i am the one that holds your prayers

shuffle fast clap'n circle smoke praise moan'n shuffle shout'n shuffle fast
sing'n shuffle dance'n shuffle fly holla prayers home circle smoke shuffle praise
we been learned to dream cause in wake we had to be dead.

(STOP DANCING)
you is free cause we was captive
you are the one we been waiting for
gaga gaga gaga/ga   gaga gaga gaga/ga   gaga gaga gaga/ga
wake now!

GRIOT. FROM DRUM
the Houma   the swamp the woods yonder
the Fon the Ibo the Yoruba the Wolof/tied lashed
lashed/opened
still fight.
the Houma with Tunica Choctaw Chickasaw
here before the before
know night and moon hear trees and earth
drumming drumming
hold on
drumming drumming
on the way
drumming drumming
the Houma the swamp the woods yonder the moon they signal with drum
untie the Fon the Ibo the Yoruba the Wolof
clean swab wrap quick here here here
up swamp through woods past yonder fly
not seen.
the Houma the Fon the Ibo the Yoruba the Wolof
free
free more.

sun spoon moon make rain
the Houma the Fon the Ibo the Yoruba the Wolof the swamp the woods
yonder the moon they signal with drum
raise trees kiss earth
open pens break doors use
stones and blades arrows and fists
fight
free more.

and so and so and so again
moon rise sun sleep
more here here here
free.
go back
free more.
over over
they childrens they childrens they
children carry they story
in cloth
in feet
with hair
when laugh
with drum
Praise memory
Praise the people
drum bend holla dance shout laugh free far a way back a woods yonder
free
free more.

drum bend holla dance shout laugh free far a way back a woods yonder
free
free more

drum bend holla dance shout laugh free far a way back a woods yonder
free
free more
free.

drum bend holla dance shout laugh free far a way back a woods yonder
free
free more
free.

(END OF FILM)

GET THE STOOL
TAKE IT CENTER

FILM (FAMILY)
sometime
a whole lot of shit just libal to happen.

(END OF FILM)

GRIOT. FROM STOOL / CENTER STAGE
one day things took a turn / and everything changed
or maybe things that already was just came into focus.
well
you ever seen'd two people that truly love each other / two people that
truly
love each other but done had so much hurt pass between them that the
old
hurts block the old love but the old love keep a growing anyway / yet they
can't make the old love new because
they can't stand to be around one the other and they can't take being apart
ummhumm
well
everything was as it had become
till change walked in one night.
she was a gray eyed gap tooth
thick liped
cookie brown woman
with tight light brown curls rumbling all the way down
to a bounce on her behind   which set amply high stretching her many
colored thin materialed dress / like a piece of rubber drawed tight.
change had enough curves to make for a long trip   and when she
walked
she carried you around and around and around with her.
so when change
walked into bettye's that night
ummmhumm
we all knew some shit was libal to happen.

change come swinging in / swirling a little dust before her as she
head straight for lushy / which is hard to do
cause lushy sit quite far back in bettye's / say
the best table in the jernt be the one bettye don't serve / which would be
any
table lushy libal to be at   she just always keep it to the back

well
change was moving towards lushy/like it was a natural thing
till somebody yell out
that's her that's her!
j.b. and kokomo look up/seem to know who change was
but instead of sending out a welcome
they packed theyselves up/got on out of bettye's
as did about four or five other peoples.
na/i didn't have time to give much thought to the leaving   cause i got
caught up
in change.
people started yelling begging for a song/i was watching her
take it all in   till all of a sudden
right there in the middle of the jernt
that woman widened she stance throw'd her head all the way
back/dropped
down a taste/open she gap tooth big lipped mouth
and i declare
the sound that came out
shook the entire room.
shit started flying off the walls/glasses was tumbling from tables and the
peoples damn near made a stampede getting to the dance floor.
i ain't never experienced nothing like it.
that woman unleashed the power of gabrielle with her voice
swinging high and low and around the room all at the same time/knock-
ing
everything
to a new place.
it took the band quite a few to pick they drool and join in.
meantime/change was shaking she hips hard as she was shaking them
walls
mixing everybody's mind up/till the confusion of so much movement
and
feeling exploded in the last note of she song.
then it got quiet.
change turn
get back in route to lushy.
i says to myself poor j.b. and kokomo was fools to leave before all this got
let out.
ummhumm
well

drool got wiped
the band start back normal
coffee go to being served
flasks get to being opened
and the dance floor got back to its usual dip.

thats when i turned
saw bettye's face
which didn't look friendly at all
oh she was smiling
like a big ole wild cat tracking its prey.
oh lawd/na
i shout but can't nobody hear me cause right then
bettye let out a yelling as she broke a pop bottle in half/move
with the jagged edge face out
na/this cause ten things to happened all at the same time
change turn round pull something from she titties/couch and smile
the dippers pause
lushy run up from back the jernt grab bettye rush she out the front door
big bill run down from front the jernt pull change out the back door
papa ann holla and faint
the band switch songs/pause
then
folk get back to things and whatnot.
except me.
i roll out front see what going on.
there i find bettye and lushy under the
figure's flavors.   the world's finest.
come get a taste.
sign/which we all reads
bettye's jernt/and
there lushy and bettye talking.
lushy say
look here bettye
it's time you let this thing go.
bettye look violent but lushy press on say
i am sorry bettye i know sorry don't make it right/but i need to say it to
you i owe you that.
lushy take a big breath then quick start
bettye i was wrong in how i treated you
i was wrong for the way i took your love for granted/i was wrong to

think that i could act any ole kind of way and that it was your job to
take it/i was wrong for the ways i leaned on you but wasn't around
when you needed to lean/i was wrong for all the nights of making you
worry with my drinking/for making you guess what was on my
mind/for blaming you for everything that went wrong/for not taking
the time to treat you tender/for not holding up my share of making our
life work/for walking out the door yelling one last time/leaving you our
home all that we had dreamt and built and still needed to do/for all the
ways that i acted a fool i know i was wrong/and i was sho nuff wrong
for fucking change bettye.
i am sorry honey.
i am sorry.
lushy stood real close look bettye deep in the eye.
just stand there breathing soft saying she sorry real low/stare
till/all the wind and flame and will and walls fell away. and the two of
them
just clapse into one the other's arms. bettye crying let lushy hold
she/lushy
crying let bettye hold she.   i crying in the corner leaning against the wall
over around the other side of the
figure's flavors. the world's finest.
come get a taste.
sign. which we all know is bettye's jernet

STAND. CIRCLE STOOL. TAKE STOOL BEHIND CURTAIN

GRIOT. WITH THE LADY
yes sir/i saw it.
i saw the damn break i saw the love flow i saw the stars sparkle i saw the
light shift
that night i saw/wasn't nothing the same
all because the dust got stirred/by change.

WITH THE LADY

FILM (SINGERS)
GRIOT INVITE AUDIENCE MEMBERS UP TO DANCE
weather man don't know
how hot it is in here
oh no/he don't know
just how hot it is

says it's ten below
knee deep in snow
but oh no i'm so hot
in here

(END OF FILM. DANCING ENDS / AUDIENCE RETURNS TO THEIR SEATS)

GRIOT. STAND BY THE LADY
duckie smooth was a handsome man.
voice river deep / smile mountain wide / eyes
shiny soft / body rippling hard
and / duckie smooth
was as wonderful to listen to / as to behold.
man always knew just what to say / how to who when
and in what timbre.

that is why bettye felt fine leaving duckie smooth
in charge on buffet night every week
cause bettye knew
that man could talk the hiss out a snake / coax sly out the fox.
yessuh
duckie smooth in charge every week / on buffet night over to bettye's.
so bettye always take that night off / it's the one night
she ain't got to cook / cause
ain't no food on buffet night   though anything else you libal to want
do be served.

na / duckie smooth mama name he john harrison lee.
but we been calling him duckie smooth since that legendary night john
lost
his cool / at the second ever buffet night / long time ago.
i was there.
in fact / i was the one name he
it just come holla out my mouth.

see
duckie smooth
do female interpretations
on buffet night.
na / as handsome a man as john is / it is surprising
at just how ugly a woman he becomes.

but he so classy/he transform from a eyesore to a beautiful and most
desirable human being right before your eyes
till/the mens the womens the both and the neithers
be batting eyes at himshe.

duckie smooth and his wife cora adam
sews all through the days
so that every buffet night
duckie smooth got a fresh getup
for each introducement of the evenings headliners.
duckie smooth fall out fancy shiny sparkley cool
seven eight nine times a buffet night
face caked/different wigs flipping in different directions for different
outfits
and cora adam/always in color coordination going round and round
collecting apprecitation fees from everybody in the joint
yessuh everytime duckie smooth swing out
cora adam right there just a collecting.

anyway
like i said
the night duckie smooth got named
was back on himshe second time doing buffet night at bettye's.
himshe come out once
come out twice
come out three times
delightful stunning with magnagamous eleganance and introducements
for the peoples.
we was all settled in for a long good time/ready to ball.
till
it did seem
we was waiting a bit too long for the forth interpretive introducement of
the
forth act.
when all of a sudden
we hears

mafucka!

then
bambambam!

out roll onto the stage
john and fathead sims
and before we know'd it fat head had
done yanked the bottom half of john's dress clean off
which really piss john off / so at that point himshe sho nuff
commensed to kicking fat head's ass
said
i
will
bust
a
new
hole
in
your
ass.
bas
tard!
john just a whooping fat head's ass   till it was over.
john then stand up / all 6 foot of himshe
wig off / face cake caked / titties crooked / and
himshe panties showing just as pink as you please
cause there weren't no dress to cover the bottom half

thats when i find myself yelling
he duck it smooth
he duck it smooth
see john
had done
ducked him manhood so smooth back you
couldn't see not a trace of it
    and i knew how much a tucking that take cause / well
anyway
i just knew
so
yessuh
that is how duckie smooth got named
on that famous night himshe loose himshe cool
at the second ever buffet night at bettye's
long time ago.

WALK BACK OF CURTAIN TO DRUM

GRIOT. FROM DRUM

big mama sway real name is isadora Africa Jr.
they been name her
she mama her mama and her mama after that first African conjuration
woman / whose real name they don't know   or won't say. everybody
call this one big mama sway cause well / you know
plus nobody dare speak she birth name / call all them generations of
power
down. but we ain't crazy / we know who she is.
hell all you have to do is feel her sing.
it's enough to drive you to rip your heart out
lay it at her feet in offering.
thats in the wee hours of moonlight.
sunshine to sunset / she be in her garden pulling weeds talking to her
flowers and herbs singing quite the different song with fingers and hips
and feet in the earth.
na / i calls her baybay
cause she my baby brother's second wife sister chile / who i promised i
would
always look after the children   and though they all grown / they still
my
baybays.
my name is cat but this one calls me aunty.

i comes by baybay's / bring ole slim
toss him on the hammock under the peach trees   let him nap whiles
i sit on the porch drink them potions baybaby serve to keep my bones
strong
   which i do think also keep my kitty purring / and tight.
anyway
poor slim don't know but he be drinking potion too. thats why he always
sleep so good through the whole visit wake so sweet
and virile.
anyway
after dinner baybay wrap her head
hang she sign out / let folk know the conjuration wo'mn is ready.
but in the sunrise
she ain't nothing but my lil baybay

playing in she garden
talking to the baybays to come.

i talk to them too from time to time.
especially this one little ole gal
she real sweet. remind me of baybay/except that one drawn to heart-
break.
see her conjuration gone be so powerful/it's gonn tip her
till she figure out how to adjust her impulses.
yessuh/that one gonn be a isdora Africa jr.   a city gurl/too far
from home.

she ain't coming for a long time. baybay
gone guide her the whole way.
and me too.
we working with her now.
listen

there go baybay singing with the trees
planting all that needs be known
deep and in the breeze.

WALK BEHIND CURTAIN TO ROCKER

GRIOT. FROM ROCKER WITH FILM

FILM (BOOKER & JOSHUA)
they met over a poem
a poem they wrote in the fields   between the digging of earth/the
laying of tracks/the crossing of lines. between the pounding of
steel/and sun
with battered Spirits/in open spaces
with no silence   they made poetry
one syllable at a time/they
conjured theirselves/love

this is how booker chang and joshua davis found each other. in
blistering sun/working days never ending/backs bent in toil/in
the company of men   they claimed each other

declared themselves
adorned each other with words. united
in heart/booker chang and joshua davis married one the other
with a poem.

love
you
live
with
me
love
you
live
with
me
my
man
my
man

for
all
time
for
all
time

i
am
yours
i
am
yours.

they quit the rails. opened shop
selling charms and things right there in they front yard
they give poetry for free.
and even us that make our own charms stop by cause
some days/you just need
a poem.

FILM (BOOKA & JOSHUA'S SONG)

kiss
me
miss
you
wish
i

touch
me
hold
you
now
i
need
your
love

will
you
be
my

baby

love
you
live
with
me

love
you
live
with
me

my
man
my
man

for
all
time
for
all
time
i
am
yours
i
am
yours.

hold
me
with
your
eyes

make
me
know
i'm
yours

give
me
all
you
have

fill
me
with
your
heart

dear.

(END OF FILM)

WALK CENTER

GRIOT. TURN / PIVOTING SLOWLY
we come in she dreams.
tickle
hug tight
stand smile Watch Pray Touch Heal
whisper worries away whisper grief away whisper loneliness away whisper
fears away
whisper saddness away
with sweetgrass sea salt and sage
copal cedar and moonlight/bring Gifts
joy/here
dreams/here
tenderness/here
Blessings/here
Divinity/here
You/here
Spirit/here
family/here
all here
Lift now
Fly now
Free now
Be now
it's okay
not alone
not alone
not alone
not alone
always/We
whisper
Love.

WALK TO THE LADY

FILM (SONG)
sun
river
you

you
river
sit

sun
heat
river

river
move
slow.

river
move
slow.

sun
moon
cross

stars
shine
soft

you
river
gaze

river
move
loud

your
head
spins

river
move
fast

your
heart
jumps

river
change
shape

your
eyes
lock

river
rain
down

river
rain
down

blood
rain
down

fill
river
thick

run

you can't.

wind
cry
names

trees
know
names

wind wail
river thunder
trees moan

you

can't

move.

you
can't
cry
you
can't
breathe
you
can't
see

river
pulls
you
in

rain
keeps
you
under

river
sweeps
you
down

river
carries
you
away

long
journey.

trees
wind
sun
river
you.

home.

(END OF FILM)

GRIOT. STAY WITH THE LADY
we calls her miss sunday morning
but she don't hardly go to church   though she do rock with sweet t
lashay/pray to god
every Sabbath.

ms. sunday morning run the jernt
back of bettye's.
it's a gambling shack
a place standing way past good timing/she
gots folks working dark corners back rooms against the walls
and on a little red lighted stage   be shake dancers/grind so hard
not a string of clothing can hang on   they bump and wiggle
into the night and sunrise/dancers drop so far down
squeeze the last note out any song   rolling
back up.
yessuh
ms. sunday morning gots a little something for anybody/just outside of
right.
folk stepping in know   all possiblities
gonn come to pass.
they is jimmy slide/he smoke a cigarette with him ass-
cheeks   suck/tight
whip the mind of many around at the sight of it.
they is sally thick/who move she hips so slow
and low/and deep into the night
till ain't nobody brave enough to do nothing but watch.
her

off in a blue light
on a table
smiling and winking and
riding
alone.
they is tucker long who gots a peeter and putter
open and unroll/let you touch
for a fee

and they is them that fill the jernt
so tender/and flush
so ready
and ripe
so full of bursting
ain't nothing but trouble in sight.

yessuh
we gives ms. sunday morning plenty room.
hard as life is around here/much as we gots to forget
much as we needs to forgive/filled as we is with knowing
bad as it feel sometime/folks bound to only can find jesus
over to ms. sunday mornings jernt/some folks
got to jump in the circle that way
through the back door.
late.

ms. sunday morning herself
come in that way. her and sweet t
come in from a long road
late
and right on time.

see/sweet t was a man last life
is na woman/feel like a man
solid and sturdy/stern and silent/pressed and polished
sweet t
used to not know why he look like a he
packed like a she
sweet t
used to not understand why things didn't fit/why he didn't make no
sense

sweet t used to want to return him   she body
early sometimes
sweet t used to couldn't wait to come back/a he again.
sweet t used to get tired.
look like
sweet t was the one everything bad happened to
the one that never harmed nobody/but always got beat
since she was a child   folk take they evil out on she.
must have been sweet t was the one that suffered our transgressions
paid the price
for our collective sins. didn't know why.
sweet t had a hard life.
sweet t had it ruff
sweet t got scars all over she body.

a man then
woman now/neither really
skin peel/heart pull apart
sweet t journey been long.
no one to talk to. no one to think about the wrong of it. no one to kiss
the
pain. no one
to see her. no one to care why
no one

till ms. sunday morning come along.

ms. sunday morning come in with the river
ms. sunday morning floated down   layed up on a rock/stretched out
sweet t found she

ms. sunday morning had got tired too.

far away
she flew
in her mind
spun open
will
running
from nothing
running

from everthing
running
for no reason / running
for lots of reasons / running
because.

she left / her body
left her mind
left / floating
with empty eyes / in silence
she left
swept away
landed in the wrong place / at the right time
ms. sunday morning opened her eyes saw
sweet t's face and cried.
said i'm home now. and
they didn't need no words. they saw it all in one the other's eyes
and knew what they knew.

was sweet t brung ms. sunday morning to us
brung herself too. said they needed a charm
a chance to make it
wanted the road to be gentle / to
open a little more kind

and so now ms. sunday morning and sweet t
they pray
in each other's arms
in each other's mouths
bodies wrapped / they make holy
every Sabbath   love

they blossom
full
raise up one the other / breathe in tongues
take in Spirits / swallow
whole
shine
perfect in the light
of Sabbath

when the jernt is closed
they lay up
in one the other
breasts full
hips open / and large
like sunshine / they move
up and down
side to side across the sky
deep penetrating
and all day / reaching
higher
higher
lift
smile
see
god
cry
wail
sing
see
each other
heat
rise
moan
burst
make
love
holy
wholy
make
love
every day
and all of
Sabbath.
when the jernt is closed.

sweet t gots a little girl in he / now
giggle giggle slip out here and there / all the time since
miss sunday morning got a hold of she.
sweet t don't understand it / but ain't mad at why.

ms. sunday morning and sweet t run that jernt together na
make provissions for the peoples.
keep the back door open

holy wholy everyday
holy holy they love
holy holy they love
holy holy love
holy
they . . .

STAY WITH THE LADY

FILM (SONG)
i never left you
i been right here
waiting this whole time
wrapped in the memory of
your smile
your eyes
the scent of you
i been dreaming awake/about
sleeping in the soft of
your breasts falling
around my heart
i been walking in the moonlight
wishing for your love
praying God give me one more chance
to love you right.

HAND OUT AFFIRMATIONS

(leave script on stool/end up back with the lady)

FILM (FAMILY)
our gurl she
carry the conjuration her mama she mama she mama she mama
and that first African woman pass on   this scare her from
time to time/cause there are things she know but don't understand
things she can do but don't know why/power she got   can't control
like her voice

it contours time in release
each note / make the Holy Ghost rise in all who feel
she don't question this
but it do make her sad. too much too big too often / alone.
can't wrap words around it / so she don't try. just keep to herself
except for times when she think she drowning
feel like a touch / some talking / a smile might save her.
she keep company then

our gurl
she hurt from feeling all the the feelings she feel
which she keep pushed down / cause she think she got to
can't stop stay sharp turn the check toss the head step on be strong
don't worry never want can't have don't rest
smile
one foot in front the other / heavy
not dreaming
whittle words
day by day
till
nothing left

our gurl don't yet understand that the pressure of not feeling / explodes
poisons the Spirit dims the vision stills the heart cripples the hearing
sickens the body makes lonely the path
which libal to make the lesser way seem right at the cross roads
so
we told she mama / to send
our gurl home
na!

STAND NEXT TO THE LADY

FILM (SONG)
You are the me i am waiting to be
deep down / i see your Divinity
and i know that we are Free.
free / like the night in flight
free in God's Delight
in the Name of
We are

flesh of the Ocean
the Sun beaming bright
Winds crossing
the Earth's might
we are
your smile
my Heart
with Sight
Free.

no more fighting
i rebuke all fears
no separation
cause we are

the Peace we Pray
the poem we pen
the bridge we make
the song
that dance
is us
and we are

free
free
Free.
cause / We are
Love.

(END OF FILM)

STAY WITH THE LADY

READ

booka chang joshua davis clap speak	conjuration she
bitty fon / dreaming dream	conjuration she
big mama sway / sing shake	conjuration she
peachy soonay / claim her power	conjuration she
jook jernt / holla dip	conjuration she
ma dear big paw uncle daddy / pray smile	conjuration she
drummer / drumming drum	conjuration she

Fig. I.2. Conjuration scene. *The love conjure/blues Text Installation.*
Photo by Jen Simmons, courtesy of Sharon Bridgforth.

African and Indian / fly free conjuration
she / says our names
conjuration / she
keep our stories
conjuration we

send she back	conjuration we
hold her hands	conjuration we
praise she laughter	conjuration we
pave her path	conjuration we
open her road	conjuration we
Bless her heart	conjuration we
join her Love	conjuration we
grant she wishes	conjuration we
give her riches	conjuration we
stand in Light	conjuration she
sits in gold	conjuration she

dresses in jewels   conjuration she
says our names

                conjuration
                   we
                  give
                   she
                  Life
                conjuration
                   we

                  here
                  here
                  here
                conjuration
                   we

                  here
                  here
                  here
                conjuration
                  We

                She . . .

CENTER
GRIOT CONDUCTS AUDIENCE

STARTS WITH THE REMEMBER SECTION
READ THROUGH
BRING IN OTHER SECTIONS
END WITH REMEMBER SECTION

i   i
am the conjure.   am the conjure.
sacrificial blood made flesh / i am   sacrificial blood made flesh / I am
sanctified by tears wailing   sanctified by tears wailing
deep in the belly / i am that sound   deep in the belly / i am that sound
released. i am   released. i am
love remembered   love remembered
the promise kept   the promise kept
the should have been   the should have been

the utterance of hope/i am
the Life dreamt

i am the answered Prayer
the manifested Light
i am my Ancestors
returned
i am the dead/and the living
i will carry on
i will come back
i will grow more powerful
i will remember
i am the one We are waiting for

i
am
the conjure
come back/to Love.

the utterance of hope/i am
the Life dreamt

i am the answered Prayer
the manifested Light
i am my Ancestors
returned
i am the dead/and the living
i will carry on
i will come back
i will grow more powerful
i will remember
i am the one We are waiting for

i
am
the conjure
come back/to Love.

remember
remember
remember
remember.

LOVE!

THANK AUDIENCE

JEN
CREW
CAST
FUNDERS
SUPPORTING ORGANIZATION

DANCE!!

CHAPTER 1

Reinventing the Black Southern Community in Sharon Bridgforth's *The love conjure/blues Text Installation*

Matt Richardson

and do the jernt be packed!
mens womens some that is both some that is neither/be
rolling all up and between the sounds
—*love conjure/blues*

The work of performance artist/writer Sharon Bridgforth depicts the early twentieth-century rural southern black community from the crossroads of poetry, theater, and fiction to creatively imagine the interstices or "between the sounds" of fixed gender and sexual norms. In Bridgforth's work generally and in *The love conjure/blues Text Installation* in particular, the South as a space where multiple sexualities and genders are central to black culture is the guiding force for the collective to heal from the trauma of the past. Of interest here is Bridgforth's use of the dramatic technique of the jazz aesthetic in her writing. The jazz aesthetic, according to early jazz aesthetic pioneer Aishah Rahman, is characterized by the acknowledgment of multiple states of reality. The jazz aesthetic in drama is open to other expressive and artistic genres including dance, film/video, poetry, drama, and fiction simultaneously.[1] Bridgforth's two published books—a collection of short stories entitled *the bull-jean stories* (1996) and a novel, *love conjure/blues* (1999)—as well as her written and directed (what she called "conducted") plays and performances fulfill jazz aesthetic criteria for incorporating multiple genres. *The love conjure/blues Text Installation*, which is the focus of this essay, is an example of Bridgforth's adroit application of the jazz aesthetic, taking its promise of multiplicity into new dimensions by exploring the fluidity of queer gender identities in a black rural setting. Performance becomes a staged enactment of unfinished stories and accompanying movements, bringing these individual movements to a shared experience. To move with the intent of integrating "lost" bodies from the collective story is a communal act of healing.

Trained in the television and film industry, Bridgforth was founder, writer, and artistic director of the root wy'mn theatre company from 1993 to 1998. She was the anchor artist for the writing and performance collective known as the Austin Project, which was started in 2002 in Austin, Texas.[2] Bridgforth's second published book, *love conjure/blues*, touches on the stories of multiple members of a single community, poignantly moving through their desires and personal histories. *love conjure/blues* lives both as a novel (written in poetic verse) and as a text installation performance piece which, while staying true to the written text, includes filmed portions. *The love conjure/blues Text Installation* traveled to select U.S. cities from 2007 to 2009 and included live performances of sections of the novel as well as video footage.

My interpretation of this work is based on my interview with Bridgforth in 2009, my ethnographic experience as a member of the Austin Project from 2007 to 2009 with Bridgforth as the anchor artist for the project, my experience as an extra in the short film version of *love conjure/blues* in 2007, my performance as a cast member of *delta dandi* in 2009, and my experience as an extra in the Austin premiere of *ring/shout* in 2010.[3] Performance scholar D. Soyini Madison describes ethnography as an embodied practice. She states that "something happens differently when your body must move and adjust to the rhythms, structures, rules, dangers, joys and secrets of a unique location."[4] As Madison argues, something happens differently to the researcher when one is moving through the performance with "embodied attention" that structures and informs his/her interpretation and analysis.[5] From my position as an actor inside *The love conjure/blues Text Installation*, I am able to offer a unique perspective on the rhythms and rules governing Bridgforth's work.

The love conjure/blues Text Installation is a one-person stage performance of a "lost" African American rural past, written in a mixture of performance, poetry, and prose. This mixture assists in giving each text a nonrealist feel and opens the space for an imagined queer black southern community. Bridgforth's work opens a space at the crossroads of various genres and in doing so allows multiple truths at once. This mixing of genres occurs not only because of Bridgforth's training as a filmmaker and dramaturge, but also because Bridgforth's writing process often includes watching actors perform the work or her reading/performing the characters before the writing is organized, compiled, and published. Embodied performance has been part of her creative process to ensure that the work *looks* and *sounds* as well as reads according to her standards before it appears in a published book (and beyond).[6]

The novel and short stories were conceived, written, and revised according to the author's textual goals as well as her performance ones. The performances prior to publication help to shape the final script because Bridgforth gains from the actors themselves a tremendous amount of new information about the piece, which she incorporates into subsequent revisions. She uses the art of improvisation or "spontaneous creation" in each performance.[7] The script (or published book) does not contain stage directions, and through minimal rehearsal the actors and the director (or conductor) find the music and movement. However, each participant is expected to bring his or her unique perspective to the embodiment of the work. Therefore, each performance is unpredictable and kinetic.

As a "conductor," Bridgforth treats the development of a piece like a jazz composition. In the tradition of jazz visionaries such as Thelonious Monk's famous studio recording sessions, Bridgforth gathers together artists whom she respects and admires such as Daniel Alexander Jones, Baraka de Soleil, Helga Davis, Omi Osun Joni L. Jones, and others to interpret the text. Her artistic collaborators are encouraged to explore movement and vocal possibilities in a short series of improvisational rehearsals using the text as a basis. During her live performances, Bridgforth improvisationally "conducts" audience participation by giving the audience members cues to interject expressions and responses during key moments of the performances. Bridgforth uses these performances as information-gathering sessions. She assesses the text through the embodied performances, audience response during the show, and in a question-and-answer period afterward. All this becomes the basis of revisions to the text before it is ever published.

Publication is not the end of the life of these texts. The improvisation and kinesis of the work lives on, often performed, reinterpreted, and reworked in multiple ways subsequent to publication, as is the case with *The love conjure/blues Text Installation*, which comes to life as its own piece years after the novel was published. This flow between different genres of expression—in this case poetry, prose, performance, and published text—is consistent with the jazz aesthetic, a technique most often associated with live theater, which is the guiding principle of Bridgforth's work. The jazz aesthetic is an artistic practice that "encourages layering of images, ideas, sound, and experience. Polyphony and multivocality are required."[8] Multivocality is an approach that does not involve a lot of thick description, but instead places all voices in dialogue with each other (sometimes layered, but not lost), allowing multiple truths at once. All of the speaking voices heard consist of either overlapping voices that are often in competition with each other or one voice that intentionally dominates the others. The overall effect is that the aesthetic valorizes multiplicity rather than singularity.

Bridgforth's deployment of the jazz aesthetic owes a debt to the work of Aishah Rahman, Laurie Carlos, Ntozake Shange, and other artistic innovators. Performance scholar Omi Osun Joni L. Jones attributes the emergence of jazz aesthetics to the Sounds in Motion artistic workshop in Harlem during the height of the Black Arts Movement dominion of public discourse on the "proper" political aesthetics for black art.[9] These early practitioners shifted away from Black Arts Movement definitions of art that served black cultural and political goals and embraced jazz aesthetic qualities that they thought would reach multiple layers of black experience simultaneously. Jazz aesthetics rely on the ability to imagine more than one event, sound, or idea at a time in order to tell stories that have not been told.[10] Furthermore, the separation from the rigid nationalism of the Black Arts Movement allowed the founders of the jazz aesthetic to "set no limit on Blackness," thereby leaving space for a broader representation of black desires and gender identities.[11] Jones expands on Rahman's definition, describing what she calls "jazz aesthetics," thereby pluralizing the process and leaving it open for evolving practices. She defines nine "foundational precepts" of the form: being present to one's feelings, breathing, "deep listening," improvisation, honoring simultaneous truths, collaboration, virtuosity, body centeredness, and metamorphosis.[12] For the purposes of this essay I focus on Bridgforth's application of Rahman's principle of honoring simultaneous truths, analyzing how it has opened up the possibilities for the representation of gender and sexuality. I explore the ways in which *The love conjure/blues Text Installation* accomplishes a layering of queer black southern experiences through Bridgforth's use of overlapping sounds, images, and texts.

Bridgforth's interpretation of jazz aesthetics reflects embodied forms of simultaneity as well as aesthetic ones. Her respect for varied and often contradictory perspectives and embodied truths comes from both her personal experience and the stories told to her by the elders in her life. She combines the stories she has heard with her life experiences and transforms them into her unique creative vision. Bridgforth brings to the stage the queer life that she envisions the elders/ancestors to have had, enabling her ability to imagine the queer parts of their lives that her elders could not or were afraid to speak aloud. This commitment to multiple truths is often incorporated into the text through the presentation of a variety of genders, including characters that are gender variant, meaning that their gender presentations do not "match" their anatomy according to social norms. As it is so eloquently expressed in the script, in this restaged setting the elders/ancestors include "the mens the womens the both and the neithers." Bridgforth adroitly uses the black vernacular custom of adding an "s" to already plural words to signify that the terms "men" and "women" are not fixed in a bilateral stasis, but are complex and creative categories. Moreover, queer genders and sexualities are the basis upon which these characters build relationships and kinship with each other. The performance provides a guide to survival and resistance that is centered on queer ways of being and creating community. In this way, black queer ancestors and elders are never completely "lost" to us. They exist in and through their representation in sound, image, and dialogue.

Sound: They Took His Drum; Hearing the Ancestors

The love conjure/blues Text Installation embraces the jazz aesthetic's tenet of simultaneity by including different forms of media. It is a simple stage. The audience sits around the center where there is a live performer, a chair, and a couple of altars. Video screens and speakers that project images and sound surround the audience and performer. Throughout the piece, the live performance and the music and sound from the speakers do not simply serve as a soundtrack for the projection on the video screens, but are concurrent performances in conversation with each other.

An excellent example of this effect takes place at the beginning of the performance. The layering of sound between the performer and recorded sound also functions as a way to layer the time represented in the piece. This layering process is exemplified in one of the first parts of the performance wherein there is a recounting of the story of the slave ancestors that is signified by repeatedly chanting, "they took his drum." "They took his drum" is an example of aural simultaneity at work in the text/installation as the sound of the drum fills the space and is layered with spoken voices of the live performer and the soundtrack. The beat of the drum is both mournful and defiant as the live performer whispers. The details of that whispering are inaudible, and the recorded voices chant, "they took his drum" along with other speech that is not clear. The fact that the voices are disembodied makes them feel otherworldly, like the whispers of spirits. The effect is a palpable sense that the live performer is creating sacred space through ritual and prayers. The performer's role as the carrier of memories becomes clear as her voice and the voices on the screen come into sync. As they both speak the words "they took his drum" the performer becomes the voice of the past that is spoken into the present. The living and the ancestors are all given a voice in the production through a monologue or music. Bridgforth's layering of multiple perspectives and voices functions as a way to aurally layer temporalities, which is a key aspect of the jazz aesthetic. As Rahman states, any given performance piece can "represent a triple-consciousness: of the unborn, the living and the dead."[13]

The piece is premised on Rahman's statement of simultaneous consciousness and overlapping temporalities wherein the unborn, the living, and the dead share the same dimension. This is achieved through what religious studies scholar John Mbiti describes as the "unlimited past."[14] According to this schema, the ancestors offer a wealth of knowledge and experience that extends back indefinitely in time and is available to those willing to seek this wisdom. This is in opposition to a Western progress narrative where society looks to the present and to the future, concomitantly dismissing the past as "backward" and elders as "out of date." According to Mbiti, West African cultures honor the contributions of the ancestors and elders and make use of their wisdom in practical ways. In the *love conjure/blues Text Installation* project, the past is a resource for knowledge; there is an epistemological reordering wherein the wisdom of the ancestors is primary and readily available in the present and to future generations through ritual, memory, and storytelling.

The love conjure/blues Text Installation makes use of this conceptualization of the ancestors as accessible beings to "close the gap" of black history. While we know some information about the lives of captured Africans in the Americas, most of their experiences, including a richer understanding of their emotional lives and sexual relationships, have been lost. Slavery is considered an archive that black people cannot access.[15] Since the ancestors are close to the narrator of the *Text Installation* project, she is never alienated from past events. The piece reaches back and restages the impact of slavery. In the performance, the diversity of black sexualities and genders is not erased. Families are not decimated by slavery; they connect to memory, reaching into the past to find a network of those who know each other and whom they have loved.

The segment "They took his drum" begins a story of slave resistance and rebellion. The live performance monologue is a story about the power of sound. The slave community drummer is so feared that the slave owner takes away his drum, and when he continues to make rhythm just using his body, the slave owner cuts off all the drummer's fingers in an effort to stop the power of the drum. However, through creative resistance, "with him mouth/make sound/low to the ground legs bend feet," he makes rhythm with his mouth and feet. The sound itself assists the plantation's conjure woman, or possessor of spiritual knowledge and secrets of communion with the spirit realm, with her plan to overthrow the master.

Imbedded within the narration of the drum is the story of the conjure woman Isadora Africa, the "first African conjuration/woman."[16] According to the legend, she leads an insurrection on the slave plantation that existed in the fictional community of the novel using only prayer, ritual, and herbs to stop the white owner and overseers in their tracks. This is enough to assist Isadora Africa in calling the force of the spirits that ushers in a wind that "lift[s] ole marsa up high in the air/drop him down flat on the floor." She uses her access to the kitchen and knowledge of medicinal plants to poison the master and overseer's food with the very fingers he took. By the end of the night, all the slaves left the plantation and "ain't no plantation no more never since that time/not on these grounds." The story is passed down through the generations and each time a conjure woman of strength is born, she is given the name Isadora.

Image: Feeding the Feeling; Juke Joint as a Site of Healing

The black southern small town in general is a liminal space in Bridgforth's work at the crossroads of time.[17] It is suspended in time somewhere between the "then" (the early twentieth century) and the "now" (the late twentieth/early twenty-first centuries when the installation was written and published and presumably when these ancestors are no longer part of the visible world). The temporal ambiguity of the performance piece is projected in the visual representations of the juke joint as a sacred space of divine feminine power, communal ritual, and gender diversity.

The juke joint setting for the performance is mostly described by the narrator/live performer and represented on the screen. We are introduced to the juke joint, named Bettye's, through a description of the club's owner, Slim Figurman, a description that is accompanied by his image on the screens. Slim appears as an androgynous figure

Fig. 1.1. Slim and Dem. The *love conjure/blues Text Installation*.
Photo by Jen Simmons, courtesy of Sharon Bridgforth.

surrounded by indistinct green and fertile woods. He is described as a "fancymann" [sic], and a trickster, who talks "so many circles / till don't nobody know what the hell / he talking about." He is the cross-roads figure that opens the door to the spiritual world of the community represented in the performance. Like the rest of the characters, he is both of this world and a queer ghostly presence that invites us into the sacred work that is performed in the juke joint.

Slim Figurman's visually androgynous image helps us to imagine the male femininity of Duckie Smooth. Later in the performance, Duckie is described as a cross-dressing performer who does "female interpretations." His interpretations of black femininity are sensual and engaging in their own way, since Duckie is not conventionally beautiful. Nevertheless, he is desirable across the gender spectrum as "the mens the womens the both and the neithers / be batting eyes at himshe." Bridgforth conjures a particularly queer femininity, creating a complex series of individual interpretations of gender throughout the text that are not assigned to any particular anatomy or sexuality. Duckie Smooth is a male feminine figure that is in a heterosexual marriage. His wife, Cora, supports her husband's performance efforts by collecting tips at each show. Duckie's marriage to Cora does not prevent him from joining the line of feminine trustees of the juke joint in Bettye's absence.

Bridgforth's specific attention to representing queer femininity is an explicit departure from other queer performance pieces. Lisa M. Anderson notes, in *Black Feminism in Contemporary Drama*, that in theater the "predominant representation of lesbian is of butch."[18] In plays such as Shirlene Holmes's *A Lady and a Woman*, Ed Bullins's *Clara's Ole Man*, and Bridgforth's *the bull-jean stories*, there is a strict lesbian butch/femme pairing that "lines up" according to anatomy, and in Laurinda D. Brown's *Walk like a Man*, feminine lesbians do not appear at all. Anderson contends that this phenomenon occurs because the "unmarked lesbian is the butch; she functions as the visible lesbian both in lesbian culture and in the larger culture."[19] In *The love conjure/blues Text Installation*, the feminine characters are the spiritual guardians of the juke joint and as such they initiate the healing rituals within. As Bettye's main singer, Big Mama Sway's embodied performance is situated at the core of the community's ritual:

> a big ole
> powerful sample of wo'mness stroll center the room. sway step
>   smile sway
> step smile sway sway she went till she in place standing center
>   inside a
> moment of stillness

Big Mama Sway is a channel of divine forces. She sways from side to side with the piano, which is the catalyst to lifting the feelings of the audience members so that the sound of her voice can help them release the pain of trauma. Florinda Bryant, a longtime participant/director in the Austin Project, represents Big Mama Sway on the screen. She sways into the center of a semicircle, surrounded by onlookers mesmerized by the movement of her hips and the swing of her arms. Big Mama Sway moves with courtly power, and in combination with the piano, her voice opens a portal to divine magic and ancestral forces. When Big Mama Sway sings, the narrator says that "some kind of hunger-spirit" sweeps through the room, until bodies hungry for release continue "feeding the feeling" until church. The community is carried to trance by the swaying of bodies, the beat of the instruments, and the open invitation in Big Mama Sway's voice. In these moments she is the holy priestess or mambo of the community, bringing the community members into the arms of spirit where they are safe enough to "stop [the] heart."

As a link to the spirits, Big Mama Sway is positioned at the crossroads between the living, the dead, and the unborn. During the day, she is a conjure woman, or healer who cultivates a garden of flowers and healing herbs, while she speaks to the "the babies to come," the unborn children that are on the way. She and the narrator are given the gift of third sight to be able to "see" and speak to future generations, to help prepare them for the journey ahead. They are the ones who will be willing and able to listen to the ancestors as they impart their stories and knowledge even after death. Big Mama Sway's birth name is Isadora Africa, Jr., but "nobody dare speak she birth name / call all them generations of power / down." At night, Big Mama Sway is the headlining blues singer at Bettye's juke joint. Bettye's is a space for queer community creation and healing ritual.

Big Mama Sway's masculine counterpoint in the juke joint is Big Bill. Big Bill is a commanding presence in the community, wearing "she suit black / hat low / glasses dark / and shoes so shinning [sic] make / your head hurt." Big Bill entices the patrons at the juke joint as she "walk / pants pull here here / here / material ripple across she crotch which appear packing a large and heavy surprise," while she nonetheless plays the piano with an authoritative vigor. Much like the relationship between the dancer and the drummer, it is the combination of Big Bill's piano or guitar playing and Big Mama Sway's voice that opens a portal to divine presence and ancestral forces.[20]

In answer to their musical prayer a deity does respond to their musical supplication for divine manifestation. A "cookie brown woman / with tight light brown curls rumbling all the way down / to the bounce on her behind" named Change appears in the juke joint, "swirling a little dust before her." When she sings, "the sound that came out / shook the entire room." The power of her voice causes the earth to rumble and the walls to shake. From the force at which she swoops in and captures everyone's attention to the multicolored swirl of her dress, Change is a description of the West African orisha (deity) Oya. In the Yoruba pantheon, Oya is "the Queen of the Winds of Change. . . . She brings about sudden structural change in people and things," and as a "mistress of disguises" she can appear anywhere without warning.[21] She walks in and heads straight for Bettye's hard-drinking ex-lover, Lushy. Change's targeting of Lushy with her charms brings about a shift in Bettye and Lushy's relationship, initiating reconciliation between the two lovers. This moment is also an opportunity for masculine redemption as Lushy goes from being a "drunk" to making amends with Bettye for her irresponsible and selfish actions. The diversity of genders represented in the Oya video segment (and in the rest of the performance piece) is foreshadowed in the Slim Figurman video toward the beginning of the show.

The video segment that signals the arrival of Change/Oya is punctuated by syncopated rhythms and the words "sometime/a whole lot of shit just libal to happen." During the taping of the Oya section of *The love conjure/blues Text Installation* in 2007, the crossing of the divine and the everyday became more explicit as actors (straight and queer) were directed to bring clothes appropriate for an early twentieth-century juke joint setting and plain all-white clothes to the taping, which created a more timeless feel. White is a ceremonial color that indicates, among many things, that the participants are ready to receive the bond with spirit that ceremony provides.[22] Once we arrived, we were instructed to pair up (femme-femme, butch-femme, transman-femme, butch queen–butch queen) and dance in the middle of the floor first to 1920s/1930s-style blues.[23] We then changed into all whites and imagined that we were listening to gospel and reacted as if we were in a black church setting where it is common to see people sway and jump in a spiritual trance. The result is a mystical scene that is transformed from the appearance of the living room, where the scene was taped, to an image of us suspended in an all-white space similar to a cube or a cloud. The white space again represents the ceremonial practice that is occasioned by both the blues and gospel. We moved seamlessly between the two modes of being, one feeding the other and both informed by our collective imagined vision of how our queer ancestors might have moved with each other in community. Part of the incredible power of being in the scene is the recognition that the reenactment of an imagined black queer community is a spiritual process of reaching across time for a connection with the ancestors. To imagine their existence is an act of stepping into the crossroads, that infinite space that makes the "the dead/and the living."

The text installation ends with the representation of two couples that represent the power of love to resist oppression. Gay men are an important part of this revisioning of black southern community. Booka Chang and Joshua Davis are a representation of black gay male love and tenderness. They are day laborers trapped in a life of backbreaking toil. In the midst of brutal exploitation, they create beauty:

> they met over a poem
> a poem they wrote in the fields   between the digging of
>   earth/the

laying of tracks . . . between the pounding of steel/and sun
with battered Spirits/in open spaces
with no silence   they made poetry

Bridgforth gives us a different portrayal of the resistance used by black
people to reclaim their humanity in opposition to crushing deprivation
demanded of working in the "blistering sun/[work] days never end-
ing/backs bent in toil." As a continuation of the plantation economy
created in slavery, the labor conditions endured by workers like Booka
and Joshua are designed to squeeze the spirit into submission. Despite this environment, the two men find each other through loving expression. Isolated in the "company of men," black men's ability to love
each other, to "claim each other" and find joy together, is a profound
act of refusal of domination. Along with images of two black gay men
projected onto the screens, songstress Helga Davis's voice croons the
words to their poem: "kiss me miss you wish i, touch me hold you now."

The final visuals of community and ritual accompany the story of
Miss Sunday Morning and Sweet T. The visuals on the screens that run
concurrent to the couple's description involve the same couples that
were in the juke joint now in ritual white clothing. The narration states
that Miss Sunday Morning's place exists at the edges of the community.
She runs the joint *behind* Bettye's joint. It is "standing way past good
timing" and "just outside of right." There are patrons and workers along
"dark corners back rooms [and] against the walls" of the joint. Those
who engage in explicit sexual performance and transactional sex have
a place in Bridgforth's schema of the sacredness of black community.
Miss Sunday Morning is another feminine guardian of sacred space.
Illicit spaces like that of Miss Sunday Morning's are usually represented
in terms of shadow and despair; however, Bridgforth lights up the dark
corners of the sexual margins with love and healing through her relationship with Sweet T.

Sweet T is neither man nor woman, but lives in the interstices of
gender: "a man last life" is now a "woman/feel like a man." Sweet T's
frustration over not having a body that matches her/his gender identity is compounded by a life of abuse and suffering. She/he was "the
one that never harmed nobody/but always got beat" from childhood,
leaving her/him with a body marked with scars. Sweet T is a symbol of
the brutality of the past that lives in the scars on his/her body. While
the narration tells of Sweet T's past, the couples on the screens frolic
in the forest in joy and playfulness. Again, queer love shows the collective a way through suffering and embracing all marginalized parts

of the black community. Sweet T lives a life of isolation and despair until he/she meets Miss Sunday Morning. Their lovemaking is a sacred prayer for wholeness, their "bodies wrapped/they make holy/every Sabbath." With the help of Miss Sunday Morning's soothing and re-assuring love, Sweet T is able to embrace the "girl in he." As a result of Sweet T and Miss Sunday Morning's union, they work together to take care of the marginalized and discarded, and "holy wholy [sic] everyday" they love each other and the rest of the community. Sweet T's transfor-mation from loneliness to his/her newfound joy is a metaphor for what can occur for the black collective when the discarded parts are enfolded into the whole with love.

In Bridgforth's work, the southern community is the locus of black queer life. It is also the birthplace of black queer identities and plea-sures—both of which are constructed as resistances to external impo-sitions from society and regulating regimes, which attempt to delimit and define black families and communities, bodies and desires accord-ing to outside norms.

Text: I Will Remember

The piece is called a "text installation" because the written text is layered throughout the performance and because the live performer reads directly from the script onstage. Given the expansiveness and possibility of the jazz aesthetic's focus on improvisation, the text is still central to the performance. The text's centrality is indicative of Bridg-forth's acceptance of her role as a possessor of ancestral memories. She laments that even though the gift of storytelling was freely given to her from the respected senior members of her community who surrounded her in childhood and that their words gave her sustenance, a significant part of the community was silenced and unseen.[24] Bridgforth writes in response to that silencing; she states in the preface to the bull-jean stories that "these are the stories they didn't tell me the ones i needed most."[25] Even in Bridgforth's autobiographical introduction, she uses poetic syntactical strategies to convey meaning. Between the phrase "these are the stories they didn't tell me" and the phrase "the ones i needed most" is a literal space, indicating a sea of emotion in the inter-stices of what was not said and her own longing. It is also the gap be-tween knowing that there was more that the elders could have said, but did not. The word "needed" is palpable in this sentence. Need is what follows the gulf of knowledge that is lost in the silence. The work emerges to bridge the gap between what Bridgforth knows was missing and what can be said in order to help quench the need and put it in the past tense. The ancestors and elders' words were needed and now they are said through the process of "creative-remembering," a reformulation of the storytelling tradition.

The love conjure/blues Text Installation challenges normative understandings of black community by emphasizing Africa-derived cultural features whereby the living and the dead exist in the same temporal space. Both the voice from the soundtrack and the live performer echo each other with the following words:

i am the dead/and the living	i am the dead/and the living
i will carry on	i will carry on
i will come back	i will come back
i will grow more powerful	i will grow more powerful
i will remember	i will remember
i am the one We are waiting for	i am the one We are waiting for

These lines from the closing pages of *The love conjure/blues Text Installation* are emblematic of Bridgforth's ability to straddle poetry, drama, and prose simultaneously as a method of bringing the text to the crossroads of past and present. The space between the two columns of words suggests that two realities are at work simultaneously, symbolizing the break between dimensions or states of consciousness. The crossroads are a space between, which is what allows for gender ambiguity, sexual fluidity, and unpredictability to flourish. As Jacqui Alexander states, the crossroads is "that imaginary from which we dream the craft of a new compass."[26] Trauma, ritual, and celebration are what bring the living, the dead, and the spirits together in the performance. The phrase "i will come back more powerful" is a reference to the eternality of spirit as elders are reincarnated in the new generation. The connection is also made to the "living/dead," those who are mired in sorrow and are still alive, but not living. There is hope for them as well through the collective strength passed down to successive generations. The link between the old and the new, the living and the dead, is not only unbroken, as each generation remains connected to the past, but also stronger, making it possible to create a new future.

Notes

1 Aishah Rahman, "The Mojo and the Sayso," in *Moon Marked and Touched by Sun: Plays by African-American Women*, ed. Sydne Mahone (New York: Theatre Communications Group, 1994), 110.

2 The Austin Project (2002–11) was a group of predominantly women of color (although a small number of white women and transmen of color also participated) who came together for eleven weeks to share in a writing workshop that is focused on the writing process. It was founded by Omi Osun Joni L. Jones, professor of African and African Diaspora Studies at the University of Texas at Austin. The production was also underwritten by the Warfield Center for African and African American Studies at the University of Texas at Austin, http://e-tap.org/history.htm (accessed March 1, 2009).

3 Bridgforth was the anchor artist from the Austin Project's inception in 2002 until 2009. The Austin Project usually had an anchor artist, producer, and director who moved the group from artistic process to performance. According to Omi Osun Joni L. Jones, the anchor artist was the artistic guide for the eleven-week series of sessions. She facilitated weekly workshops and pushed the participants to work through a creative process. At the end of the eleven weeks, whatever creative work had been done from each member (writing, film, photography, sculpture, etc.) was gathered together and assembled into a collective performance piece wherein each participant's voice was integrated into the whole story. The entire process culminated in two public performances of the collective piece.

4 D. Soyini Madison, "Staging Fieldwork/Performing Human Rights," in *The Sage Handbook of Performance Studies*, ed. D. Soyini Madison and Judith Hamera (Thousand Oaks, CA: Sage, 2006), 401.

5 Madison, "Staging Fieldwork," 401.

6 Bridgforth, personal interview, June 1, 2009.

7 Omi Osun Joni L. Jones, Lisa L. Moore, and Sharon Bridgforth, eds., *Experiments in a Jazz Aesthetic: Art, Activism, Academia, and the Austin Project* (Austin: University of Texas Press, 2010), 3.

8 Jones, Moore, and Bridgforth, *Experiments*, 25.

9 Omi Osun Joni L. Jones, "Cast a Wide Net," *Theatre Journal* 57, no. 4 (2005): 598–99.

10 Rahman, "Mojo and the Sayso."

11 Jones, "Cast a Wide Net," 599.

12 Jones, Moore, and Bridgforth, *Experiments*, 6–7.

13 Rahman, "Mojo and the Sayso," 283.

14 John Mbiti, *African Religions and Philosophy* (Oxford: Heinemann Educational Publishers, 1969), 22. See also *Introduction to African Religion* (Oxford: Heinemann Educational Publishers, 1975).

15 See Saidiya Hartman's discussion of the limitation of the archive of slavery in Saidiya V. Hartman, "Venus in Two Acts," *Small Axe* 12, no. 2 (2008): 1–14.

16 Throughout this essay I capitalize the characters' names even though they do not appear that way in the original script. I do this in order to help the reader easily distinguish the names from the rest of the essay.

17 Bridgforth's play is in dialogue with other African American fiction that represents the South as a place of creative potential, especially the work of Zora Neale Hurston. It also has resonances with other personal accounts of

the South such as Mamie Garvin Fields's memoir, *Lemon Swamp and Other Places* (New York: Free Press, 1970).

18 Lisa M. Anderson, *Black Feminism in Contemporary Drama* (Urbana: University of Illinois Press, 2008), 110.

19 Anderson, *Black Feminism*, 110.

20 For research on vodun spiritual practices and the dialogue between drummers and dancers that creates the conditions to establish contact with ancestors and with deities called lwa, see Gerdes Fleurant, *Dancing with the Spirits: Rhythms and Rituals of Haitian Vodou, the Rada Rite* (Westport, CT: Greenwood Press, 1996).

21 Luisah Teish, *Jambalaya: The Natural Women's Book of Personal Charms and Practical Rituals* (San Francisco: Harper San Francisco, 1985), 120.

22 For more information on white as a ceremonial color in Yoruba ceremonial practice, see J. Omosade Awolalu, *Yoruba Beliefs and Sacrificial Rites* (Brooklyn, NY: Athelia Henrietta Press, [1996] 2001).

23 "Butch queen" is a term used by African American gay men to describe gay men whose gender expression is not exclusively masculine or feminine. See Marlon M. Bailey, *Butch Queens Up in Pumps: Gender, Performance, and Ballroom Culture in Detroit* (Ann Arbor: University of Michigan Press, 2013) 3.

24 Bridgforth, personal interview, June 1, 2009.

25 Bridgforth, preface to *the bull-jean stories* (Washington, DC: RedBone Press, 1998).

26 M. Jacqui Alexander, *Pedagogies of Crossing: Meditations on Feminism, Sexual Politics, Memory, and the Sacred* (Durham, NC: Duke University Press, 2005), 8.

CHAPTER 2

Interview with Sharon Bridgforth

Sandra L. Richards

Sandra L. Richards: Were you exposed to theater or the other arts while growing up?

Sharon Bridgforth: I didn't grow up going to the theater, or being involved in the arts, per se. I do believe that my work is based in a black American cultural tradition and art-making traditions. . . . The piece of theater that I did see was *for colored girls who considered suicide/when the rainbow is enuf* in the Bay Area back . . . in the seventies before my daughter was born when it was in the early stages of touring. I saw it in a theater in San Francisco and that was life changing for me and helped me to continue to imagine images and music as something that can live on the page. The way Ntozake Shange wrote really freed me up, but it took me a while to find my own self inside of all this.

SR: How then did you get involved with theater?

SB: Right after I got my degree, I worked for MGM as an intern on the show *Fame* [laughs], but that intern program didn't last long. Next, I worked for Planned Parenthood. I can't remember my title, but I was the person you saw before you saw the nurse, so I took the history, the blood pressure, etc. And it ended up being an amazing thing for me, because when I moved to Texas in 1990, those skills helped me to get a job with the Health Department. There, I was a disease and prevention specialist, so I managed syphilis cases for the Health Department, which then led to my being one of the first HIV educators and testers in the community in Austin. Along the way I was collecting a lot of skills around community organizing in Austin. I was still writing, but I didn't know what to do with it. And also because Austin is a very small town, it's very progressive and pretty amazing people were very accessible. I fell in with a group of artists who used art as a vehicle for social justice. I was encouraged to continue to write and share my work. At that point, a women's theater company in Austin produced my first show. I thought they were poems. I handed them a pack of handwritten poems, and they saw it as a one-woman show, and they said, "Oh, we're gonna produce your one-woman show," and I said, "Oh, that's what it is?" [laughs]. So that kind of changed my life.

SR: What was the name of the show?

SB: *Sonata Blue*. The Word of Mouth Women's Theatre Company in Austin, Texas, produced it.

SR: And what year was this?

SB: This was around 1992, or '91. I just sat in the room while they rehearsed.

SR: Interesting, you had seen Shange's play: you saw it on the page and it was poetry, but that wasn't you necessarily. Yet you were writing poetry . . .

SB: Yeah, yeah, it was pretty full circle. I was like "That's what this is!" I started moving pretty fast after that because then I understood I had these skills that I had been collecting as an activist and community organizer. So I started my own theater company shortly after that, 'cuz I still didn't know how to do anything like how to access directors. I wanted to work with a black director, because the director of my first show was white. She was great, but to me what I was doing was spiritual and felt very much about carrying on a cultural tradition. Since I didn't know who to ask for help, I just said let me just do it, and at that point I had met Omi [Omi Osun Olomo, aka Joni Jones]. And she was the person in the University [of Texas, Austin] who was always deeply steeped in the community, and I asked her to help me and she came. I cast the company. Omi did a series of workshops using the Theater of the Oppressed model, and using the body as the site of performance, which was kind of perfect for what I was doing. And she talked a lot about African and African American performance traditions, and it just really, really helped me a lot.

My theater company was called root wy'mn theater company [laughs]. We toured. I laugh because I really didn't know what I was doing, and I really think it was just God and angels moving us along. And I worked, you know, so I paid for everything, so it was crazy [laughter]. I had my full-time job at the Health Department, and I worked as a contract worker for other organizations, so I really had like three jobs, and I wrote the pieces, and I directed and managed the theater company, and we went on the road. We had a great time! We had amazing experiences. An organization in Austin called Women and Their Work . . . were part of a performance network. They took a five-minute clip of our show to the NPN [National Performance Network] conference and we got picked up as a result of that. We toured from '93 until 1998.

And at that point I just couldn't keep doing everything, so I quit my day job. Since I didn't have or know how to access the human resources necessary to have the company move forward, I felt like I had to pick, so I said, "I will focus on writing, because that is what I feel I am really here to do." So I started moving in the world as an independent artist whose primary work is writing for performance. And the theater company—it doesn't exist anymore, because the artistic staff is different—but Frontera at Hyde Park Theater—they use the symbol "@ Hyde Park Theater" . . .

SR: Is this a successor group to yours?

SB: No. Under the artistic direction of Vicky Boom, they started producing my work. They hooked me up with Laurie Carlos, who's one of the original women of *for colored girls* . . . And so Laurie stepped in and blew my world all apart to the moon, just like really lifted my life. I consider her to be a mentor, big sister, dear friend, foremother of the aesthetic that I am working in.

In 1998, Frontera produced one of my pieces called *Blood Pudding*, which is where I was looking at my Louisiana ancestry. Laurie directed it, Frontera produced it, and everything just changed again. Omi continued to work with me as a dramaturge: sometimes she directed a couple of things and performed in a few other pieces.

SR: You say that Laurie Carlos is the foremother of the aesthetic. Would you tell me a little bit more about what you mean, particularly because her work isn't as well known as Shange's. Are you saying her work is different from Shange's?

SB: Well, I would even consider Shange and James Baldwin to be people who have informed and moved forward this aesthetic. I guess I say Laurie specifically because the aesthetic in which I am placing myself is the theatrical jazz aesthetic, and there are some attributes of this aesthetic that I think Laurie specifically does. One is the idea of walking with other artists so that you learn by doing, by driving to the store and having conversations, by bringing each other in whenever possible into the room. These interactions are always all about the process, which is finally about life. The outcome is gravy, and the outcome is also a place where you learn. I think Laurie is very specifically, intentionally committed to that. And I am, too. The people that name themselves as working in the theatrical jazz aesthetic are all very different, just like any group of people, so I am not saying everybody feels the same way or works the same way. But I do believe that in order to have the work successfully live and articulate itself, it must have movement, voice, prayer, ritual, dramatic interpretation, and music coexist. I feel like Laurie's work very specifically draws on these things, too, that's why I say that.

SR: Have you always incorporated digital elements in your performance pieces?

SB: No, that's been a newer interest for me. I've worked with filmmakers and done some CD recordings of my work, but I hadn't actually incorporated a digital part before *love conjure/blues Text Installation*. For me, the stage is a living altar. It's not so much about costumes and sets, but it's more about how the work lives in the room, the way that we can invite or provoke the audience as a witness who is responsible for what happens in the room. This digital aspect is newer.

SR: How and when did you come to view the stage in such spiritual terms?

SB: I was working with the root wy'mn theatre company in 1993. Omi did intensive performance workshops, and a dancer in the company named Anoa Monsho did a series of dance workshops for us. Michelle Parkerson directed our first piece that I called *love/rituals and rage*, produced at the Vortex Theater in Austin. Marcia Ann Gomez was the set designer. Marcia was a sculptor and an environmental activist and one of the cofounders of the Indigenous Women's Network. Marcia was the one who helped me see that what I was really trying to do was pray. She is the one that coined this idea for me of the set as a living altar. When she designed our set, she created an altar, using sculpted pieces and masks of the women's faces that she had created. And from then on it's just what I've been doing.

SR: So how might the idea of the stage as a living altar work for different performance spaces for this piece? Are there other ways in which you prepare the space?

SB: Laurie was actually the person who told me this: we don't do anything to literally invite any spirits [laughs]. We don't want that to happen because we don't know what would happen, but the idea of the spiritual quality of the stage is more about the intention and the energy we set. Visual art is one of the media the story is told through. I've worked with sculptors who have sculpted pieces that are part of the altar set, and sometimes the altar set is created with salt and sand. So, it can be very obvious, and it can be not so obvious, but the work itself is really a prayer. A lot of the idea is supported by what the words convey and how the performers use the space. So the intention is really a part of it.

SR: I'd like to be a little bit literal here, and push you a bit more. "The energy, the work itself is a prayer." Do you meditate as a group, is that part of how you set the energy, or is every person responsible for themselves? How do people know that this work is a prayer? How do they know that this is not just another acting job? Where does that emphasis on spirituality come: is it in rehearsal, or have you worked with the same people all along so that you have this shared history?

SB: I've worked with many of the same people for so long that it's kind of a shared history, but I'm always working with new people, too. It's the text itself, the process of bringing the piece back to life, and the people that are working in the process. For example, for one version of *love conjure/blues*, Helga Davis, who directed and composed and conducted those performances, was taking some text and creating vocal soundscapes with the cast members. Now, we've always performed in a circle, the idea being that the audience is part of what's going on and has to participate with the performers. But in that rehearsal process, it really did become church 'cuz the text is the road map for what happens, and it informed what [Davis] pulled out from the performers. We had an experience in the rehearsal process that blew our minds. Now whether the audience gets that or not, we're not trying to be literal or responsible for that, but our process or experience, our intentions, we weave together.

SR: You talk about being present in rehearsals. At what point do you turn your words over? Do you ever say, "Okay I am giving my work to you, I'll be back opening night to see what you've done"?

SB: I love giving the work away! But I am very careful about who I work with. By careful, I mean people who understand and respect the aesthetic. What it requires is not that you have to do more than what you are taught. You have to show yourself: what you think and what you feel, what your impulses are, and then that informs what happens. The way I've directed my work is through a very collaborative process. I would just say to my theater company: "Here's the work. What do you think?"

SR: Like giving them a poem . . .

SB: Yeah, yeah. I would ask questions like, "What do you hear?" and go from there in shaping the piece. My only thing is I do not want any words changed. I do not want an extra "Aha." I am very intentional about what I put on the page. Every "uh huh," every word is part of creating a musical tapestry. If they throw that off, it's like fingernails on a chalkboard. But how they interpret those words! I guess, that's the jazz of it. You're working within a very rigid structure but you are supposed to improvise. So it's how you choose to embody it and how you engage with other people that's the other artists' freedom. I don't wanna tell people what to do, but I do want them to stick with the written text. The text is, in that way, a musical score.

SR: So whenever you're writing, do you at times speak the words aloud? Do you hear the various voices quite clearly in your head?

SB: My process is very long. I feel things first. I usually find songs that fit the feeling, and I go through this long process of researching, once I can put a finger on the general area that the work is living in. Then eventually when I get to writing, I hear it. Then I just kind of record what I hear, and once I get as much of it out, then I read it out loud to myself, over and over again. I work with performers as I am continuing to shape the piece. I learn so much about what works and what doesn't. I can hear the things that are working from paying attention to the performers, that is, seeing how they move and speak, and hearing how they talk about the work. I usually go through one or more staged readings before I reach the point, where I am like, "Don't change anything!" I mean up to that point I need them to do what's on the page, but I don't go very rigid about it because I am really paying attention to what I am learning from them around the words. So it's a long process before I get to that point where I feel like it's finished, and I need them to stick to the music.

SR: Can you say more about how you came up with the concept for *The love/conjure blues Text Installation?*

SB: I wanted to write a jazz piece—a piece that would work as fiction *and* in performance would activate my text as a musical score, as jazz more fully than before, without me having to conform to Western play styling. Since I was in the throes of reimagining form, I leaned into my communities for support and in retrospect I can say that organically, this project became a tool for building and connecting community. It helped me fully integrate my skills as an activist, community organizer, and facilitator with my art-making tool set. The amount of support that this project received in the form of grants, crowdsource funding (before it was popular), community-based volunteers, artists working in various capacities (filmmakers, singers, actors, graphic designers, etc.), audience participation . . . is staggering when I think about it. Inspired by Helga Davis, Lawrence "Butch" Morris, and so many others, with *The love conjure/blues Text Installation* I finally put my body in the mix for the first time. I took a baby step towards the live improvisation composition technique that my art practice is now centered in. And since I had the experience of my body in the mix, later, when Omi performed as GRIOT (the character), I was able to be in an accelerated conversation with her about the text and how to best bring it to life.

SR: There are many voices in the piece that, as you say, are unborn, living, and dead. With what character do you feel the most connection?

SB: I just *love* big mama sway. Ain't nothing like a big ole powerful sample of wo'mness who can cause a hunger-spirit to sweep through a room!

SR: Your response actually prompts a question about dialect. I'll say up front that I grew up in a West Indian community in Boston and thus am accustomed to the sound of another dialect, but it seems as though, at least from looking at the words on the page, the dialect isn't quite accurate. Are you taking black vernacular speech and doing something different with it, so that it isn't supposed to be accurate?

SB: Yeah, I wasn't trying to go for a dialect even. I am more interested in words as music, so I am more interested in tonal qualities and rhythm. Inside of that, what happens in *love conjure/blues*—as book or as performance—is that some people are dead, some are alive, and some are unborn. Once I got everything on the page, I realized there was a thread where some of the information about who was who and how they were connected related to the way they talked. But that was backpedaling. Yeah, I wasn't trying to do dialects. I love tone and rhythm. There is a way I hear language, and how I heard people talk while growing up slips in.

SR: I guess some of the word choices just startled me a bit. Something like, "I saw he hanging from the tree" rather than "I saw him hanging from the tree."

SB: That's the music of it. And I do think that these people become themselves, they take on their own lives. So whether they're real people or not is not so much what I'm interested in. . . .

SR: I didn't mean to suggest that you were listening to real people and then capturing their words on the page, but . . . some word choices made me wonder whether there was a conscious effort on your part at times to break what we might think we know about black vernacular speech patterns.

SB: Perhaps. One thing I was trying to do, too, is to play with gender. I think gender is much more fluid than we usually allow it to be. So words like "himshe" is a gender choice or rather, recognition of someone's gender. . . . So, yeah, I was breaking with the conventional.

SR: May I ask what difference does being a lesbian make in your work?

SB: That's a good question. You know, I think that the way that it has served me is that I feel like . . . once I came out to my mother—and I had to fight with her—nobody else . . . I wasn't scared of what anybody else thought. So my determination to be myself came to the surface. My mother and I are very close now, but we had a hard time for a long time, but because I was committed to having my daughter know her grandmother, I worked through it, and I'm so grateful now. Having gone through that fight to be myself, I'm also determined to encourage and hopefully provide space for other people to. And then it broadens the scope of what is presented, of what I'm talking about.

SR: On your website you assert: "Art and life are inseparable and the purpose of art is the revolution of the spirit." This is a very expansive, ambitious definition of art. I don't mean to quarrel with your definition, but I do want to ask: How do you know when you've been successful? What are the signs of "the revolution of spirit"?

SB: As a touring artist, I get to return to places, and because I have been cultivating relationships, long-term ongoing relationships with a lot of artists, organizations, and communities for a long time, what I get to witness is the miracle of life and change. I see individual artists growing, making courageous, big moves. They tell me how the practice of this art form, working with me, or being with me helped them to get to a new place. That, I consider a success. When I see poets, whom I've mentored, are now professors at universities, when they invite me to visit their class, and I see how magnificent they are and that they're teaching my book, then I feel like that's a major success.

It just takes so much work to make things happen. For instance, with *The love/conjure blues Text Installation*, there was a long, communal process, and the success of it, to me, was in the making. Because people hosted fund-raising parties; people opened their doors and housed artists who were visiting from out of town; people brought us food when we were rehearsing. All the gifts that we were given during the making of the piece is the evidence of my success as an artist. . . . It is my relationships over all these years that I think has brought me that, that circular giving. So that's major success. Whenever I get the opportunity to just be in the room and see what I've built fully produced, that's major success.

Being nominated for awards—I was nominated for an Alpert Award—that's a major success for me, because I don't come from privilege, I'm more like a working-class artist, so to just be able to be in a room and have access is the sign of success for me. And I know that I'm standing on other people's shoulders. Other people have already done a lot of sacrificing and hard work, and so I don't have to go backwards, I'm supposed to go forward. And so every time I go forward I feel like that's the evidence of my success. Every day is a sign of success for me.

Part II

Machos

Directed/developed by Coya Paz; created by Teatro Luna

The ensemble for this piece included Desiree Castro (now Guzman), Belinda Cervantes, Maritza Cervantes, Gina Cornejo, Yadira Correa, Ilana Faust, Stephanie Gentry Fernandez, and Gwen La Roka. Asterisks indicate that the lines following overlap.

PRELUDE: ALL GUYS ARE NOT

ALL	Can't stand it
ONE	when a girl tells me that all men are this, all men are that they're all players, dogs, men that don't listen blah, blah, blah*
CHORUS	(*overlaps unevenly*) all men are this, all men are that they're all players, dogs, men that don't listen blah, blah, blah
ONE	Like, I hate hearing that, cuz it . . . ain't . . . true. (**beat**)
TWO	We're not all just out there to get laid, drinking beer, and be macho men.
THREE	We actually think. We have hearts. We care about things.
TWO	Don't classify, categorize or try to dissect the man I am. Cuz you don't know me.*
ECHO	You don't know me.
TWO	*You don't know my life.*
FOUR	And as for WOMEN, I don't trust THEM!

CHORUS	Mmmm mmm. No.
FOUR	Women are minefields.
ALL	*Listas para esplotar con miradas de matar.*
FOUR	You never know when they're Gonna explode. She'll kill you muthafucker.
FIVE	You can't tell a woman anything. Cuz then they want to know **everything.** (*all punctuate*) A simple question or observation turns into Well, what about this? What about that?
SIX	(*overlaps, in "girl voice"*) What about this? What about that?
FIVE	I DON'T KNOW! I just saw them on the street I don't know what they're cooking for dinner, who they're dating or what kind of underwear they are wearing. I DON'T KNOW! But my girlfriend wants to know everything!
SIX	Questions are dangerous!
SEVEN	Especially when they ask
SIX	Well . . . (*beat*)
ALL	how do I look?
CHORUS	(*assorted*) Uh Um Yeah Uh
ALL	WOW!
SEVEN	You look great! (*beat*)
SIX	("*girl*" *voice*) No. What do you really think?
SEVEN	That's when you know you're walking straight into the minefield.

EIGHT	Chances are you're going to give the wrong answer anyway so
	Don't fall for it RUN FAST AND FAR!*
CHORUS	(overlap)
	Run
	Get out while you can.
	GO!
SEVEN	There's no right answer.
EIGHT	Whatever we say, will always be the wrong answer.
FOUR	I don't even respond to questions like that anymore.
ONE	Not convinced? Okay.
FIVE	Tell the woman in your life that she's gained twenty pounds and see if she doesn't pimp slap you or stop putting out.
SIX	Naw bro, I wouldn't risk it.
	Women play a lot of mind games.
	They'll ask you a question just to see what your response is.
TWO	Just to see if that's the response they think you're going to give.
THREE	Between you and me
	there are things that don't look good on women.
	Like these shoes that I see women wearing.
	They're like Frankenstein for the feet all closed up at the top making women's feet look hideous. But will I say that to a woman?
CHORUS	Oh no.
	No way.
	Uh uh.
TWO	No fuckin' way.
THREE	What do I know about shoe trends anyway?

Transition, shift in tone, HOW TO BE A MAN.

DANIEL	Okay, so when I was young my sister got a Donny and Marie doll set, and so I immediately assumed that the Donny doll was for me and the Marie doll was for her. So I took the

Donny doll and I got in trouble and I remember it was like this big OH! I'm not supposed to play with dolls, like that's for girls. And you know that was, one of those big moments where it sunk in, like this big division you know. I'm a boy. And I can't wear makeup or play with dolls or have fancy shoes because I'm not a girl. I'm a boy. And I have to grow up and be a man.

Shift, the beginning to this is fast and rhythmic, almost overlapping, and builds in intensity. Each "be a man" should have a different inflection, implication.

ALL	Be . . . a . . . man
ONE	Be a man.
TWO	Step up
ONE/FIVE	Be a man
THREE	Man up
ONE/FIVE/SIX	Be a man!
FOUR	Grow some balls
ONE/FIVE/SIX/SEVEN	Be a man!
EIGHT	You wanna be a man?
*CHORUS	Huh?
EIGHT	You face your fears
THREE	Work hard.
FOUR	Pay the bills.
TWO	Don't cry.
ONE	Be a man.
ALL	Be. A. Man
[DAVID R]	Okay so, I was just in a relationship and the girl expected me to wash her car. And I was like, why? And she's like, "Well that's what guys do." And, you know, she didn't cook. She didn't clean. I was like, "What are you supposed to do?" And and, she wasn't fitting what she was supposed to do

so I didn't understand how I was supposed to fit what she supposing I was supposed to do. I mean, it didn't make any sense. Uhm, and I was like, "*you* can wash your car." You know, but don't push it on me to say look it's your job to because you're a man. C'mon now, am I supposed to do everything? I don't think so.

CHORUS   (*a round, every "man" sounds different*)
           Man . . .
           Maaaaaaaaaaaaaan.
           Man.
           Man!
           [repeats × 4]

ONE/CHORUS   Be a man.

TWO   Push comes to shove, you do what you gotta do.

FOUR   If you gotta take care of your wife, your kids, you do.

THREE   Gotta work hard

FOUR   Don't complain

TWO   Don't cry

THREE   Don't punk out

TWO   Suck it up

THREE   Toughen up

FOUR   Grow up

THREE   Shut up

ALL   You're a man.

JAIME   I got called all sort of names growing up in the hood u know, like ghost, powder, Whitie . . . so then I turned 16 and got the Aztec calendar tattooed on my forearm so I would feel Mexican enough, you know? It's kinda dumb—I had to get a whole sleeve tattooed before I felt I was Mexican enough . . . So it's the same thing with being a man. It's like I got to act a certain way *alllll the fuckin' time*. Like if I'm at a bar and a group of chicks walk in—even though at first glance you know no amount of liquor could cure them women of their ugliness—you still got to check them out or you're gay. Or

Machos   **93**

the pressure to be tough* . . . stand your own*, be aggressive
all them stereotypes loom over me

*ONE	Be a man.
*TWO	Stand your own
ONE/CHORUS	Be a man.
THREE	Be tough
ONE/CHORUS	Be a man.
FOUR	Not a fucking pussy.
JAIME	. . . It's ridiculous. I mean it's rare when I'm just relaxed and comfortable being myself. Fuckin' complexes, I mean if it ain't me worrying about not being Mexican enough, it's me stressing about *being a man*. At least my tattoos do the talking now. I'm fuckin' Mexican. And I'm . . . —tough—like a man "should" be. *(chuckles)* Plus, I get more chicks.
ONE	Be a man
TWO	Age old things
THREE	Same old things
ONE	Be a man
THREE	Be tough
FOUR	Play sports
ONE/CHORUS	Be a man
TWO	Drink beer
THREE	Fuck bitches
ALL	Be a man
TWO	Age old things
RICKY	Same old things. We keep repeating them, can't get over them. It's like atoms bouncing off a wall. It's like the molecule broke. Bam bam bam. Be a man. Be a man. I hate the phrase be a man. *(mockingly)* Be like me. Do what I do. But still . . . I mean, I know that I think. I know that I am considerate of other people and of women and of things like

that and I think that regardless of what I think, I want a 14 inch penis I could swing around. It's true. (*calls, jokingly, as if to God*) C'mon, give me another ten inches damn it! (*back to audience*) I'm just messing with you. I only need another five. Okay six . . . okay maybe seven. But why do I even care. But I do. I want a big old dick. I want the biggest dick in the room!

ONE   Be a man

THREE   Man up

ONE   Be a man!

FOUR   Grow some balls

ONE   Be a man!

FOUR   Don't complain

TWO   Don't cry

SIX   Don't bitch

SEVEN   You do what it takes.*

TWO   It's burned in there*

FOUR/ILANA   *Yeah.

ONE   Be a man.

THREE   Man up.

ONE/CHORUS   Be a man

DAD [DAVID M] Danny . . . Why are you crying? you can't go around crying over a toy. Shit . . . Come here—don't tell your ma I said shit—it takes more of a man to cry than a man who holds it in. But you have to cry for the right reason, you know, you know, are you going to cry because you didn't get what you wanted or Tito took your toy or because or because of something personal and emotional and in your heart. Save your tears for something that matters, me entiendes? Okay, now go play or something. I'm going to watch the game. (*calls after him*) Hey, Danny . . . you tell Tito to come in here, alright??

ONE/CHORUS   Be a man. (*underlying* MAN, MAN, MAN, MAN)

TWO	Step up
ONE	Be a man
THREE	Man up
FOUR	Suit up
TWO	Shape up
ONE	Be a man
FRANK	I grew up watching a lot of television. John Wayne, Charles Bronson and uh, Steve McQueen. I didn't realize as a kid that it was a script. And that someone was playing a part. I always thought that men had to, to somehow be: liked, and loved, and strong, and not cry. My dad was like that. My grandfather was like that. Old school macho. But I didn't know then. I thought, okay Frankie, that's how I have to be: a macho. A REAL MAN

EIGHT, FIVE, SEVEN, SIX   Man, Man, Man, Man 2×

EIGHT   Me? I learned it from my dad.

AL   Oh man! My dad, he was the type of dude, you be at home— you get home from school and you do your chores. And like me and my brother would be chillin' in the house. We would clean up our chores. Our friends would be over. Man our house was like the hangout spot.

FRIENDS, AL, *and* BROTHER *are hanging out, playing video games.*

FRIEND 1/GINO   Dude, did you tell him?

FRIEND 2/STEFAN   Yeah, man I finally got the code.

AL   Aw, no shit!

FRIEND 2/STEFAN   It's up up, down down, left right, left right, BA BA, start.

FRIEND 1/GINO   And he got that shit for free!!

AL   And he would come home, (*all freeze, tensely*) and he would like, look for stuff to fuck with us about.

DAD   Did you take out the garbage?

AL   Yeah

DAD	You walk the dog?
AL	Yeah
DAD	(*looks around*) You left a piece of garbage on the floor.
AL	And I'd be like "Whoa, why you bothering me about that piece of garbage in the kitchen on the floor? Why don't you pick it up? Like why are you bothering me about that?" He would like get so—he would come in and cut off the TV. He was looking at me like . . .
DAD	Man, if I was your size, I would beat you down right now. Go pick up the garbage.
AL	(*to Dad*) Fine. (*to audience*) He was a corrections officer. It was like living in a prison a little bit sometimes. Because he didn't know how to shut it off. He worked at Rikers Island, in the juvenile part. You know, young men. So he would treat us like we always doin' something bad.
DAD	(*calling to* AL) You sure you walked the dog?
AL	Yes!
DAD	Boy, don't lie to me.
AL	I ain't lying to you.
DAD	(*furious*) You ain't lying to me? You ain't lying to me? (*grabs* AL *by the neck and drags him roughly*) Cuz you know what I see? I see some dog shit on the floor. Clean that shit up.
AL	Fine. (*goes to get a paper towel*)
DAD	I said, clean it now.
AL	I ain't cleaning that shit with my hands.
DAD	(*throws* AL *down to his knees*) You do what I say. You can wash your hands later.
AL	(*to audience*) I wanted to—man—there were so many times I wanted to beat that man down. I swear!

I'll tell you something else he did. He was like that real traditional man so he had to make sure he raised men. So
when I was a kid, one time there was a mouse, I was like,
"Ewww it's a mouse." I was trying to run from it but it was
dead.

DAD   What are you making a fuss about?

AL   Dad, there's a mouse.

DAD   What? Come here. Pick up that mouse.

AL   I ain't pickin' up that mouse.

DAD   It's a mouse.

AL   I ain't pickin' up no mouse.

DAD   (*grabs* AL *by the neck and puts his face down by the mouse,*
           AL *is scared*)
           Pick it up. Pick it up. (*roughly grabs his hand and places it over
           the mouse*) You can wash your hands later.

AL   It was the same thing he said about picking up the shit.
           Wash your hands up. But you know, to this day, I'm not
           scared of mice and to this day, if I had to pick up some shit,
           I wouldn't mind picking up the shit. Because I would wash
           my hands. It was weird lessons like that he taught me but it
           made me stronger. You know what I'm sayin'? I had to get so
           used to life just being cold. Otherwise, you just break down
           and just cry. And he don't like you cryin'. Hell naw. He had
           to make sure he raised *men*.

           Transition, URINAL PIECE. *Four urinals are rolled out.* JANITOR *enters
           and starts mopping.* SILENT GUY *enters, sees the urinals are empty and
           looks relieved. He goes to the one farthest stage left and begins to do his
           business.* STRAIGHT-FORWARD *man enters and goes to the urinal stage
           right.* FATHER *enters, as if he is holding a door open for somebody.*

FATHER   (*talking to his son who cannot be seen yet*)
           Come on Diego! Dale . . .

DIEGO   I want to go with mom.

FATHER   No more of this—you going into the girl's bathroom with mommy, you hear? You're a big boy now, you gotta use the urinals like a man!

STRAIGHT-FORWARD GUY   (*looks over shoulder at the father and son*)

FATHER   Now look the first rule is you don't double park—

DIEGO   What is double parking?

FATHER   It means you just don't pee next to somebody, not unless you don't have a choice.

JANITOR   It's called the gay buffer.

FATHER   Excuse me, do you mind?

JANITOR   You don't want people thinking he's gay . . .

FATHER   thank you, but I got this . . .
now where was I . . .

DIEGO   Gay buffer.

FATHER   It's called no double parking—now, it's simple, you just stand up to it and pull it out, and urinate.

DIEGO   Dad . . .

FATHER   What?

DIEGO   Where's the toilet paper?

FATHER   Toilet paper? You don't wipe, you shake . . . well, before you walk away, and you don't want to make a mess . . .

JANITOR   But you only shake it three times because then it can be like you're playing with yourself . . .

FATHER   Look really dude, I got this . . .

JANITOR   I'm just trying to be helpful . . .

FATHER   I GOT IT!

JANITOR   Okay, okay . . .

FATHER   (*clearly flustered by now*)
Another thing is you don't want to look at the other men peeing okay son?
So, look straight ahead and mind your business . . . look at the wall only okay.

Machos **99**

JANITOR	You don't look down either kid, I mean you don't walk in and see people just looking down at their pee-pees while they're peeing.
FATHER	You know son, this brings me to the next thing you gotta remember . . . which is YOU DON'T TALK TO THE OTHER MEN WHEN YOU ARE PEEING!
JANITOR	Oh yeah, I hate that. I hate that I have my penis in my hand and I'm urinating and somebody's trying to talk to me. I don't like that, no.
FATHER	This is a private moment. I know you're standing right next to me but . . . It's still private.
JANITOR	*(clearly oblivious to comment by dad)* Exactly! It's a private moment, I mean I don't feel comfortable peeing out in the open to begin with you know—so when someone starts conversating with me it's like they are invading my space! That bothers the shit out of me . . .
FATHER	Yeah, well you have no idea how it's bothering me right now . . .
DRUNK GUY	*(slams the bathroom door open and stumbles in)* Yeah, this is where all the dicks hang out. Whoa! Who stepped on a duck? *(laughs loudly and obnoxiously)*

Dad hovers over young boy who is fascinated with the drunken guy.

FATHER	*(under his breath)* La puta madre . . . Come on Diego, hurry up and pee!
DRUNK GUY	Yeah, hurry up and pee. I gotta go!!!!!

DIEGO *starts to pull down his pants.*

FATHER	Hey . . . you don't wet your pants while peeing, so you better hold 'em up. And you don't want to show your butt!
DRUNK GUY	It's just butt, we all got one man! Hey . . . you done or what?

DIEGO *is staring, fascinated, at* DG.

FATHER	Diego! I told you not to look at other men!
DIEGO	But Dad . . .
FATHER	Look at the advertisements/wall only.
DIEGO	Dad . . .
FATHER	Take it out, hold your pants up, keep your eyes straight ahead, don't look at your neighbor
JANITOR	. . . or down at yourself. What? He can get in a fight that's all . . .
DRUNK GUY	You all too up tight man . . . (*overlapping*)
FATHER	Don't make a mess and DON'T TALK
DIEGO	Dad, I don't got to pee anymore . . .
DRUNK GUY	Yeah, it's a lot of stress, so much shit to remember all for a little piss . . . (*exits*)
FATHER	Let's go, maybe you can just use the stall instead . . .

Father and son exit.

JANITOR	Don't worry kid you'll be a pro in no time
MICK (SILENT GUY)	I hate urinals.

I think it's rude to have to stand in the fucking urinal and avoid making eye contact and avoid feeling that awkward tension.
I'm like fuck it I don't need the stress in my life.
I usually bypass the urinals all together for the most part and go to the toilet.
I used to make myself go to the urinal, thinking don't let them think you are going in to the stall because you have a small cock. But now I just say fuck it, I go to the stall. It makes me feel at home.
It's safer.
Because um I don't want anybody looking at my dick and I don't wanna accidentally look over at somebody which I probably would.
Urinals suck.

I don't want anyone to see my dick.

See,

One time my mom's boyfriend was wrestling with me and I was in my underwear.

I was about 10 or something, 10 or 11.

We're wrestling and in doing so he had grabbed my penis, through my underwear you know? Well he stops short and yells to my mother,

(calling out, as if he is Ralph)

"Hey honey, guess what! Mikey doesn't have anything down here!"

He might have been joking but it was certainly that kind of attitude that has stayed with me?

(chuckles at himself, but in a sad way)

And to this day, I . . . I feel that my penis is not up to snuff.

It's something that I think about every day.

I find myself wondering about my penis size in relationship to other men's.

Every. Day.

I mean, I don't know about other guys (laughter) but I look. I do that.

Like . . . I look at a man's package through his pants and think about my own in relation to it. I feel very strange about that but I do it all the time, you know. And, you know it's important for me to know that I'm pleasing my part-ner. I mean I've certainly never had a woman say you're not big enough, but that's always in the back of my mind, you know? "Is that (motions to his penis) an issue?"

Is it?

Can I make her happy with what I've got?

Transition.

TWO	4.5
SEVEN	Six.
THREE	7.5
EIGHT	Five
FIVE	Seven inches and change.

ONE	I'd rather not say.
FOUR	I've never measured myself.
THREE	I'm party size. Not too big but not too small.
EIGHT	I'm a grower, not a shower . . . but hey, give me time baby. You won't have any complaints, I guarantee.
SEVEN	Um, I think I'm smaller than other men. I think, but uh, it's not exactly the kind of thing you take a survey about.
FIVE	I finally measured myself when I was 24. I was scared out of my mind to know the size. It always looked smaller. Especially when you saw porn. It took a woman saying "it's not small" for me to feel better about it.
TWO	I'm short but I'm thick. And I last
ONE	If any guy tells you they don't think about it, they are lying out their ass. We think about it constantly. We measure it, stretch it, photograph it, find toys for it, make it look bigger by shaving it or trimming it. I even know someone who plucks it with tweezers.
FOUR	Why do we care? I don't care! so easy for me to say because, like, I've gotten so much compliments, so many on my dick, you know what I mean? Like, God forbid I should ever lose it. I know mine is very big and very nice. I don't ever feel the need to discuss it. Part of that is because it's just there, and, like, *I like it*, so there. MAN, I got a great dick!

Transition. Sound of a radio or television playing, an advertisement for a gym or men's hair removal service is playing. Underneath it some kind of rhythm or music to score the piece. ALL are onstage, they move as if facing the mirror in the morning, checking out their bodies, pinching their fat, checking their hair, flexing their muscles. They don't move in unison but they move together—it should have the sense of a common ritual marked by a few variations. Focus is on EMORY, NICK, and NOAM.

NICK	*(as if stepping on a scale)* 210 pounds.

EMORY	*(as he is about to shave, stops to look at his face more closely in the mirror)* My nose is too big.
NOAM	*(checks his hair in the mirror, indicates that he is frustrated and annoyed)* Yup, still bald.
EMORY	Maybe I could get surgery to fix it.* If I could afford it, that is.
NICK	Now I'm short *and* fat.* Great.
NOAM	Jews are the baldest people on earth
NICK	When you're the short guy it seems like you always have to try a little harder to get noticed. My whole life I heard "Ramirez if you were just five inches taller I'd be able to start you" or "Ramirez if our bigger guys had your heart we would go to state." So much for playing football.
NOAM	My friend Andy says I'm losing my hair because I always wear a hat. I'm losing my hair because I'm fucking predestined to be bald.
EMORY	My face is too long. Looks stretched out. Like a cartoon. What does she see in me? My face. My skin. Look at these acne scars. I wish my skin was better. Get one of those gels or something to clear my skin once and for all.
NICK	And now my friends are calling me Nick the Drumstick.
EMORY	I have no muscle tone. I eat and eat and I eat but I am too skinny. I wish I had more muscle.
NOAM	Both my grandfathers were bald. They say that it comes from the mother's father, but anyway I'm bald from either side . . .
NICK	And my family calls me gordo, of course. Even worse, gordito.
EMORY	What does she see in me?
NICK	I got a little comfortable after the wedding, I guess.
NOAM	The French have such nice hair.
EMORY	I wish I had a natural smile. My smile looks fake.

NICK	My wife says that she loves me just the way I am but for some reason I still get bothered. A huge fat ass.
EMORY	My fingers are so long.
NOAM	So now I use Rogaine. But, frankly. I don't think it's working.
NICK	You know I feel like a total chone when I stand in front of the mirror and look at my gut and realize that I once had a flat stomach and a six pack coming in. You know, who does that!!! What guy stands in front of the mirror and looks at his gut!! It's the most non-hetero thing to do.*
NOAM	$500 a year and for what?
EMORY	What does she see in me?
NICK	Can't tell anyone what I do.
NOAM	At least I'm not short.
NICK	I might lose my man card.
NOAM	Or fat. You ever see a short fat president? Nope.
EMORY	What does she see in me? My face is stretched out. My nose too big. If I could, if I could afford it, I would get a nose job.
EMORY AND NICK	What does she see in me?
LEWIS	(breaking in) Eh, who cares? One too many beers? Hey, I earned this stomach. It's an investment. And hey, I can always wear a hat. (beat) But the best part of being a man? CHOKE THE CHAIN SPANK THE MONKEY, PUNISH THE POPE AND MY FAVORITE . . . let me introduce you to my friend Manuela.

Transition: A MASTURBATION DANCE, stylized. TIM is setting up lotion, magazine, it has a funny slapstick feel. Just as he leans back and starts to unzip, we hear:

WIFE (VOICE-OVER)	Honey, are you in there, what are you doing? I need to pee! Honey!
TIM	My wife doesn't like me to masturbate. The funny thing is, I never even did it until I was married.

I just was a naive person, as it related to sex.

I was very interested in sex.

But I don't think I knew what we were headed towards. You know, from a very early age, I would enjoy pornography, I would look at it, but I didn't know where I was headed. I just enjoyed the feeling of arousal and then went to sleep.

Now, of course, I'm comfortable with it, I know what to do, but only if my wife isn't around.

She's caught me a couple of times, walked in on me, magazine in one hand, you-know-what in the other. Oh, she was upset!

She told me it was a betrayal, a kind of cheating!

(he laughs)

She says, just have sex with me if you need it so bad.

But the thing is . . .

The last time we did it . . .

it was months ago and well . . .

let's just say this here magazine has more life than she did.

I've been married for thirty years and I'm sneaking around like a goddamned teenager.

(laughs)

I'm cheating on my wife . . . with myself!

Let me tell you this is not what I signed on for.

Transition: Sunshine and the sound of Frank Sinatra, "How Lucky Can One Guy Be?" A stylized, 1950s sitcom feel as MR. LOYAL *enters. There is a bright, false edge to everything he says.*

MR. LOYAL	Hey neighbors!
GROUP 1	Hey neighbor!
MR. LOYAL	Will I see you at the neighborhood watch meeting tonight?
GROUP 1	Sure thing!
MR. LOYAL	Hey fellas!
GROUP 2	Hide-e-o neighbor!
MR. LOYAL	Lawn is lookin' good!
GROUP 2	New fertilizer!
MR. LOYAL	Ohh, I knew it. I knew it.

MR. LOYAL	Hi. (*puts down briefcase*) I'm a loyal man. A good father. I guess you could say, I'm a family man.

SONS enter, running on, peppy and enthusiastic, wearing sports uniforms and caps.

BILLY	Dad Dad . . .
BOBBY	Pop
BILLY	Will you play catch with us?
BOBBY	Huh Dad will ya will ya?????
MR. LOYAL	Not right now boys. Your pops is pretty busy.
BILLY	Aw shucks Dad!
BOBBY	I think you mean, Aw SUCKS Dad.
MR. LOYAL	Bobby . . . What would your mother say if she heard that language?
BOBBY	I know.
MR. LOYAL	We'll keep it just between us guys. I'll be back tonight and you know what happens on Saturdays.
BILLY	Yeah . . .
BILLY AND BOBBY	Movies!!!!
MR. LOYAL	And . . .
BOYS	Popcorn!!!!
MR. LOYAL	And . . .
BOYS	ROOTBEER FLOATS!!!!!
MR. LOYAL	(*ruffles their hair affectionately*) Alright, go throw a few for me. I'll be back tonight.
BOYS	Aw, you're the best, Dad!!!!!

They start to run off, Billy stops.

BILLY	Hey Dad . . .
MR. LOYAL	Yes son.
BILLY	I love you.
MR. LOYAL	I love you too son.

The boys exit.

MR. LOYAL	Yes . . . I enjoy family.
	Grew up in suburbs. Mom, Dad, two brothers.
	Always wanted the same thing for myself.
	I saved myself for marriage . . . Almost.
	My wife was the second person I've ever had sex with.
	Hey, I wanted to wait, but
	Hey, sometimes a fella gets tempted and Mary Jane, well, she was a skirt kind of a gal. Looked good in a tight skirt, and was comfortable with the backseat of a car. I guess that's what they mean when they say "I got lucky."
	But I knew she wasn't the kind of woman I was going to marry.
	Ellen was my college sweetie. I knew the minute I saw her I wanted her to be my wife.
	I thought, that's the kind of woman who'll make a great mom, kind of woman I'll want to sit on a porch with when we're both eighty.
	And she is. She's one helluva mother.
	I wouldn't trade her, or this, for the world.
	It's a good feeling, a really good feeling.
	Now sure, there are temptations. The thrill of a new relationship.
	It's hard to compete with that.
	But I'm a loyal person.
	I'm a good husband and a good mate and I really love her and
	at the same time . . .
	I think it would be very hard for me to be monogamous.
	My wife was the second person I've ever had sex with.
	And I put my number at around 50.
	You can do the math.
	(pauses)

Now, I know, I sound like a hypocrite.
But I love my wife.
And I love sex.
And if my wife loved sex, well . . .
But she doesn't.
Look, I'm a loyal man.
A good man.
Other men should aspire to be like me.
I'm a family man.
Want to raise my sons the way my father raised me.
So I've made the compromises I needed to make.
And you know what, if I had to choose, I'd marry Ellen all over again.
Sure would!

Snaps fingers, we hear birds chirping, everything is back to sunshine.

	Lookin' good boys!
BOYS	Thanks, Dad!
MR. LOYAL	You two are gonna be a pro in no time!!
BOY 1	Like Ernie Banks?
BOY 2	What about Babe Ruth?
MR. LOYAL	Now, if you'll excuse me, I have a "meeting."

Winks, picks up his briefcase, pulls some handcuffs or a condom out of his pocket, waves them cheerfully, and walks off whistling.

ONE	I love sports.
TWO	Love football
THREE	Love baseball
FOUR	Love basketball.
ALL	Love sports.
ONE	Sports are . . . they're uh
TWO	A metaphor for life
THREE	You struggle to climb a mountain and struggle to slide down.

FOUR	You band together with your team, your boys. It's camarade-rie.
ONE	I would describe it . . .
TWO	If I had to pick one word . . .
THREE	One word . . .
ALL	Beautiful . . .

SPORTS FANS *come running in, dressed crazy, carrying beer, snacks. They are messy, loud, and sudden.*

JEFF	(yelling)
	YEAH MUTHAFUCKA!!!!!!!!!
JACK	Yeah baby!!!!!
JOHN	Season mother fucking opener!!!!!
IN UNISON	Blue 42, Red 36, Hu Hu Hiiiiiike!!!!!!!

They cheer, body slam each other, drink, getting more and more excited, increases in volume and then goes to silent slow motion as they continue to cheer and get ready to watch the game.

ONE	Football is the sport I love.
FOUR	My ultimate favorite.
TWO	I Love. Football.
ONE	Football season comes around, I'm football 24-7.
TWO	I Love. Football.
THREE	The skill.
FOUR	The art of the game.
ONE	The brains of it.
THREE	The mental aspects involved, play called and schemes.
ONE	The brains of it (taps forehead)

FAN SCENE *comes alive again, full volume.*

Fig. II.1. Fan Scene. Left to right: Yadira Correa, Stephanie Gentry-Fernandez, and Wendy Vargas in *Machos*. Photo by Johnny Knight, courtesy of Teatro Luna.

JACK   *(takes a swig of beer as the play unfolds, he can't yell so he hums an "awwww fuck!")*

JEFF   WHAT??? What?????

JOHN   WHAT THE FUCK???????? Ah, come on!!!!! Come on.

JEFF   What, what happened?

JACK   *(with a disappointed look, he motions his hands to indicate a "false start")*

JEFF   Awwww shit man, we can't be making rookie mistakes like that

JOHN   Don't worry man. It's still early in the game, we got plenty of time to come through.
            JACK — We'll make the Packers eat shit

They CHEER, *say something crass or mean, and slowly go back into slow motion.*

ONE	It's just beautiful.
TWO	A beautiful thing.
THREE	Perfection.
ONE	The beauty of a flawless play. It's like this
TWO	everything
THREE	everything
ONE	everything has to be executed perfectly for that play to work
TWO	simultaneously executing it in a certain amount of time
FOUR	I appreciate the art of that
TWO	*Life* isn't perfect
THREE	so when you see that one perfect play
ONE	It's just beautiful
TWO	a beautiful thing

Fans come alive full speed and volume.

JEFF	*(jumps off the couch)*
	YEAH BOY WHAT'S UP NOW? GO BABY, GO GO GO!!!!!!
JACK	Come on come on come on come on . . . . . .
ALL	TOUCHDOWWWWWWWWWWN!!!!!

ONE *and* TWO *shoulder bump each other as if starting a fight.*

JEFF	Yeah, that's what I'm talking about
JACK	What?! Whatchu gonna do? Whatchu gonna do!
JEFF	Yeah Boi!!!!!!!!!

They chest bump, followed by high fives, screaming, and touchdown dances.

CHORUS GUYS	*(in unison)*
	And being with the guys

ONE	time together
TWO	catching up
FOUR	just you and your boys
THREE	your brothers
TWO	high fiving and embracing
ONE	it's genuine
TWO	it's special
ONE, THEN THREE, THEN TWO	It's like, it's like, it's like . . .
FOUR	like clapping with your own hands
THREE	but clapping with someone else

Fan scene comes alive again.

JOHN	Aw yeah, yeah muthafucka!!!!!!!
JACK	Told you, you didn't know SHIT!!!!
JEFF	Ah, suck my dick you asshole.
JACK	Fuck you pussy, You don't know shit

Fades.

ONE	Sports is full of drama.
TWO	a rollercoaster
THREE	a game of chance
FOUR	a full novella in front of your eyes
ALL	the fear
ONE	the pain
TWO	are they going to lose
THREE	or are they going to win?
JEFF	INTERCEPTION YEAH BABY (*sees something bad*) Oh shit . . . FUMBLE!

JACK	Oh no
JOHN	FUCK!!!! Shit man, who got it who got it????
JEFF	Come on Bears ball Bears ball. (*waving arms to signal ball belonging to certain team*)
JACK	Damnit. Aw shit!

They all sit down dejectedly, drink, depressed.

ONE	It's like a soap opera.
THREE	The cyclical text it goes on and on
TWO	never ending
FOUR	every year
ONE	different combinations of people falling in love
JEFF	Yessssssssssssss!!!!!!!!!!!!!!
TWO	Breaking up
JACK	Fucking Shit!!!!!!!!!
THREE	Getting revenge
JOHN	Bear's ball baby, yeah!!!!! I woulda beeeeeen salty like a muthafucka!
FOUR	And then it all starts all over
THREE	In a different formation
TWO	Over and over again
ONE	Every year
UNISON	I love sports.

FANS *final cheer, running around, slamming into each other. Transition. Lights shift.* LUIS *and* DENNIS *are sitting on different parts of the stage, wearing Cubs uniforms or, at least, pieces of Cubs uniforms.*

DENNIS	Of course, growing up, I thought I was going to play for the Cubs.
LUIS	That was my dream, as a kid. I wanted to play for the Cubs,

specifically, as a kid. Still do, I mean, yeah . . . that's not going to happen.

DENNIS   I was real young, I don't know five or six years when I first realized what baseball was all about. I remember having you know my parents bought me a Cubs uniform and you know I used to stand in front of the mirror the first day of opening day and I'd put my Cub uniform on, watch the game with my Cub uniform on, stuff like that. And uh, probably from the time I was nine years old till now, my dream has always been to play in the World Series with Ernie Banks, at second base with Ernie Banks as the short stop.

LUIS   But I love baseball. And I was good. Played in high school. Mayor Daley's all-star team. When I was 17, I got a scholarship to play for the University of Miami . . . but I didn't go. Because my girlfriend got pregnant. She decided to keep the baby. And I chose to stay. And I played at the College for a year, but the family responsibilities . . . man I couldn't go back . . . and I tried out for the Florida Marlins, made the final cuts, but uh . . . the kids and my wife and uh . . . I got a contract from the New York Mets farm system, but it was in St. Lucy, Tennessee, so, you know, my kids . . . now I have a pickup game here and there, that's it.

DENNIS   I work in a restaurant you know, but sometimes I come home and I put on the "Greatest Moments in Sports" album and you hear, Pew (**sound**), crack of a bat, and you hear, braaawwr, the roar of the crowd, and you hear Mel Allen saying—Mel Allen? He's a famous sports caster. "The sound you just heard is heard across the country six months out of the year. The name of the game is baseball." And by now I'm crying. "And if any name is synonymous about the game it would be this one." Then you hear a guy saying, "Well, I have three ambitions in my life: one to play in 10 World Series, three to hit 700 homeruns, or two to hit 700 homeruns, and three," and I forget what he says. And Mel Allen comes back and says, "His name was George Herman Ruth, but if you ask any kid in the country I—well I'll put my finger on this, he will simply be called The Babe." And, that game is just it's it's me, you know, it's a part of me. Which is, I love this game. And I still dream, still dream of playing in the World Series with Ernie Banks. My whole life, every day. I'm 63.

LUIS   I go to work, I come home. And yeah, I was a little upset, a little bitter. But I had to do the right thing. Be a man. Provide. And uh, that's the only thing—as far as like dreams and goals are, I don't really have anymore. And my wife you know, she kind of turned out, well it kind of turned out not so good. Sometimes I think, I should have taken the scholarship.

Transition, some kind of cap. DENNIS *exits,* ROY *enters, watches as* LUIS *is leaving.*

ROY   My buddy, uh, he's always talking about "I coulda been this, I coulda been that."
He tells anybody who will listen.
I saw him play in high school.
He was pretty good.
And then he married that crazy-ass bitch.
Sorry about my language, but . . . Some women.
Okay, so, he cheats on her.
And bam!
She finds out.
But instead of chasing him around with the scissors threatening to cut his huejitos off he just stands there silently . . .
Shit!
She don't talk to him for a few days but she continued to wash his clothes and make him lunch for work—
of course he wasn't eating that shit cuz he thought she had put rat poison or something in it—
Yep, she acts all normal . . .
doesn't even shed a single fucking tear.
She was normal with the kids and everything.
He was even starting to forget what he had done and was growing his balls back again when one day he walks into my bedroom and there she is with fuckin' Panchito!
He was like what the fuck!!@#$%^&* Mother fucker!!@#$%^&*
Panchito jumped off her so quick and he chased after him but that fuckin' fat ass took off bare-assed. Then he turns

to look at her and there she was dressing herself and
said "Cierra la boca cabron, I took it like a man when you
cheated so don't you go and act like a bitch."
And walked right out to make dinner.
And shit.
I wasn't there.
It's all he said she said
But I know my buddy
And I know that nowadays, anything,
if you even beat on a woman, that's—you're hitting them. a
shrug, a push,
if I even touch you with my fingernail and I pushed you,
that's abuse.
That's domestic violence.
Bullshit.
Women are the Devil. They're the fucking devil!

Transition. HIT *a Woman.*

ONE	Never.
TWO	A man doesn't hit a woman. You're not supposed to.
THREE	I've never hit a woman, but a woman has never hit me.
FOUR	Some women are bitches and they totally need, deserve to get checked.
FIVE	Yeah, I've slapped a girl before.
THREE	my friend was getting his ass kicked by his girl . . .
FIVE	that guy's not a man.
ONE	No. No. I wouldn't hit a woman.
FOUR	a real man would beat the woman, you'd rather be the guy walking down the street with everyone saying damn, he's a bad dude, he beats the shit out of his wife, than be the guys who they say, that guy's a fucking faggot, you know, his wife beats his ass!
THREE	He was in this really abusive relationship. She was crazy for real.
FOUR AND FIVE	bitches that totally need to get checked.

ONE	Never
TWO	A man doesn't hit a woman. You're not supposed to.
THREE	she would you know verbally assault him and shit, you know. She was like nasty you know.
FIVE	I've slapped my son's mother a couple times. What? Don't look at me like that, she's a big girl. She would hit me and I would hit her. I hit her back. What am I supposed to do, stand there and take it?
ONE	I wouldn't do it . . .
TWO	I say that, but who knows?? If you're going to be one of them girls who, "oh, hell no," and get in my face and push me and hit me and cuss me out?
THREE	verbal assaults you know? Like everything you know like "oh you're not a man" and shit.
FIVE	What am I supposed to do, stand there and take it? I mean she punches me. She sees me talking to other girls gets jealous and just comes up and punches me, like bam. Punches me. On the arm, in the stomach, man she aims for my face. So I hit her back. Like I said, she's a big girl.
FOUR	You don't wanna be that guy who's a fucking faggot, his wife beats his ass.
THREE	he would run from her to avoid confrontations cuz she would start slapping and she would start fuckin' punching and he would run . . .
ONE AND TWO	A man doesn't hit a woman. You're not supposed to.
THREE	Eventually it was too much and he didn't run anymore. He ended up kicking her.
ONE	Never.
TWO	A man doesn't hit a woman. You're not supposed to.
FOUR	Some women are bitches and they totally need, deserve to get checked.
DONATO	NO . . . Ope! I'm sorry I have, I'm sorry I have. My ex-wife. I can't believe I just forgot. Yes. Um, there was, when I first

got separated. My ex-wife's aunt instigated this whole situation. Tells her that I'm going to pick up my daughter and I'm never going to let her see her again. And at this time my wife, my ex-wife, she was illegal from El Salvador, (*inaudible . . .*) the whole biz. Um, I still had the power to send her back and get her deported. So without my knowledge her aunt is telling her all this . . . (*makes motion with hand*) Well then her aunt calls me at work and tells me that my wife, my ex-wife was going to pick up my daughter and take her to El Salvador and I was never going to see her again. My, my daughter is the world to me, she is everything, so I rushed down there, to get my daughter. Her aunt was taking care of her, and I go to the back room to where my daughter is and I grab my daughter and I start to carry her out of there and my ex attacks me. She actually stabbed me in the side. She's about this big but she still coming at me, with—with the knives and I turn my back to her, and she's trying to stab me and I'm trying to—trying to hold her back, but I have—I have my daughter in—in my arms, and I'm afraid she's going to hit her, or—or stab her. She has absolutely no—no consideration that I have my daughter in my arms, and I'm trying to shield my daughter, and I'm trying to give my daughter to *her* aunt and the knives are just coming at me—coming at my face, and I had to hit her. I had to hit her and I floored her. I tried walking out and got attacked by pretty much her whole family. Me with my daughter in my arms. (*small laugh*) And I'm the one that got locked up for it. Because—a—a man hitting a woman doesn't go well, anywhere, but yeah, it was a big incident. I'm the one that got locked up for it.

That's not the kind of thing I talk about you know. Not the kind of fight story you tell, sitting around at the bar. (*beat*) I'm the one who got locked up for it.

Transition, fight scene. DONATO *is exiting stage as* JOSH, GABRIEL, *and* LORENZO *are entering.* DONATO *accidentally shoves* LORENZO *with his shoulder as he walks past.* LORENZO *ignores the shove and keeps walking but his two boys* GABRIEL *and* JOSH *aren't having it . . .*

GABRIEL   Man you gonna let that pussy push you like that?

JOSH	Dude I'd knock him out!
LORENZO	Just leave it alone. It was an accident. He didn't even push me.
GABRIEL	Man, Shit, remember that time I got out of the truck when that one guy flicked me off and I punched him dead in the face and broke his fuckin' nose!
JOSH	Oh yeah! That was fuckin' AWESOME! You're a MANimal!!!!! (slaps Gabriel on the back)
JOSH	Remember the time we were at O'Reilly's and I was hitting on this hot girl, then suddenly her boyfriend shows up and the fuckers like 6' 7 and like a football captain or sum shit. Anyways so half the team comes up to me and I just start throwing stools at them big motherfuckers, but then he picked me up by the neck and was choking me, so I pretended to faint and as soon as he let me go BAM (shows round house kick) I fuckin' round-housed his ass in his fat neck cuz I couldn't reach his head cuz he was so damn tall . . .
GABRIEL	Ah shit, yeah that was crazy man!
JOSH	That shit was MANtastic! Good times! Manly times

Both Gabriel and Josh look at Lorenzo expectantly . . . beat.

LORENZO	Okay okay. Remember when we were coming back from Austin and we were walking past the Lambda Phi house and they start drunk jawing . . . And uh, so we go over there, and there's probably about . . .I don't know ten or fifteen of them. Maybe twenty. And there were probably about ten of us. And there were more coming from behind. And you two are getting your asses kicked Uhm and so I pulled out my belt like my pops used to and started beating the shit out of all them jerks! (replays event, suddenly super enthusiastic and screaming insults and slapping the belt all over stage with tons of emotion) I was like Yeah, Orale cabron! Hijo de su Pinche! Ahroa vas a saber cabron! Fuckin' showed them.

Long beat, Gabriel and Josh stare at him.

GABRIEL   That was you pussy?

JOSH   Dumbass, you got us in trouble for that shit. Why did you do that anyway?

LORENZO   *(composes himself and re-straps his belt into his loops)*
           What? We was getting our ass kicked. At that moment I thought my belt would hurt more than my punches . . .
           (trails off)

GABRIEL   Naw man, that was some pussy ass shit!!! Who uses a fuck-ing belt, you gonna use your high heel next?!

JOSH   You fag! A fucking gay belt!

They continue walking . . . offstage . . . LORENZO holds back.

LORENZO   So . . . So I threw down with the belt?! Who cares? You two were getting your asses kicked. And that ain't some gay ass shit! I know some gay ass shit! You haven't even kissed Dana yet. Oh, you're waiting for the right moment. Now that's some gay ass shit! *(pause)* Assholes! Gay assholes!
           (walks offstage)

Transition: Boy Band, I'M NOT GAY. As ERIC and RICK exit, lights shift, we hear a voice-over, cheesy, like the beginning of a music track on a CD. It should feel as though something is about to happen, like a con-cert, right before the band comes onstage.

MUSIC . . . BOY BAND comes onstage, dancing, lyrics are sung in '90s boy band style.

INTRO

HEARTTHROB 1 *(cheesy opening to a song voice-over style)*
           Girl, I know there have been a lot of rumors goin' around and we're just here to clarify a few things for ALL you beau-tiful ladies in the audience tonight. So, sit back and enjoy tonight's performance, because this one is for YOU . . . espe-cially YOU.

Fig. II.2. Boy Band Scene. Clockwise from top left: Stephanie Gentry-Fernandez, Maritza Cervantes, Yadira Correa, Belinda Cervantes, and Gina Cornejo in *Machos*. Photo by Johnny Knight, courtesy of Teatro Luna.

MUSIC *punctuation.*

ALL　　　　　　　When I hang out with my boys
Ooh it's not that way
We drink, watch sports
Occasional porn
And if there's a circle jerk
It's just 'cause we're horny
And girl I think of you the whole time

I swear we never touch
Except for that once
But baby, we were all really drunk

(Chorus)
Girl, I'm into you
Girl, I swear to you
Girl, I promise to
Stay by your side
You're my heart and soul
My perfect angel
Tell me you'll always be mine

I like women, girls, and chicks
Not interested in dicks
Except that tranny prostitute
[She was pretty cute]
Didn't know till we were in the car
By then it had gone way to far
Already paid a ton of cash
Closed my eyes, got it done real fast

And yeah, okay
I went back twice, but hey
What can I say, girl I'm not gay

(Chorus)
Girl, I'm into you
Girl, I swear to you
Girl, I promise to
Stay by your side
You're my heart and soul
My perfect angel
Tell me you'll always be mine

(Rap interlude)
Yeah I wax my eyebrows and wear a spray tan
But that doesn't mean that I want a man
Derrick Jeter does it too and so does David Becks
I'm still a total stud get lots of girl sex
Got no problem with gays, I have an open mind
My hairdresser Rico was a total find
He hit on me once, it didn't matter
I smiled at him and said, Hey . . . I'm flattered!

(Bridge)
I can always tell when a guy is gay

Wears a shirt like I've got on today
Dancing, high voice, it's all here
If I saw me in the mirror I'd think I'm queer

(A cappella "break it down" moment)

I was twelve and had a crush
Felt giddy when we touched
Finally decided to kiss
Getting ready for girls and this was practice
Making out, it felt so good
Would have done him if I could
'Til he turned to me to say
"Listen dude, I'm not gay"

I didn't want to hear
Him say he was not queer

But still I told him, "uh, yeah dude, me neither"

(Chorus)
Girl, I'm into you
Girl, I swear to you
Girl, I promise to
Stay by your side
You're my heart and soul
My perfect angel
Tell me you'll always be mine

Cause girl I'm not gay!*
Girl, I'm so into you! I promise to*
I promise . . . I promise . . . *
You are my heart and soul
Tell me you're all mine.

Cause girl I'm not gay.

Transition into F-WORD. *As song ends, and* BOY BAND *exits, lights up
on* DANNY, *sitting, talking intently to the audience.*

DANNY   I'm not gay.
              I've never, uh, had that instinct.
              But I have lots of gay friends.
              Of course.

I'm an actor!
My mom is so sure I'm gay.
Because I cry a lot, you know, I'm emotional.
She thinks I won't have kids for her, I'll automatically get
AIDS.
(thinks)
And, uh, my whole life, people have been calling me a faggot.
Can't remember a time when it wasn't faggot this . . .
faggot that . . .
I remember my brother's friends telling me stop being such
a faggot,
you're being such a faggot . . .
oh look how you're walking, walking like a little faggot . . .
I got self-conscious about that . . . thinking
I don't know how, but I better learn not to walk like a faggot.
It's the worst thing you can call a man.
Men are so fucking scared of being called anything else but
a man.
I remember going out in to the yard and my friend's dad saw
me
and all of a sudden he snatches my earlobe and pulled it
and was like
what the fuck is that
what is that
is that a earring?
You're not a fucking faggot,
you're not a fucking faggot you're a man you don't wear an ear-
ring
I didn't even have an earring.

I've been thinking about this.
Because I used to say it all the time.
I didn't even mean to be mean about someone.
I just said it all the time.

You show any type of weakness, emotion or empathy, you
get jumped on and called a faggot. You have to keep your
belt high and your emotions low.

And my dad, you know . . .
we've been trying to talk through some shit from when I
was a kid . . .

and it's hard and
we were on the phone and
I was crying and
he yelled at me.
He was like
Don't be a baby. Don't be a faggot.
I'd never been vulnerable like that with him . . . and he
stomped on it.
It's like, it's constant.
I go to the bar with my friend my buddy from next door
Steven Sanchez and he's such a horn dog.
I thought I was a horn dog but he's worse
and you know, I just broke up I'm not in the mood for the
bar
for the girls
but he's forcing so many women on me and I say
Steve, I don't want to fuck every girl that's in here,
I just want to relax, chill, forget about my problems
and of course he says,
Ah what are you, a fucking faggot????
You know, I don't want to holler at some girl on the street:
What are you . . . a fucking faggot?

And I know better, but it gets me.
If someone said it to me walking down the street it would
make me mad,
it would
it really gets me angry,
I have a reaction, my immediate
it's hard . . . I get so angry and you know
I have gay friends
I got no problem with people being gay
And I got no problem with being emotional
But it gets me.
It gets me.

Transition, shift. LESBIANS.

ONE   It's just not for me.

TWO   I'm not comfortable with it.

THREE	I don't want anyone hitting on me in the bathroom alright?
FOUR	What? (listens) No. I don't think I'm homophobic. I mean, I love lesbians. They're gay right?
THREE	Mmmmm . . . Love lesbians.
ONE	Love them.
TWO	I'd have to say lesbians make me very excited.
FIVE	I fuckin' hate lesbians.
TWO	Very excited.
THREE	Women together, it's so soft.
ONE	But not because of why you think . . . although I like that too!
FIVE	I just hate them. There's this thing inside me that's like UGH, fucking lesbians.
THREE	So gentle, the way they, the way they touch each other . . . mmmm . . .
TWO	Girl-on-girl action. Very exciting.
ONE	I think it's awesome because if I like football and the lesbian likes football . . . We can go see a football game together, or we can sit down and watch football.
FIVE	I'm just being honest. It's my instinct. When I see two, two lesbians walking down the street I just feel this ugh, this thing inside
THREE	I enjoy watching two women go at it cause it's just . . .
FIVE	The whole style, the whole thing: the shirts, the hats, the whatever . . . the haircuts, I'll be like, God! Those fucking dykes!
THREE	Excuse my vulgarness, you know? But women are more gentle and uh, two together, two together, you enjoy it more because it's softer. It's more, more . . . dammit that's as far as I can go with that . . .
ONE	So women dating other women is awesome because you

	know, if she's my friend, we can have a conversation about that too . . .
FIVE	And I think any man, any man, if he was being honest, would say exactly what I just said. Fucking lesbians.
ONE	Man! I love lesbians.
THREE	Mmmm. Love lesbians.
TWO	I have to say . . . it's very, uh, exciting.
FOUR/ELLIOT	I'll tell you what, I'm more comfortable having a gay sister than if I had a gay brother. That's their thing, but you know it would no way be for me. I don't know. I don't know, it's . . . The way gay guys act . . . I don't know, I don't really like it. They're so worried about what they wear and how much money they make. They're more materialistic. And they're more judgmental and they're not in committed relationships like they . . . kind of go all over the place with a lot of different guys. I don't know . . . it doesn't seem like a good vibe. I'm just not comfortable with it.

Transition . . . party scene, overlapping chatter, people mill about.

ALAN	*(mid-conversation)*
	Anyway, what can you do? You should just quit. Brian says why stick it out if you don't have to. Have you met Brian yet? He's around here somewhere. (**looks around, spots Brian, waves, holds up his drink, shakes it to indicate he wants another one**) He was supposed to bring me another drink. He's so easily distracted. But, anyway, he knows all about freelancing so you should ask him. That's how we met. Well, at a party. I introduced myself to him because I thought he was cute and he worked for [place] and I thought, okay, I'm a graphic designer so maybe he'd like my work. So we talked at the party and he gave me his card and so I called him and so I go over to his house and he were just talking and talking and finally I had to seduce him—all that talking, I had to pounce—and it was great, we totally clicked, but afterwards he wasn't saying much, you know, and I left and I wanted to see him again and I had left my hat at his house—no! Not like that! I really forgot it there. So I had left my hat right . . .

Brian walks up with a drink for A, rolls his eyes.

BRIAN   Are you telling this story again? Oh God. He loves to tell this story. *(switches out Alan's drink and starts to walk away)* Change the subject while you can.

ALAN   *(calling after him)*
I need a lime! *(shakes head)* Whatever. He loves this story. I don't know why he pretends not to. Anyway, where was I . . . oh! Okay . . . so I'm coming down with a flu right but I go to get my hat—it was a great hat—and this guy—this guy—opens the door and he's just wearing a towel around his waist—that's it, and wet hair and brushing his teeth and Alan comes out and he's like, oh hey, all casual right, "here's your hat and oh by the way, I made you a CD." *What?* So he gives me the CD and the hat and I leave and that guy is there in his *towel* so I'm thinking, well, I guess it wasn't really a connection, but the CD? So I go home and I'm sick so my grandmother comes over and makes me stinkyfish, which is a Chinese thing, right, we eat it all the time, but have you ever had stinkyfish? Or, more to the point, have you ever smelled stinkyfish??? It STINKS!!!!! Like permeates every-where, everywhere, like the air and gets into your clothes and your skin . . . one time we were making it at home and our neighbors actually called the police on us . . . my mom was like, well, what do you want us to do, not cook? And they're like, uh, maybe you can cook it less stinky? But you can't. Stinkyfish STINKS. But it tastes good. So anyway, the stinkyfish is everywhere, and I have a fever like a 104 and I put in the CD and it is full of all these romantic songs, really beautiful songs and I'm so confused and sick and sweating and eating stinkyfish and just crying and crying because I feel so bad, and I don't remember what songs were on it but the first song was so nice and it just made me cry . . .

Brian has rejoined Alan, with a lime for his drink.

BRIAN   Beth Orton.

ALAN   Beth Orton?

BRIAN	That was the first song—it had Belle and Sebastian and Call and Response but the first one was definitely Beth Orton.
ALAN	Okay well, Beth Orton, and I was so confused because the guy in the towel . . .
BRIAN	(laughs) Aw man . . . my friend Tim . . . he almost ruined it for me, he was in town for a job interview and he just shows up out of nowhere and was like I just need to get ready at your place and I'm like, are you kidding me . . . aw man, this is a really bad time and then Alan shows up and Tim is in his towel, all hey, wassup, and I don't know if Alan wants an explanation or just his hat so I just give him the hat and the CD and I'm thinking, fucking Tim!
TOGETHER	In his towel!
BRIAN	And Alan calls me, and he's like I'm so sick and he's cry-ing . . .
ALAN	. . . because of the CD
BRIAN	What can I say, it was a good CD. So I say come over, I'll take care of you. And he's like . . .
ALAN	I can't!
BRIAN	. . . because he stinks!
ALAN	(slight overlap) I stink! But finally I go over . . .
BRIAN	. . . and he's so sick and I'm just holding him, like rocking him, here (makes gesture of holding head to his chest) and aw man, he smelled so bad. Have you ever smelled stinkyfish?
ALAN	I told you I was going to stink.
BRIAN	It was in his pores. Oozing out. But I didn't want him to go.
ALAN	And I didn't. After that I just moved in.
BRIAN	Brought his stuff and never left. What a stalker.
ALAN	Shut up!

They laugh, smile at each other affectionately.

BRIAN	That was seven years ago.
ALAN	Seven years. Can you believe it?
BRIAN	(*fake sigh*) Feels like forever.
ALAN	Ah . . . what a tough guy. He's such a tough guy.
BRIAN	(*ruffles* ALAN's *hair affectionately*) Here we go! I'm getting another drink. (*walks away*)
ALAN	Tough guy. Playing Beth Orton! (*calls after him*) Beth Orton! He's a total momma's boy really.

Transition. Momma's Boy.

ONE	What's wrong with being a mama's boy?
TWO	I love my mom's.
THREE	Shit, my mom is awesome.
ONE	I mean, everyone always says it like it's a bad thing. Momma's boy.
TWO	My moms is like a rock, a tigress. She kept me out of trouble. Looked after her mi'jito and stuff.
THREE	If I'm hungry she'll tend to me. If I want something, I don't even have to say it, she'll just know. If I want flaming hots in my sandwich, she'll go to the store and get me some flaming hots and it's there. She's great.
ONE	Men who don't respect their moms don't respect woman. Period.
TWO	That don't mean she's not a little crazy. Man, sometimes my moms can really get on my nerves, she's in my business and shit.
THREE	I've never met anybody that's more Christlike than her. Like she'll do (*hits table*) whatever for you—if you need $300, and she has to pay her car payment with that $300, she'll give it to you. She'll just do it.
TWO	Like when I was younger, I didn't want to play baseball, right? Because I sucked. But she signed me up. She'd actu-

ally hit me so that I would go play, because she didn't want me hanging out in the streets. In my business and shit!

ONE I'm a feminist because of my mom. Because she raised me by herself and I know that wasn't easy.

THREE She cleans my room. Buys the groceries. I got it good.

ONE I respect women. Maybe too much.

TWO Sometimes, sometimes . . . uh . . . I wanted to pop her. Just get back in her face. Be like, Damn mom. Stay out of my business.

THREE I got it real good.

TWO Just so you know, I would never hit my mom. All I'm telling you is sometimes she got on my damn nerves, telling me do this do that don' hang out with so-and-so, where you going. Damn!

ONE Respecting women is why I never get laid. Because I don't want to be that asshole. You know, that asshole.

THREE All I have to do is keep her company, go to church with her once a week, that's cool.

ONE I always struggle with like you know, I really really want to talk to that woman but I don't want her to think that I just want to go have sex with her—even though sometimes that is what I want to do. I mean, I go to the bar and end up playing with the touch screen.

THREE I am in no hurry to leave.

ONE And I'm always the friend. Girls are like, "you're my best friend!" And you know that sucks. I mean I want to be friends with women, but why do I always have the be "THE FRIEND"?

THREE No hurry.

TWO But you know what? For all that? I'm not in a gang. I didn't drop out. I play ball. I stayed safe. My mom's did all right. I appreciate that.

THREE Tell me . . . would you want to move out? Hell no. I got it good.

ONE   My mom says that the right woman will come along that I
             just have to be myself.

TWO   I love my mom's.

ONE   A nice, straightforward, mom loving, feminist guy—good
             catch right? Yeah tell that to the ladies.

TWO   Now, do I want to marry a woman like my mom? (laughs)
             Nope. Gonna find a girl who minds her own business.

THREE   Shit. My mom is awesome. I'm in no hurry to move out, not
             until I find a girl like her, who knows how to take care of a
             man. Which won't be easy, I know. Because women these
             days, man . . . they are not what they used to be. They are
             not what they used to be. Girls.
             Damn! I got girl problems.

Transition. GIRLS. Men are at a bar.

*Transition, lights fade on ALAN, up on other party guests. Three guys
at coffee shop, one is waiting for his coffee, the other two are seated.
The one waiting for coffee is some kind of contractor. This is mid-
conversation.*

GEORGE   Shit. When I have a house I want stainless steel everywhere.

CARL   Better marry a rich bitch then.

All laugh.

GEORGE   Son, I'm a gangster.

Laugh some more.

GEORGE   Whatchu selling these days?

CARL   Whatchu need?

All laugh.

BRETT   Show me the menu!!!!

All laugh.

CARL	Aw shit . . . you see that car. *(all look out window)* Oh, I haven't seen one of those in a long time.
BRETT	What's that? A Charger?
CARL	Naw . . . that's made by Chrysler.
GEORGE	Sammy Sosa got one for free from the Cubs.
BRETT	Sammy Sosa. Aw, for real? Damn.

SAM comes over, carrying coffee for CARL and himself. Hands it to CARL, foamy thing with straws, comes back trying to put straws in his mouth.

SAM	Here you go.
CARL	Thanks.

Long silence. GEORGE texting, BRETT just sitting there.

SAM	I'm fucking tired.
BRETT	Me too.
SAM	That's 'cuz you wake up so early. I told you you don't have to come to work so early.
BRETT	Yeah.

Long silence. A texting.

GEORGE	Ooooh I can't wait for Saturday.
CARL	I can't wait to sleep.
GEORGE	*(long pause. Gets text)* Ah . . . this girl . . . *(irritated, keeps texting)* The other day I was in class and I was so fucking bored I was texting so much my fucking battery died.
BRETT	Damn.
SAM	It takes a lot to kill a fucking battery, like two days.
CARL	Of course that day you didn't learn nothing.
GEORGE	Yeah. *(keeps texting)*

SAM	Aw hey—you still dating that stripper?
CARL	What stripper?
GEORGE	What's her name? Candy?
BRETT	(*laughs*) Candy
CARL	Why does everybody have to be a stripper or a nun with you? There's no normal girls in your spectrum?
SAM	So why is her name Candy? Why the *fuck* is her name Candy if she doesn't strip? (*slams table with palm of hand—turns to other guys at table*) I mean Candy is a stripper name.
GEORGE	Ah, this girl!
BRETT	The same one?
GEORGE	Naw. That one is crazy. She was supposed to call me, right? she forgot. So I text her. And I tell her I'm going to call her later. I went to the barbershop, I forgot. Talked to this other honey, whatever. So she texted me, (*girl voice*) "oh guess we're not meant to be" I was like, what do you mean, (*girl voice*) "you and I," I was like oh-kaaay girl, you're on crack, show *me* you want to be with me, you know what I mean? whatever, so I go home take a shower go out to the club with my boys . . . dude she's fucking there!
BRETT	(*overlaps, sympathetically*) Damn.
GEORGE	Being all, (*girl voice*) "why didn't you call me?" I forgot! (*girl voice*) "You're an asshole." Oh! How come when I forget to call you once I'm an asshole but you forget to call me I'm not all like "you're a bitch." All these girls are fucking crazy. Even this girl I'm talking to now. Fucking mood swings up the ass.
BRETT	(*laughs*) You're the wrong guy for that type of girl.* That's why I'm not getting married
GEORGE	(*overlaps*) Speaking of the devil (*text*) (*girl voice*) "Baby, I'm just kid-

ding." Ah whatever. Fucking girls. (*texting*) You . . . are . . . making . . . me . . . Crazy . . .

CARL	Your problem is you date the wrong kind of girls.*
*SAM	What the fuck do you know? You're dating a stripper named Candy.
*BRETT	All girls are like that.
CARL	Candy is not a stripper.
SAM	Sure is. She's white, isn't she.
GEORGE	What does that have to do with anything?
SAM	It's the classic route for white girls from small towns . . . They love big cities and big city dicks.* And she probably found a strip joint to work her way through "college."
CARL	Man, fuck you. Why do I even talk to you?
SAM	Cuz I'm the smartest guy y'all know . . . and if there is one thing I know—is women! (*sings like Biggie Smalls*) "*cuz if you don't know, now you know!*"
CARL	You don't know women. You-don't-know-women. (*takes a sip of his beer and shakes head no—sure of this*)
SAM	Oh I know, what I know, and I know, that I *know*—women!
BRETT	He knows women.
CARL	Just because he knows the game does not mean he knows women.
GEORGE	Nobody fucking knows women.
SAM	Playing the game and knowing women are the same thing. You have to know how to give women what they want.
CARL	Like, respect?
BRETT	Fuck that.
GEORGE	Yeah, fuck that.
BRETT	Women don't want a nice guy.
SAM	Look, you've got to be nice, but have a little bit of bad boy in you and let it come out. Because women have an evil streak.

CARL	Are you serious?

SAM   You have to know what women want and what women are. (*to George*) So your problem is you date all those Puerto Rican girls

GEORGE   Yeah, cuz they look good, holla!

SAM   Yeah, but . . . they're crazy. You're into those Puerto Rican girls who will chop your nuts off and cut you in your sleep.

CARL   Again . . . are you serious?

BRETT   I've met girls like that.

SAM   Puerto Rican women are too dominant. They always want it their way and have to call the shots . . . Like, uh . . .

GEORGE   Hillary Clinton.*

SAM   Exactly, You might as well slap a dick on her and give her a crew cut. You know?
Same with Colombian women. Colombian women are very materialistic. When they meet a guy, they're like what do you drive, how much money do you make? They just wanna know what you can do for them. Peruvian women are better, more docile, they're more giving, not used to a fancy lifestyle; so they'll take what you can give them. Same with most Mexican women unless you get that boojy type of woman who only looks for certain things . . . That's why you got to mess with the races that are subdominant.

BRETT   Like a Chinese girl?

SAM   Oriental women

CARL   Asian women.

SAM   —they'll tend to men maybe 100 times better than a Latina would. Maybe in Chinese culture, they really respect the role of the man, the role of the woman. They stick to that role. Not like black women who want to be in charge of everything. And then they get so frustrated they want to take it out on men. At least with a white girl, you get what you want, right? (**CARL** *ignores him*) White women are caregivers. They worry about their partners, they even ask, "Hey, was I good? Did you enjoy sex? Do you want to do something dif-

ferent?" As opposed to Latinas where that's all you're going
to get. You're not going to get no more and if you don't like
that, then go find someone else. Even if you're with them,
they're like, "Oh, I don't give head" or "I don't do this" or "I
don't do that," you know? They're not open, just whatever
they want.

GEORGE   It's always what they want.

CARL   You are so full of shit. This is why you're single. This is why
          all of y'all are single.

SAM   *Single by choice

BRETT   *Don't tie me down

CARL   You know the best part of my day is waking up next to her.
          Someday you guys are gonna fall in love and regret all your
          bullshit.

    The guys make fun of him.

CARL   I have to go back to work. I don't know why I waste my time
          with any of you assholes.

SAM   I'm just telling it like it is.

GEORGE   (*gets text*)
          Sweet. She said yes.

BRETT   See you tomorrow?

SAM   Tell Candy I said Hi!

CARL   Yeah. See you tomorrow.

GEORGE   Man. This girl . . . this girl right here . . . she's fuckin' hot.

SAM   (*with transition*)
          Yeah, but she looks crazy.

  Transition. FRANKLIN.

          I don't know that word, player.
          But if you mean did I used to get girls, oh yes, but when I
          was growing up we would call it snaggin'.
          Before my wife, I was a wild kind of guy. Had a trickster

messing with my life. Cuz I wasn't walking in the Indian way.

See, as long as I got focus on being Native American, I'm okay. The minute I let my focus slip, then everything starts to slip. If you can understand that.

Now, the Indian woman has got a great, great power. She's got the power to put a stop to anything just by the way she looks. I grew up in the reservation, singing and dancing Native American style. Spoke my language. And you're an Indian man, you get your respect for all women. You're not thinking, hey I've got to get . . . you're always respectful of women and the other gender.

But I got drafted in the Army in 1972. Got out in '74.

I got back from the war and I was, you know, not thinking Indian.

I had the white man in my head, drinking all the time.

Lots of time in a bar looking for who knows what.

Playing the same game everybody out there does.

I was really good at it too.

Really good.

I could, uh . . . I mean, I was the only Native American in the circles I ran in and the girls loved it, you know?

I had even longer hair at the time.

They just loved it.

I'd always just walk in the room and say "Indian's here" and everyone loved it . . .

three or four or an hour or two into the party, and a couple of beers I'd be telling so many jokes, Indian jokes, white man jokes, I'd have everyone rolling in laughter and that's how I played it up. *(laughs)*

And I really did play it up a lot. And I knew it too.

I had a lot of one night stands.

Wild. And you know, they were all white girls.

They loved it, want to be with the Indian.

But even back then I was kinda afraid that if I got with another one, a Latino or an Indian or an ethnic lady that somehow I'd have to recognize, somehow I'd have to give that life up. They might know something that I knew. *(laughs)*

And I knew all the time that what I was doing was somewhat wrong but I was so caught up in it.

I was playing their game, the white man's game.

But when I met my wife. I knew, the minute I started talking to her, she thinks Indian. She helped me get the white man out of my head.

And sure, I still like a drink, every now and then but I don't look at another woman. Sure don't.

Because my wife can put a stop to the world just by the way she looks.

DRUNK PIECE

Four separate scenes overlap. JUAN, FRANKIE, *and* LORENZO *are at a spades table* (**Spades**). FELIX *(son) is at home, looking for his father* RUBEN, *who is at the neighbor's house getting drunk, the sounds of a block party in the distance* (**Block Party**). ALEJANDRO *is just home from work, in a small room with a chair and a record player, possibly a bedroom or a study* (**Solitary**). MIKE *and* CLAUDIO *are playing darts, holding beers, passing a joint back and forth* (**Darts**).

SOLITARY

ALEJANDRO   *(enters and sits on chair)*
Si! Ya te oi! *(He sits down and is taking off his shoes)* Sophia, I hear you! No, I'm not hungry right now! You guys eat without me! Yo se, but I just got home! Let me just sit for a second! *(to himself and under his breath)* Callate. *(beat)* Lalito! Go downstairs, dinner's ready! I don't care, I said go!

Beat, looks around, opens drawer on a small table and takes out bottle of liqueur. Takes a swig and relaxes. As other scenes begin, he begins to play the song on the record player. It is an old mariachi song.

SPADES

JUAN, LORENZO, *and* FRANKIE *are playing spades and drinking.*

JUAN	Ey, how's your brother?
FRANKIE	Man, fuck you!
LORENZO	For real man, you got a dykey ass sister
FRANKIE	Fuck you man thass my sister don't be disrespecting
JUAN	You guys get your haircut together?

LORENZO	Deja de estar chingando who's deal is it?
FRANKIE	Don't talk shit, she's younger than you and she's a principal
LORENZO	Yeah (slurring) your drunk ass can't even spell principal
JUAN	Fuck you I can drink any of youse under the table
LORENZO	Yeah, you'll probably see his sister under there eating pussy
FRANKIE	I told you to watch your fucking mouth
LORENZO	I thought your sister had the fuckin' mouth haha!
FRANKIE	But hers ain't bloody like yours is about to be
JUAN	Man, fuck this hand! Redeal.

Throws cards in and gets up for another beer. FRANKIE *and* LORENZO *protest, overlapping.*

FRANKIE	Aw hell no!
LORENZO	Damn, what a fucking cheater
FRANKIE	Thass bullshit
LORENZO	Fuck you man thass fucking cheating you can't redeal just cuz you got a shitty hand
JUAN	Man . . . lick my left nut.

All start laughing.

FRANKIE	Alright, who wants a shot?
LORENZO	Coo (pushes glass forward)
JUAN	Yeah all right
LORENZO	Fucking cheater
FRANKIE	Shut up and drink.

BLOCK PARTY

FELIX *runs on.*

FELIX	Dad!!!!! Mom's looking for you. Daaaaaaaaaaaddddddd!!!!!

RUBEN	Ey, sshh shhh. I'm right here, ching'ao man

RUBEN enters, plastered, stumbling and slurring his words.

FELIX	Where you been at?
RUBEN	Next door . . . drinking with Rico and the guys . . . they didn't think I could hang. I showed them!
FELIX	*(laughing)* Dad, are you drunk!?
RUBEN	Naw, I ain't drunk. I'm fine . . . *(long pause)* . . . hahaha fucking Mexicans got me drunk *(slightly slurred)*
FELIX	Dad?! *(leftover laugh from hearing his father slur, but in semi-disbelief)*
RUBEN	What! I'm a fuckin' Mexican, I can say that.
RUBEN	Your Grandfather . . . grandpa was a fuckin' wetback . . . that wetback motherfucker . . .
FELIX	Dad, come on . . . you sound like those white guys at work you always be telling me about.
RUBEN	Hey! Let me tell you something, I'm not a white guy, I'm half a white guy!

DARTS

CLAUDIO	Your turn man.
MIKE	*(pulls out joint, takes a long drag)* Hold up, hold up.
CLAUDIO	You gonna play?
MIKE	Yeah. Yeah.

Long uncomfortable silence, they both drink from their beers. MIKE throws a dart.

CLAUDIO	Nice.
MIKE	I know.

Fig. II.3. Quarters Scene. Ilana Faust (left) and Yadira Correa in *Machos*.
Photo by Johnny Knight, courtesy of Teatro Luna.

They laugh. Long pause.

MIKE   Te dije que te quiero? I love you, man . . .

CLAUDIO   *(looks at him, laughs)*
            I love you too.

MIKE   Nah, but . . . really . . . I really appreciate you comin' here,
            man, I do.

CLAUDIO   *(still looking at the board, awkward)*
            No es nada.

MIKE   *(long pause, smokes, long pause)*
            This shit is good.

CLAUDIO   *(picks up instantly)*
            Yeah man! It's been forever since I smoked something this
            good. That shit I get in Chicago . . . It's killing me, man. **(They
            both wince, long silence)**

MIKE   I don't think my dad is gonna make it past this week.

CLAUDIO	(like he's been waiting for it to come up)
	Yeah?

| MIKE | So, how's Chicago? |

SOLITARY

ALEJANDRO	(He changes the song on record player. He is getting drunker. He begins to check his pockets looking for something. He doesn't even know what he is looking for.)
	Isabel! Has visto mi . . . Isabel! Have you seen . . .
	(Trails off as he is continuing to look. He stops as if no big deal. Takes another swig. He mumbles something to himself)
	Lalito! Traime mis chanclas! Lalito! What, you don't hear me?! Lalito! Andale, keep it up pendejo!

BLOCK PARTY

FELIX is supporting RUBEN, trying to get him to his room.

RUBEN	They thought I couldn't hang, fuckin' wetbacks, they ain't better than me, I'm part Irish so what, I'm born here, so what? We're all just fuckin' wetbacks!
FELIX	Come on Dad, I'm just gonna sit you back down, and I will be right back.
	(exit to stairs)

He gets RUBEN upstairs and into a chair (bed?), starts to leave.

RUBEN	Don't shut that door Felix! Damnit Felix, I wanna go outside, I'm not a child! Everyone else is outside!

DARTS

MIKE	Hey, remember that Thanksgiving dinner when you came with that, what's her name? Candela.
CLAUDIO	(chuckles, remembering)
	Candela . . .
MIKE	Yeah Candela. And my dad told her she was chubby. Remember her face? (They both laugh)
CLAUDIO	Aw man, she was pissed.

MIKE	You don't tell a woman she's chubby!
CLAUDIO	Your dad, man . . . (*They both laugh, slip into a long silence*)
MIKE	Hey, you want another beer?
CLAUDIO	Yeap. It's your turn.
MIKE	Want a shot of tequila?
CLAUDIO	Yeah . . . tengo un pedo que no veo
MIKE	I'm going to miss my dad
CLAUDIO	(*overlapping as if he didn't hear him*) Where's that shot?
MIKE	Yeah I'm going to miss my dad

SOLITARY

ALEJANDRO	(*changes the song on the record again and then drinks from his flask*)

SPADES

ALL	(*pounding on table, in unison*) Uno . . . Dos . . . Tres . . . (*They drink a shot*)

EL REY *is playing.*

JUAN	Aw turn this shit up this is my jam!!!
FRANKIE	Aw yeah, man, I fucking love this song. It makes me cry and shit!
JUAN	Pinche chillón siempre esta llorando . . . kind of like your parents did when they found out about your sister.
FRANKIE	(*jumps up, knocking over chair, shoves* JUAN) I'm sick and fucking tired of this shit! I told you to shut the fuck up about my sister!!
JUAN	O que, guey? Que vas a hacer? Pinche joto igual que tu hermana.

They start to fight, LORENZO *breaks it up.*

LORENZO   Ya ya ya . . . both of youse shut up and let's play already you're fucking dragging.

He passes a bottle around, they drink, JUAN *and* FRANKIE *eye each other warily, "El Rey" by Jose Alfredo Jimenez comes on and the guys' faces immediately light up as they start singing along.*

ALL   Yo sè bien que estoy afuera, pero el dìa en que yo me muera sè que tendrs que llorar! . . .

SOLITARY

ALEJANDRO   *(is also singing "El Rey")*
Llorar y llorar, Llorar y llorar, diras que no me quisiste, pero vas a estar muy triste . . .

Song continues and then starts skipping. He takes another drink from the bottle. He screams again but this time he's screaming more to himself, in his own world.

Sophial! Sophial! Porque no vienes? Se que me oyes! Te quiero decire algo, **(softly)** Isabel. Te quiero mucho mi'ja. Lo sabes? Con todo mi Corazon! Te quiero Isabel! Tu! Me limpias mi casa! Me haces de comer! Me lavas mi ropa! Ven! Te quiero decir algo. **(beat)** Paquito! **(waits)** No me oyes? **(waits)** Que tu ya no me quieres? **(waits)** Paquito! Ni sabes de lo que yo te estoy hablando. Tu no sabes! No sabes que te quiero tambien. Como tu mama. Mucho, mijo! Con todo mi Corazon! Lo sabes?! No. NO! No lo sabes. **(to himself)** Los quiero. **(sings, alone, music is skipping)** No tengo trono ni reina, ni nadie que me comprenda, pero sigo seindo el Rey!

BLOCK PARTY

RUEBEN   *(locked in his room, shouting after* FELIX*)*
Let me out of here! I don't want to be in here! You mad because I called Grandpa a wetback! He WAS a wetback! Let me out of here! You think you're fucking better than everyone . . . waving the Mexican flag . . . you don't even speak Spanish! Getting all political on me! Fuck you!!!! Fuck you

Felix!!!! (*tries the door*) Open the door! Please, I'm not an animal, I'm your father. Let me out of here!

SPADES

The three men are singing, loudly and sloppily, arms around each other. JUAN raises his arm high, bottle in hand, lets out a grito and throws the bottle to the ground. The other two cheer, encourage him.

JUAN   Les voy a decir algo neta neta neta netisimo guey. (*points to* FRANKIE) Guey, te quiero. No sabes cuanto te quiero guey. Tu para mi eres como un hermano. Verdad brother? Fuck the Border.

ALL   Pinches gringos!

SOLITARY

ALEJANDRO   Estoy solo (*is getting teary eyed and belligerent*) Pero los quiero! (*sadly*) Chingada madre. (*softly sobbing*) Se que me oyen! Los quiero mucho! Nunca les digo, pero oyenme ahorita! (*almost too intense with a bit of madness along with the sadness*) Les quiero mucho cabron!! (*breathes hard and then hits the record player to a stop*)

DARTS

MIKE and CLAUDIO are silent, drinking their beers, and throwing their darts, passing the joint back and forth. MIKE takes a long drag, holds it in, closes his eyes, leans back and rocks back and forth softly on his heels. CLAUDIO eyes him cautiously, uncomfortably. Takes a long sip of beer and throws a dart.

End scene, transition.

ROBERT   I grew up and uhm . . . my father was the kind of person that . . .
he was old school macho—you know—
he came from a very abusive, large family.
and he grew up very lonely and in turn,
as when he got married,
he thought or his belief system was,
as long as I work and bring home the money and I provide

all the basic necessities, I—my job is done and I can go out and do what I wanna do and let the wife take care of the house. And that's how it was.

And it was a lonely life. For him. For my mom. For me.

I realized I don't want that life.

I don't want to be Macho like that.

I don't demand anything. I—I don't say, it has to be my way or the highway. Uhm, I don't think that I'm . . . that I should somehow not have to be part of a child's rearing.

Uh, I do housework.

I do yardwork.

I do car work.

I clean tushies.

I wipe noses.

I pick up spit.

You know, uh, uhm, all the things that, you know, men traditionally are not supposed to do. You know, I do it.

So, and I don't say, that she has to take my name or whatnot.

And I don't tell her, this is how it's gonna be and that's it.

So, in those ways I don't think I'm macho

But if push comes to shove I'll show you how macho I am. *(laughs)*

uhm, I, I know how to fight.

I've been raised fighting.

I fought in the streets and I fought in the ring.

And, uhm I know I can hold my own to a certain degree so to me macho is kind of holding your own. And I mean holding your own whether it has to come to a physical or your responsibilities in life. So . . .

Maybe I am Macho.

But not like my dad.

Like me.

Transition. Ending: Macho.

ONE   Macho? *(long beat)*

ALL   Macho?
           Alright, alright . . . *(laugh, shaking heads)* Macho?

THREE	Macho.
FOUR	You walk around
FIVE	you're a wall.
SIX	No emotions
SEVEN	no feelings
FOUR	Girls are beneath you male stereotypes
TWO	tenth degree that make them Latino. It says not only are you . . . you know a bad ass. But a Mexican badass
SEVEN AND SIX	A CHINGON
CHORUS	A Macho
TWO	My father died
THREE	Don't cry,
ONE	be a man
TWO	said my uncles
FIVE	you're the man of the house now
SIX	take care of your mom and your brother.
TWO	What the fuck does that mean to a nine-year-old boy?
CHORUS	Maaaaacho.
THREE	devoured by a pop culture
FIVE	you know, like they refer to salsa as being macho.
THREE	You know like, oh this is a macho sauce . . .
FIVE	Or you know if you walk into some burger joint and there's a macho burger*
THREE	*a macho burger
FIVE	cause they have jalapenos on it
SIX	or the spicy cheetos are *macheetos*.

THREE	You know like it's gotten . . . it has lost what—whatever it used to mean you know?
FIVE	You know?
CHORUS	Macho?
EIGHT	This is macho.
ONE	Jimmy De Leon—61st subway street attendant
EIGHT	I was drunk one evening coming out of a bar on the lower east side stumbling out three guys jumped me
CHORUS	Bam!
EIGHT	managed to hold them off for a while but I'm no Jackie Chan. And uh,
ONE	Jackie Chan this guy from nowhere,
TOGETHER	Jimmy De Leon,
EIGHT	comes out of nowhere
ONE	and he fends one of the guys off and
EIGHT	I used to carry a box cutter with me and
ONE	I cut one of the guys and
EIGHT	he ran off and
ONE	the other guy ran off and then there was one left and us two and
EIGHT	then the guy ran off and yeah
CHORUS	Maaaan . . .
EIGHT	If it weren't for him, I woulda got my ass beat
CHORUS	Bam!
EIGHT	Yeah
TWO/EIGHT	Jimmy De Leon
EIGHT	That was macho.
SIX AND FOUR	Maaaaan . . .

FIVE	Man!
SEVEN	There was a time you know you know
SEVEN	Macho used to be something good
THREE	That's a man
FOUR	Takes care of his family
THREE	That's a man
SEVEN	Macho
THREE	Macho
SEVEN	My dad, quiet, silent
SIX	Like Tim Duncan from the Spurs
FOUR	You know him?
SIX	You can count on him
FOUR	He scores his points, gets his rebounds
FIVE AND THREE	Doesn't say anything
SIX	Doesn't need to
SEVEN	Like my dad
EIGHT	Macho
TWO	Macho
SEVEN	Strong silent type
SIX	That's alright
TWO	Yeah, I'm a macho
THREE	A macho
TWO	Walking with a woman
THREE	She walks on the inside of the street
TWO	I hold the door
THREE	Pick up the check
TWO	Treat my lady like a lady

THREE	Maybe that's not feminist
TWO	But that's right
THREE	So yeah, I'm macho
TWO	Push comes to shove
THREE	I'll do what I got to do
FIVE	Any guy in America can be a Macho. You don't need brown skin
SIX	Shiiiit . . . the whitest guy in the country
ONE	The dude running the country
FIVE	He acts macho
CHORUS	Real macho
THREE	It gets hard I guess when you're hanging around guys and they're like
ONE	"What, you can't come to the game?!"
FOUR	Um your lady won't let you go?
FIVE	"What are you pussy whipped?"
SEVEN AND EIGHT	Pussy whipped!
THREE	And it fucks with your head
SIX	and the next thing you know you're like,
THREE	"Honey, I'm going to the game with the guys and don't give me crap about it."
SIX	And she hasn't even said nothing, and you're already jumping down her throat you know?
THREE	I guess that's Macho
EIGHT	Shit I remember my dad holding this pillow
ONE	Telling me to punch it
CHORUS	Punch it! Fight this pillow fight this pillow!
EIGHT	I was three years old and he's teaching me to fight, not to

cry, and leaving me with this image that* that's the way of boys and men

ONE   (*overlap*)
*that's the way of boys and men

SIX   Man

SEVEN   Man

THREE   Macho just means man.

CHORUS   Man

THREE   Like in Spanish. Macho means a man, hembra means a woman. Macho.

FOUR   Be a man.

SIX   What does that even mean?

TWO   Stand up

SEVEN   Step up

FIVE   Man up

ONE   Be a man.

THREE   Be macho.

ALL   Be. A. Man.

END

CHAPTER 3

Voicing Masculinity

Tamara Roberts

Midway through technical rehearsals for Teatro Luna's *Machos*, director Coya Paz and I had an argument. One of the female actors—playing a man—wore a costume that included a button-down shirt and V-neck sweater, and we disagreed over whether current men's fashion dictated that the shirt collar be worn in or out of the sweater. We enlisted opinions from various bystanders of a range of sexes and genders with no clear winner emerging from the queries. Ultimately, the costume designer's preference won out and the moment of masculine uncertainty passed. But the question remained: who had the authority on what was masculine in the production? The queer, white, Latina, female director, a frequent drag-king spectator? The straight, Latina, female costume designer, studied in styling men? The straight, white lighting designer, biologically male but whose wardrobe consisted of jeans and ragged sweatshirts? Or, myself, the somewhat trans, mixed-race sound designer? For a show that seeks to trouble the relationship between masculinity and maleness, it seems that any one of us might have held the word on the "true to life" collar position.

Machos is based on interviews Teatro Luna ensemble members and associates conducted with over one hundred men across the United States, in person and over e-mail. Additional material culled from casual interactions and even overheard conversations between men is also represented in the text. Pulling together these numerous and variant voices, the show examines masculinity from "the inside," employing the words of men as they discuss what they think it means to be—or be a—"macho." A cast of eight women perform the words of these men, switching in and out of a variety of roles. Never arriving at any one conclusion, the show explores the range of experiences of men, as well as the multiplicity of ways masculinity is performed. Ultimately, *Machos* seeks to illuminate the ways in which masculinity presents both free-doms and constrictions to the men that embody it.

Despite its focus on men, *Machos* is quite similar to the company's previous work. Teatro Luna is an all-Latina theater company that has devoted its output to explorations of the racial, ethnic, gender, and sexual identities of contemporary Latinas. *The Maria Chronicles* (2003), for example, engages the challenges faced by Latina actors when the majority of roles available to them are maids or gangbangers, while S-E-X . . . *Oh!* (2005) is a foray into the multiple manifestations of Latina sexuality. The overarching theme of these works, as well as a goal of the company's more broadly, is to illuminate the diversity of Latina lives and show that there is no—as the title of their first show claims—*Generic Latina* (2001). Similarly, *Machos* begins with the assumption that there are manifold experiences and identities within the category of man or male.

Diverging from previous Teatro Luna shows, however, is the first step in the *Machos* development process: the interviews. To create its signa-ture ensemble-built works, the company frequently turns to members' own personal stories for material.[1] For *Machos*, the company turned its gaze outward for source material, which was then transcribed and vetted by the ensemble and writing associates. The basics of the stories included in the script were selected and developed through a year-long workshop process in which the artistic team discussed recurring themes, interesting personae, and other ideas worth bringing into the show. Paz then worked the script into its final shape, determining what stories would remain and their order. Thus, while much of the text is verbatim, the ensemble shaped it through the selection and arrange-ment of the stories. The first full production of *Machos* debuted in Chi-cago in November 2007. The show had a nearly sold-out run, a sold-out remount at a theater in Berwyn (a Chicago suburb) the following Janu-ary, and went on to tour frequently around the country.

Here, I would like to step through a few of the major gestures the show makes in its journey to the heart of masculinity: the juxtaposition of multiple voices and perspectives with a more in-depth singular nar-rative, the employment of female performers, and the occasional use of camp amid a generally realist-based aesthetic. Having served as the sound designer and composer for the show, I hope to offer unique in-sights into the final performance text, as well as the decisions that led up to it. Further, as the issues raised in *Machos* continue to be explored by Teatro Luna and other artists/ensembles, I would like to acknowledge the show's strengths while also locating areas for reconsideration or growth.

The primary structural dynamic of the script is the movement from large group scenes to more intimate monologues. This form is meant to capture general sentiments on a given topic—sports, for example—and then provide an individual portrait of a single man's relationship to it. We see, then, a group of men proclaiming the poetic beauty of watching a sports game alongside a separate trio that hoots, hollers, and curses as football plays are made, all giving a sense of a range of sports-watching behaviors. This moment is followed by interwoven monologues that discuss two men's failed dreams of playing sports professionally. In the production design process, the cinematic concept of the extreme long shot and the close-up—as well as the zoom between the two—became a guiding image for articulating this contrasting form.

Costume designer Crystal Orraca chose a palette of browns, greens, khaki, and denim, presenting a uniformity of color that evoked a sea of men. From within this general wash, each performer had her own unique silhouette: a white-collar worker dressed in business casual, a grungy youngster wearing baggy jeans and a hoodie, and a sensitive blue-collar guy clad in khakis and a guayabera, to name a few. The sparse, angular, gray-brown set featured a collection of four interlocking platforms of different heights, placed at an angle to the curtain line. Designer Carolina Avalos surrounded this unit with a taller L-shaped platform upstage, providing a vantage point where actors could view each other, suggesting the ever-present dominant gaze through which men police each other in "authentic" masculinities. Lighting designer Mac Vaughey used fast fades between full-stage washes and solo spots to provide the sense of singling out one voice amid the crowd. And I created sound cues blending bold, acoustic hip-hop beats mixed with classic-rock guitar licks. Meant to sonically evoke the strength and/or brashness assigned to masculinity, I found it particularly important to highlight the electric guitar, long a symbol for male musical and sexual prowess. This musical base was punctuated by character-specific music that introduced certain scenes, the contrast again meant to expose sonic masculinity in a variety of incarnations.

The cinematic zoom of the script also illuminates the difference—and tension—between gender and sex. The long shot operates as discourse on masculinity, while the close-up functions as the lived experience of a male-bodied individual constructing a masculine identity. The opening choral sequence of the show is a perfect example of this dynamic, as the cast details how to "Be a Man." The performers stand in positions spread over the platforms and speak/rap dictums over a dissonant drum track. The addressees, presumably other men, are told to "grow some balls," "face your fears," "drink beer," "fuck bitches," and a host of other, sometimes contradictory, rules. Interspersed among these choruses are short monologues that expose the pressure men feel to live up to these expectations.

The role of performance in being masculine is undeniable. One character, Frank, says, "I didn't realize as a kid that it was a script. And that someone was playing a part," in regards to the film and television stars that served as his models for "being a man." These images do not simply remain in fictional settings, however, for he also claims: "My dad was like that. My grandfather was like that. Old school macho." Similarly, Ricky illuminates how masculinity is crafted and maintained through performative reiteration, saying: "We keep repeating them, can't get over them. It's like atoms bouncing off a wall."

As the play unfolds, we learn that the conflicting axioms of masculinity often cause confusion for men trying to perform them. In fact, the show is one long exposure to men's failures at living up to the "ideal" masculine image, revealing a gap in discourse on masculinity and lived experience. A useful model to consider this shortcoming might be one of a circle with the center point being the ultimate masculine (along with whiteness and heterosexuality). The men of *Machos* are in various ways striving toward this center point, but there is always something holding them back from reaching it: being a person of color, too thin or fat, gay, or weak. Geometrically speaking, a point is in fact infinitely small and, therefore, unreachable. These men are striving toward a fugitive ideal of manhood that only exists in discourse and in contrast to what it is not, revealing again the gap between gender constructions and the sexed people trying to embody them.

For example, near the end of the show, Franklin reveals the impossibility of ever measuring up to dominant conceptions of masculinity because of being Native American. He grew up in the cultural milieu of a reservation but, after serving in the army, he returned, "not thinking Indian. I had the white man in my head, drinking all the time." He would go to bars or parties and become the center of attention and numerous women's affections, successful at being the only Indian embraced by a white social circle. But he did so by essentially performing redface: proclaiming "Indian's here" upon arrival, telling Indian jokes, wearing his hair long, and drinking. For a person of color, performing a caricature of yourself may ingratiate you to the dominant culture, but it will never allow you fully to pass into it. Indeed, Franklin says he had one-night stands with white women who wanted to "be with the Indian," his masculine prowess racially marked and, thus, not quite positioned at the masculine center. bell hooks suggests that society must move from equating participation in patriarchy with racial success and begin "to create new norms of masculine behavior, blueprints for the construction of self that would be liberating to black men."[2] Franklin's piece reveals one man's desire to envision a new center, in which "walking in the Indian way" and being a man are not contradictory performances.

By revealing some of the complications and failures of trying to be masculine, Machos asks us to empathize with the characters onstage. We see that racial, gender, and sexual structures are harmful to everyone's freedom, including those that are in dominant positions. But when the overarching response to the stories is one of feeling sorry for men, engagement with the negative consequences of masculinity, particularly on women, can be neglected. In a section about whether or not a man should hit a woman, for example, Donato explains the circumstances of the one time he struck his ex-wife. Trying to protect his daughter while his ex-wife repeatedly attempts to stab him, Donato says, "I had to hit her. I had to hit her and I floored her." He ends up in jail for it, but we are meant to see this outcome as unjust. While this action might have been warranted in this particular case, rampant male-on-female domestic violence is obscured when only explored through this story. Masculinity may be a construction, but it has tangible effects, and the consequence on women's bodies is undercut by the choice of this anomalous voice (as well as limitations in what men might have been willing to share with female interviewers).

Additionally, in Machos, we might also miss the grave impact of masculinity on non-men by witnessing the effects of masculine violence primarily on male bodies, such as in "Clean Up Shit." While we can intellectually separate men from masculinity, dominant social discourse puts them together, and, because of this, men still wield a greater power. The flipside of this equation is that, while masculinity is hard on men, it is still overall harder on women and other genders. What is left out in the ensemble's desire to respect and empathize with the men portrayed is, for example, the fact that they ended up interviewing men in pairs so that they would not be hit on. This underside of masculinity is so expected that it was naturalized and ignored rather than spoken within the context of the performance. Ultimately, in Machos, masculinity retains its power because it obscures these facts.

Of course, women are hardly absent from the production; the biggest dramaturgical intervention in *Machos* is that women perform all of the roles. For every performance, the cast bound their breasts, applied makeup and facial hair, and stepped into clothes meant to disguise their curves. They also went through a months-long rehearsal period that included workshops in which a female drag king and several men coached them on posture, gesture, and voice production. I cannot overstate the adeptness with which the original cast—Desiree Castro, Belinda Cervantes, Maritza Cervantes, Yadira Correa, Gina Cornejo, Ilana Faust, Stephanie Gentry-Fernandez, and Wendy Vargas—performed their roles. Far from presenting generalized caricatures of men, the ensemble performed distinct, nuanced portraits of each of the characters. Not only did audiences and critics respond positively to these portrayals, the cast received a Joseph Jefferson Award for best ensemble.[3]

The choices for costume, gesture, and staging were made with realism in mind; audiences were to fully feel they were watching men on the stage. The successful portrayal of men by female actors worked to highlight the performativity of masculinity. Being masculine is shown as a construction and separate from biological sex because females are able to embody it. At the same time, the knowledge of the sex of the performers makes the audience more attuned to the choices the performers make to portray men. This extra attention to men and masculinity heightens our perceptions of these constructions, marking and making them strange. This queering of masculinity goes further in that each female performer embodies multiple masculinities as she moves in and out of roles: a "base" male persona for choral sections and additional characters for individual scenes.

This queering of masculinity also comes from the play's resonances with the predominant theatrical venue for cross-gender performance: drag shows. *Machos* differs from drag by focusing less on heightened, stylized, or kitschy performances of gender and more on its everyday performativity, but there is no doubt it similarly capitalizes on the titillation of cross-dressing. Yet, while drag is generally performed in LGBTQ venues and often to arouse queer desire, *Machos* reads more as women using drag performance to understand their male partners, siblings, and friends. This framework does—and did not—negate the potential for queer consumption, but it does suggest that the target audience is not a queer one. The show instead presents heterosexual audiences with a chance to encounter cross-dressing in a "safe" manner, without having to enter homosexual spaces. Thus, while queering masculinity, *Machos* remained somewhat heteronormative as a production.

The side effect of this is that, while having produced the show, the women onstage are marginalized from the proceedings. In several moments, characters refer to women in their lives but the play remains a one-sided conversation. Women appear as vectors within the show, vessels through which to hear the words of men.

To make the basic point of masculinity-as-construction, the original *Machos* production drew on some of the sexual and gender binaries on which patriarchy relies. Promotional materials and the lobby display featured before and after photos of the cast, suggesting the radical difference between the two. Interesting to note is that one actor, who on a day-to-day basis appears quite masculine, was made to look more feminine in her before photo, perhaps to give the after shot more weight. The spectacle of women performing as men also became the primary focus of reviewer criticism of the show. Thus, in some ways, *Machos* reinforced gender binaries by highlighting the performances as cross-dressing rather than including, say, the exploration of female masculinity. Drag kinging is as much about performers expressing themselves through masculinity, whereas *Machos* assumes no correlation between the two. The play misses an opportunity to further exploit the tension among female bodies, men's words, and masculinity in critiquing patriarchy and its assumed gender and sexual binaries.[4]

The employment of female performers does raise interesting questions regarding differences between cross-gender and cross-racial performance. While the former is seen as, perhaps, transgressive but generally inoffensive, the latter holds a difficult place in the U.S. American theater given the history of minstrelsy (although minstrel performances also often featured cross-dressing).[5] In *Machos*, the characters were clearly identifiable as men but often the racial/ethnic backgrounds of the speakers were not evident. The majority of reviewers mistakenly mapped the performers' identities onto the characters, assuming that the entire text consisted of words from Latino men. Discussing the show, Paz said to me that in drag kinging, masculinity is most apparent when attached to the performance of nonnormative race or class, something I believe is often rendered through some degree of exaggeration or stereotype in order to be legible. With the focus on realism and respect for interviewees in *Machos*, heightened racial performance would be offensive and call up a racially troubled theatrical past.

Unfortunately, though, we may miss some important nuances that disrupt racial and gender assumptions. In "Stinky Fish," for example, the main speaker tells the story of how he met his boyfriend, wearing hipster glasses and citing the indie rock artists that fueled their nascent romance. What we never learn explicitly is that the speaker is Asian American, a fact that disrupts the long-standing popular elision of homosexuality and whiteness.[6] As the rehearsal process unfolded, Paz grew concerned that the Mexican characters were the only ones that were racially visible. Through the use of Spanish and discussion of topics such as the U.S.-Mexico border, these men were most legible within the confines of realism dictated by the production. Less a critique of *Machos*, I find the inability of audiences to suspend disbelief in regard to race an interesting discussion worth further exploration.

Despite the questions I raise, I believe there are many *Machos* moments in which useful critique of masculinity does indeed occur, often the most theatrical moments as well. In one scene, a trio of men prepares to masturbate but is repeatedly interrupted by mistakenly hearing someone at the door. Entirely silent, the characters employ stylized movements, choreographed by Gina Cornejo, to a ragtime piano piece to get at the great lengths the men must go for sexual privacy, as well as the sneaking around required of perhaps not being entirely open with their sexual partners. In another episode, "Mr. Loyal" greets his neighbors and two sons in a parody of 1950s white domesticity à la *Leave It to Beaver*. His monologue reveals a life of sexual infidelity, despite his initial claim of being a faithful husband and father. The disconnect between the setting and his words critiques this particular man's vision of loyalty, as well as a greater society that affords more freedom for men to sleep around without debilitating consequence. Finally, the penultimate scene of the show engages multiple men as they drink, socialize, and sing along to old mariachi records. Alejandro sits alone, wanting space from but repeatedly calling out to his family members; Juan, Frankie, and Lorenzo play cards and proclaim the strength of their friendship despite living on opposite sides of the border. These interlocked stories reveal the ways intoxication might be the only vehicle through which some men are able to combat feelings of inadequacy and openly communicate with those around them. In all, these moments stand out from the script because, while not in a heavy-handed manner, they provide a frame and argument through which to critically engage the men's words.

I would like to offer more detail on one last theatricalized moment of the show, a send-up of a boy band. I choose this moment to expound on, first, because it is based on music and choreography not fully revealed in the script. Second, the song stood out to many audiences and reviewers and has been performed by the company as a stand-alone piece. Throughout the script development process, Paz and ensemble expressed concern over poking fun at the men they inter-viewed and there was hesitation that the boy band performance might cross this line. The end result, however, navigates the terrain between mockery and respect, lampooning masculinity but not the men dis-cussed. Homosexuality is a topic that regularly surfaced in the *Machos* source interviews: in the narratives of gay men and, more frequently, in straight men's discussions of their own queer behavior. A repeated comment the interviewers heard was the description of homosocial or homosexual activity followed by the statement "but I'm not gay." This seemingly paradoxical admission became Paz's inspiration for creating the boy band piece and she wrote the lyrics for what became "Girl, I'm into You." I composed the music, wrote additional lyrics, and did vocal coaching for the actors.

"Girl, I'm into You" features five singers' unabashed accounts of not-so-straight conquests, unfolding over a quintessential Backstreet Boys or early 'N Sync drum and synth track. The most important element of any pop song is the repeating chorus that highlights its central mes-sage; in this song, the specifics of the homosocial verses melt away with each proclamation of the chorus—"I'm into you," "I swear to you," "I promise you"—words formulated to make the hearts of every teen girl and gay boy melt. These statements are performative utterances to the fullest; despite behavior to the contrary, the members of the boy band, and the men they represent, are not-gay simply by proclaiming it so. The power of this speech act and its inability to be challenged reflect the unspoken power of masculinity to determine discourse. As Judith Butler states, the "critical promise of drag does not have to do with the proliferation of genders, as if a sheer increase in numbers would do the job, but rather with the exposure or the failures of heterosexual regimes ever fully to legislate or contain their own ideals."[7] In *Machos*, "Girl, I'm into You" is an important element in highlighting the men's seemingly paradoxical statements of sexuality, while critiquing the dis-cursive limitations of straight male sexuality.

Musical performance is heavily gendered in Western classical and popular traditions, and gendered voice parts are, like any other identity, socially constructed. Males and females are considered to have lim-ited options when it comes to voice parts; men sing tenor, baritone, or bass, and women sing soprano, mezzo soprano, or alto. These parts are considered natural and biologically determined yet, in actuality, they are constructions based on a set of techniques meant to produce spe-cific vocal sounds. Still, these voice parts are considered "natural" while those that deviate from the taxonomy are considered unnatural, incorrect, or aberrant. In the bridge section of the song, the members sing: "I can always tell when a guy is gay/Wears a shirt like I've got on today/Dancing, high voice, it's all here/If I saw me in the mirror I'd think I'm queer." And, sure enough, the members do vocalize in a higher register. Yet, within the frame of a normative boy band performance, it is decidedly unqueer and masculine.

In "Sapphonics," Elizabeth Wood describes a queer or "Sapphonic" voice as one "that refuses standard categories" and whose "flexibility, versatility, and power cross over and integrate the physical (and psychological?) boundaries of sites that produce vocal pitch and tone and are commonly distinguished in the female voice."[8] This type of voice appears when a female-bodied person either produces notes that fall outside of the traditional voice ranges, or does not disguise the "break" between female/head and male/chest voice, revealing two very different timbres within one body. Thus, a queer female voice is not one that sounds like a man but one that sounds at times masculine and at others feminine, joining the two in one person. It is important to highlight Wood's designation of the sapphonic voice as a uniquely female one. For male voices have generally been afforded more flexibility in their significations before being considered deviant. In Western classical music, singing both high and low are prized as feats for the male voice, whereas female voices are coaxed to the high end alone. Also, in Western popular music, where masculinity has always reigned supreme, falsetto has long been considered a desirable feature for male performers.

Wood details the history of falsetto singing—men singing in a high head voice—as being called a "fourth voice" or "false" to indicate its nonnormative gender and sexual connotations, as well as to distance it from normative masculine vocal production. By the late-1950s era of popular music, however, male R&B and soul singers resignified the use of falsetto as one of masculine sensuality and sensitivity. With exceptions, performers rarely use falsetto throughout an entire song, reserving it to highlight particularly important statements or climactic moments. This technique has remained a staple to the R&B, neosoul, and rock crooners of today, including artists such as D'Angelo, Maxwell, and Coldplay's Chris Martin. Following in the most saccharine of R&B's footsteps, however, boy bands embrace falsetto as a vocal standard. Much like other vocal production, falsetto is not simply a high voice, but a culturally specific device selectively employed in service of masculinity. Boys singing with unchanged voices, for example, are not performing in falsetto simply because of the register in which they sing. And boy band singers, even with lower voices, have been trained to produce these higher notes. Thus, when the female performers sing "Girl, I'm into You," their use of a higher register does not mark them as feminine but rather presents them as more masculine.

Several moments in "Girl, I'm into You" call attention to the use of falsetto. In one instance, the "baby" of the group (picture a Menudo-era Ricky Martin) sings:

> I was twelve and had a crush
> Felt giddy when we touched
> Finally decided to kiss
> Getting ready for girls and this was practice
> Making out, it felt so good
> Would have done him if I could
> 'Til he turned to me to say,
> "Listen, dude, I'm not gay."
> I didn't want to hear
> Him say he was not queer
> But still I told him, "uh yeah, dude, me neither."

The performer uses an exaggerated falsetto when singing "making out, it felt so good/Would have done him if I could," a climactic moment revealing the height of his more-than-friendly desires. Incidentally, when the character speaks the final "uh yeah, dude, me either"—delivered in a lower spoken register to sound more "manly"—the backing voices sing in unison "I'm not ga-ay." Due to the overlap of voices as well as the setting of the word "gay," we hear the character's rebuke of homosexuality right up against a colorful rendering of the word "gay," highlighting the contradictions of his statement.

As a contrast to the use of falsetto, a rap interlude falls right before the song's bridge section. Despite a different delivery, however, this part of the song also highlights the distinctly "un-masculine" masculinity of boy band performance. Dominant discourse paints hip-hop as hyper-masculine—violent and sexually threatening. But when employed in pop contexts, rap generally appears in watered-down, less racialized, and supposedly "safer" forms. Keeping in line with this style was important in highlighting the character—a straight, self-proclaimed stud talking about waxing his eyebrows—and gently lampooning his contradictory claims to masculinity. In fact, during the rehearsal process, the actor playing this role started experimenting with a dancehall cadence and delivery. While excited by the performer's musical exploration, I decided against this particular bent on the interlude. A boy band rap, just like its speaker's metrosexual demeanor, needs to be minimally risky, not too raw, and perhaps not even all that interesting.

"Girl, I'm into You" neatly encapsulates many of the issues with which all of *Machos* contends and stands as a testament to Paz's foresight and daring to push beyond the men's words and make explicit some of their subtext. The song's inauthentic, prefab style mirrors the textual critique of the limitations of sexual labeling. Regardless of the intricacies of their lives, the characters are constrained to a limited range of vocal and physical gestures, as well as a label in the negative—"not gay"—meaning only the ability to say what they are not. In my repeated reference to the contradictions of masculinity, my aim is not to suggest that indeed all of these characteristics cannot reside within men. Nor am I saying that because of having same-sex encounters, these men are necessarily gay. Rather, this song and *Machos* on a whole expose the lack of terminology for discussing the intricacies and gray areas of male sexuality and gender identity.

Laura Nader suggests, "There is a certain urgency to the kind of anthropology that is concerned with power, for the quality of life and our lives themselves may depend upon the extent to which citizens understand those who shape attitudes and actually control institutional structures."[9] *Machos* is the beginning of this kind of "studying up" through performance, opening up a dialogue on the status of masculinity and its social and political power. Revealing the impossibility of reaching the fugitive center, the show provides an entertaining and thought-provoking journey through men's relationships to masculinity, whiteness, and heterosexuality. The distinction, however, between macho as a state of being and being macho as a performance is made but reinscribed when the cast says, "Macho just means man." Interrogating masculinity but not the structure of patriarchy, future productions of *Machos* might more heartily address the role masculinity plays in perpetuating patriarchy, racism, and homophobia. So who held the authentic word on whether the collar should be in or out of the sweater? *Machos* expertly breaks masculinity away from men, but ultimately it remains the men who have the final word on the subject.

Notes

1 Teatro Luna is known for this particular theatrical style in which various stories are combined into a "variety show" on a given topic. Often fast paced and mixing humor and serious narratives, the shows resist conclusions or arguments in favor of open-ended exploration. While this form

is the company's signature, Teatro Luna has also produced several single-authored plays, often written by company members.

2 bell hooks, *Yearning: Race, Gender, and Cultural Politics* (Boston: South End, 1990), 75.

3 The "Jeffs" honor excellence in Chicago theater, the local equivalent of the Tony Awards.

4 This criticism is more about recognizing the limitations of many theatrical audiences rather than the artists' choices. Explicit discourse on matters of gender is either absent or superficial in much of the U.S. media. Paz and ensemble were tremendously intelligent in their work to bring concrete discussion of gender to diverse audiences. At the same time, the production revealed the challenges of bringing complex discussions of gender to viewers at disparate stages in this conversation.

5 See Eric Lott, *Love and Theft: Blackface Minstrelsy and the American Working Class* (New York: Oxford University Press, 1993).

6 The text of "Stinky Fish" does indeed mark Asianness through cultural references. Viewers without this cultural knowledge, however, may not recognize this context.

7 Judith Butler, *Bodies That Matter: On the Discursive Limits of "Sex"* (New York: Routledge, 1993), 237.

8 From Elizabeth Wood, Philip Brett, and Gary C. Thomas, eds., *Queering the Pitch: The New Gay and Lesbian Musicology* (New York: Routledge, 1994), 30.

9 Laura Nader, "Up the Anthropologist—Perspectives Gained from Studying Up," in *Anthropology for the Nineties: Introductory Readings*, ed. Johnnetta B. Cole (New York: Free Press, 1988), 470.

CHAPTER 4

Interview with Coya Paz

Patricia Ybarra

Patricia Ybarra: What made you want to look at male subjectivity and masculinity? What pushed you in that direction?

Coya Paz: *Machos* is our fifth ensemble-created show, and we were trying to think of new ways to talk about being Latina women. We thought, there's only so many times we can do . . . "And now we'll talk about Latina women and pregnancy." That show actually came after. We thought with *Machos* that what we were going to do was interview men about Latina women, and then perform as men talking about Latinas. It would be a way of getting at ourselves from the outside. And the project turned out not to be that at all. I mean, we have a little bit of talking about Latina women, but it's not the thrust of the project. That was our original idea about it.

When we started our training process we realized that we had to learn to move as men, because we knew we wanted to be good. We didn't want to make fun of men. And we didn't want to do bad performances of masculinity—not bad, but we didn't want to do parodic performances of masculinity. We were more interested in staying grounded and staying real, which is our way in our performances. We realized how many assumptions we were making about men and masculinity just from having to move around the room as men. Nothing about the way we were moving resembled actual men. It was entirely our construction of men. And then, sort of parallel to that, as we got into the interview process and we started asking men questions about their lives, we realized how little space there is for men to speak honestly about their lives. There's so much violence towards men who try in any way to be vulnerable or emotional. I mean we have a culture that's so invested in asking men to behave a certain way, in ways that are really punished from an early age if they don't. I don't think we went into the process thinking that, at least not collectively, but we were really struck by it early on and made a commitment early on in the process to just listen and find a way to have the process be about listening to men and commenting on that.

The kinds of discussions we had within the company were really challenging because not everyone in the company identifies as a feminist, although we identify as a feminist company. As the developer of that project, I had a lot of ideas about masculinity and performance of gender, and about the social construction of gender. But that's not a framework anyone else was working within. They were approaching it in really different ways, and really challenging some of my own ideas about masculinity. I remember one conversation in particular which got really heated because some of the women were saying how they felt really sorry for men, and that it was really sad that men didn't have the space to talk about it, and how much women participated in abusing men and keeping men in these boxes, and it was just really sad. But I feel like men still benefit from the fact that this happens. I feel kind of sad, too, but I feel sad as a woman because I feel really oppressed by men's need to behave in a certain way. We couldn't come to terms with that as a company. We sort of continue, I think, in talk-backs on things like that to have the different points of view about what's at stake. Or perhaps it's not a different point of view, but a different way of articulating what's at stake.

PY: Right. I mean, I think through queer theory, I think through feminist theory. I come at it with that theoretical framework in mind when I come to the question of anything that's even already incredibly personal. Like I already do that when I think about my dad's own anger. I'm already thinking about it in terms of class, race, all of that stuff. But you know, that's only one way in. That's only one way into the question, I guess.

CP: Part of it became: how do we make a performance that serves as that kind of introduction to gender theory, this idea that there's not anything natural about gender? And that kind of became the framing question of it. How can we at once honor the men who are spending the time talking to us, telling stories, but also raise this fundamental question of what it means to be a man? And to just use the performance to highlight the performance of gender itself both in men's lived experience and in our performance, in a way, making our performance of gender disappear. I mean, the fact that it's not parodic becomes really important to a project because people forget that they're watching women perform, and then they remember at the end, and they have to question, "Those were women, and they were being men." And so being a man is not as natural as I thought. Anyone can do that "performance," meaning women, too.

PY: Which is amazing because it sounds like, from things I've heard you say in other contexts, that learning to embody a man was actually an incredibly difficult learning process both vocally and physically. And so do you think any of that difficulty was retained in the performance? Because when you watch it, it looks seamless. I can't see the difficulty of the labor, but I know there was difficulty in the labor of learning to be a man. So do you think that embodiment actually changed how people dealt with, say, the text or the interviews as they were performing them?

CP: Our training was not just physical and vocal, but was a lot of working with men to get into the mentality, the mind frame of masculinity. We had the people we interviewed and then we also had these workshops that were designed to get material, to get men talking to each other, and pull performance material from that. But then we also had workshops that were training workshops for us where men who are our colleagues or family members or just men on our e-mail list would come and help us. It was all about them working with us. There is sort of three different modes. And then we had our movement coach. And one of the guys said, "You should spend a week not talking to each other about your feelings. When you hang out, do not talk about how you feel." And we were like, "Okay, we're going to do it." And we were depressed by the second or third day because we are so used to coming into the space of rehearsal and workshop and we always start with a check-in and "How do you feel?" We sometimes derail a whole rehearsal because someone is feeling really sad and needs to talk about it and needs a whole community intervention around what to do. That's how we work, and it makes work like s-e-x . . . *Oh!* feel like that kind of community. But for *Machos*, the exercise in not talking about our feelings was, very sad, and we abandoned it early. We just thought, "We don't want to not talk to each other about our feelings." But it was good to remember that men rarely do engage in that behavior, and so it helped us think about the kind of restraint or the way that men will talk around a problem. And it also made us appreciate how special it was the really emotional stories that men were telling us, but also realize we couldn't just approach those stories straightforwardly. We had also to understand and pay attention to the reluctance to tell.

It was that whole year of thinking as men, or trying to think about it, "Okay, how different would guys think about this?" because there was also no one man. I remember one workshop so clearly because we had four or five straight men and two gay men, and the straight men were weirdly performing for each other. Something very strange was happening where there was a real competitiveness and someone gave a prompt around sports like, "Show us what it's like to watch a game." I forget what it was exactly. But the gay men stepped out. They felt completely disenfranchised from the process because of posturing that these guys were doing. That was really telling, and we processed a lot our failure to create a safe environment for these two men in the moment. And so it's the sort of thing you can't realize ahead of time. I think we did everything we could to intervene when we realized they felt not included or . . . "We're not that kind of man, who would ever go to a bar and watch a game. It's just not what we do." So the assumption that even all the men in the group would relate to that scenario was challenged fairly early on in the process. We were not yet able to think about things like that. It was always all these good reminders. They're weird things to have to be reminded of. I think there is a tendency among women to lump men together, except when they're thinking of really specific men. We know our dad is not like that, our mother is not like that, our lover is not, our brother. But guys are that way, generally.

PY: And so I know that when you did the interviews you did some by e-mail and you did some in person, is that correct? So you had a number of different types of interviews that you were doing?

CP: We did most of them in person. We did fifty-five in-person interviews, many of them over an hour and a half long. I think the shortest one was an hour and twenty minutes. And then we also did anonymous surveys. So we didn't do e-mail interviews per se; we did these surveys because we wanted to ask questions about penis size and things like that. But we did not feel comfortable asking them to their face, and we didn't think they would be honest with us, although some men did. We have a piece in *Machos* about a man talking about his penis size, but we didn't ask him about his penis size. We asked him what he thought a man was when he was growing up. And he told us a story about wrestling with his stepfather, and his stepfather grabbing his penis and saying, "[Name of guy] doesn't have much down here." He was a little kid, but thinking like, "I'm less of a guy because I have a small penis." It was sort of a formative moment for him. And he is still very anxious about the size of his penis. But we didn't ask him what the size of his penis was.

PY: So how did you use that other survey information because it seems to me that a lot of the piece comes from these stories. Right? So did you even use that information?

CP: Yes. So one of the questions we asked in the interview is about urinals. How do you use a urinal? Because we don't know. And how did you learn to use a urinal because I know your mother didn't teach you. You know, so what's this moment of learning? So we asked them about that and based on that we created a scene. So we pulled the dialogue for each character from people talking. But it's a scene. One of the men told us in the interview that he never uses a urinal. He hates it. He always goes into a stall. He doesn't like the idea of people looking at his penis and he does not want to accidentally look at someone else's penis. And that's it. We merged that story with the man talking about his small penis. Because the man who talked about his fear of a small penis had also said he never went to a urinal. But he had not elaborated; he had gone into this other story. But we had this other guy talking about not going into urinals. So we put their stories together; we do have a lot of composites. So the urinal scene leaves this one guy who has elected to go into a stall and then some kind of zoom in on him. It doesn't zoom, but the lighting designer and I played a lot with how you go broad with lots of people and then narrow in on one and then pop back out. I kept telling him "a zoom lens" and he kept telling me, "It's not a film," and I was like, "I know, but I want it to feel like that." So we go into his monologue, and then it breaks out into a group piece of, you know, "7.5, 4 inches . . . I've never measured." So, all the little popcorn pieces of what men had had to say about their penis. Or five of them. We picked the five most interesting. How big their penis was, when the first time they measured it was. So, we did that a lot, where we used the online surveys just to get filler data. And that was the last thing we did. That was one of the last things. We were like, you know what, we just need to texture. We need some words that we can use as texture.

PY: And did the men talk about Latinidad? I mean, did they talk about being Latino as well? Was that something that came up in terms of cross section with them talking about masculinity or formative masculinity? Did they link those things? Or did you guys link those things maybe in the interview?

CP: They're not all Latinos in the play. We did ask questions about, "Do you think there is anything specific about how you identify? And how do you think that shapes your idea of what it means to be a man?" But those are sort of the least productive questions. People have not really thought through that. Sometimes we would hear something about, "Well, being a black man in America means this." But white men never thought about themselves as white men. Latino men had a lot to say. In some ways, Latinos had the strictest codes about how to be a man and how to treat women and how women should behave, even really progressive Latino men. The monologue right before the last piece, which is a group piece, is this guy, who we asked, "Are you a macho?" That's how we ended the interviews. So "are you a macho" and he said, "Well, I think I am. I'm a boxer and I like to walk on the outside and the woman has to walk on the inside of the street. But it's not my way or the highway. I change diapers, I wipe tushies. I'm a father, that's my way of being a macho. I take care of my family. Yeah, I'm going to take care of my family. Do I tell my wife she can't work? No. But I'm gonna take care of my family. So yeah, I'm a macho. Not like my dad, like me." And he was so passionate about wanting to redefine what it meant to be a macho, which is what we tried to do in the piece. Because we didn't want to mythologize machismo either, especially because even though we imagined it as a multiracial, multiethnic piece, we knew the majority of the people we'd be talking to would be Latinos. We did a third of our interviews in San Antonio. So that right there is the sort of self-selected population. For *Machos* we interviewed all over the country. And *Machos* was one of the few plays where we had a grant specifically to develop the play, and I remember when they passed us to the second level, one of the comments was, "We're really glad that you are going to expose the machismo of Latino men." And I was so shocked that they would say that because that wasn't our intent, to expose. We're not trying to sell out our men. That's not Teatro Luna's style or our interest in the project. So we thought, well, we have to be really careful about how we talk about machismo and to recognize that machismo has had a really important place within Latino communities.

PY: And not just among men.

CP: Right. I'm queer, I live with my partner, and I still love hanging out with Latino men. Straight Latino men are probably my favorite to hang out with because they, I'm going to quote the play, "treat a lady like a lady." You know, they always open the door, they walk on the outside of the street, they hold my bag with no shame. There's no embarrassment.

I grew up with that, so I appreciate that, in a way that doesn't make me feel oppressed. It makes me feel cared for. I would feel oppressed if I can't go to work or I'm expected to stay home with our child automatically, which are not issues I have to deal with since my partner is not a Latino man. If I had not been allowed to go to college, I mean there's so much machismo that has some negative things. But I think that for a lot of men and for a lot of women it's associated with a kind of caretaking of their families that a lot of men take pride in. And I think there's nothing wrong with that. But I also think that the pressure to always have to be a caretaker and that there isn't a culture that takes care of men's feelings. . . . We have a culture that takes care of men's needs, but not emotional needs. So that, traditionally, we think of having to wash the dishes, or get our father's food, or do this or do that, but never, "How are you feeling? Are you tired? You've been working so hard." That's not part of it.

PY: I think of traditional Latino drama through the ages there's a way in which every time there's a space for that type of subjectivity for a male character, it's queered actually in this interesting way, which is not to say that there shouldn't be queer Latino male characters, but there's a way in which it sort of, it's already queered, and that's even by queer authors that that happens, which I think is really fascinating, you know. I can't think of one example in which a man breaks down in that way and in which there isn't some kind of ambivalent feeling about sexuality.

CP: Yeah, we're very scared to tackle that. And I mean, that was part of the debate among the creative team. Going back to the whole thing of "I feel so sorry for men" and me thinking, well, so many of the voices that have been able to express Latinidad come from men and if they're not seizing the opportunity to talk about their feelings, that's on them. I can't help them, you know? We have so few spaces as women to talk about our lives publicly. We have a lot of them intimately, whereas men who have the public forum have not opted to talk really honestly about their life. They want to talk about a macropolitic. They don't want to talk about a micropolitic. So I don't think it's a surprise that an all-female theater is getting at the kind of emotional heart of masculinity. And it's been remarkable how many men came up to us after the show and said things like, or kind of laughing, and they'd be like, "You got me. You made me cry." And they were laughing about it then, but admitting to crying while they were watching the show, or "That's my dad, man," and they would start to cry. We'd have to process with men after the show who were really emotional.

PY: Did any of the people who you interviewed see the show?

CP: Yes, a lot of them. We were so scared every time. "Oh, it's . . . Roberto's here," you know. And that's not the real name; it's the character. And one guy, for example, came to see the show and I was shocked because I don't think we have the most positive portrayal of him. In the interview he talks about hitting his girlfriend very openly, and we included that in a piece. But we also included a monologue based on his story. He wanted to be a baseball player and he was recruited out of high school but his girlfriend got pregnant, so he elected not to go; he didn't take the scholarship. He got a baseball scholarship and he didn't take it cause he stayed home to care for the girlfriend and the baby, and then several times in his life he could not pursue a baseball career because of his obligations to his family, and he was deeply sad about it, and it hadn't worked out with his wife, and so we left it at that. Later on in the interview, he talked about hitting his wife and all these things, and we didn't want to taint the deep sorrow he felt at realizing he's never going to be a pro-baseball player, and his sorrow and his loss. "And then I turned out to be a wife beater." That wasn't what we wanted to do. So we interviewed one of his friends about the guy. So we actually have another monologue from a different guy about this guy and how he found his wife. He cheated on his wife and then he found his wife in bed with this other man. You know, "Women are the devil, they're the fucking devil." You know, and this other guy talking about that. So that's how we could sort of put those two narratives together without needing to pathologize . . . that we could tap into his sorrow that has led him to make some really unfortunate decisions, about the women in his life, without dismissing it. And so, he came to see the show five times. He loved it. He absolutely loved the show. And I was just amazed because I didn't think it was entirely a charitable portrayal. Well, not uncharitable. It was a really complicated portrayal.

PY: Right. And you can't erase the reality of that in your view, and what came out of it. You have to be true to the reality of the most extreme end of so-called machismo or the acceptance or ambivalent relationship of violence to masculinity. I mean, you can't erase that.

CP: Right. But we could show that we understood where he was coming from without endorsing where he was coming from, you know? And that happens. There's a whole section where we talk about violence against women, and we did it really carefully, because what we found, actually, is that a lot of men had hit their partners at some point and felt no ambivalence about it. They just felt like that was what those women deserved. And other men felt really strongly that you should not ever hit a woman, no matter what she does.

PY: We've talked a lot about subjectivity and how you process personal stories and yes, they in some sense reflect the macro. And you said something really interesting I didn't expect you to say but it's true in this weird way; men talk about the macro. They don't want to talk about the personal. Do women talk about the macro?

CP: Well, I think that part of it is what happens to the anecdotal is that we don't always recognize the macro in it, even though it's there. And so how can you use the performance to expose those intersections but in a way that doesn't feel didactic, so that people are coming out knowing something on a different level than they may have known before, but you haven't explicitly said, "Therefore, we say that in our lives as women, we are socialized to do x," but we can still understand it in a different way through the theater. That's something I think about a lot when I work. What are we trying to say, what's the larger movement here? I think we have within the ensemble different approaches to that or different approaches to how important that is. But certainly in a project like *Machos*, ultimately we had so much material. We clarified it. Does this come back to the question of being a man? What does it mean to be a man? What does it mean to perform masculinity? So all the stories had that in place, somehow, even though we had great stories about how men talked about their sense of being Americans, but it wasn't so tied to masculinity, so we left them out.

So what I've become really interested in, especially after *Machos*, is this question of "the other" from the point of view of the ones who are often othered. So with *Machos* to approach masculinity from the point of view of women, but trying to understand it as men.

Part III

Strange Fruit
A Performance about Identity Politics

E. Patrick Johnson

The stage has four performance areas. Far stage left has a small table and chair. The table has a mirror, cold cream, and a white face cloth; stage left has a black block with gym clothes, sneakers, and a set of two 10lb weights and a tambourine; at center stage there hangs a scrim; stage right has a table and chair with three books; far stage right has a set of steps.

A silhouette of the performer's effeminately posed body appears from behind the scrim. It is clear from the silhouette that he is wearing a dress and a wig. The performer begins singing "God Bless the Child" and walks from behind the scrim onstage to reveal that he is in drag and blackface. While continuing to sing, he walks off stage and into the audience passing out gold cards to the audience that read, "Black American Express: Membership Has Its Privileges." In the center of the card is a picture of a paper bag with a hand reaching out of it. The bag reads "Trick or Treat." Where the account number would usually appear are important dates in American/African American history (e.g., 1640, 1776, 1865, 1968, 1970).[1] The name on the card is "Dr. Colored A. Negro." At the end of the song, the performer stands at center stage and faces the audience.

PERFORMER   "Let's face it. I am a marked woman, but not everybody
              knows my name. 'Peaches' and 'Brown Sugar,'

      Slide #1 of mammy on Washing Powder Box.

PERFORMER   'Sugar,' 'Sapphire' and 'Earth Mother,'

      Slide #2 of "Nigger Hair" Tobacco can.

PERFORMER   'Aunty,' 'Granny,' 'God's Holy Fool,'

Slide #3 of Aunt Jemima Pancake Box.

PERFORMER   a 'Miss Ebony First,' or 'Black Woman at the Podium':

Slide #4 of "Mammy Yams."

PERFORMER   I describe a locus of confounded identities, a meeting
             ground of investments and privations in the national trea-
             sury of rhetorical wealth. My country needs me, and if I
             were not here, I would have to be invented."[2] That's my alter
             ego talking: Miss Hortense Spillers.

             And speaking of inventions, I bet you thought that Madonna
             invented the vogue. Oh no. I have been voguing since 1971.
             Strike a pose!

Tape of Madonna's "Vogue" begins to play.

*12 slides #5–16 of Performer "posing" as a little boy; the last slide is
Performer in clown face. After the slides, the music fades.*

PERFORMER   Mama started dressing me in drag when I was just a little
             thing.

Slide #17 of Performer as child wearing a wig.

PERFORMER   Little did she know that she would play such a vital role in
             making me the "man" I am today.

Slide #18 of Performer in drag.

PERFORMER   Now, I'm not trying to suggest some kind of ontological link
             between gender and sexuality. Oh no, no, no. I'm much too
             smart for that now that Judy Butler has taught me that the
             two are not coextensive.[3] All I'm saying is, Mama thought it
             was cute when she put that wig on my head back then, but
             she didn't think it was so cute when I started sneaking into
             her bedroom and putting it on for myself. Agency is such
             a drag for those in power! If you don't believe me, ask your
             mama!

Slide #19 of the words "Mother's Pearls."

PERFORMER   Speaking of mothers,

Slide #20 of Performer's mother with hand on her hip.

PERFORMER   that's mine. That's some pose, huh? Yep, I picked that one up real early as my mother gendered me at a early age.

Slides #21 and #22 of Performer with hand on his hip.

PERFORMER   But I was talking about wigs wasn't I?

Performer sits down at the table and begins removing makeup.

Slide #23 of Performer as child in a wig.

PERFORMER   Well, mother's wigs and I go way back. She didn't have that many, but the ones she did have were great. There was something about the feel of all that curly hair on top of my head that freed me. Those days were short lived, however, as I soon traded in my wigs for football helmets. Yes, I played on the football team—well, I should say that I warmed the bench. But it didn't matter. I was a football player. A member of the team. I only played on ONE team—not the other—and definitely not both. (**winks at the audience**) I had to live up to the five other brothers who had come before me. They had all played sports, so there was no question that their little brother would as well. See, my brothers bought into the whole black macho thing early on. Check out this picture of one of my brothers, for instance.

Slide #24 of Performer's brother pointing a gun at the camera.

PERFORMER   It's scary to think that this notion of black masculinity was what I had as a role model. Good thing I preferred wigs to ski caps. (**pauses**) But now that I think about it, I did have another brother who also dressed in drag. In fact, it was my most homophobic brother who dressed in drag in the 8th grade.

Slide #25 of Performer's brother in drag.

PERFORMER   I don't know WHAT it is about those Johnson boys and drag.
            It's the queerest thing. But I digress. I was talking about my
            mother. We have a wonderful relationship and I've never
            given her any reason to be disappointed in me. I'm her baby.

Slide #26 of performer's baby picture.

PERFORMER   Mama's baby . . . Papa's Maybe.[4]

Rapid slide #27 of lynching then slide #28 of performer's baby picture.

PERFORMER   But again, I transgress. I mean, digress. As I was saying,
            Mom and I have a great relationship, but it has definitely
            changed since I came out to her. We're now under this com-
            plicity of silence about my gayness. It's almost as if I never
            told her. But that story, my coming out story that is, is not
            a horrible one at all. In fact, it's rather amusing: She was up
            visiting me in Amherst and I had decided that it was "time."
            We were watching the late evening news when I turned to
            her and said, "Well, Mama, I need to talk to you about some-
            thing. I've wanted to tell you this for some time now, but
            I've been afraid to." And she said, "What have you done?"
            And I said, "I haven't done anything. I'm gay." And she
            looked at me and said, "Pat! You mean to tell me that you
            like other men?" "Yes, ma'am." "Why?" "Well, I think I've
            always known."

Slide #29 of performer in wig.

PERFORMER   She said, "Well, I don't understand it." I said to her, "Let me
            ask you something, Mama. Have you ever found yourself at-
            tracted to another woman?" She said, "NO." I said, "Neither
            have I."

Slide #30 of young P kissing a little girl on the cheek.

PERFORMER   Then she got it. She said again, "I don't understand it, but
            if that's the way you are I just have to accept it. You're my

child and I love you." No crying. No screaming. No Bible thumping. It was great. But we haven't talked about it since.

Slide #31 that reads "Transitions." Performer walks to center stage and begins to take off the dress.

PERFORMER   Can someone help me with this? (*gets someone from the audience to help him out of the dress*) You know black is great for giving an illusion, but it can also be very confining.

Tape of "Macho Man."

Performer steps out of dress and puts on sneakers, shorts, and a tank top and begins lifting the dumb bells; music fades when Performer is dressed.

PERFORMER   (*looks at audience*) My butch drag. Come on, you didn't think I was a femme fatale did you? But seriously, if you really want to "unveil" your masculinity, all you have to do is cut off all your hair—especially if you're a black man.

Slide #32 of the word "Hair."

PERFORMER   Now, during my college days I was the queen of big hair. Check it out.

4 slides (#33–36) of Performer with "big" hair.

PERFORMER   But dis hair is dis cursive! I mean, I've never seen so much purse grabbing, door locking, fast walking, child protecting in my life until I shaved my head! It opened up a whole new world to me! I had always theorized about how threatening the black man can be in the psyche of some white folk, but because I'm gay I thought that I would never experience that kind of race-based fear. All that changed when I shaved my head.

Slide #37 of Performer with shaved head.

PERFORMER   And then, I decided that I would use my new look to my advantage and perform hyper-black masculinity by playing

what Brent Staples calls, "Scatter the Pigeons." At a talk I at-
tended, Staples read from his work:[5]

*Performer begins to do curls with the dumb bells and voice-over plays
excerpt from* **Parallel Times** *by Brent Staples.*

VOICE-OVER "I tried to be innocuous but I didn't know how. The more I
thought about how I moved, the less my body belonged to
me; I became a false character riding along inside it. I began
to avoid people. I turned out of my way into side streets
to spare them the sense that they were being stalked. I let
them clear the lobbies of buildings before I entered, so they
wouldn't feel trapped. . . . Then I changed. I don't know
why, but I remember when. I was walking west on 57th
street, after dark, coming home from the lake. The man
and the woman walking toward me were laughing and talking but clammed up when they saw me. The man touched
the woman's elbow, guiding her toward the curb. Normally
I'd have given way and begun to whistle, but not this time.
This time I veered toward them and aimed myself so that
they'd have to part to avoid walking into me. The man stiff-
ened, threw back his head and assumed the stare: eyes dead
ahead, mouth open. His face took on a bluish hue under the
sodium vapor street lamps. I suppressed the urge to scream
into his face. Instead I glided between them, my shoulder
nearly brushing his. A few steps beyond them I stopped and
howled with laughter."[6]

PERFORMER   What amazes me about that passage is how beautifully
Brent Staples captures how empowering it is for black
men to reappropriate racist stereotypes and use them as
weapons against whites. How ironic then—and unfortunate—that in the same book, he invokes that same mas-
culinist discourse to castigate his mother's beautician:

VOICE-OVER "My mother's beautician, Gene, was the star of Saturdays.
He didn't appear every Saturday but just when he was
needed and when, as he said, 'some heads need doin'.' Gene
was a faggot. He minced and twisted as he walked. But his
body had wrenched itself into a caricature of a woman's. His
behind stuck out so that he seemed to be wearing a bustle.
He chain-smoked as he walked, with his cigarette hand at

a girlish angle in the air. His other arm pressed to his torso the brown paper bag that contained his curling irons. . . . Teenage boys hooted and howled when he passed. Gene minced more brazenly then and blew smoke—POOF!—that curled over his head like steam from a passing train."[7]

PERFORMER   And, perhaps it was a coincidence, but I couldn't help but think of James Baldwin as I listened to Staples describe this "Gene" character further:

Slide #38 of James Baldwin.

VOICE-OVER   "His voice was raspy and cawing and came out of him in a deep Georgia accent. He began his sentences with 'chile' or 'girl,' as in: 'Chile, guess who I ran into walkin' over here today?'; 'Girl, I'm glad I got here when I did. This head sho needs doin'.' His eyes were bulging and widely set, always bloodshot from drinking. The eyes, over his enormous mouth, made him look like a frog. He laughed with his head thrown back, and the froggish mouth open, showing the capacious spaces among his teeth."[8]

PERFORMER   Staples went on to describe Gene doing hair. His description of Gene's hair styling was nothing short of lyrical and flattering. I was confused. How could he paint him as a stereotypical "queen" on the one hand, and as a creative hair artist on the other. My heart began to race as it always does when I'm about to ask a pointed question of someone who's really important. But, I couldn't let this one go. (*Performer raises his hand*) "Mr. Staples, in that last section you just read, you do a wonderful job of describing Gene doing your mother's hair. I mean, your description was so methodical and lyrical and poetic. Yet, in the preceding pages, you describe Gene as a 'faggot.' Can you talk about those two disparate images?" And in the most machismo posture he could muster, his shirt unbuttoned down to his navel and his legs straddling the podium, his response to me was: "Well, he WAS a faggot. I mean, it was 1957 and that's what he would have been called. There's no other way to say it. But I tell you this, whoever plays Gene in the movie (and there *will* be a movie), he's going to win the Academy Award." Dis hair is definitely discursive.

5 slides of different black hairstyles #39–43.[9]

Slide #44 of RuPaul.

Tape of RuPaul's "Supermodel" begins to play.

Performer puts on a doctoral gown complete with hood and cap and "models" the gown in runway fashion.

PERFORMER   Now this is one gown I didn't mind wearing. And although I was glad to leave LSU, I made my mark while I was there. I even became the "poster child" for minority recruitment:

Slide #45 of Performer on LSU Brochure with quote: "I think it is very important to increase the number of minority graduate students at historically white institutions. Not only do we serve as a support system for one another, but we pave the way for and become mentors for those who come after us."

PERFORMER   As you can see, my "big hair" days continued well into graduate school! I didn't begin to lose my hair until I got to Amherst College. Yep, at Amherst my hair came out and I came out—in fact, hair loss, racism and homophobia worked together rather well there.

Slide #46 of Johnson Chapel at Amherst College. Performer stands in front of the slide.

PERFORMER   This site is named after me. It's called Johnson Chapel. It houses the English Department at the "Fairest" College— a.k.a., Amherst College. My office is in the basement.

Slide #47 of the word "Black Bucks." Performer begins to walk around the stage.

PERFORMER   What does it mean to queer a space? How does one go about that if his body is always already bound to a contradictory discourse of hyper-heterosexuality and bestiality on the one hand, and childlike docility on the other? I mean, what's a girl to do? Answer: examine the ways in which the black queer body is trafficked down those ivory halls.

Slide #48 of picture of casket being carried through a crowd.

PERFORMER   But again, I transgress, I mean digress.

Slide #49 of the words "Collegiality and 'Quare' Studies."

PERFORMER   I've always liked the word "queer" because my mother and
my grandmother used to say it all the time when I was little.
They'd say it in this thick, southern black dialect. They'd say,
"that sho'll is a 'quare' Chile." For them, queer meant "odd"
or slightly off kilter, as my grandmother might say—not
exactly straight. So, it's no wonder that my research has increasingly become more about queer studies. In fact, everything I know about queer studies I learned from my grandmother.

Slide #50 of picture of Performer's grandmother.

PERFORMER   When I went to live with my grandmother to collect her life
history for my dissertation, she brought me up to date on
the people who had moved into her neighborhood since my
last visit. My grandmother says, "Well, we got one of them
'homalsexuals' [sic] living down here." "A what?," I asked.
"You know, one of them homalsexuals [sic]." "Well, how do
you know the man's a homosexual, Grandma?" "Well, he
gardens, keeps a clean house, and bakes pies." Now, all of
these applied to me as well, except for gardening. I don't like
getting my hands dirty. Quare, indeed. Have I started trans-
gressing again? Back to Amherst.

*Slide #51 of Johnson Chapel. Performer crosses to stage right and picks
up a book.*

PERFORMER   The first queer thing: I'm standing at the copier, when a
senior colleague walks up to me holding something behind
his back. This particular colleague, you should know, writes/
theorizes about sports—race and sports, homosociality and
sports, cheeseburgers and sports, sports and sports—you
get the picture. He brings his hand from around his back
to reveal his latest book. "Patrick," he says, "have you seen
the cover of my latest book?" "No, I haven't." In a flash, he's

holding the book an inch from my face chanting, "Isn't that hot? Wouldn't you like that? Wouldn't you like to taste that? Wouldn't you like to look at that? Isn't that hot?" The cover is a picture of Greg Louganis in speedos diving into a pool of water. I look at my colleague and reply,

Slide #52 of a Klansman "hushing."

PERFORMER   It's a nice cover.

Slide #53 of Johnson Chapel.

PERFORMER   The second queer thing: The second week of October is National Coming Out Week and the LGBTA usually has events to celebrate this week of queerness. I'm running late for office hours, so I barely notice the pink and yellow chalkings lining the sidewalks. I walk into Johnson Chapel and this same colleague is standing in the hall talking to another colleague. I go into the main office, grab my mail and as I step back into the hallway, said colleague turns, points at me and says, "Oh Look! There's one. There's Patrick." He runs over to me and gives me a big bear hug. As I pry him off of me I say, "What are you doing?" And he replies, "Well, the signs outside say, 'Hug a queer today.'"

Slide #54 of lynching.

PERFORMER   But it would be the students

Slide #55 of Johnson Chapel.

PERFORMER   who would bring into clear focus the intersection of race, gender, and sexuality as they have been historically intertwined when mapping racist and homophobic signs onto the black male body. If my colleagues didn't view me as the lurking, animalistic sex machine,

Slide #56 of monstrous black person chasing whites.

PERFORMER   some of the students sure did.

Slide #57 of cover of "Capitol Pages" upon which the Performer's picture appears above the caption "Not Exactly Straight: Sexual Identity at Amherst." Performer sits down at table on stage right.

PERFORMER   Thus, the third queer thing: A student asks me to give an interview for his magazine—a special issue on sexual identity. He asks me to talk about the intersection of race and sexuality. Little did I know that this would be the cover they would use for that edition, but that's what I get for agreeing to this interview and it's harmless enough. So I think. Well, because I'm so shy and timid, I'm very candid in the interview about my experience with interracial dating in the gay community and how racism affects that coupling.

Slide #58 of quote from "Capitol Pages" about white men: "I find that I'm suspect of any white man who is interested in me. Because I want to know why. Is it because you just love black skin?"

PERFORMER   Again, never be candid in a student newspaper. It will always come back to haunt you.

Slide #59 of "Lynch Party: Everybody Invited."

PERFORMER   Before I knew it, the backlash began:

Slide #60 of quote from "The Spectator."

Tape of voice-over:

"Super, Thanks for Asking: Prof. E. Patrick Johnson of 'Black Gay Fiction' fame, in the Fall '97 'Capitol Pages' says, 'Personally, I find that I'm suspect of any white man who is interested in me. Because I want to know why. Why are you interested? Is it because you think I have big dick?"

Slide #61 of Robert Mapplethorpe's "Man in Polyester Suit" then BACK *to quote slide.*

Is it because you just love black skin?' No, Dr. Johnson, the answer is none of the above. We're interested in you because of your intentional crudeness, but more importantly, your supreme ignorance. Later in the article, Johnson mentions, 'White privilege is going to be present in any context . . . where I'm automatically going to be discriminated against because of my skin color.' We would expect that kind of jaded, extremist sentiment from some factions of the student body, but a professor should know better."

PERFORMER   But they didn't stop there. This prestigious student magazine gave me an award:

Slide #62 of "Spectator Award."

Tape of voice-over with "beauty pageant" music in the background:

"Good evening and welcome to the 1st Annual Spectator Awards, the award show celebrating our most infamous, PC, and liberal faculty. *(drum roll)* And now the moment we've all been waiting for, the announcement of our 'Bones Thugs N' Harmony' Award.'

Slide #63 of Award Star/Trophy.

And the award goes to our very own black buck of a professor, E. Patrick Johnson. *(applause)* Professor Johnson wins this award for all of his 'hard' work on yet another left-wing political cause.

Slide #64 of poster of "Positively Fabulous."

especially 'Positively Fabulous' that fucking AIDS benefit he organized.

Slide #65 of Spectator Award wording.

The plaque reads: The Macho Man Johnson knows all the tools of his trade. His equipment, we hear, is not only big, but very powerful. And he's not afraid to flaunt it. But, we'll take his word for it. Here's to the chocophile in us all." *(more applause)*

Slide #66 of list of words "Faggot" "Nigger" "Punk" "Coon" "Fudge Packer" "Abomination" in the shape of a cross.

PERFORMER   "We might concede at the very least, that sticks and bricks might break our bones, but words will most certainly kill us."[10]

Slide #67 of burning cross.

PERFORMER   But then again, we all have our own cross to bear.

Slide #68 of the word "Family."

Tape of "We Are Family." Performer goes to the audience to collect "Black American Express Cards."

PERFORMER   "Family." Now there's a word for you. It has come to mean a whole host of things within this postmodern, or post-mortem, society. But, because I fashion myself as a "black" person, I have a special relationship with the word "family." I think of love and community and struggle and pride—and inclusivity. I try to love "family" as I love "blackness"—as bell hooks suggests—as political resistance.[11] But what of my queerness? Can I love my queerness and still keep my black card?

Slide #69 of the word "Church." Performer removes hat and hood and sits on block stage left.

PERFORMER   I grew up in the church. I didn't have a choice. My mother dragged me to Sunday school AND morning worship service every Sunday. After a while though, she didn't have to drag me: I went on my own. I enjoyed going to church because there was so much to do.

Slide #70 of Morning Star Church.

PERFORMER   This is my church back home in Hickory. I remember when we moved from the old church building to the new one.

Slide #71 of Performer at ground breaking.

PERFORMER   This is me at the ground breaking. I was wearing my usher's
                uniform, which then consisted of this god awful animal
                print dashiki and a turtle neck. And, of course, big hair!

*Slide #72 of the words "Morning Star First Baptist Church: Where
everybody is somebody and Jesus is Lord."*

PERFORMER   This was our church motto. It's printed on the weekly
                church bulletin, which I receive every week from the church
                secretary. It lets me know what's going on back home—who
                died, who's on the sick and shut-in list, who's going off to
                school, etc.

Tape of "My Liberty" begins.

PERFORMER   I have so many fond memories of church, especially singing
                in the choir. I joined the church and the children's choir at
                the age of six.

Slide #73 of Performer in the choir.

PERFORMER   I was the only boy in the soprano section and I could out
                sing all the girls. I was this fat, boy soprano with a big butt
                and big voice who got the church to shoutin' every Sunday
                with this solo. The song is called, "My Liberty"—how pro-
                phetic.

The music swells and Performer sings along until the music fades.

Slide #74 of Morning Star Church.

PERFORMER   We had one of the best choirs in the area and I garnered
                quite a reputation as the little fat boy who could sing
                soprano. I was also teased about my high voice—especially
                as I got older. When I reached 15 and was still singing
                soprano . . . well, let's just say it seemed a little "quare." But
                I just kept right on singing my soprano, until at age 17, much
                to my chagrin, my voice changed and I could no longer hit
                those high notes and Sherri Shade took over the lead to "My
                Liberty"—Me? Bitter? Nooooooooooooo.
                    While I miss my church back home, I rarely go back. To

his credit, my pastor never preached a homophobic sermon, but then again, he never mentioned homosexuality at all. And although there were plenty of gay men in the church—from the choir stand to the deacon board—there was never any affirmation of gay and lesbian members. No one talked about it. If there are three things the church knows how to do well, (and I ain't talking about the Father, Son and Holy Ghost either) it's shame, guilt, and denial!

Performer puts robe backstage.

Performer begins to put on black dress shoes, black jeans, and a spandex black shirt.

PERFORMER   That's why I think so many gays are finding alternative routes to affirm their spirituality and sexuality.[12]

Tape of house music begins.

Slide #75 of Performer dancing with other men.

PERFORMER   It's Labor Day weekend in 1995, I take a trip to Atlanta, Georgia, to visit friends, to escape from my mostly white New England environment and to return home to the South to find a refuge amongst my black queer peers. While there, my friends take me to a number of gay night clubs, some are predominately white; some are racially mixed; while others are predominately African American. One of the more popular African American clubs we visit is called "Tracks" or "The Warehouse," though it is gay only two nights a week—Friday and Saturday. We go to Tracks on Saturday, arriving there just a little past midnight. (Among gay bar hoppers, it is unheard of to go to a club before midnight!) Located about a mile and half from downtown Atlanta, Tracks is indistinguishable from the other warehouses in the industrial district—indistinguishable, that is, except for the line of people that coils around the side of the building and down the block. While standing in line, we overhear the catty, yet playful conversations of those in front and in back of us: "She [he] think she cute. Too bad she ain't" (*laughter*); "Chile, I ain't tryin' to be standin' in this line all night—not with these pumps on!"; "Look, Miss Thing. I ain't got no other ID. Miss Thing at the door better not try to be shady. I'll cut her ass." In general, we cruise and get cruised, negotiate sexual deals. We're all men on a mission. I know I'm home.

Inside, my friends and I squeeze down the staircase and descend into the sea of bodies onto the dance floor. There is barely enough room to breathe, let alone move. Every inch of the space is filled with a body—fat bodies, thin bodies, hard bodies, soft bodies, warm bodies, sweaty bodies, every body imaginable. Clearly, the body is on display: There are drag queens in skintight hotpants and platform shoes. There are "butch" men donning their black leather jackets, aligning the wall like two by fours holding the structure together. There are "queens" dressed in black chiffon blouses unbuttoned to their navels and tight black jeans, who are constantly pursing their lips while looking over the tops of their retro "cat-eye" shades; there are older men (in this context anyone over 45) sitting on bar stools, dressed conservatively in slacks and button-up shirts sipping their scotch and sodas while looking longingly at the young bodies saunter across the dance floor. The hip hop contingent is sprinkled throughout the club in their baggy jeans, ski caps, sneakers, and black shades, some sucking on blowpops while others sip Budweiser. And then there are those like me and my friends who are dressed in designer jeans (Calvin Klein) and tight, spandex muscle shirts, performing middle class (acting bourgeoisie)—as if we actually have two nickels to rub together! You can smell us coming because we sprayed and resprayed cologne behind our ankles, on the small of our backs, and, of course on the front of our chests and all around our necks. We're beyond reproach. We manage to dance—spoon fashion—against the seemingly thousands of flying arms, legs, and butts. I dance with the same man all night—Kevin—a friend of a friend. Kevin and I don't mean to be exclusive dance partners, it just works out that way. We dance close. Every now and then we back off from one another as far as we can and then come together again. We kiss. We bump booties. We hold on to each other for dear life as the beat of the music, the smells of Drakkar, Cool Water, Eternity, Escape, and CK-1, the sweat drenching our shirts and moistening our bulging crotches, and the holy sexual spirit that presides works us into a shamanistic state of euphoria. Time stands still.

Around five AM, the mood of the club shifts and there is a feeling of anticipation in the air. The music shifts to—No it couldn't be!—what sounds like the "shout" music played in my church back home. Kevin and I stare at each other with a carnal intensity as the driving rhythm of the music causes us to grind harder.

Before long, the DJ, a 300-pound, African American man, dressed in a flowing white shirt, blue jeans, high-top sneakers, a thick gold chain, glittering rings on either hand, a baseball cap and diamond trimmed sunglasses, appears on the stage, and begins to do a role call of different cities:

"We got any LA in the house? Show your hands if you're from the gay mecca of DC! How about the northern children from Ms. New York City? Detroit! Chicago! We got any Boston children up in here! And last, but not least, let me see the children from Hotlanta!" We cheer and wave our hands in the air if our city is called. Then, the DJ begins to testify:

"Thank Him! For how He kept you safe over the dangerous highways and byways. Thank Him, because you closed in your right mind!

"Look around you. Somebody that was here last year ain't here tonight! Look around you! Somebody that was dancing right next to you ain't here tonight! Look around you! Somebody's lover has passed on! Look around you! Somebody's brother, somebody's sister, somebody's cousin, somebody's uncle done gone on to the Maker. Sister Mary, has passed on tonight! Brother Joe, has gone on to his resting place! But Grace, woke you up this morning! Grace started you on your way! Grace put food on your table! How many of you know what I'm talking about? If He's been good to you, let me see you wave your hands." Kevin and I, along with others, dance on to the beat of the music, waving our hands, crying, kissing, and shouting, "Yes!" A drag queen appears from nowhere and begins to walk around the side of the dance floor beating a tambourine to the beat of the rhythm. The DJ's preaching along with the repetitive beat of the music, works us into a frenzy. Intermittently dispersed throughout the music, are sound bites from gospel singer Shirley Caesar's song, "Hold My Mule."

Slide #76 of the word "Spirit."

Performer dances with tambourine in front of scrim and encourages audience to clap; Performer leaves the stage.

Slide #77 of the words "Black Is, Black Ain't": "Black Is, Black Ain't" chant begins.

As the tape fades, Performer returns wearing robe and carrying a podium.

PERFORMER   God is good. For those of you who are not familiar with the protocol of the black church, our worship services are based on a dynamic called antiphony or, as we say in the black vernacular: call and response. So if I call, you are suppose to respond. So if I say, "God is Good" you should respond with "All the time." God is Good! *(waits for response)* Thank you.

Now, this morning, I'm going to take my text from four books out of the black nationalist version of the Bible. I'll read from the book of Cleaver, Baraka, Madhubuti, and King (Alveda, that is)—not to be confused with the prophet.

The title of my sermon is "Yet Do I Marvel at this Queer Thing!"

First, I go to the book of Cleaver.[13]

Slide #78 of Eldridge Cleaver.

In this book we find a man, suffering from primeval mitosis; we see a man, trying to obtain law and order while writing letters from prison to all black women from all black men; a man, on becoming a black eunuch, prays for Lazarus to come forth; this man's—this BLACK man's—soul is on ice, as he takes notes on a native son—a black son, a queer son, Harlem's son, Emma's boy. Cleaver says of this son in Ch 2, p. 100, paragraph 12, says he: "It seems that many Negro homosexuals, acquiescing in this racial death-wish, are outraged and frustrated because in their sickness they are unable to have a baby by a white man. The cross they have to bear is that, already bending over and touching their toes for the white man, the fruit of their miscegenation is not the little half-white offspring of their dreams but an increase in the unwinding of their nerves—though they redouble their efforts and intake of the white man's sperm."[14]

A little further down in paragraph 13 he continues: "He becomes a white man in a black body. A self-willed, automated slave, he becomes the white man's most valuable tool in oppressing other blacks.

The black homosexual, when his twist has a racial nexus, is an extreme embodiment of this contradiction. The white man has deprived him of his masculinity, castrated him in the center of his burning skull, and when he submits to this change and takes the white man for his lover as well as Big Daddy, he focuses on 'whiteness' all the love in his pent up soul and turns the razor edge of hatred against 'blackness' himself, what he is, and all those who look like him, remind him of himself. He may even hate the darkness of night."[15]

Yet Do I Marvel at this queer thing. Can I get a Amen! The next passage is taken from the book of Baraka

Slide #79 of Imamu Baraka.

(or "Jones" in the Old Testament). As you may recall, Jaraka was a troubled soul—oh the pressures of beautiful black women in the system of Dante's hell—it was like Babylon revisited. Poor prophet Bones was troubled in mind—the young soul wrote a preface to a twenty-volume suicide note. Oh brother Leraka—we look for you yesterday and here you come today. But though a troubled prophet, he is author to some of the most important words of the black nationalist version of the Bible. Most insightful, for instance, is his analysis of then president of the NAACP Roy Wilkins. In chapter "Selected Poetry" verse "Civil Rights Poem," says prophet a mammal, says he: "Roywilkins is an eternal faggot/His spirit is a faggot/his projection/and image, this is/to say, that if I ever see roywilkins/on the sidewalks/imonna/stick half my sandal/up his/ass."[16] Yet do I marvel at this queer, queer thing, Amen!

Moving right along. We move to the book of Madhubuti

Slide #80 of Haki Madhubuti.

(also found in the Old Testament as "Lee"). Isyoubooti was a righteous man. A man for change. But he was cool. Change. He preached of a black Christ—change, change. In the book of "Don't Cry, Scream," verses 75–80, Haiku, re- counts an event that challenged his walk with God. Don L. Get-out-of-my-booty says, says he: "(swung on a fag- got who politely/scratched his ass in my presence. /he smiled broken teeth stained from/his over-used tongue. fisted-face. /teeth dropped in tune with ray/charles singing 'yesterday.')"[17] Oh, Yet, Yet do I Marvel at this queer, queer, queer thing! But let us move on to the last book—the book of King.

In the Black Nationalist version, you might remember that prophetess Alveda was the niece of the great prophet, Martin. Her uncle's followers, however, scourged Velveeta, and this made her very resentful. And pretty soon along came old Reagan. And Alveda and Reagan got friendly. Then Alveda got to walking on shaky ground! Don't ever get friendly with Reagan. But my God is a forgiving God. My God is a wonderful God. Amen! And he forgave old Velveeta and gave her the gift of speaking in tongues.

Slide #81 of *Newspaper clipping from* **The Daily Tarheel**.

If you have your slide projectors with you, advance with me, will you, to one of King's most quoted books, the book of Bigotry. And turn with me to chapter 3

Slide #82 of *King's quote*.

paragraphs 1–5. Read with me: "King spent a significant amount of the speech explaining why homosexuals should not be included in the civil rights movement. "God hates racism; God hates homosexuality," King said. "God loves people who have been victims of racism and homosexuals. Homosexuality is a binding lifestyle," she said. Many people she knows are former lesbians or former gay men—but she says she knows of no former blacks, King said. "If you were born that way, you can be born again."[18] Amen! Amen! Yet do I Marvel. Yet Do I Marvel at this Queer, Queer, Queer, Queer, Queer, Queer, Queer thing!

Slide #83 of empty slide.

But I submit to you this morning. That long before there
was a Cleaver. Long before there was a LeRoi Jones. And way
back there before we heard of a Don L. Madhubuti. And way
on back before Alveda. There was God. A God who said suf-
fer unto me queer children. Mother/Father/Spirit who said
it's yours, for the asking. Yours! It's your blessing. Whatever
you need. It's yours. So how can it be that you question my
authenticity?
How can it be that you question my
authenticity?
How can it be that you question my
authenticity when I am the
Queen?

Slide #84 of Little Richard.

So I ask again
How can it be that you question my
authenticity?
How can it/how can it
be?
For you see
I am the Queen
you know
the Queen who hits those high E flats on Sunday morning,
eeeeeeeeeeeeeeeEEEEEEEEEEEEEeheheheheheh
gets the sistahs to shoutin'
the brothahs to squirming in their seats
before ol' preach takes his text from
Leviticus/how/can/it/be?

Slide #85 of empty slide.

the Queen
who stands like a tea cup
hand on hip and dressed to kill
in retail
stores all over the country
ready to accessorize you out of

your heretofore tacky fashions / how / can / it / be?
that you question my authenticity?
the Queen
who serviced you last night
when she had better things
to do with her time
and who had had better
oh how can it be?
the Queen
who SNAPPED!
and gave a man a
heart
attack / on / his / manly / subjectivity / how / can / it / be?
when Queen Rustin
couldn't get his props
for being a Queen
Queen Bee
Black Queen
cause his afro-sheen smellin'
"brothahs" said not in my
black arts movement
out of shackles into the black
hands that do not know the power
of their hold on the Queen's throat
until her song is inaudible
until her song is gone
until her song is please / baby / please / baby / baby / baby /
please
mr. lee / excuse / me / mr. / haki / madhubuti
don't hate me cause I'm beautiful / how / can / it / be?
that you question my authenticity?
when Queen Langston
writin' the weary blues
for mr. charlie / blues / cause
he's blue at the "Cafe: 3 A.M."
cause his friend went away
bluuuuuuuuuuuuuuuuuuuu
blew me away
when they said he's not
gay / how / can / it / be?
when Jimmy B.

the grand Queentress
just above my head
turns words into fire next
time/Hallelujah!/says
the amen corner because they have the
evidence of things not seen in the Queen
being strangled by Cleaver's soul on ice
who dropped a dime and spread the word
ain't you heard
the Queen has no name in the street
but if beale street could talk it would
go tell it on the mountain because the
devil finds work in another country but
the Queen can't go because no one will tell how
long the train's been gone
gone/gone/gone/going to meet the man
in giovanni's room to have a rap on race
so the Queen sits
with Nikki Giovanni and has a dialogue about
whether a nigger can kill
is that a rhetorical question?
the Queen wants to know
is that a rhetorical question?
mr. don l. lee/excuse me/mr. haki madhubuti
but
excuse me
but/excuse me
can the Queen speak?
can the Queen speak of
black authenticity
can the faggot tell of His goodness
alongside Rev. LeRoi (Jones that is)
who proselytizes black art
as the black/as/the/black
as/the
blackass under his dick?
can the faggot Queen celebrate her
nubian hue like the pearls she clutches
ever so gently
can the faggot sissy Queen
serve you up a big heapin'

of blue/black
blurple?
can her high Queerness speak in
authentic afrocentric field hollers/scream/shout
we wear the mask that grins and lies
and lies on the Queen
when her voice is
anthropomorphized
theorized
televised
ventriloquized
more lies
colonized like herstory
in manifest destiny
in manifest faggotry
because negro faggotry

Slide #86 of *Living Color*.

because negro faggotry

Slide #87 of *Living Color*.

because negro faggotry

Slide #88 of *Living Color*.

is in vogue
is in vogue
as in Damon Wayans
as in David Alan Grier
talkin' 'bout they
"hated it"
as when
black face becomes queer face
as when
black race denies queer space
as when
black macho kills black homo
as when
black masculinity reads black heterosexuality

*Slide #89 of scene from Spike Lee's film **School Daze**.*

> as when
> I say gamma, you say fag. Gamma. Fag. Gamma. Fag.
> but I don't want to be like spike or mike
> or even the other mike

Slide #90 of Michael Jordan.

> but I'll step up to the mike
> to say
> that you owe me
> respect for my blood and sweat
> on your fist

Slide #91 empty slide.

> and
> you/owe/me
> black poems that
> call black people
> that call black people
> that call all people
> that call queer love
> black love
> and
> you owe me
> hi-fives and soul brothah shakes
> and
> you owe me
> what's up my niggah
> what's up on the down low
> and
> you owe me
> a space on the team
> a right in the fight
> a ride on the bus
> cause we gotta have trust/and
> you owe me
> my card/my/x/my/check
> in the blank/and

you owe me
something other than other
cause other didn't save your
black ass
it was the Queen
so how can it be
that you question my authenticity?
how can it be when
how / how / how / how
how long before we bleed brother
blood / how / long
before we get it together
how / long
before we get it together
how / long
before we get it together
how long / not / long / how / long / not / long
or Lord
I long
for the day that I
STOP
counting the t-
cells that keep us gridlocked

Fade in Martin Luther King, Jr.'s "Montgomery" speech on tape.

from brotherhood
how can it be?
brothah?

Performer walks off stage and lights dim.

2 slides #92–93 of MLK.

Performer sings "Sometimes I Feel like A Motherless Child" offstage.

13 slides #94–106 of deceased black gays and lesbians, including Marlon Riggs, Essex Hemphill, Audre Lorde, Langston Hughes, Alain Locke, Zora Neale Hurston, Countee Cullen, Sylvester, and Bayard Rustin, while Performer sings song.

Slide #107 of the word "Home."

Tape of song, "Shooz" by Herbie Hancock.

Performer comes out dressed in a white African attire and sits on steps on far stage right.

Slide #108 of the word "Africa."

PERFORMER   Unlike many African Americans, I didn't have any romantic notions about Africa before I went there. I didn't think the people there would run up to me after I got off the plane and say, "Welcome, My Brother." No, I knew that they would see me as a rich American before they saw me as anything else. But as they say, you have to go there, to know there. And so, I went on this journey to the motherland.

Slide #109 of La Bodi Beach in Ghana, West Africa.

PERFORMER   I never understood Duboisian twoness until I stood on the banks of Accra staring out into the distance—into blackness where screams bombarded my head, the ocean's ebb drew my ear to the wind.[19] Listen. Can't you hear the cries for home? But where is home? The fixed melancholy settles and the voice is mute. Listen. Can't you hear the drums? Can't you hear the muted blood-curdling screams? Listen. Speak to me, Wind. Tell me I am your child, twice removed. Listen.

Slide #110 of little girl carrying an American flag.

PERFORMER   And she appears. Wrapped in the contradictions of double consciousness and colonization. Her dress, white as my master's skin, falls just so over her posed body. I'm on the other end of the gaze objectifying her to speak against her objectification. It's a cruel irony. She carries the flag like a handkerchief to wipe away the tears that will come because of my rude invasion. Where is my blackness in all of this? I don't belong here. Her tears have told me, but she holds my flag. Where is my Americaness in all of this? I hate that symbol draped over her precious little body. This twoness is killing me.

Slide #111 of Du Bois's grave.

PERFORMER   I went to Du Bois for answers. I tried to dig him up to make him answer me. Listen. Can't you hear the cries for home? But where is home? Can't you hear the drums? Listen. "Go," he said, "and listen."

Slide #112 of little girl with flag.

PERFORMER   I give her 500 cedis and she stops crying. She drops the flag on the ground and picks it up again and looks at me. She knows. Listen.

Slide #113 picture of Edison.

PERFORMER   And he appears. Edison. He has been at the camp since 1990. Lisa and Soyini asked him to be our guide on the camp, but to me he was much more.

        He took us to a club called LIPS. Now, I thought it strange that there would be a liquor bar on a Liberian Refugee Camp, but hey, poverty does not mean you can't have a social life. So we went to LIPS. Once inside, the twoness came to me again. Ghana, Durham? Durham, Ghana? Near the back wall sat a woman with a weave half way down her back, jeans that she had to have painted on, and a brother rapping hard to her in his native tongue of Twi. At the bar sat three brothers telling lies, like characters out of some Zora Neale Hurston story or like the men that congregate at the barber shop in my hometown. They don't go there to get their hair cut, but to tell lies, drink liquor, and hit on unsuspecting women.

Slide #114 of owner of LIPS.

PERFORMER   The owner of LIPS was familiar, too. He looked like my Uncle Boot, who used to frequent the barbershop in my hometown. He showed us to a table, when I couldn't help but notice the sign behind the counter.

Slide #115 of sign up close.

PERFORMER "No unauthorized persons are allowed behind the counter. Please take notice and govern yourselves accordingly to avoid embarrassment." OK? And this all too familiar sign found in black establishments around the country:

Slide #116 of "No Credit."

PERFORMER "No Credit. Pay as you call, pls."

Slide #117 of bartender.

PERFORMER It's hot. We need something cool to drink. We sit down at a table and Edison orders two mineral waters for Soyini and Lisa, a bitter lemon for me and a coke for himself. When the drinks come, Lisa quizzes Edison about his life on the camp as Soyini listens intently. I begin to think about the night before when we got lost trying to find our way from the airport. Lisa would ask in her New Orleans accent dipped in Twi, "Good Evening, can you tell me how to get to Osu?" "Straight. Go Straight," they would always say and "straight" never meant straight. It inevitably meant take a left, drive two miles, then turn right and follow the curve—but never simply, unequivocally, "straight." We spent half the night going "straight" and it got us nowhere. "Straight," indeed.

Tape of Mariah Carey's "Dreamlover."

PERFORMER I begin to doze off when, over the fuzzy stereo speakers I hear . . . Mariah Carey?

Slide #118 of Mariah Carey.

PERFORMER "Dreamlover" no less. Why would they be listening to Mariah Carey at a Liberian Refugee Camp? Dumbfounded, I turn to Edison and ask him, "Edison, do you like Mariah Carey?" "Yes," he answers as if to say, "what's so odd about that?" "Why?" I ask in an accusatory tone. "Because she sounds like a black woman," he says. I cannot speak. My voice is muted by the instability of my own identity—of my own conventions of reading race. The African teaches the African American to listen. Can't you hear the drums?

"Dreamlover" fades.

PERFORMER   I liked Edison. There was something sexy about him. But
              I had a difficult time negotiating sexuality in Ghana—the
              natives' and my own. I had seen men in town holding
              hands, hugging, and even kiss each other, but it had noth-
              ing to do with their sexuality. In fact, I met no self-identified
              gay men while I was there. There, western notions of gen-
              der performance flew out the door. Example: Edison asked
              me earlier that day about my girlfriend—about my fiancée.
              "I don't have a girlfriend, Edison. I don't have a fiancée."
              He had no clue I was gay, nor that I was flirting with him. I
              haven't been mistaken for a heterosexual in years—I must
              be down on my job.

Slide #119 of Mrs. Powell outside her house/restaurant.

PERFORMER   We rise to leave to go to Mrs. Powell's. Mrs. Powell works
              with one of the non-governmental organizations and runs
              a small restaurant on the camp. On our way out, some
              LIPS patrons, four men, surround me—each holding a fifth
              of liquor. "Eh! EH! My American brother! EH! You buy us a
              drink? Eh! My friend, do you know your history? Do you
              know that in 17 . . . 55, the white man, he come and take
              you, he steal you from your homeland, my brother. Do you
              know that we are brothers? We are brothers, my friend. You
              buy us drink?" "I'll buy you a drink if you tell me how to
              get to Mrs. Powell's place," I say, lying. Yep. That's right. You
              know what they told me. "Go Straight."
              As we continue to walk away from LIPS, the jeers of the men
              fading into the distance, out of the blue, Edison takes my
              hand.

Slide #120 of Performer and Edison.

PERFORMER   We walk like that, hand-in-hand "straight" down the road.

Tape of drumming begins.

Slide #121 of male slave dungeon.

Slide #122 of slave dungeon entrance.

PERFORMER   Have I been down this road before? Shhhhhh. Listen. Can't
             you hear the blood-curdling screams? Shhhhhh. Listen.

Slide #123 of dungeon interior.

PERFORMER   Where am I? What is this blackness? SHHHHH, listen. The
             drum will tell you.

Slide #124 of "Door of No Return." [20]

PERFORMER   Behind that door lies the answer. Behind the door of no re-
             turn? Yes. Go. Shhhh.

Slide #125 of empty slide.

*The drumming gets louder and Performer takes off his hat and top and
goes behind the scrim; drumming ends and the back of the scrim is lit
to cast Performer's silhouette.*

Tape of instrumental of Nina Simone's "Four Women." [21]

Performer dances behind the scrim while singing:

> My skin is black
> My arms are long
> My hair is woolly
> My back is strong
> Strong enough to take the pain
> Inflicted again and again
> What do they call me?
> My name is Aunt Sarah
> My name is Aunt Sarah, Aunt Sarah
>
> My skin is yellow
> My hair is long
> Between two worlds
> I do belong
> My father was rich and white
> He forced my mother late one night

What do they call me?
My name is Saphronia
My name is Saphronia

My skin is burned
My hair is charred
My eyes bleed red
My mouth ajar
Whose little boy am I?
The one to the fence you would tie
What do they call me?
My name is Matthew
My name is Matthew Shepard

My skin is brown
My manner is tough
I'll kill the first bigot I see
My life has been rough
I'm awfully bitter these days
The senseless killing of gays

What do they call me?
My name is Faggot!

Lights fade.

Slide #126 of multiple lynching.

Slide #127 of "Membership Has Its Privileges."

THE END

Notes

1 In 1640 blacks were denied the right to bear arms in Virginia. The year 1776 marked the United States' independence from Britain. In 1865, southerners created Black Codes, which served as a way to control and inhibit the freedom of ex-slaves. In 1968 Martin Luther King was assassinated. In 1970 Angela Davis was tried, convicted, and subsequently released on kidnapping, conspiracy, and murder charges.

2 Hortense Spillers, "Mama's Baby, Papa's Maybe: An American Grammar Book," *Diacritics* 17, no. 2 (1987): 65.

3 See Judith Butler, *Gender Trouble* (New York: Routledge, 1990) and *Bodies That Matter: On the Discursive Limits of "Sex"* (New York: Routledge, 1993).

4 See Spillers, "Mama's Baby."

5 In the spring of 1995, Staples gave a public reading of his book at Amherst College, where I was on faculty and a member of the audience. The proceeding excerpts are among those that Staples read. Our exchange occurred during the question-and-answer session of that talk.

6 Brent Staples, *Parallel Time* (New York: Pantheon, 1994), 202–3.

7 Staples, *Parallel Time*, 39.

8 Staples, *Parallel Time*, 39–40.

9 See Kobena Mercer, *Welcome to the Jungle* (New York: Routledge, 1994), 230–35.

10 Spillers, "Mama's Baby," 70.

11 See bell hooks, "Loving Blackness as Political Resistance," in *Killing Rage: Ending Racism* (New York: Henry Holt, 1995).

12 See E. Patrick Johnson, "Feeling the Spirit in the Dark: Expanding Notions of the Sacred in the African American Gay Community," *Callaloo* 21, no. 2 (1998): 399–416.

13 Eldridge Cleaver, *Soul on Ice* (New York: Dell, 1992).

14 Cleaver, *Soul on Ice*, 100.

15 Cleaver, *Soul on Ice*, 101.

16 Imamu Amiri Baraka [LeRoi Jones], "CIVILRIGHTSPOEM," in *The Selected Poetry of Amiri Baraka/LeRoi Jones* (New York: William Morrow, 1979), 115.

17 Haki R. Madhubuti [Don L. Lee], "Don't Cry, Scream," in *Don't Cry, Scream* (Detroit: Broadside Press, 1969), 27–31.

18 Alveda King, "King Addresses Racism, Homosexuality," *Daily Tarheel*, February 19, 1998, 1.

19 See W. E. B. Du Bois, *The Souls of Black Folk* (New York: Dover, 1994), 1–7.

20 The "Door of No Return" is so called because it is the last door through which enslaved Africans passed before being boarded onto slave ships.

21 The author altered the last two stanzas of this song. In the original, the last two stanzas are "My skin is tan/my hair is fine/My hips invite you/My mouth like wine/Whose little girl am I?/The one with money to buy/What do they call me?/My name is sweet thing/My name is sweet thing. My skin is brown/My manner is tough/I'll kill the first mother I see/My life has been rough/I'm awfully bitter these days/Cause my parents were slaves/What do they call me?/My name is Peaches!"

References

Baldwin, James. *The Amen Corner*. New York: Laurel, 1954.
———. *Another Country*. New York: Griot Editions, 1994.
———. *Blues for Mister Charlie*. New York: Dial, 1964.
———. *The Evidence of Things Not Seen*. New York: Henry Holt, 1985.
———. *The Fire Next Time*. New York: Dial, 1963.
———. *Giovanni's Room*. New York: Dial, 1956.
———. *Going to Meet the Man*. New York: Dell, 1966.
———. *Go Tell It on the Mountain*. New York: Laurel, 1985.
———. *If Beale Street Could Talk*. New York: Laurel, 1974.

————. *Just above My Head*. New York: Laurel, 1979.

————. *Nobody Knows My Name*. New York: Dell, 1963.

————. *Tell Me How Long the Train's Been Gone*. New York: Laurel, 1968.

Baldwin, James, and Nikki Giovanni. *A Dialogue*. New York: L. P. Lippincott, 1973.

Baraka, Imamu Amiri [LeRoi Jones]. "CIVILRIGHTSPOEM" and "Black Art." In *The Selected Poetry of Imamu Baraka/LeRoi Jones*, 106–7, 115. New York: William Morrow, 1979.

Butler, Judith. *Bodies That Matter: On the Discursive Limits of "Sex."* New York: Routledge, 1993.

————. *Gender Trouble*. New York: Routledge, 1990.

Cleaver, Eldridge. *Soul on Ice*. New York: Dell, 1992.

Conquergood, Dwight. "Performance Studies: Interventions and Radical Research." TDR: *The Drama Review* 46, no. 2 (Summer 2002): 145–56.

Du Bois, W. E. B. *The Souls of Black Folk*. New York: Dover, 1994.

Fuss, Diana. *Essentially Speaking: Feminism, Nature and Difference*. New York: Routledge, 1989.

Giovanni, Nikki. "The True Import of Present Dialogue: Black vs. Negro." In *The Black Poets*, edited by Dudley Randall, 318–19. New York: Bantam, 1971.

hooks, bell. "Loving Blackness as Political Resistance." In *Killing Rage: Ending Racism*. New York: Henry Holt, 1995.

Hughes, Langston. "I Loved My Friend" and "Cafe: 3 A. M." In *Black Men/White Men: A Gay Anthology*, edited by Michael J. Smith, 30. San Francisco: Gay Sunshine Press, 1983.

Johnson, E. Patrick. "Can the Queen Speak?" Unpublished poem, 1998.

————. "Feeling the Spirit in the Dark: Expanding Notions of the Sacred in the African American Gay Community." *Callaloo* 21, no. 2 (1998): 399–416.

————. "'Quare' Studies, or (Almost) Everything I Know about Queer Studies I Learned from My Grandmother." *Text and Performance Quarterly* 21, no. 1 (2001): 1–25.

King, Alveda. "King Addresses Racism, Homosexuality." *Daily Tarheel*, February 19, 1998, 1.

Madhubuti, Haki R. [Don L. Lee]. "Don't Cry, Scream." In *Don't Cry, Scream*, 27–31. Detroit: Broadside Press, 1969.

Mapplethorpe, Robert. "Man in Polyester Suit." Photo. The Estate of Robert Mapplethorpe, 1980.

Mercer, Kobena. *Welcome to the Jungle*. New York: Routledge, 1994.

Spillers, Hortense. "Mama's Baby, Papa's Maybe: An American Grammar Book." *Diacritics* 17, no. 2 (1987): 65–81.

Staples, Brent. *Parallel Time*. New York: Pantheon, 1994.

CHAPTER 5

Passing Strange

E. PATRICK JOHNSON'S *STRANGE FRUIT*

Jennifer DeVere Brody

Currently . . . the phrase "identity politics," has become a rhetorical put-down: quite rightly, because the idea of identity as a static, naturalized, immutable essence can only reinforce the repetition of the bureaucratic "race, class, gender" mantra, in which difference is made manageable and governable at the level of institutional policies and practices. . . .

It is precisely for this reason that I want to develop the anti-essentialist theme that the work of black gay male artists . . . does indeed make a difference, not because of who or what they *are*, but because of what they *do* and, above all, because of the freaky-deke way in which they do it.
—Kobena Mercer, *Welcome to the Jungle*

Black British art critic and queer cultural studies scholar Kobena Mercer's call to highlight an "anti-essentialist theme" in "the work of black gay male artists because of what they *do*" is borne out in performances of E. Patrick Johnson's solo show, *Strange Fruit: A Performance about Identity Politics*, which was first performed in the 1990s at the same time Mercer was writing his critique.[1] Johnson's show actively valorizes "doing" in contradistinction to ontological, naturalized ways of being in the world. In concert with Mercer's understanding of doing as an active difference, Johnson's show demonstrates key concepts from the transdisciplinary field of performance studies. Indeed, with *Strange Fruit* he demonstrates that performance is a "doing and a thing done" and that subjects are determined contingently by interactions with other forms and ideas both material and psychic.[2] The focus on doing is crucial and provides at least one reason that Mercer's quotation works so well to illuminate Johnson's multifaceted show.

The second reason that Mercer's essay and Johnson's show mutually intersect is the fact that both works mark a significant political moment in the proliferation of black queer art that took place in both

Britain and the United States beginning in the 1990s. There are deep relations among and between not only Mercer and Johnson but also filmmakers Isaac Julien and Marlon Riggs and performers Djola Branner, Brian Freeman, and Eric Gupton, who made up the group POMO-AFROHOMOS (an abbreviation for Postmodern African American Homosexuals) and began performing in the 1990s at Josie's Cabaret and Juice Joint in San Francisco. This performance troupe spoofed such reverent African American realist classics as Lorraine Hansberry's A Raisin in the Sun while also in the same evening showing such fare as autobiographical sketches focused on homophobia in a black home. As such, we can understand these artistic and critical interventions retrospectively as part of a confluence of events that helped to usher in what was then a relatively new area of critique: black queer studies. The naming of the subject black queer studies is itself part of a particular moment that E. Patrick Johnson's performance fleshes out, in movement, voice, and embodied expression. Indeed, the very title of the piece, Strange Fruit, exemplifies a "freaky-deke" DOING of the sort that I believe Mercer would applaud for its antiessentialist black gay male image-making and performance.

Speaking generally, one version of this narrative about the advent of black queer performance argues that the work in black queer studies had its roots in various black feminisms from an even earlier cultural and political moment dating back to the late 1960s.[3] E. Patrick Johnson's show Strange Fruit addresses these questions of origin and enactment with flair and humor. In the show, Johnson demonstrates how to do black gay male art as a black gay man while avoiding essentialist "realist" pitfalls. The show works as an experimental documentary performance that draws on actual events in Johnson's life, while highlighting their performative dimensions. It also contextualizes them in a critical genealogy of black gay image-making. Given the show's close attention to how one can recognize black gay art, it serves as a product of its time and an index of that time's black queer sensibility. Thus, it appears not merely in the wake of black queer studies in the 1990s and at a moment in which the suturing of these terms—black and queer—came together, but significantly in the style of postmodern, antiessentialist theory.[4]

Scene 1

Johnson wrote and performed Strange Fruit: A Performance about Identity Politics throughout the late 1990s into the early 2000s. I first saw the show in the context of the momentous "Black Queer Studies in the

Millennium" conference in 2000, co-organized by Johnson and Mae Henderson at the University of North Carolina at Chapel Hill, resulting in a volume of the same name published by Duke University Press.[5] This was a year following the show's premier on the same University of North Carolina at Chapel Hill campus.

Strange Fruit is part of Johnson's larger articulation of black "quare" studies.[6] The performance, as an event, made a marked difference precisely because of its performative aspects: it was at once a DOING and a thing DONE, a comment on black gay male subjectivity and a variegated performance of this subjectivity. What Johnson DOES in and through the multiple movements that come to compose the show Strange Fruit is to produce a tentative rendering of black gay male identity politics. In the show, Johnson appears as a version of himself and as various others who come to make up his subjectivity. For example, he plays his mother, his students, acquaintances, and friends, in addition to historical figures such as Eldridge Cleaver—even purportedly homophobic folks such as black preachers and students at Amherst College. Johnson's persona in the show weaves together disparate historical figures, thereby showing a singular black gay male who is differentiated within a broader context: his story of growing up in the South, securing his first job in the North, and ultimately journeying to Ghana shows him as both singular and representative of a black queer man of a particular time, place, and persuasion.

What follows is an analysis of the first "movement" of Johnson's show, Strange Fruit, in which I demonstrate how Johnson (mis)performs his changing relationships to black feminism and femininity, masculinity and other forms of identity which are, here and elsewhere, never separate from their politics. In the show, Johnson undresses (physically) and exposes his "explicit body in performance" in order to embody the concepts with which he is concerned throughout the performance.[7] As he deftly retells and restages scenes from his life, he deploys different performative strategies to help audiences understand his changing positions and to elicit their affective responses. The cumulative result is effective and affecting, and Johnson works with and through anti-essentialism, deconstruction, and intertextuality. One of the most striking things about the show is its enactment of the tensions among and between a black gay man's performance of black femininity in conjunction with the invocation of both academic and quotidian black feminisms. It is the latter that places him in a tradition of black women and black men (including versions of himself) all of whom he (mis)performs by virtue of the fact that he is at least twice removed from any iteration

Fig. 5.1. Johnson in blackface drag. *Strange Fruit*. Photo courtesy of E. Patrick Johnson.

of some imagined, stable authentic identity from "his" past. Thus, such impersonations in the piece—of himself and others—might be deemed "misperformances."

Strange Fruit moves within and between the unique and the universal, the specific and the general. Indeed, Johnson uses his body to gesture toward the larger condition of black gay identity, and as a gesture of such an identity. For instance, in the opening of the show Johnson enters the auditorium from the back of the house (the historic space of blackness in American racism?) and walks through the audience in order to interact with them/us. His skin is smeared with black grease-paint, and he sports a black bouffant wig. His costume consists of a shimmery, sequined, black gown, accessorized with arm-length black satin gloves (see figure 5.1). His cross-dressed, blackface performance ushers in another time, literally recalling black performance from its inception on American stages through its various incarnations up to Motown and now in the present.

He meanders through the audience handing out bright yellow "credit cards" to random audience members who become part of the action, as he sings the song "God Bless the Child," made famous by Billie Holiday. The song's refrain, "Mama may have, Papa may have, but God bless

BLACK AMERICAN EXPRESS®

1640 1776 1865 1968 1970

VALID
DATES
CONTINGENT

MEMBER
SINCE
1619

AX

DR. COLORED A. NEGRO

Fig. 5.2. Black American Express Card. *Strange Fruit*. Photo courtesy of E. Patrick Johnson.

the child that's got his own," seems ironic in the face of the stereotypical version of blackness. The song, which Johnson's performance may be said to enact, discusses the problems of inheritance and individuality—of singular and plural identities—of the self-made person or, of the Other. It praises those children who can make it on their own by owning themselves. Needless to say, the discourse of ownership raises the role of slavery in the stockpiling of U.S. credit and the role capitalism plays in wedding property and identity in U.S. cultural politics. The yellow card bordered in black reads "Black American Express" (see figure 5.2).

It is "trademarked" and its "valid" dates are contingent. The membership dates run significantly from 1619 through 1640, 1776, 1865, and 1970; or, from the year the first Africans were said to have been brought to American shores, to the end of the civil rights era. Punctuating history in this teleological manner still leaves open the future of race relations. One can imagine an "update" on the show that might end with 2008 and the election of Barack Obama, for example. The card also has the effect of putting Johnson's show into a genealogy of significant events in African American and gay history. The name on the card reads "Dr. Colored A. Negro." The generic name is yet another signifi-cation of racist history that forecloses individuality for black subjects. To hold the cardstock in one's hand is to touch a simulacrum of the texts that imprint not only Johnson's performance personae but also one's own identity. The cards can be seen as the proverbial "price of the ticket" for admission to the staged event known as American history.[8]

Johnson's appearance as an apparition of a nineteenth-century blackface minstrel performer as well as his signifying on a long tradi-tion of female impersonators have the effect of disarming (and perhaps alarming) those who witness the show. Such twice-restored behavior evokes Brechtian masking that allows us to see Johnson the actor re-enacting these long-standing, interrelated performance traditions of which he has now become a part, as well as to hear his pointed com-mentary on the different political, economic, and cultural contexts under and through which such performances usually took place. In-deed, Johnson's costume is double drag: black and female imperson-ation. This choice allows Johnson to place his work in a tradition of performing blackness and, in terms of female impersonation, of rep-resenting a version of the gay male body's imagined femininity. This move also makes the force of his black male drag seem even more de-naturalized. We are prepared for the performance and instead of having the effect of making his next costume more real or authentic, his gen-der performance is just that much more of an act. Johnson is able to do this in part by his close attention not only to costume but also to his gestures, his script, and dialogue.

Later on in the opening, he explains that when his mama dressed him in wigs she thought it was "cute"; but when Johnson sought to dress himself in the wigs, then his "agency [became] such a drag" to which he adds, "If you don't believe me, ask your mama." Here I be-lieve that he moves from discussing transvestism to referencing Joan Riviere's idea of masquerade, featured in an article she published in 1929 to address the problem of working women who, having phallic power, sought to redress their potency through (hyper)feminine dress and behavior.[9] The puns, both visual and verbal, put forth in this scene show that acting on one's behalf is often a double-edged sword. We recognize and misrecognize Johnson as a "black male drag performer." Importantly, Johnson's performance demonstrates that (black) drag is not only feminine but also masculine. After having an audience mem-ber assist him in the unzipping of his dress, he changes into sneakers, shorts, and a tank top, and accessorizes not with a wig, but with dumb-bells, as he reveals his "butch drag" (see figure 5.3).

Fig. 5.3. Johnson in "butch drag." *Strange Fruit*. Photo courtesy of E. Patrick Johnson.

When Johnson removes his blackface, he reveals another mask—this one of "reality" that despite its temporal appeal to truth (in Western culture, it is what lies beneath that we believe to be real) he shows us is only another mask. This sly change of costumes reveals that under the mask of black female drag lies not an authentic "real" man but rather another drag identity—the butch or the category of "butch realness." Thus, Johnson performs onstage the dictum attributed to drag performer RuPaul: "We all came into this world naked, the rest of it is all drag"—and truthfully, even this reading may be too essentialist for Johnson's position as a poststructuralist materialist performer, which is to say that there is no nakedness to be had for any of us even if we appear to be nude.[10] Johnson plays with the notion that his story is not the unvarnished truth—everything is shellacked, varnished, or rather, subject to interpretation. He gives us his own reading of the photographs and of others—including his mother.

When he changes his costumes before our eyes, he refers to the transformative shedding as "drag droppings" (see chapter 6)—which is a kind of update of the colloquial phrase "dropping hairpins," which once was used to refer to the wearing of wigs by transvestite performers but which registers as well as a coded term for queer subjects.

Johnson's "drag droppings"—the piles of clothing that come to litter the stage—serve as a mnemonic device that recalls from whence he came, historically speaking. In other words, the action of dropping drag comes to mark moments in both real and symbolic time. We can understand and remember to see Johnson in other "personal" guises and to connect him as well to a much larger and longer historical genealogy of drag and blackface performance. His "autobiographical" performance might best be characterized as "biomythography"—a term coined by the late Audre Lorde.[11] Lorde's neologism encapsulates the mythic/symbolic at the heart of every life story and certainly proves fruitful for Johnson's selective retelling of incidents in/from the life of a southern, black gay man. This is why it makes sense that he invokes a list of mythic black female characters—from Brown Sugar to Aunty, Granny, Sapphire, and Mammy—in his opening remarks as he pays homage not only to these figures, but also to black feminist scholar Hortense Spillers's ritual citation of these "women" in the opening of her famous essay "Mama's Baby, Papa's Maybe: An American Grammar Book."[12] In a tongue-in-cheek moment Johnson refers to Spillers as his "alter ego" (see figure 5.1). As such, Johnson places or performs himself in the tradition of "marked" women when he quotes Spillers: "I describe a locus of confounded identities, a meeting ground of investments and privations in the national treasury of rhetorical wealth. My country needs me, and if I were not here, I would have to be invented." Spillers's comment, and Johnson's quotation of it, assert the foundational need for the black female in the birth of the U.S. nation-state.

Johnson follows this statement by noting that the pop star Madonna did not invent the dance craze known as vogueing, indexing black roots of white history by referring to the fact that he himself has been vogueing since 1971! This double gesture inserts black gay men into a national scene and credits them with the invention of a style merely popularized by blonde ambition—again, recalling the double performance of those bright yellow cards. It also sets the scene for Johnson's subsequent posing in photos—as a black preacher, as himself as a child, and so forth. The photographs serve to "authenticate" Johnson's penchant for performing, posing, and vogueing, and to give us a kind of "backstory" (the background photographs are projected on a scrim *behind* the performer). The use of the documentary realism provided by the photographs serves to naturalize Johnson's "unnatural" desire to pose—as a black gay male. Making comic use of colloquial phrases (e.g., playing on one team and not the other, etc.), Johnson winks at the audience members who are supposed to get the double entendre. Johnson guides us through his narrative take on the images that appear on the screen, giving the audience members a way to read and interpret what they see.

Accordingly, I want to give close readings of two telling moments in the show that resonated with me on the occasions I had to view it (on stage and screen) and, subsequently, to read it as a printed text. A redaction of the eight different movements that compose the show, which appeared on a screen behind the performer, reads:

1. God Bless the Child
2. Dis Hair Thang
3. "Quare" Studies
4. Sanctuary
5. Feeling the Spirit
6. Can the Queen Speak?
7. The Drums
8. Four Queens

Johnson explains that the title of the show refers both to lynching (referenced in the infamous lyric) and to the notion of being "strange," which is a synonym for "queer," "odd," or in the vernacular of his southern grandmother, "quare." His queer quotation of the much performed song "Strange Fruit" (he refrains from playing the song in his show—and yet the song haunts the performance as well as the title) was made more poignant by the fact that a twenty-six-year-old black gay man, Arthur Warren Jr., was murdered about the same time Johnson did this version of the show.[13] To his credit, Johnson makes the political context in which these murders occurred matter even more. In the show he produced and performed, he added new lyrics to the lyrical last movement, "Four Queens," so that he hails Matthew Shepard among others into the final song. Johnson performs a choreographed dance from behind the scrim and sings a haunting song that leaves the audience understanding the gravity and significance of the show.

Throughout the piece Johnson makes good use of his background (pun intended) as reflected on the scrim behind him. Here, the past flashes in the form of black-and-white photographs, or later, his shape is shadowed, backlit and resembling a drawing by Aaron Douglas (see figure 5.4). The doubling provided by the scrim represents Johnson's multiplicity and the (at least) doubleness of identity. It is a visual cue through which his performance materializes the tropes of blackness such as double consciousness, shadow, and polyphony in sound and

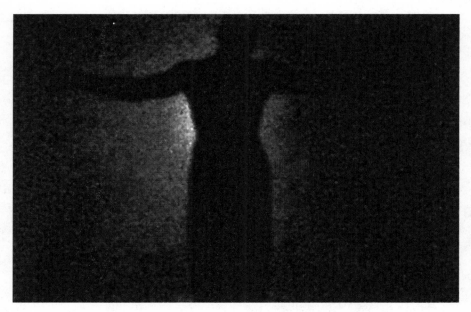

Fig. 5.4. Johnson behind the scrim. *Strange Fruit*. Photo courtesy of E. Patrick Johnson.

image. The fast pace of the show allows him to traverse a broad spatio-temporal and political terrain: from Amherst to Accra, nineteenth-century slavery to 1960s black arts, and numerous sites in between.

In the preface to the version of the show published in TDR: *The Drama Review*, Johnson claims that *Strange Fruit* was "born out of the danger [he] felt for his life." Specifically, he explains that he "felt that if [he] misperformed, even in the slightest, that [his] life might be in danger. Thus, *Strange Fruit* was born."[14] This early reference to "misperformance" suggests that Johnson understands that every performance is in some sense a misperformance. It references the fact that any form of action—(hetero)masculinity if not heterosexuality—is always misperformed. In Johnson's thinking, in order *not* to be a victim of violence against those who could be charged with the epithet effeminate, Johnson suggests that he was required to perform as a hypermasculine subject—which in itself could have put him at more risk. For in appearing to avoid being exposed as effeminate—mistakenly correlated in Western culture as a synonym for gay—Johnson saw himself *having* to perform "as a man," which was and was not a form of butch realness. It was, as it is today, a matter of life and/or death to be seen as "a real man," as masculine and "straight." The fact that one must put these terms in quotation marks indicates that they are suspect, on trial, under review—decidedly performative and not straightforward. Johnson's show unsettles, or misperforms, thereby revealing effectively and with great affect, his becoming a black gay male academic performer. Johnson's ability to perform as a masculine man (there is no ironic doubleness here) saved him from being misread as an endangered, effeminate "gay" black male. Nevertheless, this performance, this survival act, did not allay his fear of being "found out" as gay: on the contrary, the very fact that his masculinity was an act endangered him even as the re-enactment seemed to be his saving grace. By writing and performing *Strange Fruit*, Johnson said he was released, cathartically, from the fear of failing to perform normative masculinity properly. What I am getting at here is the complicated dance of redoubled action and effort that we witness in Johnson's performance of his masculinity. As we have seen, Johnson stages this transforming and transformative masculinity ex-plicitly in the opening section of *Strange Fruit*.

Scene 2. Mis(s)Performance?

For Johnson, fear was a motivating factor for his offstage persona and for his artistic practice. The show was, as he explains above, an act compelled by danger, teeming with risk and yet offering the possibility of catharsis and (safely contained) representation. Interestingly, John-son's reliance upon the term "misperformance" in his explication of the show's origins suggests to me the way in which *all* performance is a reaction to certain regulations which are therefore subject to failure and perhaps born of fear. It is no accident that the word "misperfor-mance" continues to gain traction in contemporary studies. The term was privileged during the fifteenth Performance Studies International (PSI) Conference that took place in 2009 in Zagreb, Croatia. Indeed, this event was devoted to elucidating the elusive concept-metaphor of "mis-performance."[15]

We can highlight Johnson's work by paying attention to the homo-phonic "miss" and "MIS" that precede performance (and indeed precede the actual show) to explain how Johnson's drag (at once racial, gen-dered, and sexual) gives him agency. What is "missed" here is forma-tive and performative in multiple ways. Some of the "mis" of what is lost (and found) in performance has been explained above. The "miss" references Johnson's strategic use of both feminine and masculine drag in his show. It is also a longing activated in the show by the slides of his youth when drag was seemingly innocent. While a full reading of the entire show is well beyond the scope of this essay, I hope that my short analysis of one telling section will suggest Johnson's approach to pedagogy as well as performance. So, too, I hope to convey in this writing something of Johnson's style, affect, and engagement. As a result, I leave it to other critics to (re)turn to the text(s) and to illuminate the missed opportunities inherent in this reading.

There are no clear binary oppositions in the show, no black and white, no divergence even between the object and subject of the performance. In many ways, one could argue that Johnson's show serves as a material ground and supplement to his other performances on the page and the stage. He works out his ideas about "quare studies," popular media, black arts, performance and performativity, globalization, pearls, and more in the span of this ninety-minute show. In fact, we learn from his introduction to the script that the entire performance began as an academic talk that, to use Johnson's words, "failed." Johnson has suggested a similar process when discussing the "addition" of his second stage show, "Pouring Tea: Black Gay Men of the South Tell Their Tales," which appeared prior to the release of his book *Sweet Tea*, upon which his show is based.[16] He was concerned that writing could not bring to life the different actions, gestures, and bodily illuminations that the men whom he interviewed performed for him. Thus, Johnson makes an argument that values bringing characters to life, through the body, so that their different gestures and mannerisms off the stage of the page enter into the performance arena. As a result, it is out of this "failure" of the words to cohere to the facts that remain inert and "flat" on the page in that sparse two-dimensional framework of print that Johnson shows the power of transformation vis-à-vis a living, live, and ultimately enlivened event. This short segment shows Johnson's potent mix of scholarly discourse, popular culture, and personal history. He interweaves understandings of his own identity with those offered up by historical and cultural detritus and creates a multivalent context through which to read his story.

Let us here turn to the literature distributed as part of the pamphlets and accompanying website of the Performance Studies international conference mentioned above (and eventually published in journal form). The literature, presented as a collective expression, asks the following questions, which can be related to Johnson's performance:

> What determines the success and what is the role of "mistake" as an unavoidable (demystifying) element, not only in the realization of a performance but also in its being perceived, appreciated, understood, and interpreted as performance?

Are there "good" and "bad," humorous and tragic, ethically and/ or aesthetically "acceptable" and "unacceptable" performance mistakes? . . .

Performance is intimately related to humor precisely though misperformance. Bergson defined the comic as the effect of mistake, failure, and quite literally, of slippage. What is the place of the comic in contemporary performance practice?[17]

Johnson's performance most directly addresses the question of comedy, a huge risk given the stereotype that *all* black performers can be comic. When one witnesses the entire show, one sees that a diverse range of motion and emotion afford Johnson and, by extension, other black gay men the freedom to be all they can be: they go beyond the limit or horizon of stereotypical expectation that would sentence them to be merely comic, or tragic for that matter, just American and not African diasporic, just effeminate and not also masculine and the like. This is yet another value of Johnson's carefully crafted show.

In the article about the piece, Johnson generously shares some production history of the show and, in the process of doing so, reveals the work that expectation and surprise along with performance and performativity do to structure such staged encounters. In this provocative autoethnographic piece, Johnson speaks for and as versions of himself. This "versioning" and impersonation are crucial to avoid the essentialist trap heralded in the opening of this essay. Among the other important interventions in the piece is Johnson's discussion of his queer or rather "quare" childhood. Enacting the prescription if not the directive offered by Eve Sedgwick's witty and brave lecture-cum-essay "How to Bring Your Kids Up Gay," Johnson puts his queer childhood on display.[18] The set piece defamiliarizes the queer as an adult sexual figure and represents a queer youth in both senses of the term. As such, Johnson provides a much-needed rejoinder to outmoded Freudian concepts that equate homosexuality with "infantile" sexuality and instead gives his audience a new way to think about the origin of sexual difference and gender performance.

Another innovation, in terms of representations of black gay men, is Johnson's candid and painful section on his time at Amherst College where he was vilified in the student newspaper and addressed disrespectfully by some of his colleagues. Incorporating tidbits from the extant archive gives gravitas to this section and shows that the academy is anything but a refuge for certain subjects. Like home or youth—or indeed blackness—it is a place or space that can both make and unmake

Fig. 5.5. Johnson dons African garb while recounting his trip to Ghana. *Strange Fruit*. Photo courtesy of E. Patrick Johnson.

you. Certainly forms of black masculinity make and unmake Johnson as he both enacts and relates various others that shape his narrative performance.

Strange Fruit intervenes in our perceptual thinking about major topics in postmodern African American studies such as diaspora, sexuality, gender, class, region, and the academy itself. It has tangible effects for both the performer and the audience. A leitmotif for the show appears in the idea of memory as well as memorialization and queer quotation. Johnson's work also addresses transnationalism in the long section he has about his travels in Ghana (see figure 5.5). Here again he attempts to expand the boundaries of blackness by defamiliarizing it from its stereotyped limits as something "homegrown" and confined to the United States. Instead, he gives us a show in which a black gay male identity can and cannot travel across time and space "intact." His misrecognition in and of Ghana changes the scope of the show and suggests, as he does in his other works, that there are many blacknesses to perform.

Scene 3

By way of conclusion, let me repeat what I said about and wrote of Johnson and Henderson's achievement in the conference "Black Queer Studies in the Millennium": "There is a motion, in theory black and queer, that is afloat, afoot, running afoul in an effort to move certain certainties." It is clear that *Strange Fruit* was and is such a motion.

Strange Fruit, the full-length solo performance, required Johnson to be multitalented: more significantly, he required himself to sing, to dance, to act, and to stage the show. During the many iterations of the performance over the last decade, Johnson became, night after night, an "actionable body," to use Tommy DeFrantz's apt neologism.[19] Such actionable bodies change the world—not only for the active doers but also for those active, archival witnesses who encounter such political, performative movements and speech.

Notes

1 Kobena Mercer, *Welcome to the Jungle* (New York: Routledge, 1994), 222.
2 For performance as "a doing and a thing done," see Elin Diamond, introduction to *Performance and Cultural Politics*, ed. Elin Diamond (New York: Routledge, 1996), 4–5.
3 See Roderick Ferguson, *Aberrations in Black: Toward a Queer of Color Critique* (Minneapolis: University of Minnesota Press, 2004).
4 See Dwight A. McBride and Jennifer DeVere Brody, "Plum Nelly: New Essays in Black Queer Studies," *Callaloo* 23, no. 1 (Winter 2000): 286–88.
5 See Jennifer DeVere Brody, "Theory in Motion: A Review of Black Queer Studies in the Millennium Conference," *Callaloo* 23, no. 4 (2000): 1274–77.
6 E. Patrick Johnson, "'Quare' Studies, or (Almost) Everything I Know about Queer Studies I Learned from My Grandmother," in *Black Queer Studies: A Critical Anthology*, ed. E. Patrick Johnson and Mae G. Henderson (Durham, NC: Duke University Press, 2005), 124–57.
7 Rebecca Schneider, *The Explicit Body in Performance* (New York: Routledge, 1997).
8 See James Baldwin, *The Price of the Ticket: Collected Nonfiction, 1948-1985* (New York: St. Martin's Press, 1985).
9 See Joan Riviere's "Womanliness as a Masquerade," *International Journal of Psychoanalysis* 10 (1929): 303–10.
10 It is interesting to note that Johnson appears as a nude on the cover of his

coedited book *Black Queer Studies: A Critical Anthology*, in Houston Spencer's aptly titled 1999 photograph "Whole."

11 Audre Lorde, *Zami: A New Spelling of My Name—A Biomythography*. Berkeley, CA: Crossing Press, 1982.

12 Hortense Spillers, "Mama's Baby, Papa's Maybe: An American Grammar Book," *diacritics* 17, no. 2 (Summer 1987): 64–81.

13 Interestingly, we await a show about his death even as Moisés Kaufman's company, Tectonic Theater, has immortalized Matthew Shepard, whom Johnson also remembers.

14 E. Patrick Johnson, "Strange Fruit: A Performance about Identity Politics," *TDR: The Drama Review* 47, no. 2 (Summer 2003): 92.

15 Marin Blažević and Lada Čale Feldman, "MISperformance," *Performance Research* 15, no. 2 (June 2010): 11.

16 E. Patrick Johnson, *Sweet Tea: Black Gay Men in the South—An Oral History* (Chapel Hill: University of North Carolina Press, 2008).

17 Program for the fifteenth Performance Studies International Conference, Psi 15: Misperformance, June 24–28, 2009, Zagreb, Croatia, available online at http://www.blogbird.nl/uploads/psi/130812085135460_psi15-program.pdf (accessed October 8, 2015).

18 Eve Kosofsky Sedgwick, "How to Bring Your Kids Up Gay," *Social Text* 29 (1991): 18–27.

19 Thomas DeFrantz, introduction to *Dancing Many Drums: Excavations in African American Dance* (Madison: University of Wisconsin Press, 2002).

CHAPTER 6

Interview with E. Patrick Johnson

Bernadette Marie Calafell

Bernadette Marie Calafell: One of the things that really strikes me about your performance is the multiple voices of women of color, whether that be your grandmother or in the use of song and even some of the references you make throughout the performance. Can you tell me a little bit about what you feel is the connection to those voices?

E. Patrick Johnson: I always wanted the piece to be an homage to not only the women in my family, like my grandmother and my mother, but also to black feminists, because I credit black feminism with my own awakening about gender and sexuality. And, so, the reason why I open the show in drag and blackface—which is pretty provocative and confronting for people—is because I wanted to try to engage a conversation about the relationship between the history of black women and black gay men, because I think there's a lot of overlap there. So, that's why I open the piece with Hortense Spillers's piece, and wanting to frame the performance that way followed by those pejorative images of black women. That was always in the back of my mind when I was putting together the piece and then, of course, my grandmother was a very important person in my life. I wrote my dissertation on her and she just taught me a lot about how to make a way out of no way or what de Certeau would call "making do." And so it was very important to me to find a way in *Strange Fruit* to honor her as well, and then of course my mother and I are very, very close—I'm the youngest, I'm her baby.

BC: I remember!

EPJ: But she had to work through my being gay in her own way and she loves my partner now . . . but that topic was not discussed for some time. And then she had to confront it when my partner and I had a commitment ceremony and she worked through it and she's fine. That's the long way of saying that black feminism, the women in my life, and the relationship between issues facing black women and black gay men anchor the piece.

BC: I think part of what is resonating, too, is this idea of the "theory of the flesh." The body plays such a prominent role in your performance. First, obviously through your actual body in performance. But also in your various discussions of hair and in the images that the audience sees. And it's so powerful because I think it really evokes for us, visually, sensorially, all these different feelings . . . the theory of the flesh that Gloria Anzaldúa and Cherríe Moraga talk about. And what Patricia Hill Collins talks about as the kind of intellectualizing in the everyday. We really see that in action through your personal narrative as well as in the images. For example, a really powerful moment for me in the performance is when you discuss your former colleague showing you the cover of his book and we can quickly see the image of the Klansman. I mean that is the theory of the flesh right there, that body knowledge. This illustrates to me the haunting and the continual presence of history and how, as people of color, we feel that through the body in ways that are kind of intertextual. So can you talk a little bit more about the importance of the body and the theories of the flesh in your work? Those intertextual moments are really striking.

EPJ: One of the reasons why I chose the title of the piece, *Strange Fruit*, is because of Billie Holiday's song "Strange Fruit" and this notion of exorcism, exorcising blackness, exorcising one's sexuality. Because this is a personal meditation and autobiographical piece, I wanted to talk about how in different contexts part of my identity was exorcised or people tried to exorcise part of my identity. And I wanted to try to find a way to do that without it being so solipsistic and sort of "me me me me me," to find a way to open it up and I was thinking about lynching and about the imagery of lynching. You have such a visceral response when you see images of lynching. And so it all came together when I decided to use all of those images up and against my own body on the stage. You have E. Patrick's body there before you, but then it's a body in relationship to the other bodies, through image, on the stage. What does it mean for me to be standing before you as this black gay man and then have this image of a Klansman? What does it mean to have me on the stage and then have this image of mammy, or a lynching, or whatever that image happens to be? I was trying to make some kind of connection between my physical body as it is before you as the audience, and the various representations of my body in history as they've been depicted mostly by white people. And so, for me the one hundred and twenty-something slides throughout the show were meant to have this ongoing dialogic, sometimes dialectic, relationship between the image that you were seeing on the projector and my own body because, as you know, I'm doing lots of things on the stage . . . undressing on the stage, I'm lifting weights on the stage, taking off the blackface, in a robe. As you said, all the senses are being used and I wanted the audience to feel that kind of sensory overload, but have my body be the through line throughout the entire performance.

BC: I think it's really powerful because in performance we're always trying to find ways to bring the body, right?

EPJ: Right.

BC: There's just a lot of work now in performative writing and such, but the intertextuality of the actual performance and your body, we feel it in a way that you don't necessarily always get with other modes of representation. So I thought that was really striking and significant. One of the things that you touched on and I'm really interested in and that I've been thinking about too with a lot of my students is this idea of the politics of personal voice within performance studies. It's what D. Soyini Madison calls this "sea of auto-ethnography." How do you negotiate the personal with the political, social, cultural? Could you say more about this within the larger politics of the field and the discipline?

EPJ: Well, I sort of want to do a throwback to 1970s feminism, that the personal is political, but I do think that there was this moment, I don't know exactly, I couldn't pinpoint a year or even a decade in which this happened, but I think it happened in the late eighties / early nineties. There was this self-reflexive turn in performance ethnography, well in ethnography in general and anthropology as well, which I think was good because, given the history of anthropology where you "go native" for the six months or year or six years, whatever, then come back and write it up . . . that's problematic. And then a number of anthropologists critiqued that and said, "What are the politics of the anthropologist's, the ethnographer's body in the field? And we need to talk about that and theorize around that." And I think that was a good thing, but I think what happened is that it went to the other extreme where the ethnography became more about the ethnographer than about the people that he or she was studying. And so what I think Soyini is pointing to is that we shouldn't call that autoethnography, that's autobiography. As opposed to autoethnography, which is using one's own community to talk about issues there rather than going outside of one's community, which is very different from just talking about myself. For *Strange Fruit*, I think it's both autobiography and autoethnography. Autobiographical in the sense that I'm sharing some of my personal stories of things that happened to me in my life, but in each of those movements—that's what I call them—there's always a point where it opens out, where I'm talking and connecting to broader issues, whether it be about slavery, or homophobia, or whatever the case may be. Within the field I think a lot of people are still trying to negotiate that tightrope, because it is very hard. It's very difficult to craft something about yourself that doesn't always turn inward. One of the ways I try to resist that is by incorporating theory, performing theory. In the middle of talking about coming out to my mother, I start talking about Judith Butler and I start quoting writers. That's a way to move it away from the personal to the political by using theory as a frame . . . and also making theory accessible.

BC: Yeah. I think you do a beautiful job in the performance with that because your story's there but we see what that means within a larger political, social, cultural context. That's one of the things that I've tried to talk to my students about . . . thinking about how theory can work with the personal voice.

EPJ: The other way I try to do that is through the other media, through the images and through the music and dance and all the other things, the voice-overs.

BC: Yes, definitely. Going off of that idea about the blending of theory in your work, you've published a lot of scholarship and performance work, and I think they come together in a nice way. That's really public scholarship, and when I'm reading, when I'm listening or I'm watching the performance, I hear the iterations of your published work and I think that's really significant. Can you talk a little bit more about that kind of relationship between the performance work and the published work, because, it's all there.

EPJ: Well, you know, it's funny that you say that because, whenever I'm writing something—an article, an essay, whatever—and I've always been this way, I never mean for it to stay on the page. I've always been a person who needs something to be performative, so my writing is performative, and so in *Strange Fruit*, there are actually chunks of the script that are lifted directly from an essay that I've written like "Feeling the Spirit in the Dark." That's a whole segment in there. For me, my written scholarship and my creative scholarship go hand in hand and they feed one another. If you were to tie me down, and not let me do one without the other, that would be the death of me. Because I really am invested in how art feeds scholarship and how scholarship feeds art. And what I love about this field is that it allows that relationship to flourish. I think it's important for people who are artists to not be afraid of theory. . . . And I think it's so important for theorists to not be afraid of art. I find, particularly in theater departments, that practitioners are always suspect of the scholars and the scholars sort of scoff at what the practitioners do. But it doesn't have to be that way. That's why I'm happy that in performance studies you don't necessarily have that divide, that binary between theory and practice. And so for my own work, everything that I do is about blurring those two genres.

BC: Can you talk a little bit about the pedagogical function of your work or the activist function or the social justice function of your work?

EPJ: What I always hope that my work does is expose certain ideas and issues to people who hadn't really thought about those ideas in that way. For instance, what does it mean for someone who was reared in the South, in public housing, to all of a sudden find themselves at a small elite college in the Northeast as a faculty member? By performing these experiences, the colleague who makes a homophobic comment or the colleague who makes some offhanded comment about there being too many football players admitted into the school or whatever . . . I think that when those moments are framed and presented, replayed before us, we really get to see why they are problematic. I'm hoping it's doing that kind of pedagogy. I'm also hoping that my creative work is exposing some of my own contradictions. For instance, given my background, why am I at this private institution? Some would see that as a contradiction: "Why aren't you at a public school given your background and your politics?" I never want my work to be seen as precious or unproblematic because I'm human and I am as vulnerable as anyone else to critique—and I think critique is good; it's what keeps us going in the academy. But what I hope ultimately is that people find some kind of resonance, or resonances, with their own lives and some of the issues that they've been working through, in my work. And sometimes that's about making them see something different, whether that be racism, classism, homophobia, or whether it's about how we as humans negotiate the contradictions in our lives. I often described *Strange Fruit* when I was performing it as a train ride and everybody starts out at the train station, and some people get on the train, some people don't, some people get on and get off at different points, some people stay for the whole ride, but it's hopefully the fact that everyone has come to the station—they've come to the theater to see it—[it] means that something about the show has sparked an interest in it and they come away with something being changed or moved or thinking about something in a different way than what they did when they first came to the theater.

BC: Could you talk a little about what performance does for queer theory and what queer theory does for performance?

EPJ: I think that both of those terms are, and this is going to sound cliché, contested terms, but they're also useful in the way in which they are employed and deployed because there's so much elasticity in the term "performance" and in "queer" and I think that's what's productive about both of them. One of the things that I think has happened, however, is that when people start to define those terms in narrow ways, that's when they become unuseful and sometimes unproductive because, for instance, in queer theory there were so many writers and theorists who wanted to privilege sexuality as the a priori identity without strongly considering the other identity markers that specifically people of color carry, or even working-class people, or gender, or all the other identities that we inhabit. That was really problematic to me and didn't speak to my own truth and my life situation. I found that performance was one way to call attention to that, and so in *Strange Fruit* you see me in all these different roles: a son, a grandson, a professor, a church boy, the preacher, the American in Ghana. All of these things pivot around my race, around my queerness, and so performance and queerness in that way are wonderful to use together in tandem because it really does call attention to the fact that identity is performative, but there are moments in which the body is situated materially, and there are material effects to inhabiting this particular and specific body. I find sometimes in queer theory and sometimes in performance theory, especially those theorists who are more interested in performativity as opposed to performance, that they forget that although, yes, my blackness is a performance, it's still a body in a particular moment in history—time, space—that at any moment it's vulnerable to violence, to threats, to whatever. And we have to talk about both. We can't just talk about performance without talking about performativity and vice versa, and we can't talk about sexuality without talking about race and class and all those other things. I think they're wonderful terms and theories that have emerged around those terms, but I think we have to be careful in how we theorize around them. So one of the ways I try to do that is use performance as a medium to do both.

BC: There's a couple of specific moments in the performance that are really compelling, particularly the moment in *Strange Fruit* is that transition from when you discuss Brent Staples, the transition to RuPaul, and then enter in the doctoral garb. That's a really powerful moment there. Can you elaborate on this part of the performance and what was informing those kinds of performative choices for you?

EPJ: There's a lot of changes onstage. I can't take credit for this term, but I refer to those costumes left onstage as "drag droppings." That's Bryant Keith Alexander's term; I have to give him credit for that. But in terms of the choices that I'm making there, that doctoral robe just came in handy so many times. When I started to use the doctoral robe to talk about when I got my PhD . . . I was like "Oh! This is the same robe that my minister uses." And when I started to do that spin I noticed how it bellowed out so that I'm on this runway. So it was this multifunctioning costume: it becomes a dress, it's a doctoral robe, it's the preacher's gown . . . and it's also the professorial garb, because I'm also talking about my experience at Amherst. So it was the multifunctionality of the costume itself that led me to those performance decisions, because moving from Brent Staples to RuPaul to the Black Arts Movement when I'm a preacher was all facilitated by the robe, even though those are very different things; that robe symbolized all of those things, in each of those movements. It was really the costume that drove those performance choices.

BC: That's interesting. Another part of the performance is where you challenge the question of authenticity. When you start discussing, say, the queen who does this, the queen who does that. This is one of the most powerful parts of the performance to me, particularly when you ask repeatedly: "Well how long? How long?" What was it like writing that piece, both in terms of the actual process as well as the kind of affective space?

EPJ: Well, I am a really big fan of the Black Arts Movement, and the poetry that came out of that period because it's so performative. But what my soul was resisting was the homophobia and the sexism of that poetry, so I wanted to find a way in *Strange Fruit* to pay homage to that period and that era, but also critique it. So "Can the Queen Speak?" is a poem, a poem/rap/sermon that I wrote to pay tribute to that period at the same time that I'm critiquing it. You're right, it's a defining moment in the performance because it goes from a kind of playful send-up of the Black Arts Movement, vis-à-vis this preacher character, to a hard-hitting, serious, almost rap/sermon. And for me it was about driving home the point that even though this period in African American history was very important, and those writers were very important, and the civil rights movement was very important, it's also important that we pay tribute to the black LGBT community that also contributed to that movement. The silence around the contributions of the black LGBT community to the civil rights movement, for me, paralleled the silence of the black church around HIV/AIDS. That's why at the end of that poem, I end with "How long? How long? How long?" which is riffing off of [Martin Luther] King, and I make some reference to T cell counts, which is about the silence around HIV/AIDS in the black community and in the black church. That is followed by those images of black LGBT activists: Audre Lorde and Marlon Riggs and Essex Hemphill, and all of those folks that came before me.

BC: Throughout *Strange Fruit* we see your discussion of politics, authenticity, community, and identity. Another part I thought was really powerful, was when you asked Edison if he likes Mariah Carey, to which he responds, "Yes, because she sounds like a black woman." And you say, "My voice is muted by the instability of my own identity—of my own conventions in reading race. The African teaches the African American to listen." And to me that is so significant in terms of authenticity and identity. Can you tell me a little bit about that moment?

EPJ: Oh God, it was so surreal, because everything about my trip to Ghana was discombobulating, because like many African Americans who take that trip over to the motherland, the homeland, you come back just sort of in a daze because it's never what you think it's going to be. And so I was called "Obruni," which translates to white man, or American, by Africans. I'm like *wait*. And then to see men holding hands, and greeting each other with a kiss . . . it was so bizarre, but this has nothing to do with sexuality. So being on a Liberian refugee camp was one experience, and meeting Edison, who was taking advantage—and I want to be careful here—who was trading on the fact that I was American and gay, even though he's not, but flirting with me to get some kind of economic gain. (And I'm still in touch with Edison, by the way, he still calls me and asks me for money.) But that line, particularly, "African teaches the African American to listen," was that moment of: You need to take your own advice about assumptions around race and culture, because after all, you've written a book on it, but here you're confronted with this whole notion of racial performativity, because Mariah Carey is black, but yet my own authenticity scale didn't have her high up on that blackness scale. And so it was a teachable moment for me, because I was being taught by Edison to not make authenticity assumptions about people's race, or how they self-identify based on my own sort of random authenticity scale. And it was a very powerful moment for me and continues to keep me on my toes about the assumptions that I make about people around race, class, gender, and all of that, and also how my Americanness is read around the world. You know, that I'm in this context, in the United States; I'm read as x-y-z, but once I leave that space I'm something else first in the eyes of the foreign other. I'm not necessarily a black queer from the South; I'm an American. And having to come to terms with that is confronting because I don't think most Americans think of their American identity, because we don't have to really confront that, whereas people who come to this country, they definitely have to confront their nationality, oftentimes I think because Americans are some of the worst bigots and xenophobes that there are in the world, but we don't necessarily have to experience that. So for me, going to Africa thinking I was going home . . . I wasn't totally naive about that, but I also didn't expect to feel as distant from Africans as I did when I went there . . . and that it would be a distance that they evoked toward me. I wasn't their brother; I was American.

BC: Yeah, and I think that's a really beautiful moment, because we see these layers, these intersectional layers, these global layers. And then that reflects this kind of performative moment.

EPJ: And that's why there's a line in there about the little girl. I'm taking a picture of her to speak to her plight, but that's still a colonial gaze. . . . So it's really complicated. And I had to work through all of that.

BC: You end this performance with such a powerful image: the door of no return, and then your silhouette and the singing. Can you talk about the choices you made in changing the last two stanzas, of four women and ending with "membership has its privileges"? That last part of the performance really . . . you feel it.

EPJ: I'll start with "the door of no return." When I was in Ghana I went to Elmina Castle in Cape Coast and saw "the door of no return." I was paralyzed by staring at it, and how narrow it is. But it is a threshold, from the Old World to the New World, from one identity to the other, from space to place in the de Certeau sense. Symbolically it was functioning on many different levels, and because that Africa scene was the last part I just wanted to use that as moving from the Old World to the New World into lynching, which brings us back to my original motivation for doing this performance, which is all about exorcism, because you know we have the middle passage and we have slavery and we have lynching, so that dance that I do behind the scrim is trying to marry all of that history and bring us up to the present. . . . We've just gone through the door of no return, which is in Africa, and gone through the middle passage and slavery. Nina Simone's song "Four Women" is talking about these different types of women—the sapphire, the mammy, et cetera—but I also change one of the names of the women to Matthew Shepard and try to show the relationship between sexuality and feminism, and so on. I also wanted to move away from a focus solely on blackness and gayness by showing how Matthew Shepard was murdered speaks to the way in which black people have been murdered. So replacing the last line of the song, "My name is Peaches," with "My name is Faggot" was a way to make a connection between the epithets women are called—"Peaches" is slang for "whore"—and those that gay people are called, and that I have been called. Thus, I embody Matthew Shepard, I embody those black men and women that have been lynched, and I embody the faggot, all of that—to talk about the body—it's all there in me. I end with that image of lynching because those people were lynched because they didn't have the privilege of membership. And so membership does have its privileges. And it actually brings us back to the beginning of the performance, where I'm handing out these American Express cards and the symbol in the middle of the card is a bag with a hand coming out of it and it says "trick or treat" and the name is "Dr. A. Negro." And then the credit card number is all of these significant dates in black American history, like 1865, 1955, all strung together. And the expiration date is "contingent." So, yeah, there's a lot going on at the end of the performance, and I don't know if everybody's getting what's going on. The other thing about shows that I do is I like to add layers of stuff, to give people enough to sort of chew on, to try to figure out "What is all of this going on?" I hate didactic performances, and it's so easy to do that, so I wanted to have these different layers, and that's why the Africa scene is the most poetic and symbolic. . . . There's a lot of symbolism going on there, it's not necessarily literal in any way.

BC: Where do you see your work going in the future? And the other question that goes off of that is: At the end of the day, what do you want people to remember about E. Patrick Johnson?

EPJ: I don't know where my work is going, except to say that I always want to do work that is political, and not political in obvious ways, but political in a sense that it's bringing voice to people who may not have the status or privilege to give voice to their own stories, that's what my new work is doing. I always want my work to be smart and not just thrown together without being considered and being workshopped. I also want my work to be fun. Even in the darkest moments of *Strange Fruit*, of which there are some, I think there's always humor; I think humor is a healing agent, even for those things that are really difficult. And I also want my work to last over time. I don't want it to be something that no one remembers. And in terms of where my work is going, I don't know, I sort of let the muse perch on my shoulder and tell me.

Part IV

Ah mén

Javier Cardona

Translated by Andreea Micu and Ramón H. Rivera-Servera

Ah mén is a hybrid dance-theater piece in which six actor-dancers get dressed and cross-dressed to explore and critique "masculinities" through dance, theater, music, and video. This written text only contains the words uttered by the actor-dancers (verbal text), and some stage directions. Of all the choreographies and visual documents that are generally projected onto a backdrop screen as a part of the piece, you will only see titles, in chronological order, and the music cues that accompany them.

Ah mén premiered in May 2004 at the Puerto Rican Institute of Culture's 45th Puerto Rican Theater Festival. In January 2005, it was showcased at the International Festival Teatro a Mil and the 5th Feria de Artes Escénicas del Cono Sur, in Santiago, Chile. *Ah mén* has also toured across university campuses of the University of Puerto Rico system.

PROCESIÓN/PROCESSION (THEATER ACTION)

Theater is in the dark. The song "El Dios nunca muere" by Les Miserables Brass Band becomes audible. Gradually, a procession of four men appears marching upstage following the beat of the tuba with each step. The group is dressed formally in slacks and blazers, carrying a fifth man's rigid body upside down. All are wearing nylon stockings over their heads, giving them a "Coneheads" look. The march-procession ends in front of the audience. The group slowly turns the man they've been carrying up and over the shoulders and down the back of one of the carriers and he lands, feet on the ground, facing the audience. The rest turn with him and, crouching, slowly remove the stockings from their faces. Milton, the man who has been carried stage front, speaks to the audience as the others embrace behind him.

Fig. IV.1. *Ah mén*. Photo by Miguel Villafañe, courtesy of Javier Cardona.

MILTON	Helping the child to reach freedom and responsibility is extremely difficult in a society that does not define men through universally accepted texts. It was through ancient tales and books that, for a long time, men were taught their inherent obligations to life. Those sacred texts fed culture with customs, traditions, rites, rules and even absolute truths. But, unfortunately, today our children and youngsters are currently growing up in confusion, without a culture grounded in texts such as the Bible, the Torah, the Quran—which is so in style—or some other volume of mythological tales.
	But without getting too abstract, and in order for you to understand why I'm saying all this, tonight I have here the Warriors for You Theater Company. *(asks for a round of applause for the group)* And we'll have one of the group members tell us why they are here. Carlos, come over and tell us!
CARLOS	*(to the audience, with youthful energy)* Greetings and good evening everyone! We are a bunch of young people going to different communities with a mission. We bring you theater as a present. This play—which is a surprise—is part of the "Intervening in Your Community" project. Willy Colón tells us in one of his songs **(With restrained enthusiasm the bunch of young people next to Carlos utters the following as if delivering a creed)**: "Palo que nace doblao jamás su tronco endereza" (A tree born crooked shall never straighten its trunk) **(Carlos continues)** But I have to confess to you, my brothers, that ever since we began this project we've straightened up hundreds of trunks. **(Milton and the young men clap cheerfully)**
MILTON	Fantastic!
CARLOS	Milton, if you allow me, I'd like to thank Stream of Life, Inc. and Pro Seed, among others, for being a source of inspiration. Because they are pushing us every day to get involved in this, vigorously. I hope you enjoy what we're presenting you tonight with all our love and respect. Thank you very much. *(applause)*

MILTON	Let's give the boys a few minutes to get ready and then we'll start. (*Carlos, Milton, and the others exit and the performance begins*)
GROUP	(*We hear a group of actors backstage*) Eeeeeeeeeeeeeehuaa!

HOTWEELLYS (CHOREOGRAPHY)

With music by Edward Grieg, "Peer Gynt"—Suite No. 1, Op. 46, "Morning" three men return to the stage, still in their blazers, slacks, and nylon stockings. They enter quickly, mimicking the light steps and flowing, fluttering arm movements of ballerinas to match the flautist's notes. One of them is holding Pedrito sleeping in his arms. Trying not to awake the child, he places him in the arms of one of his partners while the third dancer, bent down to one knee, flaps his arms graciously in their direction. Pedrito is again handed off to another dancer as the two unburdened men playfully hush the crowd before helping as Pedrito is gently laid on the floor. They preen over the sleeping boy until Mother-Woman enters suddenly with a broom, industrious as always, and herself preens for the audience. She doesn't see them men as she begins to sweep, but they see her and flee, terrified. She sweeps and spins grandly in her large, billowing skirt. She smiles as she brushes the last corner of the stage, exiting as a voice-over begins.

LA OBRA (THEATER ACTION)

Along with the music, we hear the narrative—voice-over—of a female voice with the "stereotypical" intonation of children's storytelling.

"Once upon a time, there was a very poor woman who lived with her son Pedrito. They had Fortunata, a strong healthy cow that produced lots of milk. But, because they were ignorant, they didn't know what to do with all the milk Fortunata produced. Then, one good day, Pedrito's mom decided it was time to sell the cow." (*During the "voice-over" the Mother-Woman returns to the stage with a basket tied with the end of a long, heavy rope. She takes out a red-checkered picnic blanket and two glasses that she fills with a pint of fresh milk. When all is set, the Mother-Woman calls Pedrito, who is still sleeping. While waiting for him to wake and stagger over, she does her morning reading: How to Win Friends and Influence People, by Dale Carnegie.)*

MOTHER-WOMAN   Pedrito, Pedrito . . . *(Pedrito wakes up, lazily stands up, and walks towards the picnic. While they have breakfast, the Mother-Woman tells him . . . , with sadness.)* It's time to get rid of Fortunata. *(She unties the rope from the basket and hands one end to her son. The other end of the rope is never revealed.)* So, you take her to the market and turn her to whomever pays you the most. This way we'll be able to improve our quality of life. *(Pedrito pulls the length of the rope across the stage, waving farewell to Mother-Woman as he does. She grabs the middle of the rope, yanking it to encourage the other end's movement and Pedrito turns and gallops off stage. The Mother-Woman also exits. Pedrito returns onstage, humming "Tengo una vaca lechera" and playfully spinning the rope's end. He is stopped in his tracks as an ominous but sweet, god-like voice begins calling his name.)*

OLD MAN   P-e-d-r-i-t-o, P-e-d-r-i-t-o . . . Where are you going with Fortunata?

PEDRITO   *(Slightly confused, Pedrito looks for the origin of such a mysterious voice. A repetitious bang sounds the arrival of a human shape wearing a floor-length furry coat with a hood. Pedrito answers, afraid but curious.)* To the market, to sell it. Mom says it's time.

OLD MAN   Humm!, so it's time? . . . *(Taking bold steps across the stage, he licks his index finger and points it to the sky to determine the direction of the wind. He hurries a few more steps and throws himself to the ground to place his ear on the floor. With agitation, rummages the floor then tries to stand up asking for Pedrito's help. Walks away.)* Come, look what I have here. *(He opens his coat majestically and shows a bag of beans tied to his belt. He sings an open note loudly and with vibrato, hailing this revelation. He continues singing while Pedrito runs back and forth in awe and confusion.)* I'll give it to you in exchange for Fortunata.

PEDRITO   *(looks at him but quickly turns his gaze away)* Are you crazy! Mom will kill me if I go back home with that.

OLD MAN	(takes the bag, cups it in his hand, and extends it upward in Pedrito's direction) Oh, but they are magic! And they're worth more than money, kid. So come on, dare, try and be brave, don't be afraid. You can do it!
PEDRITO	(Almost hypnotized, Pedrito reaches out with his hand, slowly approaching the Old Man. He simultaneously drops the rope and takes the bag from the man's hand. The rope falls to the ground and, as if alive, retreats from the stage. Now Pedrito has the bag in his hands.) Thank you!
OLD MAN	My pleasure, kid. (Then, offstage, we hear the Warriors Theater Company singing the tune of "Bippity Boppity Boo" from **Cinderella** as Pedrito joyfully skips around stage)
PEDRITO	(Pedrito cups his hands to yell good-bye to the Old Man from across the stage, as if a big valley separates them) Good-bye, good man! (He continues to skip and dance his way home)
OLD MAN	Go on! (answers while both exit the stage in different directions)

The Woman-Mother enters the stage holding a vibrant, operatic note. She grabs her skirt and dances with high-kneed excitement when Pedrito's voice cuts in to announce his return home.

PEDRITO	(yelling) Mom, Mom . . . !
MOTHER-WOMAN	(Mother-Woman looks out the imaginary window and sees her son coming back. She runs to welcome him. When they meet, they grab each other's hands and spin around many times, laughing loudly. When they finally let go of each other's hands, they are pleasantly dazed from the spinning.) Ay, my bionic little man. Look at me in the eye. (approaches him with open arms) No matter what, I want you to remember something: I love you! (She hugs him furiously, sobbing)
PEDRITO	Ay Mommy . . . me too. (They hug each other tighter)
MOTHER-WOMAN	(Thunder is heard. Abruptly, Mother-Woman lets go of Pedrito and, keeping her back to him, she wanders the stage exasperated and muttering to herself. Tries to smile, and like

speaking to herself, says) I'm such a fool. *(Finally, she ad-dresses Pedrito)* Tell me, how much did you get? *(Mother-Woman notices Pedrito is weeping. She looks about in case someone is watching her and crosses over to him. She lightly slaps at his hands and pulls him aside. Drying his tears and adopting a tone of concern.)* What would your father say if he could see you like this? *(She steps away from her son and sighs before shifting to a happier tone)* So, tell me, how much did you get for Fortunata?

PEDRITO   *(with enthusiasm)* Guess?

MOTHER-WOMAN   *(nervous but playful)* Ay Pedrito, stop playing around and tell me already, I'm so anxious.

PEDRITO   Okay, okay, okay, okay *(Pedrito makes a wild cartwheel that ends with his arms in the air and he shouts ta-daaaaa! Stepping, turning and making stereotypical karate-chopping sounds, he uses both hands to point to the bag of beans tied to his belt from a variety of different positions.)*

MOTHER-WOMAN   What's that? *(confused)*

PEDRITO   *(proudly pointing to his belt)* Mom, what do you think?

MOTHER-WOMAN   B . . . but . . . What's that bag? *(still confused)*

PEDRITO   *(happy)* It's mine . . . *(worried to see that Mother-Woman is annoyed)* . . . And yours too! *(Tries to hand the bag to her. She steps back, rejecting him.)*

MOTHER-WOMAN   *(desperate, about to pass out)* A bag of be . . . ?

PEDRITO   *(very worried)* But Mom . . . they're ma . . . gic . . .

MÁMATE (CHOREOGRAPHY)

Mother-Woman begins to physically break down and the sounds of deep bass drums play. She thrusts her chest downwards and throws her arms down with the sonic rumble of Alberto Ginastera's "Invocación a los espíritus poderosos." She dances in angry exasperation, taking up the whole stage with her movements that variously pummel the air, stomp the ground and run laps around the stage. She pauses near Pe-drito, who is cowering, and continues her rampage by throwing flailing punches through the air as she crosses the stage. Slowing, finally, she twirls toward Pedrito and takes the bag of beans from him and dramatically throws it to the ground. The bag is torn. Seeds are scattered all over the stage. She herself falls down, exhausted, crying. Milton enters with the Warriors for You Theater Company.

REFLEXIÓN (THEATER ACTION)

MILTON (to the audience) Pedro and His Beans! A big round of applauses for these actors, c'mon! (*The actors playing Pedrito and Mother-Warrior clasp right hands and clap each other on the back with their left. Mother-Warrior jumps lightly from right to left foot, like a boxer, as a young man from the Warriors for You Theater Company rubs his shoulders. They are all proud.*)

(*Milton brings Jorge closer to the audience*) I'd like to pause for a moment to thank Jorge in particular, for his composure, because this stallion has the courage to play the role of the mother, day after day, only to spread a message that is just and necessary. And let me assure you, he's not at all confused about who he is. Jorge, boys, thank you! (*Jorge and Pedrito grasp each other and exit proudly, satisfied for having accomplished mission*)

(*One of the young men in the group puts a wireless microphone on Milton. Milton starts his speech over.*) After enjoying such a convincing presentation, I'd like to reflect some about it. Meanwhile, boys, let's clean up this mess of seeds here, but do pay attention. (*The young men from the Warriors for You Theater Company enter with brooms. They start sweeping the floor as the background music by Arvo Pärt, "Silouans Song," begins to play. One of them sets up a lectern in the middle of the stage with a plastic base that looks like a Greek column. The lectern is held together and stabilized by stainless steel wire. On top of the lectern/column lies a big, bulky book. Milton will lean over this tome from time to time during his speech. Before they finish their task and exit the stage, Milton begins delivering his monologue.*)

Although this theater piece is over, I'd like to begin my reflection talking about theater. As I was watching these boys act, I was wondering . . .—and I share it with you—Why is it that we have theater, huh? What's the goal of the performing arts if not to be our weapon to incite, to spread the word? But, my friends, while we're here together using theater to spread the message, at this very moment, sodomites and other kinds of perverts walk around with their hidden agendas, trying to confuse us with immoralities and to destroy our basic institution. That's why Jorge, Carlos, Rodolfo, Ricky and all the other boys have to keep at it. (*yells in a military fashion*) Warriors!

GROUP   Yes!

MILTON   Warriors!

GROUP   Forever!

MILTON   Don't give up!

GROUP   No, sir!

MILTON   Don't surrender!

GROUP   No, sir!

MILTON   Now, what just happened here, huh? What is the subtle parable that we get from this magnificently staged story? Is this just about the stupid behavior of a brat? No. If we possess some rational intelligence, we'll be able to see beyond that. Here, we have a mother-woman that trusts her Pedrito's sense of responsibility about the selling of Fortunata, because she naturally feels it's time to bring out a new man from under his wet bed sheets.

In Fortunata, the cow, we have our metaphor: she produces milk. A predominantly feminine image, although not exclusively, since other things also produce milk. On the other hand, we have the Old Man that gives the boy a bag. An obviously masculine image. No offense, but these bags, I mean . . . sorry, this bag!, contains the seeds! Which is nothing other than . . . what brings life. Bag, seed, life! Seed, bag, life! Behold the blunt vigorous metaphor that is revealed before us.

When we intellectualize this apparently simple story, we tap into a rite of passage. The Old Man, or Old Gentleman as the wise surrogate of the absent father (*comes to his mind*) Freud . . . ! Just so you see how even psychology is a part of this . . . has given the seeds of life to the boy, testosterone among them—elementary biology. In the meantime, the boy, as an exchange, from man to man, gives him Fortunata. Which is nothing other than . . . What is Fortunata in all this? What is Pedrito giving away when he gives away Fortunata? Breastfeeding! Fussiness! Bad habits! And it's only then that Pedro—not Pedrito—is on his way to becoming a great man.

Let's look at Mother-Woman's reaction. Look at the multidimensionality of all this. The mother becomes hysterical. This is a very normal reaction in a woman. But seeing her as just perturbed would be to underestimate her. She's doing her job, even if she doesn't say it, even if she suffers in silence. It's time to stop being hypocrites and stop victimizing our women, our partners in struggle. Nature is not democratic, no matter how much we're led to believe it is. Things have an order for a reason. That's why she's been created. In all this, she is part of a bigger plan. It's why we should not be surprised at the sentimental scene—when she hugs the boy, tells him she loves him (*Milton runs across the stage with his arms open wide in preparation for a hug*), she's really saying good-bye to that weak, passive, sentimental, co-dependent, infant without responsibilities.

Ahhh!, and I know you could say that she's mean because she punished him on purpose. I want to tell you something, and I hope you don't misunderstand this reflection. Punishment is healthy, even physical punishment. Some lashing with the belt, a good slap in the face is never too much. Quite the opposite, they make our boys stronger and they activate their self-esteem, their sense of self.

Let me give you a specific example. (*takes some time to think, looking at the big book that is on top of the lectern*) Okay. Imagine your son goes to war. That's not so difficult to imagine, so imagine that. Imagine your son goes to war and the enemy takes him prisoner. You know that our military has a code of honor and that they hold secret, vital security information, both national and international. Look, when exposed to physical and

psychological torture by the enemy, your son will automatically remember the punishments and deprivations
he suffered as a child and that will give him strength
and focus. Because he'll know that his unbreakable manhood is being tested again. If he doesn't survive, he'll die,
as a martyr, for the freedom of others. But he'll be remembered as a hero.

My brothers, in *Pedrito and His Beans*, the Mother-
Woman punishes her son, but only to conceal the deeper
truth. Because when she throws the bag of beans to the
ground, she's really breaking the cycle, allowing her son
to free himself and initiate the arduous road to masculinity. (*Lights and sound begin breaking down*) ¡And that,
my brothers, is an act of ma . . . ! (*Lights go dark; we cannot see Milton anymore. We only hear his voice, without the
microphone.*) Hello . . . , lights! Jorge, lights! Jorge! Boys!
Oh my God . . . Boys . . . Maybe there's a blown fuse?
Boys . . . Ey, lights . . . , here. Lights . . . For God's sake . . .
ligh . . . (*We can't hear Milton anymore*)

FROM THE TIPI (THEATER ACTION AND CHOREOGRAPHY)

In the dark the music begins again: sinister high notes of a violin.

HIM	God has run out of light.
YOU	That's cool, I was getting really bored.
HIM	Me too.
YOU	Let's play.
HIM	Indians and cowboys!
YOU	Oh Yes!
HIM	I'm the cowboy.
YOU	Oh, but I wanted . . .
HIM	No, no . . . you're the Indian.
YOU	But you don't look like a cowboy either.
HIM	Neither do you.

Ah mén **253**

YOU	Oh man . . . Okay, but then it's my turn after.
HIM	Okay, (*short pause*) Pa!, Pa! . . . I killed you.
YOU	What! We haven't started yet!
HIM	Oh yes.
YOU	Oh no. (*short pause*) So you missed!
HIM	(*annoyed*) Ah no, I killed you.
YOU	Okay, okay . . . You wounded me!
HIM	But, how do you wanna play Indians and cowboys if you're not letting yourself die?
YOU	You die.
HIM	Cowboys don't die.
YOU	Liar!
HIM	Haven't you seen the movies?
YOU	I don't know how to die.
HIM	Then learn.
YOU	Why don't you die?
HIM	I've done it before.
YOU	Liar.
HIM	Look, the truth is, the truth is one doesn't die at all. Just . . . a little bit. It's . . . like . . . ay, I don't know, forget it . . . anyway . . . at the end you feel really good.
YOU	I don't get it. (*short pause*) Does it hurt?
HIM	Ummmm . . . , yes and no.
YOU	What do you mean, yes and no?
HIM	Is like . . . , going to heaven! You suffer a little bit, but then . . .
YOU	You haven't been to heaven!
HIM	I know, but they say it's awesome.

YOU	(*short pause, hesitant*) Okay. Let's die, just a little bit. But both of us.
HIM	Together?
YOU	Yes, at the same time.
HIM	Aren't you a man?
YOU	Yes, but we're not playing that.
HIM	Well, yes, a little. Indians and cowboys are men.
YOU	Yes but . . . Come on, don't you want to?
HIM	Well . . . yes . . . but . . .
YOU	Aren't we friends?
HIM	Uhum. (*short pause*) Okay. Together. But just a little death.
YOU	Just a little. Oh, please. Wasn't you the one who died before?

The music plays and lights come back on. "Addio Colonnello" and "Per Qualche Dollaro In Piú" by Ennio Morricone. "You" and "Him" stand side by side in dim lighting. They stuff their hands in the pockets of their track pants, stopping and staring before engaging in simultaneous kinetic, gymnastic movements. They variously sit, roll, run, and lunge in a small circuit onstage. Their movements become increasingly athletic as the Spaghetti Western sounds of a mouth-harp and whistle take over the classical music. Soon, Him circles You, who is standing with eyes closed and vibrating, and joins in. Their dance becomes increasingly athletic, if aggressive. Their athletic stretching and exercising poses morph to rhythmic pelvic thrusts. They grasp each other by the shoulders and put their heads together and down in the typical start position of a wrestling match. Breaking briefly to give each other pounds, they return here before sauntering to the opposite end of the stage. They sit then lie down next to each other, exhausted.

HIM	You know what? I liked it.
YOU	Me too.
HIM	Oh God, look . . . lights are back. (*both standing up*)

YOU	Oh yeah, what a crap.
HIM	What's that? (*walking toward an object that is placed in the corner of the stage*)
HIM	A chain!
YOU	(*picks up a thick golden chain with a medallion*) Wow, it's so cool!
HIM	(*trying to take it away from him*) Lemme see it.
YOU	I found it. (*You dodges Him's advance. You starts walking, paying attention to the chain and medallion. Him follows You.*)
HIM	I wasn't gonna take it. Daddy has one that's cooler than that one. (*They exit*)

AH MÉN (VIDEO)

Actor enters pushing a baby stroller. The lights dim as video projection comes from the stroller. In the video, we see pictures of male chests featuring chains and big metalic medallions. The deep bass guitar lines and congos that play are from Blo's "Chant to Mother Earth." This visual document is a photographic project made in Puerto Rico and New York City between 2002 and 2004. When the projection comes to an end, lights come up slowly with the music "Deconstruct Me" by Lume Lume. The Nudo (Tipo 2) choreography starts.

Progresively, we see the rest of the segments-pieces that compose the show.

NUDO (TIPO 2) (CHOREOGRAPHY)

Music: "Deconstruct Me" by Lume Lume

DES-VISTO O DES-NUDO/DRESSED OR NUDE (CHOREOGRAPHED THEATER ACTION)

Two men wearing only white briefs are in the middle of the stage, facing opposite directions but each holds his arms locked together above his head. They twist rapidly from the waist up, grunting with the exertion. They begin to dance separately but similarly articulating stretches of arms and legs that highlight their long and lean bodies. They create short phrases with their bodies: a boxer's stance, an arm raised like a crane, crouched leaps that carry them across the stage. They incorporate rigid interpretations of yoga poses such as Tree and Downward Facing Dog. At times their movements come together, but break down eventually, as when they move into a comical shuffle toward center stage. The lights dim and a spotlight centers on one long, lean dancer with a shaved head who begins a sprightly solo to the sparse music. He is alone onstage as he dances. In a modified Downward Facing Dog, he wiggles his whole body to lie flat on the floor and he rolls side to side.

A man dressed in blue enters and stumbles upon the body on the floor, lying still, face down, and dressed only in underwear. He stops, stares at him, looks everywhere, comes closer with a certain curiosity. Using his foot, he pokes the body softly. The dancer lying on the floor doesn't react. Using his foot, the standing dancer pokes him again and turns him face up. He steps back, cautious. He stares. Comes closer again. Hesitant, he places his hand upon the other's chest, perhaps to feel his heart. Then, he brings his ear closer to the other's chest. Listens. Stands up quickly. Picks up the dancer from the floor, and helps him on his feet. Now the motionless dancer's body becomes animate and the two slowly reverse roles. The dancer, now mobile, places the other on the floor and walks away to collect a set of blue clothing from a dancer who has entered the stage.

VUELA/FLY (STRUCTURED IMPROVISATION)

Music: "La costura de Dios" by Gustavo Cerati

As the man begins to dress himself in blue, the lights come up and a lone drum beat plays, music by Gustavo Cerati, "La costura de Dios." Three more performers dressed in blue enter and circle the stage with their eyes fixed on the motionless body. After a while, the group comes together and picks the performer up from the floor and lifts him over their heads. The performer comes alive but as if asleep, turning and flipping in the air in a dream stage facilitated by the hands of the other men in the group. They bring him down. He lands inside the group, becoming a part of it. The actor-dancers weave their hands together, maintaining the circle in counterbalance. They let go of the hands and, suddenly, drop down to the floor. The group splits in two trios.

Fig. IV.2. *Ah mén.* Photo by Ricardo Alcaraz, courtesy of Javier Cardona.

RECOLECTORES/COLLECTORS (CHOREOGRAPHY)

Silently, the two trios start dancing simultaneously two different versions of the same basic choreography that features kinetic chains of movements instigated by full-body rolls, body balances and claps. Often the dancers toss their companions through space, only to have the third in the trio stop the motion and toss him in another direction. The two trios' movements are often replicates, executed similarly but separated by only moments. Eventually, one of the trios stops moving, and while watching the other trio in their execution of the choreography, starts singing together.

CHOIR   "Señor te ofrecemos el vino y el pan, y así recordamos tu cena pascual." ("Dear lord, we offer you the wine and the bread, and this way we remember your paschal supper.")

At the end of this choreographic sequence the two groups switch places, the trio that was dancing is now watching and singing, while the other one dances. They execute similar movements as the previous dancers: stark, sharp lines as their bodies are variously pulled from the ground and held atop the bodies of their brothers. Soon, the singing group joins in the dancing and after that, as both trios are now dancing separately but together, they also sing together. The trios trade places as the singers turn dancers and the dancers turn singers, kneeling, watching and singing gravely. When they conclude singing they begin dancing once more and both trios perform the same movements at the same time. The six are soon dancing in silence, concluding the final set of movements at the same time: one dancer is held by the hands, face up with feet on the ground. Each trio runs across the stage rapidly several times before two members leave the stage altogether. The remaining four arrange themselves in a stark square as new music begins to play.

ENDEREZA/STRAIGHTEN UP

To the sounds of the piano and violin of Drumhead's "Autobody," the four dancers, two in dark blue uniforms and two in light blue, begin dancing in similar movements that are only slightly off-beat from one another. The sharpness of rapid leaps and claps transition into slow balances on one foot. This short piece ends with the dancers jogging as a group around the stage. Three leave the stage and one is confronted by a new dancer who has emerged from the shadows.

Music: "Autobody" by Drumhead

SALSITA RARA (CHOREOGRAPHY)

The two actor-dancers walk around the stage and have the following exchange.

ACTOR-DANCER 1   Keep fucking with me, I'ma punch you.

ACTOR-DANCER 2   Look that asshole has never written shit. (*Both men hit the ground with their hand simultaneously, and begin to dance to the tune "Por el pecho no" by El Gran Combo de Puerto Rico. Their movements are exaggerated elongations—in time and physicality—of the salsa movements inspired by the playful horns of the music. They dance side by side; over the course of four beats they may step only twice, throwing their legs high in the air and twisting their bodies out in movements reminiscent of partner-dancing. Actor-dancer 2 finishes the duet by throwing his partner suddenly to the ground. The "Gigante coraje" choreography starts.*)

With his partner lying on the ground, the dancer begins gesturing as if sword-in-hand. A series of strong man poses are followed by his bracing his body over his partner's, kicking each leg out as if goading a skateboard to roll. He pauses, watching his partner as if assessing his still body. Jumping up again, he swings his arms and balances on either foot as if on a tightrope before exiting the stage with the strong slow steps borrowed from a Western movie.

Music: "Amor maldito" by Corporación Latina

PRIMERA HORDA (CHOREOGRAPHY—BOLERO WITH NEWSPAPER IN HAND)

Music: "Amor maldito" by Corporación Latina; "Caballo pelotero" by El Gran Combo de Puerto Rico

PLAY STATION (THEATER ACTION AND CHOREOGRAPHY)

Carrying briefcases, the cast enters the stage. They ready to wait. They may be at an urban train station or some bus stop. They just wait, newspapers poised in front of their spaces. In a slow two-step they sway their hips gently and move in a 180 degree turn. The newspapers become unbearable, confusing presences attached to their faces and the dancers' bodies arch backward as if burdened by a heavy load. They slowly land on their backs, casting the newspapers aside and punching the air with their arms and feet aggressively. The four move together on their backs until the fifth eventually returns to life again. They rotate through a series of shared movements on the ground, leaping up to become a set of jockeys in the midst of a horse race and ending quietly strolling with their briefcases. Man 2 enters with a flower-print briefcase singing to himself a song from the soundtrack of the film "Un homme et une femme" (A Man and a Woman) by Claude Lelouch. The men in the group spot him and stare at him with gravity, uncomfortably. One of them—Man 3—smiles slightly like approving of the briefcase with big flower-print.

MAN 1   (to Man 2) Hey, hey, you. *(asking about the briefcase that Man 2 has)* What's that?

MAN 2   *(as if searching for a coherent answer)* I left in a hurry and . . . that's the first thing I grabbed.

MAN 1	(with disdain) It doesn't suit you. "Birds of a feather . . ."
MAN 2	Yeah, yeah . . . "Flock together" . . . I'm metrosexual. (keeps walking but turns around to ask the group) Is it here where one's supposed to wait? (The group makes an affirmative gesture to his question. He walks towards the group, places his briefcase next to the other briefcases, and waits with them.)
MAN 3	(discreetly, smelling himself and smelling around him, makes a comment) It stinks like macho!
MAN 1	(confrontational) You said something?
MAN 3	¿Me? No. (A certain tension has built up in the group. After trying to go unnoticed for a while, picks up his briefcase to leave.)
MAN 1	(to the group) Go look what he has there. (Group grabs him. After some struggle Man 4 takes the briefcase from Man 3, checks its content and finds out he has a stuffed little pig, which surprises everyone. There's astonishment, laughter, shame, discomfort, and anger within the group of men.)
MAN 4	(teasing Man 3) Oh, look at that, a little pink toy! Oink, oink.
MAN 3	Give me that.
MAN 1	(aggressively, takes the toy away from Man 4 and from a distance offers it to Man 3) Do you want it? C'mon, take it.

When Man 3 steps to grab the toy the whole group jumps on him. The men start beating him up in choreography. After a while, Man 4 takes some Hulk-like giant fists out of the briefcase.

MAN 1	(loudly, to the audience, with arms and hands open over the head as if he was talking to the crowd in a Roman coliseum) I have a hand with five fingers that I can bring together in a fist! (Man 4 puts one of the giant fists on him) I have another hand with . . . ! (Man 4 interrupts)
MAN 4	(reading out loud the instructions for use that he finds inside of one of the giant fists) "Caution: Intended for dress-

up fantasy play only. Do not strike any person, animal or object."

MAN 1   (takes the fist away from Man 4 and hits him in the face with it) You speak when pigs fly!

The group makes Man 3 stand up. He is visibly hurt. Strongly, Man 1 hits Man 3 twice with his giant fists. These blows make Man 3 fly with the impulse of the group's movement lifting him. Man 3 ends up knocked out on the floor. The group of men exists.

LA LINDA MANITA

Three dancers return to the stage and dance aggressively to the blown out vocals of "Interludio" by J-Squad. They dance around the beaten Man 3, pointing their fierce bodies in the direction of his limp body. They boast. The music cuts out and they briefly kneel to sing a lullaby. The music comes back and they shake their risen fists in triumph.

Music: "Interludio" by J-Squad

PATO

The aggressive dancers leave the stage just before Man 3 retur consciousness and crawls himself into a sitting position. He writhes across the stage in pain while a man sits silently dragging a rubber chicken towards him from across the stage. As Man 3 moves he works himself into stronger and stronger poses—though he is never able to fully stand. He crouches his way to the chicken and lies down grasping it.

Music: "Silence the Tongues of Prophecy" by Qubais Reed Ghazala; "Poverty" by John Zorn

FLOCKING

The lights go totally black and four dancers stripped down to their blue pants and red tank tops engage in elegant and quiet movements. One leaves almost immediately, and two others join as quickly. Taking up the breadth of the stage, they move in unison. The short piece ends with all five crouched as the lights raise.

Music: "Aart to Have" by Steve Roche

*Still in their crouches, the five dancers throw themselves to the ground
before the music can begin. Only the sounds of their feet and shoulders hitting the ground punctuate the space. For many movements the
dancers' full weight rests on their left arms. They are stilted but strong
gestures that find the dancers pushing and shoving their weight across
the floor. Soon, a man enters with pants for everyone. They strip down
to their underwear and change clothes. The seams are ripped out of
each pair of pants. The dancers gather the torn pant legs and tie them
into elaborate briefs as the music begins. This final piece is slow, deliberate, mournful. The dancers move gracefully, following the movement
of a knee or hand with all of their attention. They rest. They face the
same direction, sitting with their arms braced upon their raised knees
and the lights dim.*

Music: "1/1," *Music for Airports*, by Brian Eno

THE END

CHAPTER 7

Homosociality and Its Discontents

PUERTO RICAN MASCULINITIES IN JAVIER CARDONA'S *AH MÉN*

Celiany Rivera-Velázquez and Beliza Torres Narváez

Javier Cardona has a long artistic trajectory as an actor, dancer, and cho-reographer. He has been identified as one of the most influential voices engaged in dialogues about race in contemporary Puerto Rican perfor-mance.[1] In his performance piece, *Ah mén*, he and his collaborators—Jesús Miranda, José Álvarez, Yamil Collazo, Lidy López, and Eduardo Alegría—trouble Puerto Rican masculinities by challenging notions of rigidity, virility, and violence associated with Latino macho swagger. *Ah mén* offers a unique and necessary exploration of gender performance on the Puerto Rican stage by exploring and, at times, even mocking the investment that Christian religiosity has in heterosexual masculinities. The piece also illustrates the negotiation of same-gender desire during sexual awakening and childhood play, establishing a clear link between hypermasculinity and homophobic violence. *Ah mén* achieves all of this without ever explicitly claiming to be talking about gay or queer iden-tities.

Cardona is best known for his 1996 solo performance *You Don't Look Like*, in which he presented a fierce critique of the ways blackness is set apart and often erased from the Puerto Rican national imaginary.[2] In *You Don't Look Like* Cardona staged a delicate interplay between satire and reality that prompted audiences to rethink deeply rooted cultural assumptions that marked blackness as other. By exploring the relation-ship between the racialized body and the limitations of its represen-tation, he prompted audiences to critically engage with colonial and colonizing tropes of the black body as uncivilized, hypersexualized, or dangerous to the viability of the Puerto Rican nation.

To question racist stereotypes in Puerto Rico is to challenge the nation-building process itself. In *Ah mén* Cardona continues to ask simi-lar questions about the idealized constructions of Puerto Rican bodies by focusing on the prescription, transmission, and enforcement of nor-

Fig. 7.1. *Ah-mén*. Photo by Ricardo Alcaraz, courtesy of Javier Cardona.

mative masculinities as maintained by social institutions such as the family, church, school, and the state. Indeed, *Ah mén* challenges heterosexism by exploring how same-gender, especially male-centered, social arenas can never be fully disentangled from queer readings or practices because the boundaries between the social and the sexual are always blurry. Through representations of fundamentalist reverends, allusions to queer-themed 1990s salsa songs, and reinterpretations of fairy tales such as *Jack and the Beanstalk* in a Puerto Rican context, Cardona calls attention to the fictive nature of masculinity and femininity.

Preacher Parodies: Troubling Homosocial Authority

Ah mén begins with a lugubrious procession. A group of four men in black suits and ties enter the stage and slowly cross it on the diagonal, carrying another man's stiff body on their shoulders. Each step they take follows the rhythm of somber marching music. While their ceremonious movement and formal clothing imbue the scene with the solemnity of a funeral, the performers also wear nylon stocking headdresses shaped to make their heads look like the tip of a condom. The headdresses undercut the solemnity and make the scene a bit risible. As the procession comes to a halt, the men carefully turn the stiff body upright and gently prop it up on the floor.

Slowly, the statue-like figure takes a breath and comes to life. After greeting the other men with handshakes and hugs, this character—played by Cardona—addresses the audience in a calm yet authoritarian voice reminiscent of an evangelist preacher.

"Helping boys reach their freedom and responsibility," the preacher states, "is a really difficult endeavor in a society that does not define its men through the use of universally accepted texts."[3] The preacher explains that while in the past young men learned their absolute truths through sacred books, in contemporary culture, boys "grow up in confusion without a culture that is based on sacred texts like the Bible, the Torah or the Koran." Then the preacher introduces his minions, the men that carried him center stage, as members of a community-based theater company called Guerreros para Ti (Warriors for You), and invites one of them to talk to the audience about their project *Interviniendo en Tu Comunidad* (Intervening in Your Community).

As one of the minions explains, Warriors for You "is a group of committed young artists." Instead of stating what it is they are committed to, the young artist quotes the chorus of Willie Colón's popular salsa song "El Gran Varón" (The Great Son): "palo que nace dobla'o, jamás su tronco endereza" (a tree born bent will never straighten its trunk).⁴ The chorus of this song is so popular that the young artist pauses so that the other members of the group (and the audience) can join him and finish that phrase. He continues enthusiastically saying: "I want to testify that since this project started we have straightened hundreds of trees!" Afterward, all the men applaud, and the preacher addresses the audience again; he asks them to give the men a few minutes to prepare before performing "the play."

The preacher's conservative opening speech is reminiscent of the popular fundamentalist TV and radio evangelist preachers like Yiye Ávila or Jorge Raschke. These real-life and influential preachers in Puerto Rico are invested in indoctrinating their followers, as well as their state representatives, against the calamities of same-sex marriage and other queer practices.⁵ As performance scholar Isel Rodríguez explains: "Raschke's religious-activist campaign advocates a wholly Evangelical, extreme-right-wing Puerto Rico where gay sexuality features as the common detonator for Puerto Rico's social and political ills." Cardona's preacher captures the essence of how religious and political figures of authority recur to popular prejudices, false claims, and nonsense promises to gain and retain power.

Instead of mocking Ávila and Raschke by imitating their exaggerated hand gestures and dramatic voices, Cardona's preacher is soft-spoken and self-contained, yet equally paternalistic. However, there are slippages in what the preacher does and wears that undermine his homophobic discourse and reveal the irony that lies behind this character. For example, while his solemn expression, erudite tone, and formal attire command respect, the condom-shaped headdress comes to symbolize the ridiculousness of his extreme investment in manhood. Additionally, the simple mentioning of the names of the organizations that fund the Warriors for You project, such as Chorro de Vida Inc. (Spurt of Life Inc.) and Pro Semilla (Pro-Seed), exaggerates the deep investment the preacher's theater company has in reproduction-oriented messages. The many phallic references in *Ah mén*—from the performers' headdresses to the social-straightening rhetoric of Warriors for You— serve to satirize the penis as the ultimate symbol of "real" masculinity and the dominant fiction of ever-adequate, family-oriented male subjectivities.

Furthermore, Warriors for You's allusion to "palos doblaos" (bent trees) works as a metaphor for "twisted" gender and sexual expressions. The company's theater project, *Intervening in Your Community*, is reminiscent of the Christian ex-gay movement in which persons who once identified as gay or lesbian have turned away from such social identities and behavior for religious reasons. The movement is based on the assumption that people who experience same-gender desires can modify those patterns and thus abate their "twisted" sexuality. The "warriors," then, come to represent the ways right-wing organizations use theater as their tool for their version of an antigay agenda dressed in social-justice rhetoric.

Sociologists Christine M. Robinson and Sue E. Spivey explain that the ex-gay movement "seeks to advance an ambitious anti-gay social agenda that includes undermining legal family recognition of same-sex relationships, adoption by LGBT people, and protections from discrimination based on sexual orientation and gender identity."[6] By including these critiques toward the beginning of Ah mén, Cardona frames the performance with a strong statement against the overwhelming noise evangelical fundamentalism creates in the Puerto Rican public sphere about gender and sexuality.

Cardona's preacher parody is an indictment of cultural institutions that indoctrinate people by ignoring, misrepresenting, or degrading difference as abnormality rather than educating them. Through the preacher, Cardona critiques authority figures who use religion to encourage intolerance against groups of people generally devalued in society. Moreover, these figures use intolerance to sustain modes and means of political and financial gain that privilege heterosexuality. Ultimately, Ah mén makes visible the ways in which the Church perpetuates and sustains stereotypes of normative femininities and masculinities.

Coming of Age: Troubling Homosocial Childhood

After satirizing the oppressive discourses of the country's guardians of morality, Cardona takes his critique a step further. Ah mén's next scene, titled "La Obra" (The Play), presents the preacher's crew, Warriors for You, demonstrating their theatrical "straightening project" in action. They enact a "Puerto Rican-ized" version of the fairy tale of Jack and the Beanstalk renamed Pedrito y sus habichuelas (Pedrito and his beans).

The group's story follows the original fairy tale, Pedrito and His Beans, wherein a boy is sent to the market by his mother to sell their cow. On Pedrito's way to the market, he meets a stranger who offers to trade a bag of "magic beans" for the cow. The stranger is an older man who carries a crooked walking stick; he asks Pedrito, whom he seems to know, why he is taking the cow to the market. The boy shyly answers: "Because my mom says it is time." The old man acts surprised and hurriedly looks at his surroundings before declaring: "Yes, it is time!" Opening his flamboyant furry coat and pushing his pelvis forward he says: "Pedrito, look what I have for you . . . ," pointing to a bag of beans secured under his belt, very close to his crotch. The boy first refuses the bag, fearing his mother's reaction, but the man encourages him: "Don't be afraid, make an effort, be brave. You can do it!" Pedrito then reaches for the bag of magic beans from the man's crotch and places it under his belt, next to his own crotch.

Pedrito returns home and proudly shows his mother the bag of magic beans.[7] She is furious when she realizes that her son has made such a bad business deal and throws a temper tantrum as the boy watches in awe. Finally, she takes the bag of beans and smashes it against the floor. The bag breaks and the seeds spread all over the stage. At this point, the lights come up to full strength and the preacher from the previous scene returns; he claps his hands and asks the audience to join him in thanking the young performers of Warriors for You.

The preacher takes a moment to congratulate the actor who played the mother for his courage for performing a female character. He asserts poignantly: "And for the record, for him, there is no confusion," as if to dissipate any doubt about the actor's heterosexuality. The preacher goes on to explain the symbolism of the play, which, according to him, narrates how a new man is born. As the preacher is explaining that the cow represents Pedrito's innocence and that the boy's adventure symbolizes his journey to masculinity, the lights unexpectedly go out. This staged electrical failure interrupts the preacher's speech, and he is forced to leave the stage in order to solve the technical problem.

Ah mén suggests that this "new man," in some way, was queer and that Pedrito's road to normative masculinity was going to be, indeed, very long. After all, the boy exchanged the cow for beans from a man whose walking stick, furry coat, and gestures suggested queer masculinity. Furthermore, unlike the original fairy tale in which the beans grow into a giant beanstalk that will eventually take the boy to his journey to adulthood, in *Ah mén*'s version, there is not such a happily ever after.[8] There is no beanstalk to climb, no giant's castle in the sky to sack, no valuables to be gained, no better family life. In this coming-of-age story that ends with a spilled seed motif, a disgraced boy, and a hysterically disappointed mother, there is a long road to heteronormative masculinity. Pedrito's untouched potential for heterosexual masculinity has now been disrupted in the same way that the unexpected blackout has interrupted the preacher's moral speech. This sudden transition points out that the audience has also been spared any further lecturing of the "right" ways of being masculine within heteronormative constructions of masculinity.

Presumed Queer: Policing and Violence in Homosociality

In "Play Station" Cardona distinguishes which gender slippages are allowed within homosocial spaces and which ones are not. This is arguably the most intense, active scene in the play. It choreographs the beating of a man who critiques hypermasculinity by uttering the words "qué peste a macho," a slang phrase that literally translates to "it stinks like macho."[9]

"Play Station" begins with five of the dancers wearing blue overalls; each one picks up a briefcase and lines it up with the others on one side of the stage. They all stand still in formation behind the briefcases with their arms crossed. All of the men are awkwardly silent and hold a neutral gaze as if they are all patiently waiting for something to happen.

The silence is interrupted; a sixth man enters the scene humming a jolly tropical tune. This last man, who happily strolls across the stage, sports a small flowery briefcase, which he swings merrily. As he is about to exit the stage, a self-proclaimed leader from the lineup asks him aggressively: "Hey, what's up with the flashy bag?" In response, the man with the flowery bag retorts, as if noticing the bag for the first time: "I was late and it was the first thing I grabbed."

The man in the briefcase lineup responds with an angry tone: "Well, it does not suit you!" The rest of the men stare at the man with the flowery briefcase with disgust. Understanding that his masculinity is in question, the man with the flowery bag defiantly replies: "I'm a metrosexual," as he joins the lineup and waits with the others. With a deliberate gesture he places his flowery bag right along the other briefcases in the line.

The briefcases symbolize a particular kind of upwardly mobile heterosexuality. The five men standing behind them, in turn, perform widely accepted and normalized ways of embodying masculinity. After a few minutes of uncomfortable silence, another man in the lineup, who until now had remained quiet, interrupts the silence. He sharply utters: "It stinks like macho up in here." This utterance challenges not only the performance of "toughness" observed in the stern facial expressions and physical posture of the rest of the men, including the self-proclaimed metrosexual, but also the fiction of these culturally learned behaviors.

As the man walks away from the lineup, following his critique, he becomes a suspect of gender deviance. At a signal from the lineup's leader, the others mobilize to stop the fleeing man. At this point in the scene, the man with the flowery bag, who originally seemed a figure of defiance, proves to be in compliance with the normative behavior since he also joins in the attack of the man who dared to utter "qué peste a macho." Following the ethos of "you are either with us, or against us," the group bullies and harasses the man who dared to name and critique the performance of machismo. In searching his bag for some irrefutable evidence of something weird, of something queer, they find a pink stuffed piglet. Since the man is already considered a traitor to masculinity by virtue of his comment, the concealment of something childlike and effeminate makes him a threatening "infiltrator" of the homosocial space, which is always assumed to be heterosexual.

This "evidence" propels the mob to beat him up, thus stripping the man of his humanity. In a carefully choreographed dance sequence, the mob throws him from one side to the other. He is stepped on, stomped over, dragged, and pushed around. He tries to fight back, but after the beating, he collapses on the floor. The mob proceeds to dance, celebrating its victory. Throughout the course of the scene we see how the self-proclamation of metrosexuality seems more acceptable than the explicit challenge posed by a phrase like "it stinks like macho." The comment uncovers the tacit behaviors of policing and surveillance that sustain homosociality as nonhomoerotic. In other words, individual critiques of how representation of maleness has transformed from rugged and virile to subtle and stylized are more acceptable than a critique of the systematic policing of gender performance that happens as "business as usual." These challenges are the object of irrational hostility and tend to incite physical and emotional violence.

This scene highlights the bullying, gay bashing, and hate crimes experienced by many boys and men who do not seem to conform to appropriate performances of maleness. In their study of the social contexts and functions of violence, public health and family science scholars Jeffrey Fagan and Deanna Wilkinson explain: "Street codes emphasize toughness and quick, violent retributions for transgressions of one's sense of self or insults to one's repudiation. Such transgressions become grievances, and a response is mandatory."[10] Thus, in order to maintain status it is necessary for men to respond to such transgressions in a timely and aggressive manner in order to safeguard their own unquestioned positions of normality. This enactment of violence in the play traces how gendered relations of power are intolerant of, and oppressive toward, sexual desires and practices oppositional to dominant social norms.

The scene that immediately follows "Play Station" is "Pato." *Pato* is the word in Spanish for "duck" and is used as a derogatory term in Puerto Rico to refer to gay men similar to the way "faggot" is used in English. Queer studies scholar Lawrence La Fountain-Stokes explains that to be called "pato" is a "quite disconcerting and at times traumatic event, for it is to be marked as queer, strange, different, sexually or gender non-compliant, or simply marginal."[11] The title of this scene refers to the distress, pain, and damaging impact that such popularly used tropes have on men who do not perform normative masculine behavior.

"Pato" begins with the battered man from "Play Station" alone onstage. He slowly tries to stand, but keeps falling; it is as if an invisible force keeps pulling him down. After he manages to sit on the floor, he struggles and moves desperately, as if trying to escape from an invisible straightjacket. While this is happening center stage, a rubber duck is dragged through a thread, left to right, across the back of the stage. Center stage, the dancer eventually gives up fighting with himself. He slowly manages to move toward the back of the stage and lays down next to the rubber duck in a fetal position. A solemn silence invades the theater.

"Pato" represents the emotional distress, the storm within, that is inherent to the individual acknowledgment of alternative gender and sexual expression. In this scene, Cardona allows the audience to experience the stage as a "healing" space. The man onstage embodies the trauma, contradictions, and frustrations of not fitting in. This scene enacts the aftermath of violence; the most traumatic and catalytic wakeup call toward a long road to embracing one's own difference. It shows the intense solitude and frustration of being read as different. It further manifests the idea of being violently estranged from self and others because of a hidden secret of sexual preference.

Conclusion

Ah mén challenges religious and political affiliations that feed off of populist and patriarchal constructions of nationalism. The performance parodies Caribbean and Latin American moralistic discourses that thrive in their condemnation and exclusion of those who do not conform to normative gender expressions. Toward the end of the play, however, a sudden transformation occurs. In one of the last dance sequences, six men comfortable in their half-naked bodies dance in solidarity as if they had overcome the pressures of society and cultural stigmas. Through the combination of theater and dance, *Ah mén* reclaims the emotions, affect, and the senses not only as human characteristics but also as healthy ways of being a man in the contemporary world.

Notes

1 See Jossianna Arroyo, "Mirror, Mirror on the Wall: Performing Racial and Gender Identities in Javier Cardona's 'You Don't Look Like,'" in *The State of Latino Theater in the United States: Hybridity, Transculturation and Identity*, ed. Luis A. Ramos-García (New York: Routledge, 2002), 152–71; and Lowell Fiet, *El teatro Puertorriqueño reimaginado: Notas críticas sobre la creación dramática y el performance* (San Juan: Ediciones Callejón, 2004), 338–42.

2 In *You Don't Look Like* Cardona enacts characters stereotypically associated with blackness—such as the basketball player, the Rastaman, or the rapper—in order to ridicule the pervasiveness of racism within Puerto Rican popular culture and entertainment industries. For more on the pervasiveness of racism within contemporary Puerto Rican popular culture, see Yeidy Rivero *Tuning Out Blackness: Race and Nation in the History of Puerto Rican Television* (Durham, NC: Duke University Press, 2005); Bárbara Abadía-Rexach, "La negritud en la música popular puertorriqueña" (master's thesis, Universidad de Puerto Rico, 2006); Maritza Quiñones Rivera, "From Trigueñita to Afro–Puerto Rican: Intersections of the Racialized, Gendered, and Sexualized Body in Puerto Rico and the U.S. Mainland," *Meridians: feminism, race, transnationalism* 7 (2006): 162–82; and Isar Godreu, "Folkloric 'Others': Blanqueamineto and the Celebration of Blackness as an Exception in Puerto Rico," in *Globalization and Race: Transformations in the Cultural Production of Blackness*, ed. Kamari Maxine Clarke and Deborah A. Thomas (Durham, NC: Duke University Press, 2006), 171–87.

3 Cardona's original text is in Spanish. All citations are from our transcriptions of the performance recordings available in the video archives provided by the artist. The translations are our own and differ slightly from the published translation included in this volume.

4 "El Gran Varón" was popularized in 1989 by the Nuyorican singer Willie Colón. The song tells the story of Simón, a young man from a Puerto Rican family in the island, who migrates to New York City. One day, the father visits Simón unannounced, only to find out that Simón was a cross-dresser. Estranged by his family, Simón dies of AIDS alone in a city hospital. While this song is generally remembered as a sympathetic attempt to tackle Latin/o American machismo, and the suffering caused by the AIDS pandemic, it has been heavily critiqued by the LGBTQ Latina/o communities and its allies. Although it made issues of stigmatization and abandonment

experienced by queer men visible, it lacked the critical punch necessary to destabilize larger myths and dichotomies of the queer body as deviant or disease ridden.

5 These two preachers' concerns with issues of gender and sexuality have roots in the ongoing efforts to revise Puerto Rico's civil code in order to include the possibility of same-sex domestic partnership, changes to gender in the birth certificate of transgender people, and other changes that would positively affect the LGBTQ community. The Commission for the Revision and Reform of Puerto Rico's Civil Code was formed in 1997. The reforms concerning LGBTQ citizens have been very controversial, especially in light of the 2015 U.S. Supreme Court ruling, which legalized gay marriage. These discussions are extremely significant to the livelihood of queer Puerto Ricans because in 2010 alone, there were ten gruesome murders of members of the lesbian, gay, bisexual, transgender, and queer community in Puerto Rico and several life-threatening attempts that resulted in victims being severely injured and emotionally scarred. For more information on the GLBT civil rights movement, visit the website http://prparatodos.org (in Spanish).

6 Christine M. Robinson and Sue E. Spivey, "The Politics of Masculinity and the Ex-Gay Movement," *Gender and Society* 21, no. 5 (October 2007): 650–76.

7 A man in drag—an unusual casting decision for a theater company supposed to be highly moralistic—plays the mother's character. There are historical points of reference in theater history for this convention. For example, the emergence of boy performers in female roles in England during the seventeenth century resulted from a conservative prohibition against women on the stage. A similar case developed in Japan's kabuki theater. In both instances, prohibition of women onstage led to a queering of the economies of spectatorship. See Michael Shapiro, *Gender in Play on the Shakespearean Stage: Boy Heroines and Female Pages* (Ann Arbor: University of Michigan Press, 1994).

8 See Maria Tartar, *The Annotated Classic Fairy Tales* (New York: W. W. Norton, 2002).

9 "Qué peste a macho" is an expression that was popularized by the queerly ambivalent character of Vitín played by Puerto Rican comedian Sunshine Logroño in his television shows in the late 1980s and early 1990s.

10 Jeffrey Fagan and Deanna Wilkinson, "Social Contexts and Functions of Adolescent Violence," in *Violence in American Schools*, ed. Delbert S. Elliot et al. (Cambridge: Cambridge University Press, 1997), 55–93.

11 Lawrence La Fountain-Stokes, "Queer Ducks, Puerto Rican *patos*, and Jewish-American *feygelekh*: Birds and the Cultural Representation of Homosexuality," *Centro Journal* 19, no. 1 (2007): 194.

CHAPTER 8

Interview with Javier Cardona

Jossianna Arroyo

Translated by Ramón H. Rivera-Servera

Jossianna Arroyo: How do you approach the making of a performance? Where do you find inspiration for your work? How do you conceive of and distinguish between a theatrical scene, dialogue, and choreography? What comes first, dance or dialogue?

Javier Cardona: I don't really have a formula. Usually, when I cook I do so without a recipe. Creating performance is like cooking; cooking for oneself or for someone you love . . . or do not love so much. It is a kind of "domestic" labor: from inside out and from outside in. Cooking is vital, it is ritual, it is necessary. It is food . . . for our brains.

You begin with your utensils. Then you go on collecting the various ingredients, spices, protein. Sometimes you even play with whatever is left in the refrigerator or the cabinet. You throw it all in the pot or the skillet. You mix, add, cut, stir fry, season, taste or let others taste, adjust, let things cook (sometimes over low heat, sometimes high), you let things rest and taste again, adjust. Then you serve, eat, and let others eat. A full belly leads to a happy heart. That's what the popular saying teaches us.

Inspiration does not really just come to me out of nowhere before I begin a performance. What overcomes me is a yearning to do by myself or with others; to dialogue with or without words, through gesture; with objects and technologies. Creating and performing a new piece is at once rational and visceral. It is executing one or multiple actions in unison, fueled by pleasure or concern. Sometimes without really knowing exactly why I perform. What is it that I desire? The necessity of doing . . . is a desire, a physical and mental urgency to move, to reflect, to celebrate, or to repudiate something . . . and to share with others. Creating and performing a piece means venturing into an activity that pleasures and perturbs my very self and making a conscious decision to get messy with it, to dance really close with it so that I can later exteriorize what is possible for me to show about this encounter. Performing about something becomes commentary or dialogue when shared with those who witness in the audience.

The need to create performance comes from my life experiences as a subject and object of our shared consumer market. My body is part of this consumer society—my physical body in particular, which I inhabit, but it is also inhabited by many other things. My body, just like many others, is a subject and object of labor, exploration, pleasures and pains. In performance, my body is not just there to create the event onstage but it is also intent on finding places where I may find and lose myself.

Throughout the ages the body has been domesticated and, in turn, used to domesticate others globally. "Domestic affairs." I am not sure why, but I very much like this term from the English language. Despite the fact that the body is a space of simultaneous writing and reading, of articulation and disarticulation of discourses, it and its actions on display continue to be a space for reflection, for resistance, and for the construction of utopias (utopia as a space of multiple possibilities). The body is nebulous territory, unsteady, difficult if not impossible to control, to codify.

I work with this body, through the multiple and diffuse possibilities it allows me to explore, the stories and narratives it helps me find and create, and through the limitations and privileges previously imposed on it by imperial and hegemonic corporeal geographies.

The body is always present, even if at times it pretends not to be. Scenic actions are fueled by and led not just by the body onstage but by the influences exerted by other "bodies": original, borrowed, or stolen texts, objects, music, visual and aural technologies. In my performance piece *You Don't Look Like*, for example, the handheld mirror I use emerged out of sheer coincidence. But that small mirror introduced multiple meanings to the narrative of the piece. This mass-produced object was created by the Disney Company where, among other things, girls and also boys are sold the white beauty of Snow White. Like so many, I, too, was born and grew up consuming the ideals of heteronormativity and white beauty promoted by Disneyland. Now, as an adult and through my own performance work in pieces like *You Don't Look Like*, I look in the mirror and question all of that while the deflated merengue tune by Wilfrido Vargas seeks to find the reason for my disturbing questioning, but at the same time the refrain of that song, "Mami qué será lo que quiere el negro"/ "Mamma, I wonder what the black man wants," questions my questioning.

So far I have been addressing the issue of creating performance . . . and in a way I have to go back to correct or clarify myself some more on this issue. When it comes down to the truth, I am not sure "creating" is the best word to describe my approach. I don't think that I have created anything new. Much of what I seek to express, say, and do through performance has been thought of and done before. What I do think is significant and unique about creating a performance is the physical and mental acts of play. By play I mean the act of remembering and of amassing a wide range of things to arrange in a common space. Creating is a particular act of composition and decomposition where we assemble meanings that reveal realities that subvert the norm. To create is to throw the world in a pot to move, stir, add, and remove, so that we can later serve and savor. Notice that I return to food and cooking as concepts for performance. If there is anything one truly creates with performance it is precisely that metaphor that makes it possible for us to reach other worlds with counternarratives.

JA: When you developed *You Don't Look Like* for audiences in the Caribbean, you encountered some difficulties translating Puerto Rico's racial problems to other contexts. Could you speak about some of these issues?

JC: What happens is that to be or to figure one's self as black or dark skinned in Puerto Rico is perceived as foreign. It is not local. It is seen as an import. Translocal? For example, this also happened to me when I performed the piece in the Dominican Republic. To be black or dark skinned was assumed to refer to Haiti or to being Haitian. In Puerto Rico, the theater and film roles I have been offered as an actor have always been foreigners, not local, not national, it is to be from over there . . . from the islands.

In New York City, many Latinas/os read me as "moreno" or African American. They are often surprised to hear me speak Spanish and I tell them, "Yes, I am moreno." They respond sympathetically and understand quite well the appropriation: "Yes, but you understand me." And, of course, I understand them. Within this collective imaginary that I am a part of I am Jamaican, Cuban, Dominican, Brazilian. And almost always as the last alternative, *boricua* (Puerto Rican).

JA: Would you classify your performance work as queer? Why or why not?

JC: I am not an expert in queer theories. I am also not an expert on matters of race. I am not an expert at anything. I think that by assuming a critical stance, I know, and at the same time I know very little about everything. The more I learn about things, the more I realize how much more there is to learn.

I am many bodies at once. My scenic work is just the same: messy, cluttered with things that sometimes become articulated into coherency and other times become disarticulated, nonlinear, complex, or abstract. I can see myself as queer because I am unique, without necessarily wanting to perform the "other." I believe in identities as fictions, in how self-perception can change how we see or assume ourselves differently across time and contexts. I believe I see myself as queer because I refuse essentialist binaries that seek to construct a reality hierarchically more real than other realities. I see myself as queer because I am, purposely or not, subversive and politically conscious of many of my actions, though not all.

Making theater and dance, and engaging in other sensible communicative and expressive practices, has given me the opportunity and the ability to think and perform myself in diverse ways on and off the stage. I can affirm myself in many different ways. For example: "man," "gay," "black," "Latino," "Puerto Rican," "educated." But, what do all these words mean? How are all these etiquettes of being performed together or separate? For who and for what reason do I perform them? Am I a "role model" for local or global export? What am I supposed to be when I affirm or am affirmed in all these categories?

I do not like categorizations much because they flatten, empty, or homogenize me. Oftentimes these categories are meant to box me in. Defining what I wear, what I eat, what I read, what I hear, how I cook, how I behave, how I think, how I act, how I practice sex. How to classify myself? Sounds like biology. Like filling in the bubble in a multiple-choice test. It sounds like Darwin and the species.

Although I can and sometimes assume myself to be "man," "gay," "black," "Latino," "Puerto Rican," "educated," and "queer," among other things, and although all of these "identities" shape my complex constitution as a human being, none fully defines my history.

At the end of the day, I think it is not my role to define what it is I do. I do things out of necessity, desire, pleasure, anger, solidarity, reflection, exchange, dialogue, community, provocation, doubt, to exorcise others, things, and myself.

JA: How do all these intersectionalities (race, gender, sexuality) appear in your performance work? How do you translate them thematically?

JC: I am never a single one of those things alone. I am a package of intermixed and tangled things in constant flow. In the very act of living, we negotiate and perform many realities at once.

I think that the imagination and creative play allow me to loosen up, to create biographies and other stories, modeled and interconnected with and because of very concrete social circumstances. Additionally, play enables us to create other realities, other possibilities for communication, relation, to impregnate and be impregnated, to give birth. To invent lives. To help us translate our own living texts, to bring all these categories together: metaphor, contradiction, happy accidents, and uncertainty.

JA: What is your relationship to theater and performance critics and scholars?

JC: In Puerto Rico? Which critics of theater, dance, or performance? Criticism is very sporadic, on the surface, participatory and inclusive. What usually appears in local newspapers or magazines are reviews. I know there are folks who every so often will write interesting reflections, mostly via web-based platforms. Susan Homar wrote about dance for some time in the *San Juan Star*, *Diálogo* (the University of Puerto Rico monthly magazine), and *El Nuevo Día*.

Lowell Fiet in *Claridad* is one of the few, if not the only one, who persists at maintaining a serious and articulate practice at theater criticism in Puerto Rico. He has labored constantly and insistently to articulate and disseminate a critique of contemporary theater. Through his writings, Lowell has documented an important part of the island's theater history. But Lowell does not write all that frequently about dance works that cross into the realm of theater as does the work of many colleagues and friends like Viveca Vázquez, Teresa Hernández, Eduardo Alegría, Karen Langevin, as well as my own. Puerto Rico lacks multidisciplinary criticism interested in the kinds of hybrid, in form and content, performances that characterize our work.

There are also, both on and beyond the island, academics and scholars with specialties in literature, race, gender, cinema, political and social sciences, who have produced articulate, interesting, and illuminating critiques of my work and the work of other multidisciplinary artists in this scene.

Among these critics, I don't think there is a consistent or devoted practice of performance criticism. There are the critiques coming from Rubén Ríos-Avila, Mara Negrón, Yeidi Rivero, Celiany Rivera-Velázquez, Lowell Fiet, Susan Homar, Gilberto Blasini, Rubén Nazario Velasco, Juan Rodríguez, and you, among others, who have engaged my work and that of my colleagues. Aside from documenting the local scene, they create interesting dialogue and exchange of ideas. Although I am to some extent recognizing that there exists a community of critics, I also must remark on the existing resistance or inability to play with the hybrid aesthetic discourses of a genre like performance.

JA: Do you think that a nationalist focus limits criticism on the island?

JC: The discourse of nationalism has been historically, for the most part, exclusionary and undemocratic. Sometimes the problem is one of too limited a perspective or angle. How to articulate nation while recognizing, and sometimes celebrating, the constant contamination of culture? The nation is also a project of constant transformation and contradiction. Not always, but almost always, the nation or the nationalist project gets articulated as something pure and coherent, without deviations. The nation is also a personal imaginary grown from diverse and hybrid collectivities.

JA: Are your collaborators queer? Do they work or negotiate queerness in their collaborations with you? How do you enter that kind of dialogue?

JC: Eduardo Alegría has been one of my most frequent collaborators since I began my career. Unfortunately, a lot of the work we did in the early years of our respective careers went undocumented. Some pieces have been poorly documented.

The conciliation of dance styles, creative approaches, and dialogue between Eduardo and me has been very interesting and rich. *Trepa paredes* (Wall climber) was a piece about quotidian horniness and shared solitude. We created the piece around the architectural environment of Centro Dharma: doors, frames, corners. My work with Eduardo has opened a space in which to play and create fun possibilities. The piece ends with Eduardo and me devouring in one whole swoop a roasted chicken delivered by a young man.

Another piece we did was *Tipos del Paleo* (Guys from the Paleo Age). Two men travel backward in time to the Paleolithic age (our own crazy idea). By then Homo sapiens was in existence, I think. These two men were on a trip to find something they never lost: being men. Perhaps Eduardo reads the piece differently. Housewife floral-print housedresses, long-sleeved flannel shirts, a pair of empty luggage pieces, a pair of cigarettes, tennis and white brief underwear were all elements worn and played with during this back to the past journey. The piece was an initiation ritual of sorts. What kind of initiation? In some way we danced our quotidian gestural masculinities.

I have always benefited from the fact that Puerto Rico is a small country where everyone knows each other. I would have never been able to develop *Ah mén* without Rosa Luisa Márquez and Miguel Villa-fañe, who generously granted me access to their Old San Juan studio for rehearsals. For most of my pieces, and for *Ah mén* specifically, auditions have not been necessary since I am familiar with all of my collaborators. I work with gay and straight dancers. And collaborating with them for nine months is how *Ah mén* came to be.

JA: Larry La Fountain has been working with the term *transloca* to address the work of Puerto Rican performers in transit between New York City and the island and at the same time dealing with queer themes. Do you consider yourself transloca?

JC: I imagine "trans" to be related to the multiple back-and-forth traffic between here and there. *Loca* is a popular, colloquial, humorous, and derogatory term to pinpoint someone who does not behave "according to proper norms and etiquette." Loca is similar to *pato*. The only difference is that loca is the feminine term for crazy, and pato is an animal. Loca and pato are an effeminate man, with mannerisms, queenie. I am not devoted exclusively to the exploratory search for my femininity or my locality.

Larry's term suggests movement, constant displacement of something that will always be with us: roots, *pasteles*, music, love, the escape, *sancocho* stew, the *cafrería* or vulgarity of transiting the local. Transiting through that small island (Puerto Rico) from within or from afar is always an odyssey. Trans-loca, trans-local . . . I think of Juan Flores's concept: "Cultural Remittances" or "Remesas culturales." Every time we send or transport something out, we bring something else in with us. I move between here and there, carry things in and out. I pick up and drop off. Abandon and anchor (temporarily).

After all this, what do you think? Am I transloca or not? Is it the transvestism of the loca or the local? I think it is Larry La Fountain's task, and that of other critics, to "loca-lisarme" (locate or place me). What I do know is that I am not loca as in crazy. But there may be critics and other folks who might read me that way. We all have the right to read and interpret in different ways.

Larry La Fountain is a good example of scholars who are skilled and persistent and who insist in documenting and reflecting on the queer artistry required to be boricua on the island and beyond it. I would love to dialogue with him more to find out if he thinks of his own work as a critic as fitting the label of "transloca."

Part V

Dancin' the Down Low

Jeffrey Q. McCune Jr.

ACT I

R. Kelly's *"On the Down Low"* plays as pre-show music, then fades out. Enters the exuberant DJ on a mobile apparatus, like a DJ Booth with turntables, which has at its background an enlarged DL sign. DJ, the disk jockey, is onstage spinning on a set of turntables in a spot center stage, with a large metal fence upstage of him.

DJ	Good Evening, Good Evening, Good Evening. Welcome to Dancin the Down Low, the show that's gonna let you know a little more about this thing folks call—black men who identify as straight, even when they re-mix the tune every now and then and get down and dirty, or down and clean, with another brotha. They call themselves men on the down low. Some sistas call them male (*mixes real fast—sister moves to gate*)
SISTER	Hos!!!
DJ	But nobody really know, no one really knows how they get down, between the sheets, who they meet, or how they handle the heat—the pressure of being black, male, and somewhere on the sexuality scale—but, hell it's not like sexual "ambivalence" is racially specific.

For example, DL brothas are kinda like the white brothas at the golf course, who got a wife and kids at home and sometimes when he's in the country club restroom, he knows his only chance to get a peek, or to engage his fantasy—that thing that all his life has been called the lowest of the low, a little u know what—is from the guy standing next to him in the stall right behind them. OK . . . not quite like that, but almost. How do I know? Well . . . the DJ knows almost all things. (*scratches*) Maybe it's a little more like when the machismo-thing get Latino brothas all wrapped up in how he does his "man" thing—that the only way to do his thang is somewhere outside of the glares and stares of those who seem to measure how manly his performance of man is. Something like that, but it's not quite the same. In fact—the difference is in more than the name. One brotha said (*mixes on turntable*):

BROTHA	Brothas always gotta be on. We gotta be this, we gotta be that, we got history chasin us, we got family and community dependin on us.
DJ	That's why it's not as easy as what one of the sistas told me (*mixes*):
SISTA	The Down Low? The Down Low? These men need to come out of the closet, get it up high, bring it out, put it up front!
DJ	(*sarcastically*) Hmm . . . Is it that easy? You ask me, it sounds kinda cheesy? Keepin it real—gay black men don't even come out, so DL men?—you need to sing a new shout. Re-

mix it a little, maybe ask the DJ for a new tune, cause the day for the chorus of comfort, is not coming too soon. And a brotha said (*slow mix*):

BROTHA   How can folks even ask for us to "be honest," when for so many years they been asking us to lie?

Chorus gets louder—speaking lines and overlapping.

SISTA   keep it on the down low-puh!—

BROTHA   Family and community depending on us—

SISTAH   Come out the closet!—

BROTHA   all these years they been askin us to lie.

Chorus descends in volume, lights descend, and the voice-over overlaps.

OVERHEAD CHORUS   Vibe Magazine Introduces the HomoThug! Hip-Hop and its New Homo Vibes (*automated voice*)

There is no homo in hip-hop! (*male voice*)

This is the anatomy of a media frenzy! (*automated*)

All this talk about the DL, what about the folks who are af-fected and infected by them? (*female voice*)

DL, literally down low, is a vernacular term used to describe black men who have sex with other men, who typically identify as "straight," and maintain relational ties to women. (*automated voice*)

DL, what's that? Now I know we, black folks, used to do stuff on the "Down Low" all the time—trying to keep out of white folks' eye. Now they talking about DL, I guess that's just a shortened version these young folks now came up with. (*older grandmother voice*)

68 percent of all new cases of HIV-AIDS are heterosexual Black women. (*automated voice*)

They had to get it from somewhere . . . but really, what we doing now that they got it? And what we doing to prevent other folks from getting it? Right. (*male voice*)

To their wives and colleagues these DL men are straight. (*automated*)

I would've never thought that my husband was sleeping with anybody—let alone another man. (*female voice*)

To the men they have sex with, they are forging a new exuberant identity. (*automated*)

Ain't nothing new about the DL—what's new is HIV. (*deep male voice*)

To the gay world, they're kidding themselves. (*automated*)

They a bunch of fags in thugs' clothing. (*male voice*)

To health officials, they're spreading AIDS in the black community. (*automated*)

DL is not synonymous with HIV. (*female voice*)

DJ   (*scratches—in a way that all the voices blend together like a tape slowly rewinding and speaks, while shaking his head*) Just Another Portrait of a Violent Black Man Acting OUT!! This is your DJ, re-mixing this visual rhyme, showing you new, more complex portraits of black men—in real time. (*rewinds and plays "on the down low" re-mix—then fades to black*)

DJ's booth is moved further upstage. The stage space is transformed into a basketball court. A drone is heard—and fades away. Panting is heard onstage. Echoes of African Drums are playing in the distance, soon to be replaced by the bounce of the basketball. The lights come up and the "guys" are playing basketball, dribbling on beat, panting off-beat, and shooting periodically against the hoop, which hangs upstage. Strangely, they are all holding balls and trying to get them into the hoop, one by one. There are verbal exchanges (masculine in texture and tone), grunts, pushing and shoving, constant body touching, and David falls on top of Michael, and it's a weird pause—the other members slide the ball off stage left and right. They tend to the scene and when they reach David and Michael downstage, they get up as David pushes him off. They get up and it's David's turn for his free-throw and they position themselves. After they align themselves for the free-throw shot, David concentrates and they slowly leave David onstage by himself, as if he has only been imagining the scene all along.

DAVID I tried it once. (*alone on the court—shoots basketball and misses*) I tried it twice. (*shoots again and misses—then turns around to the audience*) Did you see how he gon push me off him like I was some fag or somethin? This nigga now lost his mind. It took every bone in ma body, not to haul off and punch that nigga in his eye. You don't punk me. But it's just a game right? It's just a fuckin game. Yeah . . . he try to punk me and he the faggot ass nigga, ain't got no girl—can't really play no ball—and if you ask me—got mo sugah in his tank than a dip stick. You know them candies with the stick you dip in the pack of sugar. (*smirks*) He kinda remind me of the first dude I ever let suck my dick. This dude was sweet. Like them cats you see on TV—wrists all limp and shit. This nigga kept staring at me in the shower one day—this when I was in high school—I almost said "what the fuck you lookin at"—but he seemed to know just the right moment to turn away. I don't know if he was starin at other guys—but I know that one day we was sittin up in the locker room, right after swimming, and he gon stare at me while I'm at my locker. I looked back at him this time—gave him a look like "what the fuck u starin at?" and he just kept looking. Then he gon do this thing with his jaw and tilted his head, as if I was to follow him. I thought about it for a minute. Shit . . . It's just some head. So . . . I went with him—back into this corridor where don't nobody go. He told me that the only people that come in here are the cleaning folks, late at nite. He was right. That nigga sucked my dick for bout an hour. He act like my shit was going outta style. After I bust, I just walked away and went back to the locker. I grabbed my shit and jet before he came back.

(*defensively*) I ain't no fag or nothing like that. I'm just a brotha who like to get his dick sucked from time to time by another nigga, with no strings and no bonds. I like my bitches. Ain't nothing like good pussy. Ooh——weee! Nothin like it in the world. I remember one time this punk gon tell me his ass was like good pussy. I said "nigga please!"—that shit cracked me up. I wish I would stick my dick anywhere near some nigga's ass. Now, me and my girl might do dat sometimes. But, it ain't the same. With a dude, it just don't seem right. That was the first time I had done some shit like that—and that was just lettin some nigga durb on my dick.

Every now and agin I dip off and let some dude durb me down. But, mostly I try to lay low—deal with my females and just try to make it. Shit, a nigga gotta get paid first.

If I'm ever gonna have a wife, kids, my own crib, I gotta do what I gotta do. Ain't no nigga gon be able to help me get there. So . . . a brotha gotta keep his house in order, do the damn thang. This one female, Sheila, she love me like no other. She keep saying "D, when you gon marry me, when you gon marry me?" I tell her—"one day baby, one day." (*He smirks slyly*) Knowing damn well I don't know when one day is. I just know, if I was to marry her—me, her, her son, we gotta be strap. We gotta have something. Right now, I ain't got shit. So how am I going to marry? How can I even think about building a family with fifteen cents? Shit . . . how the hell I'm gon be able to do anything with her that's deep, when—Really, it's not so much I can't control it. I'm young, I like sex, what can I say. It's like an addiction, but not quite. Cause it ain't no problem. It's just human nature. Females, Dudes, whatever . . . a nigga gotta get his where he can, when he can. I ain't sufferin or nothing . . . I get mine. Right now, I guess I ain't ready for all that family shit. But, I will be. Cause this getting old. I'm getting tired of doing this dance—back and forth and in-between. (*black out*)

Lights up. Onstage are four pairs. Four men are dressed in all black and their partners are in varying colors and outfits. Furthest downstage right is one couple as they engage in what seems to be a heterosexual romantic moment. Stage left is two business partners who are at work. Furthest upstage, center left is a pair of men clearly flirting with each other. Upstage, center right is another pair. DJ is at the booth, when he scratches, the couples re-pose and construct a new social or sexual setting. This continues twice more. They exit as if pedestrians on the streets of Chicago.

DJ   (*at DJ booth-singing*) Danc-in the Down Low, Danc-in the Down Low. (*to audience*) So what you say (*in female voice*) "DL ain't nothing but an abbreviation for Dick Lover, honey, and that's that." (*sharp scratches*) Or . . . (*in deep male voice*) "Sound to me like a brotha just confused?" Yeah . . . Some are and Some aren't . . . but that isn't new news. . . .

MICHAEL **(walking down the street, outside of house)** Every day I come home from work, when I get off the metra stop at 71st, I get excited to see my little girl Jacoya (her momma's choice), my wife Tricia, and of course King-Kong—that's the little chi-wa-wa Tricia insisted we have, so I insisted we name him king-kong instead of to-to. What the hell—is this the wizard of oz? She tripped me out with that. **(looking at the house)** Yeah, this is my piece of the American dream. My little piece of happiness, prosperity, all the things I've worked for in my life balled into one. I would give anything to have it all over again the same way. **(reflexive pause)**

Like the other day—Jacoya came over to me and she say "daddy, is it OK when I grow up that I want to be just like you?" I say yeah, but you better make sure you a little like your mom too. She says "But, I'm already like her." **(smiles-smirks)** My little girl—a little woman admiring her dad. You don't hear that too often. Shit . . . when I was growing up, I just wanted to know who "dad" was—that's not to say my moms never had a stable man in her life—but they were often fleeting. Yeah . . . but growing up, I don't remember who I wanted to be like—Magic Johnson, Kool Moe Dee, Bill Cosby—just anybody who seemed to make it out the hood into the good life.

My little baby girl wanted to be like her daddy. On one hand, I was elated. But, deep down inside I was thinking she really might be better off trying to be like her mom. A bro-tha right here—gotta whole lot of work to do. But . . . I know what she means when she says she wants to be like me. And that's touching—that she looks up to her dad and sees the undying love I have for her and my wife.

DJ **(comes out weeping . . . then stops)** Ain't that beautiful? Naw . . . serious. I can feel that. Like the music, the madness, the dance—that's where it's at. **(enter Lorraine reading—short pause)** But, what I can't seem to get a feel of—is all this hoopla over these E. Lynn Harris novels, or whatever. Well . . . here come Lorraine with *her* review of the Harris sagas—that seems to have taken the black sistas world by storm—showing brothas living it up and laying it down on the DL.

LORRAINE **(reading a novel—stage right in a chair)** Oooohhhh fine! This man got it going on. You know how you read a book and you wish you could be right inside of the book—you know just rubbing your body against the fine, ex-football star turned businessman of whatever novel you encounter. I don't know about you—but I'm living, eating, and sopping up every hunk of imaginary chocolate that I encounter page to page in this here E. Lynn Harris novel. Baby I have read every E. Lynn Harris Novel since 1992, starting with *Just as I Am*. Now I probably should've started with *Invisible Life*—that was actually the first one—But, my girlfriend had read *Just as I Am* and her girlfriend had given it to her and her girlfriend's girlfriend had given it to her and her girlfriend's gay friend, I don't remember his name, told her about it— so I figured it must be good. And good? . . . yum . . . yum, yummy . . . it's Hot! **(slows down)** So hot I'm reading it for a second time. Ooh . . . **(looking at book)** *Any Way the Wind Blows?* Blow baby, blow me away with John Basil Henderson, that sexy chocolate man. Now, I know he gay, or bisexual, or whatever—but he is sooooooooooooooo Luscious. If I could wrap him up, turn him straight, and make him mine, I would devour him, honey. Yes child—I would have to have me a "Basil on command." Come here Basil—Can you score a touchdown on me, I mean for me? I would be his field goal or whatever he needed me to be. You can not find men like that these days. Damn shame—always the good ones. Shit . . . I understand why Kyle, Bart, Raymond, and all the others had to go that way—I mean they was real gay anyway—but this was a straight brotha—turned out and over to the other side. And this sistah, talented singin-sista, Yancey just been a damn fool. My girlfriend just told me that one of his books now became a stage play—Not a day goes by? **(talking to the book)** Too many days went by before Yancey, Ms. Braxton, realized her man was what?—creepin around with another man. She all distraught—saddened and brokenhearted— fool! Here is a woman in a novel that need to read the novel that she in—for herself! Maybe that'll bring her some insight.

But Ms. Yancey got Basil right together though—she wrote her first single about him—named it *Any Way the Wind Blows*—she say:

(attempting to sing in a smoker's wanna-be cabaret singer voice)

Dobedobedobedobedobe. . . .
You said I was your lady
As sweet as candy baby, and I fell for you
But then one day I come home
To find you're not alone
(She begins to perform a version of a run—DJ cuts in and scratches—as Lorraine continues to sing her sad melody—screeching as if she is at the climax of the song)
(almost crying) *This can't be true . . . it can't be true!!*
You were in the arms of another man
That was more than I could stand
I had to let you go.

Fuck letting him go honey—I would've cut his throat. You come back to me—after being out in the streets—and with another man—child, pleaz. Mr. Butcher would have had his ass all over the house.

What they call em now—DL Brothaz? I wish a man would—I'll become a DL expert. I'd be doing cell phone checks, credit checks, and even ass checks. He'd say "what you doing down there?" I'd say nothing. Knowing dog-on well that I'm trying to see if my man been doing the do—with another dude. You gotta do what you gotta do, sistaz. I'm serious. These men are a trip. First you had to worry about them out here with another woman—now a man. You got to wrap up, strap it up, and do whats best for you. Ladies, you don't even have to question—if yo man is a man—just take him down to the clinic—yall go together. **(speaking like an infomercial)** Get tested periodically. Make it a family outing or something. I go, you go. We both go in— like we don't know. Yall know what I'm talking about.

But, for real these books got me right together. Opened my eyes—let me see—that men are just what they are— M.E.N. MEN! And that means that they will Mess up Every-thing for a Nut! **(DJ joins her)** Hm!

DJ Hmmmm . . . is that what it is. Men mess up when doing the bis! Another DJ said E. Lynn Harris Books are like her bible for understanding the DL. Well representation can be bitch— Shit—cause when I looked at his books—as the brothas on *In Livin Color* used to say "hated it!" E. Lynn Harris novels doing the same thing these other novels do—playing the same ol song of brothas who are dirty, deceitful, dumb, and too selfish to think about you. That narrow story was old about two centuries ago. It's just re-playing itself over and over . . . Yeah . . . I know some of us ain't shit . . . but there's some brothas out there, like me, who got a bad ass mix.

TRICIA   *(comes in carrying laundry basket—walks and picks up pair of Michael's socks by the coffee table)* Don't ask me why, but every night—this man takes off his socks in the same spot and at the same time. Talk to his Mama and she'll tell you the same thing. *(smirks)* The things we do. *(sits down)* Michael and I met while in college, in the laundry room of our dorm. He was an aspiring young businessman and I was a blossoming young teacher. A perfect match. Our worlds are so different, but yet so similar. *(picks up picture of family off table)* It was after our first year of dating, we found out we were pregnant. We got married. We were happy. We were in love. I have never seen a man who loves his child so much. Our daughter Jacoya—she's three. The most precious baby girl in the whole wide world. The name was my idea—I know it's "ghettofabulous"—but I liked it. If I could tell you about the back and forth we went on between naming our daughter Jacoya or Michael and naming our dog Toto or King Kong. We split—I won and he won. Jacoya was it and King Kong was the godforsaken name given to our little Chihuahua. Now, though we may bicker form time to time—Michael is the man of my dreams. *(looking at magazines)* Even though he lacks a little organization. *(straightens magazines)* But Really . . . I used to pray to God—"send me a man who is faithful, honest, fine as hell, and can take care of the business." OK . . . the latter part is usually written out when talking to God. But, Michael could throw down tho—talk about laying down the pipe. That man had it down to an art. Hm.

      But really . . . Michael is an all-around type of man. Jacoya and I can be at home—waiting for "daddy" to get home from work and he knows—if he's going to be late he calls ALL the time. But when he gets home—It's like the house lights up immediately. It's like I always saw my family. It's kinda the family I wished I had had. While my family was not bad, it always felt empty—my dad died when I was two years old. So, I never knew him. Now my daughter had the opportunity to experience the magic of a dad's touch. Michael, never lets us see him down either. He might've spent his day getting down and dirty with the boys in the office and he would come home and be just as sweet and nice—as if everything is alright all the time. It's amazing— I would've never thought I would find someone like this. Growing up—while we had everything—my mom never found that man who could bring a smile to her face unceasingly, or to ours. But, she had Jesus. And I swear, it was Jesus who helped all three of us, me and my older sisters, to be the people we are today. All of us have gone thru college, done something with ourselves, and made families. My mom still says "it was cause we were a praying family no matter what." That's true . . . but it also helped that we had been in good schools, and had good teachers, and had a great mom too. Ooh . . . I gotta get these clothes in the wash before I pick up Jacoya.

(*rises and walks downstage of the coffee table*) You know folks say "the grass is greener on the other side"—but you don't really know til you get there. I had spent all my high school years and the first couple years in college—single and alone. Then I met Michael. When we met, in that cold basement of Cather Hall, it was not supposed to happen. Cause Michael, to me, was a stuck-up pretty boy—the type that either want one thing or wouldn't want me at all. I thought. But . . . I was wrong. (*lights dim on Tricia—lights upstage come up on Michael*) When I came in the room—Michael turned around and looked at me once. Then he did a smooth double-take. I almost dropped my hamper . . . cause he was wearing like basketball shorts and a tank top. He's slimmed down a bit since then, but he still has that nice frame. And I knew— when I walked up to the washing machine next to his—that this man was the man of my dreams. I knew that moment was like a dream come true, only to be followed by years of love, happiness, and serenity. I don't know what I would do without my baby girl, my wonderful husband, and God's grace. Without them, I would be nothing.

(*lights up on house—enter Michael w/ briefcase, mail underneath his hand, and flowers*)

MICHAEL	Hey Sweetie. Happy Sweetest Day.
TRICIA	Thanks, but you know today isn't Sweetest Day.
MICHAEL	I said Sweetie's Day and you my sweetie. *(They kiss—he sits down on the couch)* Here sweetie, here's your mail.
TRICIA	Thank you. I'm going to run and get Jacoya from school.
MICHAEL	Alright baby. *(lights fade)*
TRICIA	*(with hamper, flowers—to audience)* God is good.
DJ	*(DJ begins playing a gospel number and cuts in)* "God is good— *(gestures to audience for response)* and All the time— *(gestures to audience)*. Now God is good all the time, but sometimes the records we play for ourselves has scratches. Alright. Now yall heard a little sermonic prose, I'll return you to the episode of "every rose has its thorn."
MICHAEL	*(reading a magazine at the table)* You know life ain't all about sex. Some of these magazines would have you believe it. I have seen more ads in here about Viagra and penis-enlargement than I needed to see for a lifetime. And if you listen to some of my guys, on and off the court, as they talk about the things that keeps them proud—you might think there is nothing in the world but good lovin, and easy livin. Sex is good—especially when you have someone special like your wife to share it with—but, that's not all life is about. Nah . . . life is about being happy—having friends and family—making the best of what you got. It's just sometimes your flesh interfere with what you wanna do. Sometimes I think it's deeper than the flesh, even deeper than the sinful spirit—but like something you have inside of you, but the world doesn't allow you to freely explore it. You just left to deal—all by yourself, keeping everything on the low. You know how you feel something, or like when you don't know why you feel the way you do, or just how you know you really want one thing, but you also really want another. And then when you have your cake and you can eat it too—it still don't seem like you got everything together. You probably like, "What the hell is he talking about?" I'm just rambling. I know.
(confessionally) OK. So me and my best friend fuck around.

We been doing it for a while. Yeah, he (Yes he!) and I do shit together that I can't go into too much detail about. But, all I'll say is that it feels good and right when I'm doing it— but afterwards this burden of guilt comes over me. It's like when you a kid and you know you wanna play mommy in the game of house. But, it just don't seem right. OK, bad example. It's just . . . we been best friends for over 10 years. We met in college, same frat, same everything. This was my guy—my ace. We were the flyest dudes on campus, pretty boi extraordinaires. Come to find out, we both was pulling the girls and the fellas at the same time. I found out—cause one night I was messin around with this fool and he got a call—and when he got off he said "That was my boy Greg." I said "Greg who?" He said "Greg Crockett." I said "He get down?" and this cat, with no hesitation, just said "Yeah."— like no big deal. He started describing him, talking about what frat he in, where Greg was from, and a whole bunch of shit I didn't think he should know. That's why I say you can't just fuck with any old faggot ass motherfucker—tell all your business and have yo shit out there. I just took note.

So, the next time I hung out with Greg at my little studio apartment in Carbondale, I just asked him—I said "Yo-u get down?" He said "What?" Trying to play stupid. I said "Ya know . . . you get down?" He knew what I was talking about—I could tell by his smirk rather than a frown. Finally, he say "Every now and then." And as if he was interested, he said "What about you?" I said "Nah . . ." He said "Then why you ask me?" After that, I just tackled him and said "Yeah man! . . ." and from that moment on, we was buddies. (looks down at magazines and sees pic) Now, we both got families and shit—we do what we supposed to do—and when we need it or when we want it—we get up. It's just us tho—ain't no gay shit. Ain't no other nigga ever suckin this here. Or nothin. I guess me & Greg got an unwritten agreement—it's just us. We do the damn thang and proceed as normal.

DJ   (setting up computer on table) I know—I'm a DJ—what can I say—I'm multifaceted. But, did he just say "normal?" One would think Normal men know what they want—either a man or woman? Right? (waits for audience) Wrong. Black men and the desire for other men—in this world may almost seem an oxymoron or should I say, it is moronic to think that black men—or black women for that matter—wouldn't have sexual desire for those of the same sex. That's why we need to start payin closer attention to our history. This ain't new. There are new figures in the equation. But Maalik & Antwon always been around. Go to the library—look it up—read all in between the lines. You'll see it. Just might be under a different name. Chk-chk-check it out . . .

ANTWON   (*begins typing and waits for it to load*) These computers are always so damn slow. By the time your page load up, your time is up. But, it's free, right. I ain't complainin.

MAALIK   (*on the phone*) Shit . . . this line always so damn busy. How many niggas calling?!
(*overhead*) This month's sponsor is the Las Vegas nuggett .com for gambling and SPORTSBOOK. You've reached the Chicago beehive—if you got some minutes to blow, blow em with us. If you into the adult hardcore don't do it here.

(*presses 80*)

For the live rooms, press 1—for the bulletin board press 2, for the one-on-one press 3.

(*Maalik presses 3 quickly*)

(*woman's voice*) to go to CB press 1. (*He presses 1 quickly*)

Record your introduction message at the tone, you got up to forty seconds:

MAALIK   (*deepening his voice extensively—almost sounds like another person*) Hey wasup—this attractive nigga out south on the DL, bisexual—I know yall prolly tired of hearin that shit—cause I am too. I'm saying . . . but that's the truth with me man. . . . I don't like feminine niggas at all. . . . Not attracted to feminine at all. . . . I only hang with straight niggas. . . . And if I can't bring you around my homies . . . I work, go to school, shit like that. . . . Lookin to hang out with a nigga—see what ya look like—if something happens, it happens. Only into tight guys tho—people be confused about what is fine—but that's what I'm looking for. Money maker, right here.

ANTWON	(*huffs and puffs*) Finally. You'd think you'd be now died before this shit load up. Aight-aight. Let's see what these brothas talking about. See if any brothas online—mostly white cats up on here. Shit . . . I figured gay.com, couldn't be too many brothas up on here anyway. But shit . . . if there were any—I figured they would hit me up before anybody. With a screen-name like DLsmooth, brothas was bound to know what was up. I'm tired of doing the back and forth on these message boards. By the time you actually get a brothas number—shit . . . it's been two or three weeks. I'm tryin to be on something. Right now. I tell these dudes—straight up—I'm looking for femme cats only! I want niggas that scream like bitches, act like bitches, that's mobile, and can be at my crib within 15-20 minutes. I ain't got time to wait and I ain't about that public shit. Nigga right here tryin to fuck, getting his dick durbed on a little bit and that's about it. (*woman's voice interrupts*) Record your name at the tone:
MAALIK	Mark—the paper chaser. (*immediately clears his throat back in regular voice*) Mama—I'm on the phone! (*hangs up*) Damn— I thought she was sleep. I'm trying to make an early morning hook-up and she gotta wake up and pick up the phone. Shit, I guess I'll have to call later. I'm trying to be on some money makin shit too. Gotta make that paper, man. Help my moms out as much I can. A broke niggas ain't gon be able to do shit. These gay dudes—be lovin this—they pay up too. My stuff be makin niggas scream and moan and shit. Females don't be wantin to pay—but you know these brothas be layin down the cash. I had this one dude give me a hundred twenty-five to suck my dick. For real yo. This other cat was gone give me fifty—but when he saw the piece—he was like I can give you seventy-five. Cats on da line be thirsty tho— and half them brothas be lyin. Say they look like usher and be lookin like the church ursher. That be killin me. Say they 6'0 165 and be like 5'11 and 200. believe me—it make a difference. I be like—why you gotta lie. If you fat just say you fat. If you ugly just say you ugly and I'll tell u either got a go—or the rates just went up. These brothas don't recognize, I ain't sufferin, this is a job—not a fuckin hobby. I got females from here to Wisconsin, in line to be my baby momma, whatever. For real yo.

ANTWON	*(reading and laughing at message)* Ha! This nigga asked me to pay him—nigga you should be paying me. I wouldn't never pay nobody for sex and I definitely ain't putting myself out there like that. *(He types and speaks)* "Hell Naw!" They be trippin. *(looks at the screen)* Bigbottom, that's his screen name, just told me that he could be at the crib in 15 minutes, looking pretty tight too. Nice ass, smooth body no hair, latino brotha, about 5'9, 145—just my type so far. *(chatting)* you bareback? He say "huh?" like he don't know what it mean. *(writing back)* You know—like no rubber." No? Shit, this nigga don't want this then. *(He types and recites)* "you don't want this then." *(reading response)* why? Why? Cause a nigga right here don't need no rubber—*(types and recites)* Clean cat, DL cat, masculine cat, ain't got shit. These guys be killin me. What a brotha like me gon have?—I don't get down with every brotha I see, I'm strictly a top, rarely suck dick—I'm just a drilling machine, who does his job well, I might add. *(looks at screen)* This little brotha look like he really got it going on too. *(reads response)* "sorry man, can't do it—but good luck." Whatever dude—fuck you. Let's see what these other fellas on. *(pause)* Damn, all that time wasted—I could've been had some ass on the way. That's what I mean—that's why I hate this shit. It takes too much time. Either you wanna get down or you don't—don't waste my fuckin time.
MAALIK	This one chic, she told me, we can be good for each other, make a family, she'll help me out til I get on my feet. What I look like—a punk. I gotta hold my own—be independent first. I can't let no female support me. By the way, just for the record, I don't let no nigga kiss on me, I don't fuck no other dudes. I don't get no type of excitement from that. I just let em suck on my dick . . . if I do anything, I might play with they nipples or something. I nut, they pay, and I be up—that's the way it is—that's the way—
MAALIK'S MOM	*(from upstage)* Maalik Leroy Terrell Jenkins—get your behind down here—Right Now!
MAALIK	Yes mam! *(He gets up)* We'll talk later. *(runs upstage)*
ANTWON	*(angrily)* Damn I got ten more minutes and this fuckin monitor blows out. Looks around for help.

(enter James [actually DJ], the "fix-it" man)
(looks with recognition) Yo man, wasup, yeah . . . this computer keeps messin up or something. Can you fix it?

JAMES   Nah man . . . I just take em back and replace it. But, I can get another but it'll be like 10 minutes.

ANTWON   Shit!
            (James picks up the computer)
            (aside while looking at James) Damn.

JAMES   (picks up the computer—looks at Antwon with a gaze that is obviously more than eye contact) Alright man.

James proceeds toward the stage left exit and Antwon follows.

DJ   (enters singing) On the Down-Low, Down-Low. (moves the table where the computer) You see that dance—from the screen to the telephone—all that work to get there groooooove on. (thinking) Hmmm. I guess a virtual world promises much more, when you trying to keep it on the down low, keeping this dick thang from messin up the flow. You know it's like spinning a re-mix, while being committed to the old song. You keep re-vising over and over, until you get it right, or until its gone.

He repeats chant—"on the down low"—until two bodies are seen onstage.

THE DL DUET Two dancers appear onstage—one upstage and one downstage. They both are on the street—pedestrian. They are choreographed to express everyday tension, erotic tension, and a heightened feeling of conflict about the overlap. The dance is brief, specific, and punctuated to accentuate tensions.
            (DJ pauses the dancers pose as they end with a tender caress)

DJ   Yall stay right there. I want David to see this—it's beautiful. Brothas do ur thing—just be safe. (quick pause) Sistas too.

David enters and observes the scene.

DAVID   What the fuck dude? (The dancers exit) What is that shit?

Don't they know this ain't no fag country, it's a free country, but ain't no fag country. Jesus. I was not ready for that. Not today. We was just up in class today. . . . I'm trying to finish my GED . . . and I . . . we got to this one dude, I now forgot his name. Um . . . James something . . . they used to call him Jimmy B or something like that—He was a homo. But, he used to keep it on the low. Well . . . at least that's what he believed in, but his shit got out there too much. James Baldwin, yeah. The guy that teach the class, he started reading some shit from *Giovanni's Room*, some crap about these two gay ass white dudes. I was like I don't wanna hear that shit. Get sick of that shit. Fairies running around and shit. Be a man. Get some balls. Get Jesus. *(He smirks)*

I was at one of these things they got now—with my girl— she asked me to go—she told me that they was talking about "gay brothas who are married"—and I was afraid if I didn't go, she would think I was a fag or something, or that *(mockingly)* "I wasn't being a supportive mate," or whatever. Well, turned out—it was some dude there talking about DL cats—and I just sat there and listened. One sista said, after the speaker guy say he asked some dudes if they could take a pill to not like men—would they?—she yelled out something like "the pill is Jesus." And I wondered what Jesus she was talking about. Cause I now tried that pill since I was a shorty. And it ain't worked. I was messin wit dudes—before females. People always thinking, u know, that u like females before dudes. Naw . . . that wasn't me. 25 years of sittin in a pew—listening to preachers preach, getting low at the altar asking God to stop this. Cause I really don't like feeling like I can't control my shit. Maybe that's what I should be askin for—is control. Cause this whole desire thing don't seem like it's leavin. I mean, I don't feel like I have to . . . but it feel damn good. Another dude is another dude, I know that. It's weird. My ma say these desires for men, is of the flesh and not of the spirit—or some shit like that. I hear her when she be screaming at the screen when she watch Springa. It be funny—cause she be so real. I don't know why she be getting so into it. *(slightly mocking his mother)* "all these sinners on the TV . . . and you wonder . . . wonder why the world is going straight to . . ."—*(to the audience)* you know where. People on TV got they own lives, they own crosses to bear. Just like us. I don't know what's up wit mine. Like I smoke weed, but that's natural. This shit with dudes . . . uh . . . naw . . . it just don't seem right. I mean—I can't get it. I can't tell if it's the years of church that's now messed me up or just that I know deep down, I want a family and kids and the whole damn thing . . . but others dudes ain't included. I mean it's like I got a plan, and that plan don't include another man. (**He pauses**) Damn that rhymes. I always do that shit.

Ya know, I'm a poet right. And I always write these poems about things like my car, my girl, my moms (sometimes), and even got one bout my shoes. But, none about dis type of shit. I mean that's kinda funny.

Cause . . . I could write a poem about the way I have to check myself not to wreck myself. (**smirks**)

But, for real . . . no one wants to hear a poem about how
    I've had to balance between my desire, hold it back
    and hold it in
To avoid being beaten, put out, or fired.
Everyone wants to hear a feel good poem, right—about
    me "finding myself, coming out," or how do these
    churchfolks say, "my deliverance?"
Deliver me from that jungle of madness that tells me that
    a man has to raise a family, to be a pillar
In the community.
Deliver me from the streets that told me that to cry is for
    punks, a real man only cries in the dark,
Deliver me from the world that can't let up and just see
    that I ain't gay/straight, neither in no closet or bi.
Buy me back the moments where my father told me that
    men can only live on pussy alone, while my body felt a
    man's, and didn't really like women for their "pussy"—
    but the woman's touch,

I guess TV got folks thirsty for knowing who is, when is,
    where is, how is, and how to know when there men
    are on the DL
Why?
So they could have a show called
Straight Eye for the DL guy.
As if I am not straight.

Don't hate—just appreciate.

Why people try to front like its new shit.

Black men been fuckin around with other men like everyone else. Look at Jimmy B.

Just too scared to show it—cause we so worried about
what white folks think about us.

We gotta be the saved folks.

You know how much—how much trouble I've went
through to save myself the trouble of struggling to fit
in somebody's "saved folk" box.

I say save us from the fucked up world that would rather
keep people down than pick them up.

You know . . . save us from the preacher who tells us to
watch our desires that's desiring Sister Jackie, while
also desiring brotha Mike.

Save us from our parents, who more concerned about re-
producing than producing children that can love ALL
of themselves.

Save us, Save me from the hate that eats up
my soul—forcing me to sell out for the salvation that
does not save, but Kills.

God, save me from having to write fuckin poems that no
one really wants to hear.

But, nobody wants to hear a poem about that, see . . .

Nobody wants to hear this, do u?

*David stares at the audience for about 30 seconds and lights fade to
black.*

ACT II

*Scene opens with David still staring at the audience. He stares for
about 15 seconds and exits. Upstage center—Antwon stands with back
turned to the audience, with a kneeling guy giving him fellatio.*

ANTWON   What are yall starin at? (*man exits—Antwon turns around*)
Yall never seen a man get his dick sucked? Now I know
you didn't think that I was going to spend all this time tap-
dancing on the keyboard—to never get this—(*gesturing*)

tongue-tapped by some young, hot slim stud, who knew how to serve it, save it, and suck it again.

I mean come on . . . I spent the last two months going back and forth. I really didn't even know if I could do this shit no more. I mean . . . it's one thing to talk a whole game . . . and another to do it. I mean a brotha live his whole life chasing after females, ain't easy trying to get with dudes. This gets tired, gets old. Especially when brothas be lyin. Like one dude, said he would me at the park, right? I'm at the park—we met in the parking lot—and he suppos-edly in a navigator, and I see this car pull up—like a pinto or something. First lie. Then, brotha get out the car—he had tinted windows—and he is feminine—but he think he a woman. Now I like fem cats—but not like that. If I wanted a female—I would've called up Latoya, Tracy, or any of the other girls who know how I do it. But, that's not what I was on. I was on some hot DL shit—and females were not in-cluded. I can have that—all day every day. But, here I am putting my shit on the line for this. The next two guys— don't get me started . . . They couldn't do nothing for me. Maybe if I was a bit more naïve. But, one cat—we talked on the phone—and I could tell he was the type that "pro-gay marriage" or something. I mean you do you—but I'm not about to be caught up. I ain't trying to have no relationship with no man. Bad enough (*pause*) I got this thing going on right here. I'm just looking for a brotha to go down on a bro-tha, no returns, and maybe if you lucky I'll tap that ass after you tapped this (*pointing to dick*) right here. But, you know this really ain't all that. I mean this like a little side thing . . . shit . . . I got other shit to be doing than trying to convince some nigga to come over here, or even go out and meet some dude that may or may not look like what he says he looks like. So . . . honestly, I really was getting tired of this shit—quickly.

Then one day, I was up on some hot chat like men4now and this fool hit me up with an instant message and he had his pic up—it was all good on his end. And you know it was all good right here. He was a Little cat, smooth body, nice frame, fem but still a man—ya know? And he said he could jump on the ail and be in the Rogers Park area in like

30—I guess he knew where I was from the profile. Well . . . I had learned from a previous encounter, that dudes at your house can get out of hand—when you tell them to leave and your girl coming over in like 30 minutes. Just a little messed up, just a little bit. But anyway . . . I told him that we could get down at this park off the lake. It was late—so I figured, as usual, no one would be out. (lights dim)

He met me at the park. I remember me standing at the rock and he coming towards me. (Guy enters) As he got closer, it was clearer that he was a brotha that not only told the truth but left out a few details. A few good details. My dick was hard before he even got close. Well . . . one thing led to another. He looked at me. I knew he was satisfied. And I said "wasup"—he stepped closer. (The guy steps closer) and he touched my shoulder (Guy proceeds to touch shoulder). He tried to turn my head and get me to kiss him and I took his hand down and placed it—here. (places his hand there—they freeze)
(Man enters and says, "Are you gay?")
Naw, (pulls his hand away) I ain't no faggot!

And he walks behind me and begins to rub my chest.
(Guy rubs chest)
(Man enters and says, "Are you bisexual"?)
What? Naw . . .

And he continues to play with my nipples and he tries to kiss on my neck. (Guy tries to kiss on his neck)
(Man enters and asks, "Are you a lesbian?")
Huh?

Then I turned around and he dropped (Guy drops to his knees)
(DJ enters and says, "Are you DL")
(Antwon pulls guy up and he exits) No I'm not DL—Who is that? I'm just a brotha just trying to live. I'm on the DL—but shit can we talk about something else. Let's talk about the weather—the sky—shit . . . let's talk about what I do every day. How I work for a company that continues to fuck me over—cause I'm the only black guy on the whole floor—running around like a fuckin chicken with his head cut off for $10.00 an hour—and they still refuse to provide health insurance for their workers. Let's talk about my moms dying

from cancer who also doesn't have healthcare—whose expenses are so high—that as I try to pay them I can't even afford to have my teeth cleaned. Shit . . . Let's talk about the fact that every day somebody asks me questions that I don't have the answer to—like I should always have the answer. You wanna talk about the down low—well, the down low is how I make do with what I can, when I can, under the circumstances that I can. Let's talk about my bills—oh no, you don't want to talk about my bills. Let's talk about me. Yeah . . . (*pauses*)
I'm Me. (*blackout*)

OVERHEAD   (*The beginning instrumental of Fifty Cent's "In da Club" plays and repeats*)

Scene opens with Shawn and a few guys dancing, some against the wall, a couple ladies in the distance. They dance to the lyrics:

> My flow, my show brought me the doe
> That bought me all my fancy things
> My crib, my cars, my pools, my jewels
> Look nigga I got K-Mart and I ain't change.
>
> And you should love it, way more then you hate it
> Nigga you mad? I thought that you'd be happy I made it
> I'm that cat by the bar toasting to the good life
> (**They all scream together**) You that faggot ass nigga trying to pull me back right?!

SHAWN   (**still grooving**) Yeah, that's the shit right there. Fifty is hot—this the joint. (**looks up at audience**) I know what you thinking? What the hell am I doing at the gay club? I know . . . I thought the same thing. Matter fact, I was scared I was gonna walk in—see a bunch of feminine guys running around to Madonna, Whitney, Cher . . . and stuff like that.
        (**dreadfully recollecting**) I remember the first time going to one of these clubs. I was in New York—me and my best friend Drew who also gets down, went to this club called the Warehouse. It was a frightening experience to say the least. I remember we both wore our hats so far down over our face—the most you could see was probably my smile and his goatee. We wore real big clothes, trying to conceal

our bodies and our identity. Now I don't know who would have known me in New York—being I was from the western suburbs of Chicago. But, we did it. We got in that place and we could barely move, I don't think we wanted to move. That was the first time I ever saw a group of guys together, like that, in one space. Brothas was lookin fly—there was some feminin guys and some tight, masc brothas too. I was not about to dance with no guy tho—I just was standing and watching. You know, a distant observer? Cats was all in my face—Kinda felt like either they knew I was not getting down like that—or they thought my shit was tight. (smirks) Both. Now I'm not saying I wasn't looking to get down with a nigga—cause me and Drew was definitely lookin to get a little low—before we got back to Chicago. But, a nigga wasn't gay—and I Know them guys up in there could feel it. This dude got right up in my face—cheesin and grinning— I was like "nigga pleaz! You better step back with that shit." He looked at me like I said something wrong. You got a let brothas know what's up. If you don't, they'll get the wrong idea. Now I wasn't that bogus all the time. I mean, dude was kinda broke down. If he had a been a little more tight—more DL with his shit—a brotha mighta had to let him get a taste. Ya know . . . Well . . . um . . . So . . . we just really spent a minute there and then we left. Wound up leavin after some guy tried to get up on my boy—and he felt uncomfortable. He got up on his ass and started grindin or something . . . (recalling) put his hand on his ass or . . . Well whatever . . . Drew don't get down like that—AT ALL. So he was like—let's be up.

So . . . now . . . I just guess I've gotten to the point where I can go—but I make sure folks don't know me—you know— like my name and stuff. Keep a low profile. While, I definitely felt out of place, I was kind . . . uh . . . anxious, I guess. Maybe excited . . . but that really isn't the right word either. Well, anyway, whatever I felt really had little to do with the hot, and often sweaty bros in the room—but the way they were. There was a way that the brothas, in these clubs, seem to let down their guard to a point where they seem to experience a real sense of freedom. Not no rainbow flag, gay pride type of freedom. But the freedom of just being human, a person—someone not defined by what he's supposed to be, but what he is. Yeah . . . in this club man . . . all types of brothas can chill.

("In da Club" starts again—Shawn dances—a few fellas return, DJ kindly pushes some out against their own resistance, they stand with minimal movement. And the party continues until the fade to black.)

Classical music plays—two women sitting in the beauty salon—waiting to get their hair done. Tricia and Lisa reading their respective magazines—Tricia talking about the new book by J. L. King—and Lisa puts forth another point.

OVERHEAD *(in the voice of an announcer, DJ in disguise)* Introducing . . . the hardest working man in sex business—the king of the erotic jungle—everybody's problem and solution—the million man, and woman, hunter—the new and thriving hormonal pulse within the black community itself, the sensationalized . . . DL King:

DJ AS DL KING *(Dressed in a doo-rag covering his face partially and loose jeans and T-shirt, walking slow—a hard stroll—stoic and stiff)*

I like pussy, I like dick.

That's it. That's all.

I like any thing that walks, or talks.

And most of all . . . I like to fuck . . .

(more exaggerated) I like pusssssssssy! . . .

I like pusssssssssssY! I like dickckckckkck!

Begins a drum roll with his mouth—progressing to the drum-major march. Starts to drum the "Camptown Races" lyric.

This is dedicated to all my sistahs who need to know what her man is doing, this is for my daughter—*(waves hi)* hey sweetie—who just learned that men are not to be trusted. This here song, lyric, whatever is for all those who are trying to understand the psyche of a black man.

(sings and dances) I like pussy, I like dick. do-dah, do-dah.
I like to use my stick, all my live-long day.
All my live long-days, that's what people say
All I do is use my dick, I like getting laid.

I like pussy, I like dick do-dah, do-dah.
I was born TO BE A PRICK. *(speaks) get it?*
I know my humor is kind of sick, do-dah, do-dah.
But, that's cause all I think about
is pussy and dick
All my live-long days, All my live long days
I am sex, and sex is me—
I guess I might as well be gay.

And its just that simple. (He ends with a big smile and it
slowly descends)

(taking off costume) This was dedicated to all those who don't
mind staying in the dark. *(Lights quickly fade to black and
lights fade up)*

LISA   One night, I was at this bar type/club place and this guy
says to me—"you know lesbian relationships are OK with
me, when and only when, a man is present." *(pause)* What
type of crap is that? It is not lesbian relations if a man is
present. I ain't no lesbian tho. I am just a woman who loves,
enjoys, and understands her body. Not as a tool for male
enjoyment—I will never be a video ho—and definitely not
to be mistreated and abused—I value myself cause no one
else seems to. Just look at us on the magazines, on the TV
screen, don't nobody really care about the black female, or
male, for that matter. It's all exploitation, if you ask me. You
know all this talk about the DL—got me kinda chuckling—
OK, HIV/AIDS ain't no laughing matter. But, it ain't all about
that, ya know. These are people—*(mockingly)* in the journey
to understand themselves. For real, tho. These brothas ain't
confused—they trapped. Trapped in between what they
know they feel and how everything in their world tells them
they should feel.

I wait for the day my man finds out that me and my girlfriend Rina are doing the thang—every now and then. I
know he's going to want to join us. I told him I dip every
now and then. But, he thinks that was a phase that came

before us. I heard him tell one of his friends, on the QT, that "his stuff keeps me satisfied and that's what keeps me with him." The nerve of this man. What makes him think my desire, attraction, or lust (yes lust) for another woman is contingent upon his sexual performance. Hmm . . . check one. If he had the biggest somthin somthin in the world, I would still find that I have feelings for other women. Check 2. He know he wrong for sharing my business with some other brotha—and his sex really ain't that good. Check 3. The whole reason why I feel like I got to keep my shit DL is because he would want to get involved, and me and most likely Rina would have to make room for the ego that would probably take up more room than his dick. Sorry, I'm being mean again.

No, seriously tho. This fool has asked me to let him see me get down with another female. Talking about "it would excite him just to watch." It's not going to excite me. In fact, it would not only embarrass me—but it would take away from the pleasure that I feel when me and another woman are able to do our thang, without being under some man's eye. So, I refuse regularly. And he drops it quickly. And we go on and proceed as usual. Ain't no shame—just gotta keep it real.

DJ

And keeping it real is what we gonna do. Uh-oh—women on the down low—are we go hate on them too? The question that seems so important in this moment—rather it's the desire or disease—that puts us on alarm, or better yet, which one is pleasure and which one is harm? Now, looking around this dance floor, I would say it was a little of both. But, how can we judge a woman/man, who is never able to sing their own song. Not lie, to tell the truth, but to make the tune their song, cause the world we live in is so incomplete, that every word made universal—it's always already wrong. Yall feel that beat? *(Drums are heard and Tricia enters)* Or offbeat I should say. I can feel the pain, the joy, the pleasure, the sadness of yesterday. I can feel the mourn of a mother—whose pain—comes from never having say—in what song she would sing, or what rhyme she would write.

TRICIA

I have never wanted to kill somebody I love more—than when I found out that this man I was in love with, my husband, was cheating on me with another man. When I say that I could have killed a man—I really could have. This was no laughing matter. But, I didn't. I read in the paper somewhere, like the *Washington Post*, about a woman whose husband infected her with HIV and her child, who died at 26 months. That could have been my little girl. That's so wrong. But, I don't think these men are thinking about that when they stick their dick in whatever Tom, Dick, or Harry they are out there screwing around with. I don't think they think about the pain they cause their family, their wives, and the damage they do to our integrity. I don't think these men think. Why not, huh? Why does it take for us to be hit with a life-changing illness for men to realize what they should've and could've done. Why did it take that bastard—me contracting this fuckin disease for him to leave me the fuck alone. Why, huh? Tell me why? Who is going to take care of my baby girl if god forbid something happens to me? Not him—his momma, his sister or his brother—my folks?—huh?—why should this be the lot to which our lives are cast—as women—as mothers—as those who have been fucked over in the most royal way.

(*pause—slowly speaking with great emphasis*) Yes I am angry with him for not having at least the decency to protect himself outside of our marriage; yes, it was embarrassing to know that my man needed satisfaction from another man—making me feel that I was not enough. Sure, I was pissed off cause I didn't have a choice in having my life changed forever. All those things have contributed to my long nites of pain and suffering.

Last week, I went to my weekly meeting, where we talk about issues of the disease in a group of mostly black women and a couple men. This one gay guy was talking about what he experienced growing up—from nearly getting his brains beat out to the everyday listening of "fag," "punk," and "sissy"—the latter is something I really never think about it. It's like hearing "nigga" everyday—pushed in your face. No damn wonder—they gotta be proud. Listening to Reggie, that's his name, I kinda got angry. At first, because everything about him reminded me of Michael—was he ever fuckin around with him? Or someone like him? Or . . . I don't know. Then, I wondered—if this brotha who seemed so confident had all these issues, on top of other issues, what was going through Michael. Don't get me wrong—I ain't excusing shit. Nada. Nothing. Zilch. A lie is a lie. And the lie is that he said he loved me and me only. But still . . . when I began to hear, I mean really listen to Reggie, I became enraged with my own hate for them people, black people's hate—always closing doors on people. Now what? Now look—all that hatred—disdain—disgust—and ignorance seems to be back-firing—bleeding right into our own backyards. Men aren't so able to explore and express their sexuality. So, they in turn get with sisters after their years of repression and suppression—creepin and shit. And of course, if he did tell me that he was on the DL—I was going out the door. Why? Cause that's all I know to do. When he told me—I wanted revenge. I didn't know if I should kill him, sue him, or what? But then I had to put all this in perspective. And the reality is—there is a disease out here called AIDS and if you don't want it—you got to do what you need to do. This disease has changed everything. I mean this aint the first time in history men fucked other men when they was married—or men have cheated period—shit, look at our last president. The point is things do change with time. Disease comes and hopefully goes—people evolve, change, shift, and we have to learn to cope with the changing moments, changing situations. No matter how hard it is. I just take it one day at a time—do what is necessary. I mean, what else can a woman do?

DJ   A professor, or graduate student or something was talking one nite with Cheryl Burton on Channel 7 and he said something like this. (*points to speaker*) Listen Up.

OVERHEAD   "The DL journey is marked by years of responsibility and commitment to the race, an attempt to negotiate one's masculine ideals with one's sexuality. The key part is to get the community to realize this, as well as see how this complicates the simplistic equation that DL men=HIV.

This moment is interrupted by chaos.

WOMAN #1   To hell with that.

WOMAN #2	That's Bullshit. A man need to be a man and just come on out with it.
WOMAN #1	If he gay . . . he just need to say he gay.
LISA	(in agreement) Yeah . . . what they said.

Three brothers come in—They begin talking over each other.

MAN #1	And what if he ain't gay.
MAN #2	Yeah . . . have you ever been attracted to another—
WOMAN #2	If he fuckin another dude . . . he gay
MAN #1	Maybe he bi-sexual—maybe we don't feel like we have to say who we are—
WOMAN #1	This is just fucked up.
MAN #2	We all fucked up one way or the other.
WOMAN #2	Yall some faggots
MAN #3	Bitch!

DJ enters.

DJ	Stop!

Missy is heard with her infamous "Rewind" and the scene does just that—they go back to their original combative positions.

DJ	This is a DL exclusive. (DJ stops the action and directs the action like a disk jockey-conductor) Here's what they wanted to say.
WOMAN #1	I am so sick and tired of brotha after brotha treating me like shit. It's like, it's like—they think this a game. Why can't a man be a man?
MAN #1	I'm trying to be the best man I can for these bitches. Yeah, I get down—but that ain't even the thing—it's just something, don't mean shit. I like my females—been getting down with them since I was like 12. I understand why they be trippin—

but it ain't just easy to be up—like—"yeah, I fuck around wit dudes"—hos be done blown your head off.

WOMAN #2   So now, you think you found you a good black man—all professional, good-looking and masculine. He turn out to be just a punk motherfucker. You know what—if I could find a good wholesome man, like my dad, now granted he cheated on my mom too—but he was real with it, AT LEAST. And it wasn't with no other dude. The bible say Adam and Eve—and Steve shouldn't never replace Eve.

MAN #2   When I was 12, I remember my father taking me on what he would call "father-son rides" and these would be all about "checkin out the ladies"—he would say "Boy when you grow up—you gon have all the ladies." A player indeed. He never told me how jacked up it could be—having females—and dealing with the multitude of problems they seem to have. You know my father never really even told me how to treat a woman—but I tried my best never to treat a female I was kickin wit—the way he treated my moms. No matter what—I WON'T EVER TURN OUT LIKE HIM!

WOMAN #1   Momma always said there would be men like this. "No good, good for nothins, with no jobs, no money, no damn sense." She wasn't far off. I long for a good black man—who's honest, caring, and loving. A good man is hard to find—ain't that what they say. But, why? Huh . . . cause they either in jail, on the DL, or just messed up from the floor up. I need to find a brotha who's cool with who he is, where he came from, and knows where he is going. I'm sick and tired of being tired of these tired brotha.

MAN #3   My dad, instead of ever saying "son, be you," he said "son be a man." And it meant all this stuff—stuff that seemed more stressful than helpful, that I never fully understood. Until now. Then, later on my boys would say the same type of shit, like "don't be a pussy—be a man," as if the two were always in opposition. I guess they meant don't be a punk, crying or being soft acting or something, but I never fully understood. I know I'm not the only cat who don't understand all of the rules. But, what I do know is that whatever they are—these unwritten social rules—is quite frankly bullshit.

Dancin' the Down Low   **315**

Music and slow fade to black. Michael enters center stage with a cup of water and pills on a small table.

MICHAEL   You know I never thought it would be like this. I mean what does a man do, when he has lost the only woman he has loved, the only child he has brought into this world, and deferred his dreams to a deadly, unpredictable disease. I never thought I would be sitting here, with nothing, staring at pills, thinking about the shoulda, coulda, wouldas of a life gone so wrong. This got me messed up. The whole thing— Tricia, Greg, (*pointing to medicine*) this shit. It's all overwhelming—it's all more than I can handle. It's all ridiculous—the cost of living a lie, right? The cost of doing things out of order. The cost is plenty. I sometimes wonder what my life would be like had I never known Greg. What would have been different? (*pause*). Why did he lie? He told me that he was negative, he told me that I was the only dude he was fuckin around with. But how do I know?—I mean he coulda been dealin with me and another woman, or even another man. Regardless, he fucked things up for me. He really did it this time . . . fo sho . . . yep, he pulled it. Ya know, I don't blame being on the DL for what has happened, but being on the DL and not doing what I know was right— like protect myself, my family, my life. Now I'm left to pick up the pieces. Or at least make peace. Tricia don't even really want to talk to me. And you know . . . I don't blame her. I lied to her, I deceived her, I cheated on her—and there is really no excuse. I Know . . . I just don't know. I mean, how does a man find it in himself—to forgive himself for the unnecessary anguish and pain that he causes his family, his baby girl, himself. You know—(*getting more upset*) I wanted to do right—I wanted to be the father I knew I needed to be. I was trying, I never meant to hurt anyone. I never meant it to turn out like this. I wasn't out sleepin around—I was with one dude—trying to keep it tight and in order—Of course, I knew that wasn't right. We had a marriage, a kid, a home. A happy home. And now that's shot for shit cause I, me, I fucked up. You know it's fucked up—how you want to be right and you can't do right cause you know being right may get you killed too—or even that telling the truth may destroy everything you worked for. I wasn't trying not to tell the truth—I was trying to save her from it. That's it—that's all. I was trying to be me, and that meant being the man I am, while understanding my own desire—I guess my own yearnings. This ain't easy. It really ain't easy. But, it's too late. The damage is done. (*pause. Slow fade to black*)

"Fresh Prince" intro is heard.

DJ   (*dancing at the booth*) Here's a little story all about how, my life got flipped turned upside down. Yall remember that? (*stops dancing, laughs, pauses*)
Well tonite, you've seen small glimpses into various DL men's lives. I wish I had time, but this track is almost up. I've mixed and re-mixed many songs tonight

> To end with one.
> Not an easy one.
> Not a simple one.
> In fact, no one story, or picture could ever show the full experience of these men or these women,
> No rap, by itself, has ever saved the world.
> But if we could begin to re-mix and re-arrange our priorities, question the majority, and let go of this so-called sexual authority—we might be alright. (*scratch*)
> If we can check-chkchckchk-check ourselves, before we wreck ourselves
> Strappin up, before wrapping up—
> Talkin before tappin
> And begin to see that black folks have never been uniform,
> And our choice to deny our multiplicity,
> Our complexity, our multiple sexualities
> In order to be safe
> Has not saved us from the sorrowful reality
> Of Dis-ease.
> Please. . . .
> Like Missy say "Black people better wake up."
> And see the history that has proceeded us and the future which lives ahead of us.
> Rewinding and Fast-forwarding past the pain, finding

Dancin' the Down Low   **317**

ways to eat, breath, and holistically live—shall I say
again? And again and again.
What will it take for us to see that we must re-imagine
our community, not ridding of so-called enemies, but
welcoming our friends.

(*brings out David*) Is he our friend or our enemy? (*poses
David*)
(*brings out Maalik and Antwon*)
Are they brothers still, even though they desire both man
and woman? When do they become brothas of the community, before or after the media paints their face (*takes their
smiles and turns to frowns*)
How do we account for the long history of DL bros, from
slavery to heaven knows, (*looking up*) and believe me he
knows? (*brings out Shawn*) Can we make room for a brotha
who knows how important it is to be a pro at getting out the
way of white surveillance cameras, often, or oddly, survey-
ing the dance floor in envy and hate?

Can we see beyond a black man's deceit and see his des-
peration? (*brings out Tricia*) Can we see our sisters as cautious, without framing them as victims of the Black man's
heat? But, what about re-mixing this—and seeing black
women as the casualties of this homophobic haterism, that
spins in and out of every fiber of this thing we call (*mocking
Bush*) A—mur-ick-a.
Yeah America—take that. Chck-cchk-chk—the DJ has
come—spitting a rhyme that does not relinquish black
people of their responsibility,
Or deem white people, in their force-fitting categorizing and
unfair economic, social and political standards, void of accountability
For people of color's inability to just be—or to be free—or to
be free to just be.
Change has to come. A challenge has come, HIV has come
and has not gone. Change must come. (*Other cast members
enter stage paired—male-male, male-female, etc.*) If that means
sistas and brothas, becoming models and getting HIV and
AIDS test all as one—Then we must do it. Brothas on the DL,
wrapping it up at all times, DO IT.
Change may require us to change the boundaries we

have set—that space between the DJ booth and the dance floor. Between God and the land, as we imagine it. Between mother and son, wife and husband, partners, sisters, brothers, friends.

America needs a re-mix.
America needs a change.
America needs love.
Black America needs to Live.

The DJ says live.

The whole cast proceeds to play ball. The game begins and they move as if dancing . . . aggressively passing the ball, blocking, pushing, shoving, falling, and moving to the rhythm. This continues until the final shot is hit. They freeze. Lights fade to black.

Center Spot light on DJ.

DJ   (DJ *appears onstage—in the booth—mixing "on the down low"* [remix], *while pictures of black men are made more clear but remains slightly blurred. His light begins to fade, as the song plays. Black out.*)

CHAPTER 9

Queering Black Identity and Desire

JEFFREY Q. MCCUNE JR.'S *DANCIN' THE DOWN LOW*

Lisa B. Thompson

> What is of concern to me is how is it that being on the down low, how is it that this descriptor, this way of life, how is it that this has become the image of black gay men?
> —Keith Harris, "In the Life on the Down Low"

> For closeted black gay and bisexual men, the down low is a way to validate their masculinity. For straight black women, the down low is a way to avoid the difficult issues of personal responsibility. For white America, the down low is a way to pathologize black lives. And for the media, the down low is a story that can be easily hyped.
> —Keith Boykin, *Beyond the Down Low*

Over the past twenty years, U.S. representations of black male subjectivity have gradually grown more diverse and complex. The images of black manhood in the public imagination now range from President Barack Obama and LeBron James to Wayne Brady and Lil Wayne. Even representations of black gay men are increasingly varied. In popular culture, images of black gay men are slowly expanding beyond the ultrasassy snap queen diva to encompass more diverse performances of masculinity. Contemporary television representations of black gay men run the gamut from those portrayed on the ever popular *RuPaul's Drag Race* to the ensemble series *Noah's Arc*, not to mention the CNN news anchor Don Lemon, who surprised many viewers when he came out of the closet in his memoir *Transparent* (2011).

African American theater and performance culture has often been a space that features narratives exploring the lives of black gay men. More recently, work by black gay male playwrights and performance artists increasingly challenges and complicates conventional and overdetermined representations of black gay men in American popular cul-

ture such as the image of the feminized, campy black queen popularized in the somewhat infamous sketch "Men on Film" from the 1990s
hit comedy series *In Living Color*.[1] Plays such as Brian Freeman's *Civil Sex*
(2006), Tarell Alvin McCraney's *Wig Out* (2008), Colman Domingo's *A Boy
and His Soul* (2009), and E. Patrick Johnson's *Sweet Tea* (2010) present narratives and representations of black gay masculinity in ways that disrupt established one-dimensional stereotypes.

Amid this broader range of portrayals, the popularity of novels
such as E. Lynn Harris's *Invisible Life* and *Just as I Am*, J. L. King's confessional exposé *On the Down Low: A Journey into the Lives of "Straight"
Black Men Who Sleep with Men*, and R. Kelly's wildly popular melodra-
matic rap opera, *Trapped in the Closet: Chapters 1–22*, another black male
figure has begun to dominate the black popular imagination, the image
of the black man who is living his life on the down low.[2] Although the
definition is often contested, the down low or DL commonly describes
black men who do not self-identify as gay, but who sleep with men and
whose primary relationships are often with women. Jeffrey Q. McCune
Jr. takes up this figure of the down low African American man in *Dancin'
the Down Low*. The play seeks to give voice to and place center stage a
figure and community that, by their very definition, are often reluctant
to be identified, let alone stand in the spotlight. The play not only features men who live on the down low, but it also reveals the experiences
of many of those whose lives are impacted by their actions. McCune's
rendering of this figure seeks to challenge the dominant depictions of
these men as predatory, selfish, self-loathing, and insensitive; instead,
he shows them as complex men who represent a diverse segment of
the African American community. McCune's piece also seeks to com-
plicate ideas about black gay identity and sexual desire.

Despite the critical and political interventions of black queer theorists, cultural producers, and activists, popular notions of what constitute performances of black gay identity remain contested from outside
and within the community. In many circles there remains a narrow
range of sexual as well as performative behaviors that can be constructed as identifiable and acceptable for and among black gay men.
I am particularly interested in the ways McCune's play explores the
pressures, expectations, and subsequent performances of black masculinity and how they form a vice that helps shape performances of
black males' sexuality in the public sphere as well as in private lives.
Dancin' the Down Low challenges many of the common and quite vocal
criticisms of black men on the DL, while at the same time exploring the
consequences of such deceptive sexual practices.

The play's preshow music features R. Kelly's seductive bass-driven 1995 song, "Down Low (Nobody Has to Know)." The ballad immediately signals to the audience that this is a story about those who chose to "keep it on the down low" and adamantly believe that "nobody has to know." McCune's choice of the controversial crooner's hit song featuring Ronald Isley's luscious hook not only captures the heightened intensity of sexual secrets but also seems to anticipate Kelly's aforementioned *Trapped in the Closet* music video serial, with its multinarrative rendering of sexual secrets and closeted sexual identities among a wide cross section of blacks in Chicago.[3] Kelly's larger-than-life persona and the song's popularity help to heighten the audience's anticipation of the show and reveal that it will be one that focuses on sexual secrets. McCune weaves Kelly's "Down Low" throughout the show. Its urban sensuality not only evokes the joy of the nightclub, but immediately creates an atmosphere that foregrounds illicit sex within African American culture.

In both his scholarship and his creative work McCune endeavors to challenge conventional understandings of the closet and simplistic depictions of DL culture. In his essay "'Out' in the Club: The Down Low, Hip-Hop, and the Architexture of Black Masculinity," he suggests that "these men challenge this overdetermination of the closet as a container of shame, pain, discomfort, and anxiety—offering a counternarrative of discretion as a tactic of survival." The same issues of survival are a central theme in his play. *Dancin'* considers the tactics many black men adopt in order to survive in American society and particularly the choices made by men who are on the DL. McCune asks for a more racially nuanced notion of what it means to be "out" and goes on to argue that "the closet may be an insufficient trope in critical discussions of the complex sexuality of men of color." McCune argues that the DL is an extension of "a historical black cultural practice of 'quiet as kept' and 'be still and know'—adages which have encouraged many black people to safeguard information, not for deceit but survival." While his essay also bemoans "the linear and incomplete media portrayals of these men," his play goes a long way toward addressing this problem.[4]

Various members of the African American community find themselves involved in the down-low phenomenon, and McCune tries to approximate that reality by including a wide range of characters. In a series of vignettes, we learn about the lives of what McCune describes as "black men who have discreet sex with other men, who engage in low-key queer activity and describe themselves as being on the 'down low' (DL)."[5] The breadth of the play's exploration of the DL phenomenon includes the frustrations and experiences of black men who do not identify as gay, as well as women who are angry about feeling betrayed not only by a partner's infidelity and deception, but also by his sexual choices and desires. The audience is first introduced to David, whose disdain for the gay lifestyle is palpable, but whose desire for uncommitted sex with men is equally strong. Antwon, a single man who has no conflicts about his sexual desires, searches for partners on the Internet. He encounters Maalik in a chat room. The young Maalik cruises for men who will pay him for sex and also brags: "I got females from here to Wisconsin, in line to be my baby momma" (299). There is also Michael, a father, husband, and professional, who feels tortured by a secret life in which he sleeps with his best male friend.

Dancin' also presents black women's stories. The women include Lorraine, a single woman obsessed with E. Lynn Harris's novels; Tricia, a mother and wife whose husband is on the DL; as well as Lisa, a black woman who also operates on the DL. Since McCune does not include age, or other physical descriptors, each character comes to represent every man or woman. This lack of specificity allows a director and/or reader to imagine sexual diversity within the black community more broadly. McCune's refusal to fix or describe the characters physically disrupts stereotypes and assumptions about those on the DL.

Dancin' opens with the DJ's prologue in which the disc jockey not only sets the show's tone with music but also acts as an omniscient narrator who introduces its major themes and concerns.[6] He is the interpreter and guide, much like the role of the club DJ, who acts as a director, controlling the action (or dancin'). The DJ is the central character that helps advance the plot and create transitions (mixing). The DJ explains that the play explores the phenomenon known as the down low and defines it as "this thing folks call black men who identify as straight, even when they re-mix the tune every now and then and get down and dirty, or down and clean, with another brotha." The DJ also challenges the idea of the down low as a purely black phenomenon because "hell, it's not like sexual 'ambivalence' is racially specific" (286). The DJ, a figure of authority, omniscience, empathy, and knowledge, spins and remixes tunes as well as conventional ideas about the people who populate this urban landscape.

The opening scene presents DJ doing just that. Instead of a helpful conversation between black men and women who are gay, straight, or on the DL, voices erupt and the scene quickly devolves into chaos. Each voice hurls angry insults that end only when the DJ silences them. He then "direct[s] the action like a disk jockey-conductor" and explains that the following conveys "what they wanted to say" (314). The DJ's ability to control the discourse and redirect it in order to get at a larger truth simulates what many hope can be achieved within the broader black community where there is a need for less demonizing and much more sympathy toward the various subject positions of those involved in this "down low" drama.

The DJ relishes his role as the play's narrator: "This is your DJ, re-mixing this visual rhyme, showing you new, more complex portraits of black men—in real time. (Rewinds and plays 'on the down low' re-mix then fades to black)" (288). This notion of the play as a "visual rhyme" evokes hip-hop and the rhyming integral to rap music and, along with it, the attendant masculine posturing central to hip-hop culture. The opening scenes also include a chorus of vitriolic voices that announce: "Vibe Magazine Introduces the HomoThug! Hip-Hop and its New Homo Vibes" (287). Another male voice interrupts, insisting: "There is no homo in hip-hop" (287). His voice is followed by yet another male who asserts: "They a bunch of fags in thugs' clothing" (288).[7] The culture of hip-hop and its black hypermasculinity presents one site of allure or pressure that shapes contemporary performances of black masculinity, and, in the play, hip-hop culture has a profound hold on black men's imaginations, particularly among those living on the DL. McCune's scholarship suggests that hip-hop culture and queer culture are a "dynamic duo." He asserts, "These two world-making apparatuses disrupt norms, interrogate new ground, and encourage exploration outside the domains of normativity."[8] While directly mentioning hip-hop culture, Dancin' makes it integral to the DL, but the play presents it as only one set of pressures that define notions of authentic black masculinity and influence DL culture.

The play suggests that another nexus of stress for black men comes from the overdetermined heteronormative discourse within the African American community that advocates the establishment and maintenance of intact, nuclear black families to counteract racism and discrimination. Michael and Tricia, two central characters in Dancin', both privilege a conservative model of black survival and success, and worship the black American dream. Shaped by narratives of middle-class respectability, the couple hopes to create and maintain the perfect black family, but their life together is part fantasy and part reality. Michael gazes upon his home and admires his "piece of the American dream. My little piece of happiness, prosperity, all the things I've worked for in my life balled into one" (291). Tricia's description of their family is no less than ideal. She calls her husband "the man of my dreams" and the answer to her prayers for a man "who is faithful, honest, fine as hell, and can take care of the business" (294). Tricia confides: "I don't know what I would do without my baby girl, my wonderful husband, and God's grace" (295). Their story line allows *Dancin'* to fully explore the possible impact of DL on the black family and how the DL lifestyle is at odds with the Christian, heteronormative ideology that calls for a very particular performance of black manhood to participate in the black American dream. Although the family is considered a site of comfort and support, for Michael the family is a place where he can only express one side of himself. Michael conceals his sexual desires and relationships in order to live up to his wife's dreams and the larger black community's longing for ideal families with fathers at the helm. Called upon by a less-than-understanding community to adhere to a particular script, Michael and men like him reveal only a part of themselves.

The DJ figure and the title *Dancin' the Down Low* reference the significance of music and dance for both the black and gay communities, and more important, the figure and the title evoke the relevance of music and dance to black gays who occupy the intersection of both cultural forms. Indeed, the word "dancin'" with its dropped "g" (similar to the term "DL" or "down low") is generally associated with black vernacular. The idea of dance itself calls to mind notions of bodies, dancing both alone and together, of trying to discover the same tune, to find a dance partner who understands one's rhythm. Dance also raises the specter of empowerment, and in this case, the body engaged in sensuality, flirtation, and pleasure.

The title evokes the notion of dance, and the term "dancin'" signifies African American vernacular, which, in this context, is as culturally specific as the phrase "down low." But dance also has multiple meanings that resonate in the piece as well. While the club is a site for people to engage on the dance floor, the dances that many of the characters find themselves engaged in include sexual encounters. The dance is also the way many of the men in the play pivot between identities and worlds. They are engaged with or partnered with women, while also actively pursuing clandestine sexual relationships with men. Dancing is about movement; it is a creative refusal to be fixed in place. It can also mean to dance around something—a strategy to avoid an answer or commitment, or to dance around the truth. McCune's use of this metaphor operates in multiple ways. In one scene, "The DL Duet," the dance becomes literal: "Two dancers appear onstage—one upstage and one downstage. They both are on the street—pedestrian. They are choreographed to express everyday tension, erotic tension, and a heightened feeling of conflict about the overlap. The dance is brief, specific, and punctuated to accentuate tensions. (DJ pauses the dancers pose as they end with a tender caress)" (301). This choreographed exchange between the two male dancers allows the audience to imagine the dance these men find themselves performing in both public and private spaces. Their duet ends with a show of tenderness that belies the macho callousness of the previous monologues. Their dance reveals sensitivity and caring between black men in what is scripted as a chance encounter between two strangers who are not "out" in any conventional sense.

As I mentioned previously, the DJ is a central figure. It is not only because of the prominent role of music in the piece, but also because he operates as the play's moral center. He is critical of all the players, be they male, female, gay, straight, or on the DL. At times, the DJ's comments appear somewhat didactic as he advocates for safe sex practices and chides the broader black community for being unwelcoming to black gay men, but his message (and perhaps McCune's) suggests that there needs to be a more comprehensive approach to HIV and AIDS that takes into account the complexity of human sexuality. Making one segment of the population the scapegoat (especially when its identities and motivations are more complicated than popular perceptions allow) is an insufficient response at best: "DJ has come—spitting a rhyme that does not relinquish black people of their responsibility, / Or deem white people, in their force-fitting categorizing and unfair economic, social and political standards, void of accountability / For people of color's inability to just be—or to be free—or to be free to just be. / Change has to come. A challenge has come, HIV has come and has not gone" (318). *Dancin'* calls for broader accountability as well as the dismantling of this emergent stereotype of the DL black man as a predator contaminating the community.

McCune's attempt to counter simplistic and disparaging images of black men helps bridge fissures between the black gay, DL, and broader African American community. Keith Harris notes that "the black gay male as image is disallowed, unable to signify within the political agenda of 'unity, atonement and brotherhood.' . . . It is in this miasma of presence, absence, and permission that the communitarian, cultural production of the 'in the life' identity is lost and the down low rises."[9] The black men in McCune's play choreograph a delicate dance that allows them to sway between worlds and even dance with the voices in their own heads. While Harris describes "being on the down low" as "perhaps the greatest act of cowardice in contemporary identity politics," McCune's depiction of DL men suggests that their lack of choices, demands from the broader black community, and the limited range of performances for black manhood or masculinity all contribute to their predicament.[10]

Although the metaphor of dance calls up the club as a site of encounter, desire, and community, the play also uses other settings such as the basketball court, the workplace, the street, the home, and even cyberspace to render the lives of DL and black gay men. Like the diverse characters in the play, these multiple settings allow McCune to present the DL black experience as ever present and logistically diverse.

McCune's queer representations and performances of blackness in the world of the DL even include the depiction of black womanhood. Lisa enjoys sexual relationships with women and insists on keeping that part of her life separate from her primary relationship with a man. It is also hidden from her public life and persona. Yet, aside from Lisa, the women's voices and narratives in *Dancin'* are not as complex as the men's. The play does not include women who are friends with men who identify as DL. Also, although useful as comic relief, Lorraine is a nearly hysterical black woman who is a rabid fan of E. Lynn Harris's novels and relies on the books to help her detect DL behavior in potential lovers. She explains: "Now, I know he gay, or bi-sexual, or whatever—but he is sooooooo Luscious. If I could wrap him up, turn him straight, and make him mine, I would devour him, honey. . . . You can not find men like that these days. Damn shame—always the good ones" (292). Lorraine is a self-interested and desperate woman, whose rendering teeters on buffoonery. She goes on to describe the violence she would inflict on a cheating lover. The redeeming moment in her monologue comes when she encourages women in presumably monogamous couples to get tested for HIV/AIDS. As a reader of Harris's novels, she stands in for all single, straight black women who happen to be interested in his work. For the piece to help shift opinions about this phenomenon, black women's depictions must be as complicated as those of DL men. McCune presumes that these readers are lonely women hoping to make the protagonists straight or objects of their affection. He never suggests or suspects that some of their interest may be about them feeling titillated by the narratives. If all desire is complex, contradictory, strange, and even queer, we must consider that some black women readers may have an erotically voyeuristic investment in Harris's novels.

It is important to stress that McCune's decision to include the voices of black women, particularly one who is romantically involved with a man on the DL, helps extend the conversation beyond the ways men perceive their roles or the expectations of black masculine performance. The voice of characters such as Tricia, whose husband, Michael, infected her with HIV (and even the voice of lonely Lorraine) reveals black women's anger, betrayal, vulnerability, and hurt. Of all the women, *Dancin'* allows Tricia to have the most extensive character arc. She grows to understand and forgive her husband's betrayal and eventually becomes more accepting of gays after being in a support group for those with HIV. She confides: "I became enraged with my own hate for them people" (313). McCune's piece imagines the possibilities of a hard-fought forgiveness. Michael's story also develops further so that audiences can imagine the remorse felt by African American men in his predicament.

At the end of *Dancin'*, Tricia has abandoned Michael. He is taking his HIV meds and questioning the high "cost of living a lie"—a sentiment that seems to be at the heart of the play. Lies cause Michael great suffering; they cost him his wife and daughter. His lover Greg's lie about his HIV status costs Michael his health. Notions of truth—be they political, cultural, or personal—as well as the pressures of performance shape the narrative and the lives of the men depicted within the play. The show does not fault men for being on the DL; rather, it considers how perceptions of authentic black manhood and anxieties about performing black middle-class respectability influence their choices, whether disclosing their sexual practices or using protection during their sexual encounters.

McCune's *Dancin'* engages with the kind of "moral imagination" called for by cultural critic Thomas Glave. In *Words to Our Now*, Glave speaks of needing a "moral imagination" that is "intellectually vigilant, never slipshod; politically agile and astute, never complacent; vulnerable and receptive to, aware of, the wider world at large . . . and always, without exception, compassionate."[11] Black men who are considered on the down low usually find themselves as targets of moral indignation. McCune's rendering of black men living and loving on the down low is, above all else, a compassionate representation that allows audiences to be privy not only to these men's revelations but also to the reflections of those whom they love and hurt. Glave emphasizes the importance of black gay writers writing about their own community as an act he deems morally imaginative considering that we live in "a world that continually seeks to write us *out* of existence, literally or otherwise; one that seeks to truncate us, caricaturize and demonize us, when it isn't ruthlessly busy simply ignoring us."[12] McCune's play avoids the pitfalls of demonization and stands as a remarkably tender evocation of this notion of moral imagination. *Dancin'* brings depth and complexity to the lives of men whom many, from both within and outside the black gay community, consider pathological or cowardly.

In *Beyond the Down Low*, Keith Boykin chides the broader African American community for imagining then constructing and vilifying a black gay closeted bogey man: "As a nation, we would rather talk about the down low than talk candidly about racism, homophobia, and AIDS, and about our collective responsibility to find solutions for these problems."[13] The DJ in *Dancin'* articulates a similar message that insists on conversations that lead toward deeper more complicated truths about black sexuality and performances of masculinity. African American literary critic Maurice Wallace warns that even after dispensing with "a singular black masculine identity" in order to establish notions of "an increasingly nuanced plurality of black masculine identities" we risk "the reconstitution of masculinity into smaller, subtler regimes of heteronormativity and patriarchal prerogatives in black contexts."[14] Yet, for McCune, there is hope for an alternative vision of black masculinity that is evolving, inviting, and complex.

Shawn, a young man in *Dancin'* who loves hip-hop music, describes the clubs he frequents as utopias for black men on the DL: "There was a way that the brothas, in these clubs, seem to let down their guard to a point where they seem to experience a real sense of freedom. Not no rainbow flag, gay pride type of freedom. But the freedom of just being human, a person—someone not defined by what he's supposed to be, but what he is. Yeah . . . in this club man . . . all types of brothas can chill" (308–9). Shawn rejects the restrictive notions of gay identity that define pride and the closet in ways that do not take into account race, class, and culture. *Dancin'* advocates for a safe space where "all kinds of brothas" no matter how they identify sexually can find solace and acceptance. Like Shawn, the play celebrates the kinds of spaces where "DL men and black gay men re-mix the closet, in the act of *queer worldmaking*"; but, *Dancin'* also insists that those occupying that world must understand the true price of belonging.[15]

Notes

1 Although the television series *In Living Color* is nearly two decades old, the much disparaged, often buffoonish stereotype of the black queen continues to dominate representations of black gay identity. The fictional reviewers Blaine Edwards (Damon Wayans) and Antoine Merriweather (David Alan Grier) left an indelible impression on African American culture.

2 Tyler Perry's film adaptation of Ntozake Shange's choreopoem *For Colored Girls* (2010) features a black man on the down low. Married to Jo or the Lady in Red (Janet Jackson), Carl (Omari Hardwick) is sexually involved with other men and subsequently infects her with HIV. This character was created by Perry and was not in Shange's Broadway show.

3 *Dancin'* was written before Kelly's legal troubles tied to sexual assault charges and his sexual relations with young girls and what many perceive as acts of sexual deviance with those same underage girls. For brilliant discussions of R. Kelly's *Closet*, see C. Riley Snorton, "Trapped in the Epistemological Closet: Black Sexuality and the 'Ghettocentric Imagination,'" *Souls* 11, no. 2 (2009): 94–111; and Tavia Nyong'o, "Trapped in the Closet with Eve," *Criticism* 52, no. 2 (Spring 2010): 243–51.

4 Jeffrey Q. McCune Jr., "'Out' in the Club: The Down Low, Hip-Hop, and the Architexture of Black Masculinity," *Text and Performance Quarterly* 28, no. 3 (July 2008): 299.

5 McCune, "'Out' in the Club," 298–99.

6 The DJ explains: "How do I know? Well . . . the DJ knows almost all" (286). In the performance of *Dancin'* at Northwestern University's Wallis Theatre on April 23, 2004, the actor actually said, "The DJ knows all things," which makes him a truly omniscient narrator.

7 These sentiments are reminiscent of the views articulated in the voice-overs and talking heads featured in Marlon Riggs's classic semi-autobiographical documentary *Tongues Untied*.

8 McCune, "'Out' in the Club," 302.

9 Keith M. Harris, "In the Life on the Down Low: Where's a Black Gay Man to Go?" (2006), Beyond Masculinity, http://www.beyondmasculinity.com/articles/harris.php, 147.

10 Harris, "In the Life on the Down Low," 150.

11 Thomas Glave, *Words to Our Now: Imagination and Dissent* (Minneapolis: University of Minnesota Press, 2005), 35–36.

12 Glave, *Words to Our Now*, 37.

13 Keith Boykin, *Beyond the Down Low: Sex, Lies, and Denial in Black America* (New York: Carroll and Graf, 2005), 5.

14 Maurice O. Wallace, *Constructing the Black Masculine: Identity and Ideality in African American Men's Literature and Culture, 1775–1995* (Durham, NC: Duke University Press, 2002), 15.

15 McCune, "'Out' in the Club," 300.

CHAPTER 10

Interview with Jeffrey Q. McCune Jr.

John Keene

John Keene: I would like to begin by hearing your thoughts about your work in general.

Jeffrey Q. McCune Jr.: I like to create work that has an aesthetic quality that's not only going to attract people to the narrative, but also accent the complexities and contradictions and the mysteries that are our everyday lives. There's a way in which you can flatten a life just by "keeping it real." You almost flatten it. I think that my job as a director and a playwright, and particularly as a director, is to frame moments in a way that the audience will not only get it but also get the layered complications and complexities, and that they don't miss that. My thing is . . . never make it easy for your audience.

JK: Do you mean layered complexities of meaning? Of experience?

JM: Yes.

JK: And what else?

JM: The world. The world we live in, the contexts. So that we get a feeling of these spaces. Recalling *Dancin' the Down Low*, there are all these different spaces: there was the basketball court, there was the club, the living room. I wanted folks to feel like they were there in the living room. . . . One could just throw a chair onstage and call it [a] living room, but there's something about the language of the text, and the direction of the body on the stage, that will make that living room actually live, or "pop," as dancers say. I like the idea of making this happen because things should pop for the audience. The audience should feel like they are in that living room, in that club, they shouldn't feel like this is some type of simulation of a club, but more so like, "I really was there." You can do that as a director; you can't be certain of that as a playwright. So it was really nice in *Dancin' the Down Low*, or even in the earlier piece, *Din Da-Da*, that I was able to write these realities, to reconstruct and re-present them.

JK: Let's talk about your doctoral training at Northwestern University. Specifically, I'm interested in hearing how you feel it contributed to your work as a director and a playwright.

JM: I think particularly of the work of Dwight Conquergood and E. Patrick Johnson, who were particularly helpful in teaching me how to do ethnographic writing. As you write and study up culture, there's a way in which you have to have what Dwight Conquergood calls an "ethical compass." *That* acts as the impulse for your pen, so that the pen seems to write in those moments of high stakes. And for me, the work that I do—particularly because my work deals with critical issues and is often taboo and sensitive, loaded—I think that writing in those critical moments is sometimes at once easy and difficult. And what I mean by that is that it's easy in that one of the things I learned as an ethnographer from Dwight, from E. Patrick, and from Mary Weismantel, and other folks in the performance studies department, is that language used by those with whom you speak can be, is, always already dramatic, performative, and representative. And that there isn't a lot you have to do to the narrative to make it interesting because most narratives are compelling by the very nature that we are narrative-loving people. And so I think that was really helpful, because there were these moments when I was writing *Dancin' the Down Low* that I wanted to craft it, shape it. But I found out something that Dwight told me in a seminar: that there was more drama in the breaths than there was in the directorial possibilities. My direction was not going to bring it drama, but what was going to do so were the moments of breathing. So if you notice [in the performance of *Dancin' the Down Low*], some of those freeze-frame moments are really breaths, are really a moment not only for the audience to think but also for the characters themselves to think and process, and to show that there is a process going on, whether that be my process as a playwright, or that be the process of the character, or the process of the audience. The audience is also processing, what just happened? I utilize breath a lot, but I think that the people with whom I speak utilize breath a lot. So it's really a theory of the flesh. It's not something I created but really something that came out of the bodies of the folks I'm speaking with.

JK: That's fascinating. In terms of performance theory and studies, what you're saying doesn't sound strange, but in terms of traditional and conventional dramaturgy, it sounds to me as if it might be unusual. While you were a graduate student, did you do any study of traditional dramaturgy at all?

JM: Not in graduate school. Most of that happened when I was an undergrad theater major, and so I took a lot of courses that were conventional, like Western, non-Western, and twentieth-century theater. I studied the tropes of theater and got a sense of the conventions. The point at which I began to move outside the tradition, the canon, and more conventional forms of presentation happened when I got to Northwestern. I just found a different voice. Now I'm working on another one-man show called *See Saw*, and I realize that my voice is always evolving. But I think that the voice of *Dancin' the Down Low* came out of the ethnographic research, and so my talking to folks in such an intense way, this deep listening that I was engaging in, made it much more possible for me to reproduce the sound of voice, the sound of breathing, talking. The music choices in the piece were songs that were often mentioned in the context of talking with the men with whom I spoke about the phenomenon of the down low. One of the things that I think is unique about *Dancin' the Down Low* is that I didn't change much of the ethnographic field notes; so I actually extracted them from the formal, traditional scholarship and transplanted and remixed them, creating an arrangement. The power of *Dancin' the Down Low* on some level for me, at least from looking at videos of it now, was the ways in which it juxtaposed these various narratives, and the narratives were speaking against each other, with each other, sometimes contradicting each other. Looking back at the arrangement was the really fascinating part for me. But I think that was my hardest work. Who would speak where and when, and who would connect these voices. Then you have the DJ, who all of a sudden becomes this omniscient voice that knows everything, and who can with his hand minister to the people so to speak. I think that in this case DJ acts as one of the ministers who's not about sanitization, but more about representing the fullness of experience, and challenging the experience the audience members are having. So at the moment that the audience is getting comfortable with the deviance of some man on the down low, then all of a sudden, the DJ punches it and says, "Whirrrrp. Not so fast." And it's interesting to do that. The work for me was what I had to do artistically, but what was easy was that the men with whom I spoke were complex, their narratives were complex, and they themselves lived complicated, complex lives. They were just so generous that the details were overwhelming. I had a lot of material to work with.

JK: It's enlightening to hear you move from your discussion of your ethnographic work to the process of writing the piece. Let's step back a bit and let's talk about the genesis of the project. The "down low" is a topic that reached a fevered pitch in popular culture a few years ago. What in particular led you to focus on this topic for your research and then translate it into this artistic piece?

JM: It started when I did a piece called *On the Down Low* as my performance project in my first year of doctoral studies. You have to do a recital in performance studies, and in my piece I looked at different figures throughout history who articulated what I would call a "down-low positionality," a kind of commitment to a politics of discretion that was a response to racist regimes that surveilled black bodies, and forced them to want to run from "the gaze," or at least hide from the gaze. "The gays."

There was also the idea of the overdetermination of "gay," and so in some senses "down low" is an escape from the overdetermination of "Gay" with a capital "G." One of the characters was someone I had met and talked to, but I hadn't anticipated doing a full-length play that was based on multiple voices of men on the down low. I had done this *On the Down Low* piece to deal with the relationship between history and the present, and carve out the genealogy of the down low historically. James Baldwin, Langston Hughes, Eldridge Cleaver . . .

JK: Claude McKay.

JM: Claude McKay. So, I tried to bring all of that in and talk about the homoerotics of male-male life that we often don't talk about. This performance piece prompted me to realize that there was richer material here and out of that came an interest in talking to men on the down low and locating them via the Internet, going to traditionally black male spaces, spaces that seem to offer a different kind of energy, and by that I mean a certain je ne sais quoi, that was bravado, that was loaded and oozing with proper masculinity. I figured that would be more of a comfort zone for men who had this idea about masculinity as it relates to sexuality. For them there's a certain proper way to do manhood that represents heterosexuality, or heteronormativity. I started talking to guys and having conversations and going on the down low myself, because there's a way in which I had to, at different moments, negotiate my own sexual visibility, the ways in which I was operating within a register of the politics of visibility. I had to play that down and return to the politics of invisibility, and I'm not calling that the "closet," because I don't talk about it as such. I actually think that was a down-low moment and I was operating within the politics of discretion. In those spaces I would have conversations with folks. I would say, "Are you gay?" And they would say, "I don't . . . describe myself like that." Sometimes that would be the first answer. Or they might say, "I am right now." In that context then, but outside of that context it's not an option for them. Economically, socially, religiously, it's not an option, in terms of all these other spaces that inform their lives and inform who they are.

JK: Did you then make appointments to talk to them further?

JM: Yes. I would negotiate times with them to talk more. That was mostly in virtual space. I'd be on the Internet, talking with folks who use the term "down low" within their online ad or profile heading, or describe themselves as being on the "DL," and I would schedule appointments and talk with them via the phone or via online, or in person. I began to write a dissertation based on those interviews, those conversations; in the meantime, I guess, I was also writing a play. I wrote *Dancin' the Down Low* as a way to perform activism while also at the same time producing theater. And so for me, *Dancin' the Down Low* was a corrective to the media's discussions of down-low men, particularly concerning the demonizing narratives around just plain-old cheaters without explanation, with no gesture towards the social, economical, or sociopolitical issues black men are facing. I also was thinking about it in terms of activism in the sense that it was correcting this sense that all DL men are carriers of AIDS to black women, when in fact, as you know in the play, most of the men aren't dealing with women at all, and I intentionally chose those narratives because I didn't want to reinforce that idea that all the down low is about is black men who have sex with men while having wives or girlfriends, right?

JK: And being carriers of HIV/AIDS.

JM: Right, and being carriers of HIV/AIDS and passing it onto their wives and girlfriends and children, et cetera. I thought that narrative was being overplayed, and so I wanted to construct a new narrative, a remix so to speak, of the down low. I wanted this narrative to be full, and to include some of the questions around deception, some of the questions around honesty, but I also didn't want the conversation to stop there. I wanted the conversation to then deal with the other questions on the table when we start to talk about discreet practices of sexuality, why they exist, and sometimes I think the play asks why do we need to concern ourselves with people's politics of sexuality, and why do we assume that the politics of visibility are somehow more healthy than the politics of invisibility, or the politics of discretion.

JK: One of the things I found fascinating was how the play returns again and again, in every narrative, to the question of masculinity. It excavates popular narratives about masculinity and manhood, and one of the most fascinating scenes involves the DL woman, and what she articulates comes back to a conventional masculine view of female sexuality. Please say a little more about how these issues of masculinity and manhood underpin the play.

JM: I think that there were a few things that I was trying to work out, or I should say that the men themselves worked out or complicated. There is this rubric of masculinity, this traditional way of understanding oneself as a man, that involves a certain linear narrative: this is what I must do to qualify as a man. In every narrative in the play, as you pointed out, these men are engaged in an articulation of "I have to do this to be a man." To be a man in this proper sense means that I cannot a-b-c-d-e-f-g. I cannot have sex with another man. I cannot use the "g" word, "gay."

JK: About myself.

JM: About myself, right. They can use it about others as a way to define themselves as not that. One really interesting thing about many of the men with whom I spoke and about the men who are represented in the play is that they speak of gayness as that which "I'm not, I'm not that type of guy."

JK: A negational definition.

JM: But I think that it's interesting because it's a negation, but at the same time it's an affiliation. It's a really interesting negation-affiliation dialectic that I think is common. Because clearly, to say that one is not something there has to be a moment of identification as well.

The second thing I was trying to work through in *Dancin' the Down Low* was the notion that all men's investment in masculinity comes from the same source. Meaning how one learns to be a man or how one understands what manhood is is diverse, is complicated, is dynamic, and it's not simplifiable, and so even with some men in the play, they're learning this from all different angles, even in the context of a gay club space, masculinity is being understood differently by multiple men, they're having this moment of where do I identify, this kind of over-stimulation, which is what I experienced when I went into that space as an ethnographer: overstimulation. So, one of the things I wanted to show was that masculinity is always in process, always dynamic, and always rich. It's always contradictory and always hard to pin down to one specific location of production. I learned how to be a man from this experience, and then two seconds later, I learned how to be a man from *this* experience. Then I also think that what was key to me to making the play work and key to the narratives as they were presented, as they were given to me, was that there was a tension between the ideals of black masculinity and individual sexuality and desire. And I think that how folks work that out was what made each character interesting. You have one gentleman who's working it out on the phone line and trying to figure out, really rehearsing, how to make himself sound more mas-culine or "trade," more convincing, which speaks to a constancy of the performance of what is *man*, what's properly *man*, what's properly top, and speaks to gendered notions of sexuality. Then you have another guy who operates within the virtual space and the park, and who's try-ing to figure out how to market himself in that space, how to market his desires. At the core of it, of all the characters, is this question about how do we resolve what is assumed to be a tension between the black masculine self and queer sexuality. How do I resolve that or do I? Some-times I think that the simple answer is, the down low produces a solu-tion for that.

I also think that the other point that the play tries to make is that the down low is not exclusively sexual. The play is critiquing a down low that preceded the down low, in terms of folks who don't want to talk about sexuality, they keep it "on the down low." Folks who don't talk about sexuality at all, who don't have these conversations. It's that very secreting of sexuality that creates this kind of politics of discretion for men on the down low, so what I'm saying is that there is a down-low culture within black vernacular tradition that justifies the presence of the down low in the sexual realm, as if we were to talk about down low in other settings. I'm thinking about my grandmother saying—and I think I used this example in the postperformance talk-back—"Miss Sally will let her in the front door on the down low." That's a setting where clearly the politics of discretion are working to keep the relation-ship between my mother and Miss Sally in check and intact.

JK: There it's race and class as opposed to sexuality.

JM: Exactly. There are all these different tensions that produce the necessity for a down-low politics and that's one of the things I was trying to get at in the play, along with the fact that I wanted to say that there are institutional pressures and policies that affect folks' decisions to be discreet about their sexuality. There are also effects that are created by discourse. As more people demonize these men and talk about queer sexuality as being the vector of contagion for HIV/AIDS, the more folks want to retreat from visibility, because they say I don't want to make myself subject to the violence of this gaze, of folks saying I am the embodiment of HIV/AIDS. That's what happens. Now there is this new *dreadful bisexual*, as Cathy Cohen might call it, of the 2000s, as opposed to the bisexual figure of the 1980s. I tried to undo and deconstruct those types of mythologies.

JK: Let's discuss the play's DJ. I read him as a marker of queer sexuality, especially in his relation to House music and clubs, his role as a "minister" to the characters and audience, and so on.

JM: I did read the DJ as making the audience comfortable with talking about complicated ideas about sexuality. The DJ is giving them the groove about sexuality in ways that most ministers are not able to. The music gives license to this conversation around sexuality. One of the things that I'm thinking about in terms of the DJ was that he connects different characters to each other. Men who we might think are not alike or have similar issues, he reminds us that their lives are connected by the confines of race, gender, sexuality, and class, and the DJ is a person who is able to smooth over the complexities and complications of sexuality. Also, the DJ in one sense is a magician; he's able to create magic and serves as the most mythical of the figures. He uses these mythical and magical powers to frame moments and is able to suspend things. So he moves past being the minister and becomes a God figure because he's able to suspend time and play with it, even though part of remixing is to play with time and setting. He constructs the space. You watch him move within the space, move the booth, set the scene, change everything. What I tried to do with the DJ was to give him that type of magicianship, to give him a certain type of power, but I was careful not to allow the DJ to be me, because although in certain senses he's an incarnation of Jeffrey the playwright, I wanted the men's stories to guide him versus him guiding the men. I really wanted that to be clear: part of ethnography and part of the experience and experiment was to allow the narrative to dictate where we were going. If you noticed, some men were talking from the phone chat line, but also talking about how they met in parks, the Internet, the clubs. They shared space. They had a purpose, to carve out one particular space, and that was the joy of it, and so the DJ could make that link and say, some people go to the club, some people go to the Internet, and so on. The way ministers do. The DJ is able to mix all those worlds together and show how they're interconnected, show how the woman in the living room reading E. Lynn Harris is still very much connected to the young man in the living room on the phone line, chatting, trying to do his thing, or the ways in which the guy getting head in the park is connected to the other guy at the club who is giving him head in the park. It's really interesting to see those worlds collide and come together in such a way to show the beauty of the complication of our world-space. I was reading at the time Fiona Buckland's *Impossible Dance*, and she talks about queer world-making, and one of the things I was frustrated by in the text is that she's still talking about queer world-making as if that's where queer bodies exist, that's what makes it a world. She does bring up the imagination but she doesn't quite push it, because I think the real queer possibilities don't happen, or transgressive possibilities don't happen in the sense of just the bodies, it's what the bodies do, and the DJ makes the bodies move. That's something I was interested in.

JK: Earlier you mentioned activism, and there's a didactic aspect to the play. There are moments where some of the characters urge the audience to get tested. It's wonderful and powerful, in part because you didn't place it alongside the piece's narrative, but integrate it into the story.

JM: Part of what I was working with there was the idea that the down low has always existed and what is new is HIV/AIDS. And if we know that HIV/AIDS is the new piece, then there are new things we have to do. The character Lorraine urges that you get tested regularly, that you make sure that you know your partner's status as well as your own, and that you're very clear about what you expect. This is a part of the agreement; this is something we must do. For me, that was largely a theoretical concept I've been working through, which is that the more that we get heterosexual culture in particular to think about HIV/AIDS as a possibility, the more we have heterosexual brothers and sisters who will go get tested, do what they have to do. I'm also interested in the gender dynamic, in the sense that in the United States sisters demand that your man get tested. There's such a concern about your man's sexuality, but knowing it or not knowing it is not going to solve the problem, which is HIV/AIDS, so it's the behavior that's leading to the transmission, not the fact that your man is queer, or bisexual, or tri-sexual, or whatever. Those things are not going to make the difference. What's going to make the difference is the choice-making, the decision-making, the process that you go through to ensure your safety and the safety of your partner. I also wanted to make it clear that it was not just one-sided, so DJ does the corrective work again and says that everyone needs to be safe, needs to get tested regularly. I didn't want to leave it where it is in the hands of women to control their mates, so to speak, but to provide a narrative where black women can say, here's what we *can* do.

JK: Thinking about the audience and the discussion, I'm interested in hearing about how black queer people, black gay men, have read and responded to your exploration and articulation of this concept of the down low.

JM: There were many different responses, and I'll talk about the most striking ones, which I've actually heard more of, not in relation to my play but in relation to the down low as a subject. I often felt particularly during the talk-backs that many gay men spoke and responded to the down low as something they were not. They engaged in the very same kind of negation-affiliation dance that I think happens a lot with men on the down low, which is that I'm not that type of guy, I'm not gay. I found a lot of gay men saying things like, "This is just wrong what they're doing to their wives and girlfriends," and it really became a way for them to lift themselves up, to have this moment of elevation, when they know that historically they've been in a position of subordination, of subjugation, of being subjected to the same violences that they're now committing against these other bodies. I really hurt when that happened in talk-backs. I would find myself wanting to get a little heated, because I thought, what work are you doing here? You're reinforcing these narratives that are going to impact your life and livelihood, because at the end of the day, all queers are the same, right? [Both laugh.] A queer is a queer is a queer to a lot of folks, so you're implicated in the down-low conversation. But I also felt that black straight men, black heterosexual men, knew that they were implicated in the down-low conversation; how we handled that conversation would also affect their lives. So now at the close of my book, titled *Sexual Discretion*, I talk about this guy who actually got frustrated, because every time he would go out with women and tell them what he did for a living and mention his hygienic process, like getting his nails manicured, they would call him suspect. Part of that is the residue of this down-low conversation that continues to say, those who do these type of things are questionable suspects, potentially down low. I think now we're reaping the repercussions of that in this moment, and it's really quite interesting to think about the ways in which that conversation has impacted multiple communities. Whereas most folks think that it's always going to be a contained demonization, that we can get away just demonizing certain people and things and it's not going to bleed over, but the bleeding always happens; it bleeds over and your blood gets spilled along with everyone else's. Your tea is spilled with everyone else's.

Part VI

Cuban Hustle

Cedric Brown

CHARACTERS

Narrator—30-something Black American man.

Félix—30-year-old Afro-Cuban. Ideally would be slightly lighter-skinned than the Narrator, but still distinctly black.

Ben—40-something American man.

Policeman—30s–40s white man.

Señora Silvia—50-year-old Afro-Cuban woman.

Note: Ben and the Policeman could be played by the same actor.

> *Lights up to the sound of a Cuban guaguancó. The Narrator and Félix quickly enter the stage from opposite sides while facing each other and begin to dance the guaguancó, Félix as the rooster and the Narrator as the hen. They do not touch.*

VOICE-OVER OF NARRATOR   The Cuban rumba *guaguancó* is sometimes called the dance of the rooster and the hen. Born in the black barrios of Havana and Matanzas, this pas de deux is unlike its appropriated and stylized descendant, the ballroom rumba, a now-distant relative. Here the rooster struts along with the rhythm set by the clave, drums, and song, aiming to circle and impress the hen with his majestic and intricate movements. His ultimate goal is to plant the *vacunao*, the "vaccination," with a pelvic thrust, a subtle tap on the inner thigh, or the drop of a handkerchief. The hen both entices and coyly deflects the rooster, but ultimately succumbs to the *vacunao* if out-maneuvered or out-charmed.

> *Narrator steps forward as Félix continues to dance in the background.*

NARRATOR   (*to audience*) Since I have the benefit of telling the story from the end, the present, I'll say that I'm ambivalent about the way things went down. Was it love or money? In the moment, I knew what was happening and only wanted to see one interpretation of it—mine.

Félix steps forward and does a vacunao. Lights and sound out. Félix exits. After a pause, lights fade up on Narrator.

NARRATOR   (*to audience*) When I first told my mother that I was going to Cuba, her lyrical and light "Ahhh, Cuuuba!"—no doubt accompanied by images of palm trees, conga drums, and cigars—was followed by a pause and the comment "Now why do you want to go *there?*" I don't have any ancestral or family ties to the island, but I've always felt connected to this ominous paradise, AK-47s and fatigues among fertile green mountains and cane fields.

Cuba had been in my imagination for a long time. I knew that something serious had gone down there, a revolution that greatly intensified the nuclear anxiety of the Cold War. The Bearded Ones looked to the North and said "*No tenemos ningún miedo de ti*"—we're not afraid of you! I remember reruns of "I Love Lucy" and the most identifiable Cuban on U.S. television, Desi Arnaz, playing the black-haired and heavily-accented Ricky Ricardo. I remember reading about Fidel Castro's warm reception by black Americans at the Theresa Hotel in Harlem after he was treated rudely downtown. I remember being afraid of a *Marielito* invasion after hearing that Castro had put hardened criminals and "retards" on the boats. I remember a photo of a white factory worker in *Ebony* magazine with the caption that said "U.S. immigration policy favors Cubans over Haitians, as most Cuban workers are white." I remember the giant Alberto Juantorena's brown Afro framing his bobbing, twisting head as he ran to two gold medals in the 1976 Summer Olympics in Montreal. I remember learning the words to *Guantanamera* in the seventh grade, and thought for years that it was a Mexican party song. I went to Cuba on a dare with myself. Things were different then; there was a sense of possibility and connection with the world that didn't require stripping down at the airport or wearing Canadian flags on travel gear. If you were brave and ingenious, you could get to corners of the globe without much notice.

When I first arrived in Havana, I walked around a street celebration on the waterfront. I laughed as I asked myself "Where am I, Detroit?" The crowd was nearly all "black"! When I say black, I mean those folks who would be claimed as black in the States, including mixed-race people—mulatto, trigueño, etc. Racial identity there defies our one-drop rule. This brown-skinned spectrum allowed me to blend in and move around somewhat inconspicuously—until I opened my mouth. Six years of high school and college Spanish still left me grasping to understand the verbal warp-speed of Cubans, but I eventually made out just fine. Before traveling to Havana, I had a chance to watch the stunning film "Soy Cuba," a 1964 Soviet-produced documentary—some would say propaganda piece. Through a series of beautiful black and white vignettes, the story of pre-Revolutionary Cuba is told with the voice of the island narrating in poetic verses during the transitions between each scene. The first vignette shows good time Americans gambling, drinking, and smoking fat cigars in a jungle-themed bar filled with a stable of Cuban women at their disposal. One guy ends up with a gorgeous brown-skinned woman who reluctantly calls herself "Betty." When Betty's client asks to see how she really lives, she sighs and takes him across town, over open sewers and unpaved roads, to her shack. When her boyfriend, a fruit vendor, drops in the next morning and catches them, the John rushes out, gets lost in the maze of shanties, and is surrounded by a group of tugging, begging children. The narrator asks "Why leave now? You wanted to see it; why not see it all?" It's ironic how history repeated itself after the fall of the Soviet Union. But this time, the clients aren't necessarily American, but from other parts of the world, bringing pale skin and thawed out libidos to the sunny island.

Lighting transition marks Félix's entrance.

Narrator continues:

In Havana there weren't any gay clubs or bars. I was hanging out on *La Rampa*, the city's hub of social activity, to find out where the rotating party, the *fiesta de diez pesos*, was happening on this warm, perfect Caribbean night. When I noticed him gliding up the street like a dark angel, our eyes locked.

NARRATOR   (*nodding to Félix*) Hola.

FÉLIX   Hola. Haven't I seen you before?

NARRATOR   I don't think so; I haven't been out here before.

FÉLIX   Ahhh, I can tell. Are you Jamaican?

NARRATOR   No.

FÉLIX   Canadian?

NARRATOR   (*smiling*) No. Almost!

FÉLIX   Ahh, *Mexicano!*

They both laugh.

NARRATOR   No, *de California.*

FÉLIX   Ahh! Which city?

NARRATOR   San Francisco.

FÉLIX   San Francisco—with the little trolley cars! The city *de los gais!* What brings you to la Habana?

NARRATOR   (*shrugs*) I always wanted to see it. I guess I've been curious about Cuba.

FÉLIX   Curious about Cuba. Well, welcome. Come, let's get a sip of Café Cubano—(*flirtatiously*) one of the many things you should taste while in Cuba (*chuckles*). I'm Félix (*extends hand*).

NARRATOR   (*shakes his hand*) *Mucho gusto.*

NARRATOR   (*to audience*) We went to a small café around the corner packed with other men. I bought two tiny cups of *cafecitos* that were strong, black, and bittersweet. We sat and continued to further introduce ourselves. He was quite handsome, not "phoine," but pleasant to look at. His skin was an unblemished cocoa; he had dark wavy hair (that was probably his original texture) and he was a little shorter and stouter than me.

FÉLIX   (*to Narrator*) I'm 30 and I was born and raised here in Havana. I just finished a degree in *contabilidad*, accounting.

NARRATOR   (*to audience*) I'm not sure how much time had passed before most of the guys in the café started to move out of the café and spill onto the sidewalk in front en route to dancing and drinking at the fiesta. There was an incredible swirl of men and noticeable electricity in the air. I followed Félix, who negotiated a ride for us with one of the unofficial *taxistas* out front. Félix and I crammed into the little Fiat with two other people and rocketed off through the still streets of Havana. Félix put his hand on my knee as he pointed out the landmarks whizzing by.

FÉLIX   (*pointing*) There's the *Universidad de la Habana*. And this is the *Stadio Olímpico* and the Ministry of Communication. And that is the *Plaza de la Revolución* and the famous mural of Ché Guevara. There's the . . .

NARRATOR   (*to audience, interrupting*) We headed in the direction of the airport, 25 kilometers outside of town, so I figured that we were going to be in a somewhat remote area. I could see my mother's face at that moment asking "What are you doing in a speeding car in a foreign land—one with a dictator at that—with people you just met, going to some party out in the middle of the country?" But somehow, I knew we were going to be alright.
(*Latin house music begins to play.*)
I paid for the cab ride and the cover charge to get into the party, which was at a large patio in what seemed like the middle of the woods. Hundreds of men mingled on each side of the crowded dance floor in front of the bar and bathrooms in the back. Félix gripped my hand tightly as he led me through a spicy salsa/house mix, bringing our faces close enough to feel the sweat evaporating off of each other's skin.

FÉLIX   (*shouting over music while dancing*) Do you like it?

NARRATOR   (*shouting*) Yeah! It's marvelous!

Félix and Narrator continue to dance for several beats. Félix twirls Narrator a few times; they stumble. Félix catches the off-balance Narrator. Their faces are close together. They kiss.

NARRATOR   (*while still being held by Félix, to audience*) Just like in the movies: on a dance floor, under a gorgeous, starry sky with a hot Latin man.

They kiss again. Lights and music quickly fade. The lights go up on Narrator and Félix seated across from one another.

NARRATOR   (*to audience*) Félix and I agreed to go on a dinner date the next evening. Because Cubans weren't allowed in tourist hotels, I used much of the day to catch up on my sleep—alone. When I later left my hotel, Félix was at the appointed place waiting, looking spotless and scrumptious. He decided to avoid the state-owned restaurants and take us to a nearby *paladar*, one of the citizen-run private restaurants tucked into the front rooms of someone's house. I found out later that he got a small commission from the owner for bringing me there.

FÉLIX   (*signaling to waiter*) Otra Cristál, por favor.

NARRATOR   (*to audience*) That's his third beer.

FÉLIX   (*finishing his meal*) Ah, *perfecto*. They have the best pork in Havana. (*looks at Narrator's plate*) How's the *arroz con pollo*?

NARRATOR   (*nods*) It's good, it's good. That was a lot of food! I'm full—I can't eat any more!

FÉLIX   Well, give it to me!

NARRATOR   (*hands over plate*) Wow, what an appetite! (*chuckling*) You must be pregnant!

FÉLIX   (*makes sour face*) Nooo! Soy *macho*! No, I'm not pregnant, man. I just like to eat. Soy *puro macho*.

NARRATOR   Sorry. Just a little joke. (*to audience*) 'Scuse me, *puro macho*!

Lighting changes as Narrator and Félix walk.

NARRATOR	I'm having a good time. I wish I could spend more time with you before I have to leave tomorrow.
FÉLIX	I do too. I want to keep in touch with you. *Eres muy cariñoso*—you are very caring. I want to leave this place. There's no hope here. There are no jobs for people like me. Unless you're a good party member, you end up working for almost nothing. I want . . . freedom.
NARRATOR	You wouldn't ever get on a boat, would you?
FÉLIX	No, no, no. That's too dangerous. I would never do that. I know of possible ways, though, that are safer. I just need some help.
NARRATOR	*(pauses)* Well, maybe I can. You have to tell me what to do, though, because I have no idea.
FÉLIX	Well, for starters, you could go to the dollar store and buy my family some basic things. My mother needs some good lotion for her hands. They're dried out from always washing clothes. We also need some soap. I could also use some new clothes.
NARRATOR	I don't know if I can help with the clothes right now, but maybe tomorrow I can get the other things for you. Let's meet tomorrow.
FÉLIX	The Hotel Alemania. It's in Centro Habana not far from where I live with my mother. There's a café on the first floor. Let's meet at noon.

Narrator nods. Félix gets up, looks around cautiously, goes to another spot onstage, and gestures for Narrator to follow.

FÉLIX	Thank you.

They kiss. Lights go out briefly then come back up on Narrator.

NARRATOR	*(to audience)* For a short time, during the economic crisis dubbed "The Special Period," the Cuban government legalized the use of U.S. dollars. Dollars-only stores sprung up in the city, where many of the items which are in scarce supply in Cuba's peso economy—just about everything—were avail-

able in the dollar stores. My hotel, a tourist-only destination, had one, where I bought lotion, deodorant, aspirin, soap, and pens. I got envelopes and paper. I bought a nice shirt and put everything in a cheap backpack so that the handoff to Félix would look more inconspicuous. This was as close to James Bond–like international intrigue as I was going to get, buying contraband goods for my lover (if a three-day affair counted) and handing them off in a café before walking away without an emotional good-bye.

Félix enters. The men sit down. Narrator places backpack in third chair.

NARRATOR (*to audience*) God, I wanted to kiss him so badly. He was even more gorgeous than I'd remembered him before. Or maybe he appeared so because I was leaving in a few hours and thought it quite possible that we would never meet again.

NARRATOR (*to Félix*) I put a few things in the bag that I think might be useful for you. I even bought pens and paper so that you can write me in the States.

FÉLIX *Gracias.* I'll be sure to write. You'll get a surprise around your birthday in three weeks.

NARRATOR I look forward to it. Keep your faith. Something good will happen. I'm going to try to be helpful.

They grasp hands innocuously.

FÉLIX I will never forget you.

NARRATOR I won't forget you either. (*jokes*) And remember my birthday.

FÉLIX (*smiling sadly*) I will.

NARRATOR Be careful.

FÉLIX Travel safely. Don't forget me.

Félix picks up the backpack and gestures for Narrator to walk first. He looks around cautiously and follows Narrator several beats later. Lights out. Spotlight comes up on Narrator.

NARRATOR   For some reason, people always expect to tell and hear post-vacation travel stories of sun, sand, sea, and sex, and this occasion was no exception. Everybody wanted juicy details, and I didn't disappoint—even though I had no sex tales to speak of. I was enchanted. I couldn't forget Félix. I charmed my friends with his handsome photo and turned them on with tales of rum-sweetened tropical passion. But my friends were also realists, some of them wondering aloud how we'd make anything work across a distance and language barrier, not to mention a 40-year-old embargo. Of course I dismissed their concerns with a faith that people are bigger than rules and that love is bigger than governments. Isn't it? Never mind that I wasn't quite in love, only having interacted with this man for a little over three days. Nevertheless, I was tired of being alone. Even in the one-time center of the gay universe, dating rarely happened for me, if it happened at all. Blackness is not popular here, and black men are still second-class erotic citizens, being neither exotic enough, next door enough, or in the eyes of some, trustworthy enough. To add insult to injury, the last guy I dated at that point told me that I wasn't masculine enough for him. Félix didn't seem to worry about any of these things.

Ben enters.

NARRATOR   My crazy friend Ben told me, in the way that only older black queens can:

BEN   (*looking at photos*) Chile, I knew that you needed something *imported*. This little domestic stuff here won't work for you.

NARRATOR   (*to audience*) Félix and I relied on emails and the occasional letter, expensive to send and slow to arrive, to convey our heat and hope. Who says that the art of letter writing was lost to the quick fix of email? Maybe the modern day scribe prefers the feel of pen and paper, but for two trying to find love over the miles and beyond an embargo, email was a saving grace.

     I especially loved the many nicknames; every positive, beautiful, affectionate title he could think of.

Cuban Hustle **353**

FÉLIX   *Mi oceano. Mi tesoro. Mi amorcito. Mi fresa y chocolate. Mi sol. Mi cielo.*

NARRATOR   My ocean, my treasure, my strawberry and chocolate, my sun, my heaven. His letters made me swoon like a middle-aged woman holding a velvet-lined treasure box full of memories. Only my good times weren't only going to be relegated to memories. I was going to have my cake and eat him too.

Lights fade to a spotlight on Félix.

FÉLIX   *Mi querido y estimado amor,* I hope that these words of love and caring find you healthy and happy.

Mi amor, I am very happy in knowing that you always have me in your thoughts and in your heart, just as I have you in mine. My dear mother and sister are very happy with the photograph of you, and feel like they know you already. They want to know you in person someday. I like that you have told your family about me. Now you will have a new member for Christmas festivities! *Mi amor,* I feel a great longing for you and I want to be near you RIGHT NOW to give you all of the love and caring that I feel for you. I am sure that side by side we would be the happiest in the world. It is strange that I feel that I have known you forever, and something has awakened in me that I haven't felt for a long time, and never this strongly before.

Mi amor, how the memory of your kisses drives me crazy, your warm hugs and your sweet and passionate way of looking at me—how all of these things still bring a vision of you to my eyes. I am loving you and needing you little by little. Take care of yourself and love me a lot. Don't get with anyone else, okay, since I am CUBAN and I'm jealous! I love you and only you and I want you in my life as I will be in yours.

Can you imagine what would happen if I were there with you, what I would do with you, this crazy Cuban that you have on your hands? I will love you like no one has ever done before; I will take you to a place in love where you have never been. I will kidnap you with my caresses until they carry you to that same moon that you saw the other night and thought of me. I will fill you with kisses and I will make you feel inside who this *gran Cubano* is. IMAGINE. Writing this letter has made me a little nervous and agitated . . . horny! I want to feel you RIGHT NOW!

I want to ask you a favor and hope that you don't take this badly. *Mi amorcito*, you were able to appreciate the conditions that you saw when you were here in Cuba, and the great needs that we Cubans have. I want to see if you can, within your possibilities, send me $100 so that I can buy shoes and clothes and have a dinner in my home for my birthday, which we will hold in honor of you. I want to make a dinner for my mother, sister, and a few friends—the ones that you met and who always ask me about you. I also want to buy different kinds of medicine that is available at the dollar store. With the peso, there is nothing but sadness— you can't buy anything with the peso, especially medicine. But don't become sad, *mi amor*, my mother and sister and I will be very thankful for the help that you are going to provide.

Mi amorcito, please don't be upset by my request because I need your help in this moment, and I don't like asking for it since I really only want to love you and to be loved. *Mi cielo*, if you are going to send the money, please tell me (through email) the number that the *Werter Yonio* people give to you so that I'll be able to get the money here in Cuba without a problem.

Mi tesoro, I am very happy to know that you have made plans to return to Cuba in January to study at the University—I wish it were sooner, *mi amor*, but I know that that is impossible since you have to work to be able to visit me and be at my side. You will improve your Spanish and help with my English and we will have a grand time together. *Mi amor*, when you come to Cuba, don't reserve a hotel for the entire time, since (like I explained to you) here we have *casas particulares* that you can rent and I will be able to be with you all of the time. We are a pair, *una pareja*, and it doesn't matter to me what other people will say since there are always people who don't agree. *Mi carino, te deseo* and I always think of you wherever I am. I tell you, *mi amor*, that we should always trust each other so that things will be a little bit better for us. So you can spend a few days at your hotel and a few days in the *casa particular* with your true love.

Mi amor you also should bring with you your driver's license so that we can go to the beach and to other tourist places here in La Habana like Soroa and Viñales and discos to dance salsa and spend moments of happiness together. *Bueno mi amor*, I love you and will be together with you very soon. I always have you on my mind. Be sure to tell me the day and the hour that you will arrive in Cuba so that I can wait at your hotel.

Bueno, mi amor, I don't want to close this letter and thoughts of you but I must leave this moment as time is passing. I love you and will not forget you. I am very happy that you are coming back.

Bueno mi amor, I say good-bye caringly, and send greetings from *tu cubanito* that loves you and won't forget you. A big kiss on all the places where I didn't give you any before. Until the next letter, take care from your *Cubanito* that loves you always *Felicito*. What a wonderful name—this is what we will call our children.

Chao.

Light changes. Narrator enters.

NARRATOR   I was trying to figure out whether I loved him, whether I loved his country. Both of them were simultaneously enchanting and hard edged. I was trying to sort through my feelings, which led me back to the fading crown jewel of the Caribbean, La Habana. And to Félix.

One afternoon, Félix and I were strolling down the Malecón, Havana's famous seaside concourse. The four-laned Malecón winds along the northern shore of Havana, offering a panoramic view of the skyline, with the fabled Nacionál and Havana Libre hotels sitting majestically on top of their respective hills. People in the city wander along this mighty boulevard, hoping to catch a breeze sweeping in from the Florida Straits, or to be cooled by playful sea spray as the powerful waves pounded the rocks just beyond the Malecón wall. You can catch a glimpse of the social lives of *Habañeros*, Havana's residents, being played out along the walkway: tightly knit groups of teens performing fierce free flow raps to polyrhythmic syncopated beats. A father and son cast-

Fig. VI.1. *Cuban Hustle*. A Havana police officer (DaMon Vann, center) confronts the Narrator (Robert Hampton, left) and Félix (Marlon Bailey, right). Performed in "The Hard Evidence of Existence," The Thick House Theater, San Francisco, September 2006. Photo courtesy of Cedric Brown.

ing fishing lines into the rough tide. A lone couple gazing off across the waters, perhaps dreaming of La Yuma, the United States, and the good life that lies just 90 miles to the north.

Félix and I walked slowly, re-acquainting ourselves with the physical presence of the other and making small talk.
(*Policeman enters hurriedly*)
The peaceful aura that shrouded us was shattered by the abrupt approach of a machine gun–toting man dressed in the dark blue militia jumpsuit of the *policía*.

He first aimed his order at Félix, who, upon seeing the officer materialize out of nowhere, had already reached into his pocket to pull out the always-required ID card.
(*Félix hands ID to the policeman, who scowl-facedly scrutinizes it and flicks it back to Félix.*)
Each time the officer moved his arm, his machine gun swung.

POLICEMAN   (*to Narrator*) *Identificácion. Dámelo.*

NARRATOR	(*to audience*) Showing the confidence, or perhaps muted arrogance, that the privilege of U.S. citizenship can bring while abroad, I handed over my California driver's license—my passport was safely tucked away in my hotel. The officer's sandy white face twitched with displeasure as he looked at both sides of the license.
POLICEMAN	(*demanding*) What is this?
NARRATOR	My identity card.
POLICEMAN	Where is your passport?
NARRATOR	(*to Policeman*) In the hotel.
NARRATOR	(*to audience*) At that point I was awash in adrenaline. I didn't want to endanger Félix by further annoying the officer with a too-slow response. I tried to put together my flustered Spanish in order to finish this ridiculous interruption of our crime-in-progress—walking down the Malecón.
POLICEMAN	Which hotel?
NARRATOR	Mélia Cohiba.
POLICEMAN	Where are you from?
NARRATOR	(*to Policeman*) California. (*to audience*) My license says. It translates like directly, you fuckin' idiot.
POLICEMAN	Where are your parents from?
NARRATOR	The United States.
POLICEMAN	How do you know each other?
FÉLIX	We're friends.
NARRATOR	(*to audience*) Félix was obviously afraid of the officer's power, but put forward a brave face in front of the posturing policeman.
POLICEMAN	(*repeating agitatedly*) How do you know each other?!
NARRATOR	(*to audience*) The picture was clear to us all. He'd caught two *maricones*, two black ones at that, walking down the street together.

NARRATOR   *(to Policeman)* We met here in Havana.

POLICEMAN   Ah, ¿sí? Well, what's his last name?

NARRATOR   *(to audience)* He threw out this zinger of a question, hoping
                to corner me in a lie so he could haul Félix—or both of us—
                off to do God-knows-what.
                    "Meléndez," I countered with the confidence of a man
                who'd gone to bed repeating the same name in his prayers
                for six months.
                    "Félix Meléndez Teller," adding his mother's family name
                for good measure.

Policeman exits stage.

NARRATOR   Satisfied that he'd made us sweat enough for one afternoon,
                the officer grunted and stalked off. Félix and I walked for a
                few minutes in stunned silence. I immediately wanted to go
                home, back to a place where I could demand my Miranda
                Rights and call my friend at the ACLU to ask about a racial
                profiling lawsuit. Instead, I was here with Félix.

FÉLIX   I'm used to it. They always stop the black ones. Especially
                if they think you're with a *turista*. Fortunately, you remem-
                bered my name.

NARRATOR   Later that week, after a night out at one of the famous "ten
                peso" dances with $5 drinks, I slipped the hotel guard a $15
                bribe to let Félix come upstairs to my room. Cubans are for-
                bidden to go to hotel rooms with foreigners, presumably
                to cut down on prostitution. Nevertheless, tonight was the
                night. We were finally going to get to consummate this re-
                lationship. I was finally gonna get what I'd come all this
                way to get, my very own sample of the world famous Cuban
                pinga.
                    Cuba is a phallic country. Reminders are everywhere,
                from the fat and thick *platanos* hanging from trees—peeled,
                sliced, fried, and served with *moros y cristianos*—to hand-
                rolled Cuban cigars—long, sleek, earth brown and fragrant—
                to the shape of the country itself, rising slightly north in the
                west, like being hard in the morning before getting out of
                bed. Reminders were in the full-to-bursting baskets some
                fellows sported in tight jeans, or the delectable family jew-

els hidden from view but strongly implied by lounging hands stuck down the open first button of denim cut-off shorts. *Pinga* was in the air.

Félix's was like a long cone, thick at the base and more slender at the top, capped off by a mushroom peeking sleepily from under a hood. It stirred and flopped around like a drunken snake, probably reflecting the state of semi-sobriety of its owner, who was somewhat uninterested in the whole scene. The early morning silence was punctuated only by the constant buzz of the overhead light and an occasional slide of skin against bare sheets. Félix kept trying to finger me, but I certainly wasn't having any of *that* tonight. The whole experience was anticlimactic, to say the least. And both of us fell asleep.

At 6:45, the phone's loud ring jarred me from sleep. The security guard from the lobby spoke softly but firmly: "It's time for your friend to go." And Félix refused to get up!

NARRATOR   (*to Félix*) That was the guard! He says you've got to go now. Get up! You're going to get in trouble!

FÉLIX   (*sleepily*) No I won't. Don't worry about it.

NARRATOR   (*to audience*) I didn't know whether they would arrest both of us or not, so I wasn't taking no for an answer. No way was I going to some rotten Cuban prison à la "When Night Falls" over a piece of dick that I didn't even enjoy! No, his ass was gonna get up and outta here. I even tried pushing him off the sheets, but he kept saying:

FÉLIX   (*sleepily*) *No, no te preocupes!*

NARRATOR   (*to audience*) Only a few minutes later, as I grew tired of tugging and pleading, there was an insistent knock on the door. That got his attention—Félix sat right up in bed and started scrambling for his clothes. I could hear my heart pounding through my ears as I approached the door, suddenly furious and regretful that I'd gone through with the whole thing, as a vision flashed through my mind of my mother visiting me in a Cuban jail, her saying, "Well what were you thinking? All of this for some sex?"

The guard wasn't taking any risks, nor was he taking no for an answer. He came upstairs to personally escort Félix out of the hotel before his shift ended and before Félix's stubbornness got us all in trouble.

Lights out. Lights come up on Félix and Narrator bringing in bags. Felix begins putting away groceries.

NARRATOR   (*to audience*) In order to be able to spend some time together without having to dodge the distrusting gaze of hotel security, I followed Félix's advice and rented a *casa particular* from Armando, a friend of Félix's with family in Miami and an extra apartment in Vedado. I had to pay for four days up front in cash dollars, but at least we finally had privacy without an immediate time limit.

FÉLIX   (*turns on radio, tunes into a guaguancó*) Mi amor—come, try this rumba. (*demonstrates the male steps of a rumba*) Make sure to keep your arms moving. (*encouraging*) There! Keep moving your hips. This is like the, ah, Cuban Hustle (*laughs*).

NARRATOR   (*laughs*) Well, the U.S. Hustle went out of style 20 years ago, but I'll keep trying!

FÉLIX   (*keeps dancing*) See that's the difference between here and La Yuma. The *rumba guaguancó* never goes out of style. It's a part of our roots, our *Africanidad*. It's a story of life, of survival. How else do you think we make it?

*Félix ends rumba with a pat on Narrator's groin (a **vacunao**) and exits. Music and lights fade to spotlight on Narrator.*

NARRATOR   (*to audience*) I finished stacking the vegetables on the counter for later, and put a pot of water on the stove to boil for dinner. Félix called me from the bedroom.

FÉLIX   (*from offstage*) Ven acá.

NARRATOR   (*to audience*) Ven acá. Come here. When I walked into the room, he was lying on the bed, magnificently naked, with his legs spread wide, fully aroused.

FÉLIX   (*from offstage*) Ven acá.

NARRATOR   (*to audience*) From our first tryst I hadn't remembered his body to be so beautiful, especially his chest of wide and taut pecs. His arms and shoulders were thick and bundled like carved wood. He was physically splendid. I slid onto the bed and straddled him, kissing and caressing all the while. He pulled at my shirt, taking it off over my head while I moved further down his body, sucking his chocolate kiss nipples, licking his underarms, and nibbling his treasure trail. I'd just reached further south when . . .

OFFICIAL   *(knocking on door from offstage)* Fumigación!

FÉLIX   *(enters, holding pants and cursing)* Coño! We have to leave the building for 15 minutes while they spray for bugs. Turn the water off and put the food in the refrigerator.

Félix exits.

NARRATOR   *(to audience)* We left the apartment, both blue-balled, as the other residents filed out of the building in an orderly manner. Two young women held clipboards and wore matching dark grey uniforms, watching everyone leave. The hundred or so residents of the building stood outside, much like folks do during a fire drill, while young men with big canisters of bug spray walked into the building to set off the debugger bombs. Since we wouldn't be able to re-enter the apartment for at least twenty minutes, Felix said, we walked down the street to a little square and sat underneath a sprawling tree.

By the time we came back to the *casa particular*, the *fumigación* had unsurprisingly left a heavy pesticide scent all throughout the building. We opened all the windows in the apartment, hoping to catch some sort of cleansing breeze, but that didn't work. Félix started coughing, which lasted throughout the night, a deep, bronchitis-sounding hack. So between my nausea from the sharp and heavy pesticide scent, and his cough, we ended up tossing out any erotic plans for the evening, and instead slept spoon-style, with me holding him while he spasmed through the night.

They lie down; the lights fade to black.

NARRATOR   The next day, Félix invited me to his apartment to meet his mother. They lived in Centro Habana in a neighborhood that reeked of stagnant water and rotting garbage. Their apartment was two stories up, in the back of what was probably once a grand mansion built around a courtyard. The courtyard still existed, with laundry lines strung from one side to another, and the building had been carved into smaller apartment units for a multitude of families, judging from all of the kids running around squealing and playing. Initially I was concerned about the somewhat decrepit building, much like many of the places I'd seen in Havana, with steps missing, walls peeling, and bare lightbulbs hanging. But with makeshift repairs in place, the residents went on living the best they could under the circumstances. This seemed to be the general way of operating—do what you can to get by with some dignity.

Félix was dedicated to his family. Just like me, he was close to his mother and didn't talk much about his absent father. His mom was on the young side, giving birth to Félix when she was 20 and to another child, his sister, when she was 30.

Señora Silvia comes onstage as if she's working in the apartment.

NARRATOR   She looked like a still, hot cup of coffee with a dab of milk—brown and smooth.

The Señora and Félix hug and kiss cheeks calmly, as normal. She gestures warmly toward the Narrator.

SEÑORA SILVIA (*shaking hands and kissing Narrator's cheeks*) Buenotheea micarino, muchogutoenenencontrart!

NARRATOR   (*to audience*) She smiled easily and spoke nicely, although I could barely understand what she had to say because of her accent and the speed of her speech. She epitomized the reputation of Cubans for dropping consonants and word endings and sloshing everything together. I'd always look over to Félix for a translation into slower Spanish.

SEÑORA SILVIA So nice to finally meet you. Félix has told me all about you. You've really helped our family with your gifts.

NARRATOR   (*pauses uncomprehendingly, looks at Félix, then answers*) Thank you Señora. It is a pleasure to meet you as well.

Cuban Hustle **363**

SEÑORA SILVIA   I'll make us some café. Would you like some?

NARRATOR   (*not understanding at first*) *Sí, sí Señora, gracias.*

Señora exits and brings in café for the three of them. They begin to chat and Félix shows Narrator various photos.

NARRATOR   (*to audience*) We spent a nice afternoon there in the sunny, clean apartment, a definite contrast to the outside surroundings. I enjoyed having a closer glimpse at Félix's life and family, and got to peek at his three-year-old nephew, Luís, who was sleeping.

Señora and Félix exit. Félix returns after a beat.

FÉLIX   *Tesoro*, can you give my mother $20 for an iron? Her iron broke and she needs a new one. That way she can take in other people's laundry so she can make some money on the side. Especially to help out with Luís's expenses. It's just $20.

NARRATOR   (*to audience*) How could I say no, the so-called rich American who sent money down to them every month? How could I say no sitting in her living room after she'd been so nice to me before, genuinely, I thought?

FÉLIX   (*puts hand on Narrator's shoulder*) It would help us so much. (*in near whisper*) Do it for me.
(*kisses Narrator on the cheek*)

NARRATOR   Oh all right. (*to audience*) I was definitely annoyed. I was on a strict budget while in Havana and knew that this would cut into my per diem that I had set aside for both of our expenses, since I was paying for everything. (*takes out pouch from front pocket and unfolds a $20 bill*)

FÉLIX   Mami!

The Señora reenters the room, wiping her hands.

FÉLIX   Give it to her.

NARRATOR   No, you asked for it, you take it. Here.

FÉLIX   No, give it to her. This is a gift for her, not me.

NARRATOR   (to audience) Had my command of Spanish been good
                enough while mad, I would've said "I thought I was doing it
                for you." But I never think of the good comebacks until later.

*Narrator sighs and hands folded bill to the Señora, who snatches it
with an embarrassed smile or smirk.*

SEÑORA SILVIA *Gracias, querido.*

NARRATOR   (to audience) ¿Como se dice "sucker"?

*Lights out. Félix and Narrator remain onstage in dark. Félix laughs
drunkenly while making moaning/growling noises.*

NARRATOR   Wait. (with emphasis) Wait!

Félix continues making noises.

NARRATOR   *Suave, suave . . .*

FÉLIX   (mocks him) *Suave, suaveee . . .*

Narrator makes noise of discomfort followed by a louder yelp.

NARRATOR   Aw, shit. Stop . . . stop . . . (intensely) STOP!

*Dim lights rise, with just barely enough light to see. Narrator and Félix
are at opposite sides of the stage; Narrator glares at Félix, who is initially expressionless, then contrite. Félix walks toward Narrator and
holds out his hand, which Narrator takes after a few seconds. Félix
kisses his hand. He gently pulls Narrator for a few steps across the
stage, then drops his hand. Narrator continues to follow Félix. Félix
walks across stage, lights a candle, and kneels in front of an altar (can
be real or pantomimed).*

FÉLIX   (in soft voice) *La Virgen de la Caridad del Cobre.* The Patroness
                of Cuba. We also call her Ochun. Orisha of love and money.
                (He crosses himself and prays, visibly concentrating)

*Félix remains kneeling in prayer. The light changes. Narrator approaches
Felix, cradling his head in his hands. They stand still for a few beats.*

NARRATOR   (*in soft voice*) Yes. I do.

> *Félix rises. They hug but do not kiss, and walk back across the stage to Narrator's first position in the scene. They stop and kiss. Lights fade to black. Narrator makes breaths of pleasure and passion in darkness.*

NARRATOR   (*soft voice*) Yes, I love you.

> *During this scene, spotlights come up on Narrator and Felix in different areas of the stage to show a passage of time.*

> *Spotlight goes up.*

FÉLIX   El 28 *de enero. Mi amor*—I know that you feel desperate but don't worry because I will keep loving you. *Bueno mi amor,* I will tell you that I fixed my teeth—it went very well and I am very thankful to you. Okay, you will see little by little. *Mi tesoro, saludos* to you mother and friends. Don't feel depressed. I love you and want you and adore you very much. My mother sends greetings and hopes you are well. Until soon, *tu lobo.*

> *Spotlight changes.*

NARRATOR   (*reading letter*) February 5th. *Querido amor,* I am here every day in Cuba with a great longing since you left for your country. I was very happy with you here giving your love. Destiny separated us but I am sure that someday we will be together. *Mi amor,* I hope the days fly by because (as you know) I want to see you again but I understand that you have to work.

> *Spotlight changes.*

FÉLIX   (*reciting same letter*) *Mi cielo,* as soon as you're able, if it is within your means could you send me $50? Like I explained to you, I want to repair my room in my apartment since whenever it rains my bed and clothes get wet from the hole in the roof. You can understand this since you have seen this with your own eyes. I don't have money to write you like I want because I have to buy a phone card for the computer for $5.

Spotlight changes.

NARRATOR   (*reading same letter*) I also ask that if you can, please send money for us to be able to communicate more and more.

Spotlight changes.

FÉLIX   *El 12 de febrero. Hola mi amor.* Remember that I was waiting to tell you a surprise at the end of the month? I got a visa to Russia! I am happy and very nervous. I once thought it couldn't be, but it may indeed happen and I am very anxious. As you know, I have to pay $400 to be able to travel. My sister is going to help with the air ticket. She's going to send me $1200. *Mi amor,* I need your help now more than ever. This money that I have asked you for is for Cuban immigration.

Spotlight changes.

NARRATOR   (*reading the letter*) $300 for the immigration and $30 for the visa and $20 for the airport tax. My love, you don't have to send the entire $400; you can send $200 by 16 March and the other half by 16 April since I will travel the first week of June. Please send the money on time so that I can go to immigration and start my departure from Cuba. Please tell your friends that we need their help. *Bueno mi amor,* I love you and miss you. Until the next time . . . *Tu lobito.*

Spotlight changes.

FÉLIX   *El 19 de febrero. Hola mi amor*—I want to send you St. Valentine's day greetings. Here in Cuba this is the day of lovers and is a very happy day for us. I want to give thanks to you because I received the money that you sent and now I can buy the materials to fix the roof like I told you about. I mailed another letter to you in order to save minutes since a phone card costs $5. Well, you know. *Bueno,* I want to send a big kiss for your enchanting *nalgas* that are so marvelous and that I love to adore and another kiss for your sweet lips. My love, I need you and you need me. I love you and don't forget. Don't get with anyone else. For you, *mi amor*, a big kiss on all your body. Until soon, *tu lobo feros*.

Spotlight changes.

NARRATOR   *(reading)* February 23rd. Mi amor, I am buying materials for the roof little by little. You asked me to buy a CD of the group we saw at the Café Cultural. If you send me the money, I will gladly buy it and send it with someone who can bring it to you. *Bueno mi amor*, this is short because no time is left on the card. Until next time, I love you and won't forget you.

Spotlight changes.

FÉLIX   *El 8 de marzo. Hola mi amor—todo bien. Bueno mi cielo*, don't worry—as soon as I receive all of the information and details of the trip I will tell you everything, okay. Now I have to wait for permission from Cuba and I will go on the 20th of this month to see if I can get the *permiso de salir* to be able to leave Cuba and as soon as the officials authorize my trip then I can get the ticket with the money that my sister will send.

I will also tell you that I received the money that you sent together with the letter. *Tu lobito* is very anxious to be close to your side to adore you and give you all the *calor* that you need. I'm going to use a little to buy us food and a phone card and I will put this money in the bank until my departure so that I won't be able to touch it. This is only for my trip and I will save it better in the bank. *Bueno mi querido*, I won't say good-bye, only "adiós until the next letter." *Tu lobito* who loves you always.

Spotlight changes.

NARRATOR   *(reading)* April 17th. MI AMOR—THIS IS VERY IMPORTANT! I NEED $2000 TO PAY FOR MY TRIP BECAUSE MY SISTER CAN NOT HELP ME WITH ALL OF THE EXPENSES! I BEG YOU TO ASK YOUR FRIENDS AND FAMILY TO HELP YOU TO HELP ME. I NEED THIS MONEY BY THE 27TH SO THAT I CAN BUY MY TICKET BY THE BE-

Spotlight changes.

FÉLIX   *El 27 de abril: Hola mi amor.* I hope you are well. *Bueno mi cielo,*
         first I want to give you a million thanks for all of your help
         that you always give to me. For this reason I am always
         thankful to you and will always love and treasure you.
         Please also thank your friends for being generous enough
         to help with the money. I look forward to soon meeting and
         knowing all of them and being able to thank them myself
         in person. On Monday I will deposit the money in the bank
         until the hour of my departure arrives, and when it comes
         I will inform you of where you can find me and we can be
         together and very happy. Okay, I love you the most in the
         world and as soon as God desires, we will be together again.
         Muchos saludos to all of your friends who have helped me
         and have supported our love and friendship. Here on this
         small island there is a heart that loves and wants you. A
         million kisses on your body and your sweet mouth. I will
         never forget you. *Tu lobito.*

Spotlight changes; still focuses on Félix.

FÉLIX   *El 14 de mayo. Mi amor,* do not worry about all of this money.
         I promise you that I will start working and will make all that
         I can make when I am there with you. Do not worry. I don't
         want you to be upset, but this is the final and only chance
         that I have to leave.

NARRATOR *(reading the same letter) Mi amor,* my mother is also asking
         for this favor; she is here by my side asking for your help.
         She is crying and I am also because I might miss my flight if
         I don't have the *permiso de salir* that I need from Cuban im-
         migration. Please ask your friends who brought me letters
         and all the others. This is the last opportunity that I will
         have. Please do not be upset. Do not lose confidence in me
         because when there is not trust between two people then
         the relationship dies. You know that I love you and need
         you and want to love you by your side, not from far away.

My mother is very worried and has high blood pressure and is crying every day about the problems we have and don't know how to solve. If you can help me with 400 more dollars then I will find the $100 more that I need. Please do what you can by 5/29 or I will lose my ticket and . . .

FÉLIX AND NARRATOR   (*together*) This is my last chance to leave Cuba so that we can be together and happy. When you send the money I will call you to give instructions on where I will be and how we can be together.

FÉLIX   *Te amo.*

Lights fade to black. Spotlight rises on Narrator.

NARRATOR   Félix disappeared. Disappeared with the money and the speck of a dream that I conjured of us living together here in the States.

I sent word to his mother through a traveler to Havana who hand-delivered a message to their apartment. La Señora wrote me 11 anxious pages of a letter in neat looping script, worried about her vanished son, worried about her family's economic situation. She knew he was going to leave, but for her own good Félix wouldn't tell her when or where he was going.

If I were only sharing from the end, the present, I would tell you that I'm ambivalent about the way things went down. Was it love or money? Was I a *Papi Riki*, a sugar daddy, or did we really have a connection? Did he really love me or was I outmaneuvered; hustled? In the moment, I knew what was happening and only wanted to see one interpretation of it—mine. I'd like to think that we had something real, even underneath the ambiguity. Speaking for myself, if I had to buy love, buy adventure, so be it. Félix—and Cuba—changed me, made me more confident and open to possibilities, which lie literally around every corner. But this, of course, is said with the benefit of hindsight.

Lights fade on Narrator.

FÉLIX   (*as voice-over*) Mi querido—I send you greetings on the second anniversary of our meeting. I hope that you are well. I

have thought of you often on my long and difficult journey. After many tribulations, I have landed in Spain. Barcelona is a beautiful city. I am sure that you would appreciate it. I have decided to stay here because of the language and cultural similarities. I can also become a citizen in two years.
(*pause*)

I also now have a *novio*; we have been together for two months. It is going well.
(*pause*)

Mi *querido amigo*, I thank you for all that you have done for me. I hope to never forget you.

Chao.

THE END

CHAPTER 11

Love and Money

PERFORMING BLACK QUEER DIASPORIC DESIRE IN *CUBAN HUSTLE*

Marlon M. Bailey

As the lights come up marking the beginning of the show, I enter the stage of the Thick House, an approximately one-hundred-seat black-box theater in the Mission District of San Francisco, California.[1] It is a full house, and the performance of *Cuban Hustle*, authored and directed by Cedric Brown, draws black queer people from all over the Bay Area. On this occasion, mostly black gay men witness and participate in this theatrical examination and reflection of, and appreciation for, the lives of black gay men in particular—and black queer lives in general.[2] It is opening night, September 15, 2006, for a performance that takes the audience on an experiential journey of desire, love, and loss between two black gay men across diasporic space.

Upon my entrance, I can hear the penetrating rhythms of the rumba *guaguancó* music throughout the theater. This music creates just the right ambiance that helps to transform the theater space into La Habana, the capital city and hub of Afro-Cuban culture on the island. Playing the role of Félix, I move slowly downstage to the center, while the Narrator, played by Robert Hampton, proceeds through the audience toward the front of the stage. When we meet at center stage facing each other, I begin to show the Narrator a basic rumba step. Guaguancó is a very sexually erotic dance performed by a man and a woman, representing the vitality of Cuba and its people. Yet our rendition, danced by two black gay men, transgresses convention and adds a black queer twist to this typically heteronormative dance. As the Narrator quickly catches on to the moves of the rumba guaguancó, the dance of the rooster and the hen begins. The audience roars as the Narrator begins to roll his hips to the rhythm. Incited by the audience's cheers, I (as Felix) strut and high-kick around the stage, raising my hands and shoulders, using quick and jerky movements as I pass behind the Narrator. As a performer but not a dancer per se, I use my experiences dancing in black gay clubs to help me connect with guaguancó kinetically. Throughout the dance, audience members vocalize their excitement and interest as I strut to the rhythm of the clave, drums, and song, attempting to impress the hen with my majestic and intricate movements. Still rolling his hips, the Narrator both invites yet deflects my advances. But after a brief stint, the *vacunao* (the vaccination) happens—I touch ever so gently and strategically the Narrator's crotch, and he succumbs to the vacunao—he is charmed. The dance performance is an appropriate metaphor for the overall story. The audience is soon aware that Félix ultimately seduces the Narrator with his beautiful smile, his handsome face, his sex appeal, and his irresistible charm. The audience members become participants in and observers of this communal expression and representation of black queer desire.

The Narrator is the protagonist of the performance piece, and through his memory the audience travels through alternative landscapes of desire and comes to understand why and how a black gay man from San Francisco, California, pursues erotic possibilities in another black diasporic space to contend with his erotic marginalization at home. Regardless of the fixed location, these erotic possibilities occur in a black queer milieu where blackness is both desired and desirable. Although the Narrator's relationship with Félix, an Afro-Cuban, is constituted in part by different positions of power and socioeconomic locations, these landscapes of desire cannot be understood solely through geopolitics or socioeconomics. Rather *Cuban Hustle* serves as both a way to illuminate the complexities of black queer marginalization in the United States and of exploring the black queer diasporic subject's ability to imagine and experience spheres of sexual desire and love that extend beyond geopolitical and national boundaries.

In this essay, I examine three dimensions of the performance of what I theorize as black queer diasporic desire. Chiefly, I explore what it means when black diasporic subjects with different yet similar experiences meet through and at the site of queer desire and how this connection, illustrated in the performance of *Cuban Hustle*, portends erotic possibilities for black queer subjects worldwide. First, I argue that the performance illustrates the connection that is forged between these two black queer men. For instance, the Narrator and Félix are marginalized by race and sexuality in their respective societies in different yet similar ways. Hence, they are similarly situated, meaning that the social location that each of them occupies in his home country is similar in significant and instructive ways, though the men themselves live in separate geographic locations. Like the characters in the performance, black queer people—including those in the audience—share similar but not identical social locations and experiences, even as they live in different cultural contexts throughout the diaspora. Thus, the mostly black queer audience joins with the performers and is able to connect to and participate in the performance of black queer desire, as evidenced by the audience's active engagement in the performance event.

Secondly, the overall performance event illustrates the similarities between the black queer audience members and the performers; the story resonates in some way with all those assembled, and the audience members recognize one another's shared identities and similar experiences. This performance, then, is an expressive practice that creates the space for what some black cultural theorists call an African diasporic "mutual recognition" across difference that, in turn, produces new forms of consciousness.[3] Various factors play a role in the Narrator and Félix's relationship, including nationality, socioeconomic status, and sexual identity. Although it is short-lived, the characters' relationship is initiated through a mutual recognition of themselves as black queer subjects who desire each other, in very complicated ways, across diasporic space. Likewise, the black queer audience members recognize the connection between themselves and the performers. The audience members are also familiar with the factors that underpin the relationship forged by the two black queer subjects. Therefore, I suggest that the performance event constitutes a communal witnessing and practice of black queer diasporic desire.

Toward the beginning of the performance, the Narrator, facing the audience full front and center stage, poses a question about his relationship with Félix, asking, "Was it love or money?" (346). In order to address this question, in the final portion of this essay, I suggest a rethinking of what constitutes black queer diasporic desire or romantic relationships forged between so-called first world and third world subjects, as portrayed in the performance. Romantic relationships such as the one between the Narrator and Félix tend to be dismissed as inherently exploitative and utilitarian. Yet, *Cuban Hustle* requires a more nuanced reading of this relationship, one that reflects the complexities of the lives of the black gay men involved. Mutual recognition plays an essential role in illuminating how desire is sustained, even in the midst of inequitable socioeconomic conditions. Therefore, the performance demonstrates powerfully the possibilities of experiencing black queer love and desire across socioeconomic situations, cultural milieus, and national boundaries.

Similarly Situated as Second-Class Erotic Citizens

Deploying a black queer diasporic analysis can reveal not only the conditions and constraints under which black queer subjects live but also the transcendent possibilities of alternative sexual and sociocultural geographies and imaginaries. One of my central claims is that black queer people are excluded from conventional forms of belonging within black and queer communities no matter where they live. This marginalization within, as well as exclusion from, black communities means that black queer people are similarly situated across diasporic spaces, and this facilitates a mutual recognition between them.

Elsewhere I argue that African diaspora studies has, both historically and in the present, often theorized diaspora as the result of various forms of forced dispersal and migration, such as slavery, famine, war, natural disasters, socioeconomic depravation, and other crises.[4] These forced dispersals and migrations amount to displacement from a geopolitical, material, and, at times, cultural space. Put another way, people of African descent both in the United States and in Cuba have been displaced from an imagined or real African homeland primarily through the transatlantic slave trade that transported black people from their ancestral homes. Arguably one of the most violent forms of cultural destruction visited on an entire people, the transatlantic slave trade slaughtered countless Africans and destroyed families and communities. Former slaves and their descendants, involuntarily dispersed and displaced from their "homelands," reconstituted communities and created new forms of belonging in various geocultural sites throughout the world, thus creating what we refer to as the African diaspora.[5]

However, re-creating community in various locations throughout the world has put people of African descent in precarious positions, at once a part of and estranged from the host-lands in which we are situated. In order to reestablish the forms of belonging upon which diasporic cultures are based, black people in the United States and in Cuba created communities of survival by, in part, consolidating around heteronormative gender and sexual relations, and family and kinship forms. Many view this conformity as a necessary prerequisite for black people's laying claim to national citizenship. By representing oneself as a normative and respectable subject, one proves oneself as deserving of full inclusion in the national polity of the respective host-land.

African diaspora scholars, however, have failed to take into account the lives and experiences of black queer people in their theorizations of diaspora.[6] To begin to redress this problem, African diaspora scholars must reexamine the theories of dispersal and displacement in ways that move beyond geopolitical rupture and instead bring into focus the cultural networks of belonging that consolidate around heteronormativity and that necessarily marginalize and displace black queer people. In this regard, queer studies has made a major contribution to the theorization of diaspora via a reconceptualization of displacement. According to David Eng et al., queer diasporas emerge as a critical, theoretical intervention that makes it possible to reevaluate the forms of displacement and ostracization from conventional forms of belonging—such as biologized familial, kinship, and community structures—that queer people often experience. The concept of queer diasporas also provides the theoretical tools to examine the means through which displaced people create new forms of affiliation, belonging, and social practices.[7] For instance, black queer people are necessarily excluded from or marginalized within heteronormative black family and community formations; thus, black queer displacement and marginalization are best described in terms of social displacement and marginalization rather than in exclusively geopolitical terms. What the performance of *Cuban Hustle* shows, and what the audience is a coperformative witness to, is a connection that is forged within a diasporic milieu where blackness and queerness converge. This performance illustrates the means through which black queer people connect with one another under often hostile conditions.

As an African diasporic space, Cuba has a large Afro-Cuban population;[8] however, the racialization to which its black population is subjected enforces its marginalized position, which is rarely acknowledged or commented upon by the government. Cuba is too often represented as a racially homogeneous society that is devoid of racial discrimination, when the reality is quite the contrary. Dark-skinned Afro-Cubans experience a great deal of racial discrimination in all sectors of society, including among white and mulatto gay populations.[9] And as the cultural anthropologist Jafari S. Allen argues, antiblack racism among "neoliberals and neoconservatives" alike in the United States academy and in Cuba have silenced the perspectives of those Cubans who self-identify as black or of African descent on issues of race, gender, and sexuality.[10] Thus, Afro-Cubans, especially black queers, have limited venues and opportunities for redressing their own marginalization.

The displacement and marginalization that black queer people endure inform my discussion of what the Narrator refers to as "second-class erotic citizenship," or what I suggest is erotic marginalization.

After returning home to San Francisco following a brief but exciting and memorable time with Félix in La Habana, the Narrator, still sitting at the table where they said good-bye, seemingly only moments ago, turns to the audience and sighs while shaking his head. The audience members laugh and in a crescendo of voices yell, "whooooooooooo!" in unison, testifying and expressing their empathy with the Narrator. He tells the audience how he feels about the trip and the ecstasy he experienced in Cuba and with his new paramour. In his short mono-logue to the audience, the Narrator explains that he is of two minds about his experience. He feels trepidation about falling head over heels for Félix due to the many obstacles they are likely to encounter. But then he describes being a "second-class erotic citizen" in the Bay Area, which clearly resonates with the audience. He says, "Blackness is not popular here, and black men are still second-class erotic citizens, being neither exotic enough, next door enough, [nor], in the eyes of some, trustworthy enough." During this poignant moment, from offstage, I can hear the audience members affirming his statements by saying, "yes chile," as though the Narrator is delivering a sermon that captures their sentiments exactly.

The Narrator's statement speaks to a reality for many black queers in the Bay Area. Out of the very small population of black residents in San Francisco, and an even smaller number of black queer people, black gay men are the least desired in San Francisco.[11] A 2007–8 study on race mixing and partner selection among gay men in San Francisco con-firms the Narrator's point. According to H. Fisher Raymond and Willi McFarland, black gay men or "men who have sex with men" (MSM) were reported as "the least preferred as sexual partners." The study attrib-uted this to a variety of factors that made black gay men or MSM less likely to be chosen as sexual partners by other racial or ethnic groups of gay men and MSM.[12] Therefore, when the Narrator says, "Dating rarely happened for me, if it happened at all" (353), the mainly black gay audi-ence members in San Francisco identify and connect with him—as evi-denced by the responses in the theater—as they are likely to have simi-lar experiences with dating, romance, and sex in the Bay Area. This call-and-response moment illustrates how performance and those as-sembled produce an important discourse through which black queer people can comment on our lives and contend with the silence and in-visibility we experience in the Bay Area.

Feeling the crowd's affirmation, the Narrator continues his mono-logue filled with indignation: "To add insult to injury, the last guy I dated at that point told me that I wasn't masculine enough for him"

(353). To this, I hear a cacophony of comments like "What?" "Uh huh," and "No chile!" from the audience. In so doing, audience members express their empathy with the Narrator and his frustration with and critique of the femmephobia that exists in gay communities. Clearly the Narrator is tired of being alone, and his encounter with the handsome, sexy, and charming Cuban man is the first time he has felt desire and intimacy coming from another black man—let alone anyone else—in a very long time. The opportunity to be recognized and desired by another black gay man is just too good to pass up, no matter how unlikely the relationship's longevity may seem.

While it is unclear whether Félix suffers from erotic marginalization in Cuba, it is indeed clear that he occupies a social location similar to that of the Narrator in the United States, as both a black and queer man.[13] As stated above, black people in Cuba are among the most discriminated against groups in the country, and black queer people are even more marginalized. As the political scientist Ian Lumsden confirms in *Machos, Maricones, and Gays: Cuba and Homosexuality*, Afro-Cuban *maricones* (gay people) are demeaned as effeminate when they do not live up to the stereotypes of black men as inherently masculine. As a result, they are subjected to racism and homophobia among the gay community as well as in Cuban society.[14] Since many Afro-Cubans live in poverty, as Félix does, race and class discrimination converge to shape the particularly difficult conditions under which blacks, like Félix, live.

As the characters' similar social and cultural location is revealed, the performance further elucidates aspects of the two men's black queer diasporic connection and garners empathy from the audience. For instance, although he is educated, Félix and his family are among some of the poorest people in the country. Neither the Narrator nor Félix is wealthy. Again, both are marginalized in their respective societies because of their blackness, queerness, and working- or lower-class status. *Cuban Hustle*, therefore, brings into focus the shared forms of marginalization to which black gay men in these two African diasporic spaces are subjected, a discussion of which is absent from dominant discourses on and studies of diasporic blackness and sexuality.

During the rehearsal process, the director, Cedric Brown, asked us not only to draw from our own experiences as black gay men living in the Bay Area but also to listen to and explore Cuban music and dance to get the sound and style of the country and its people into our bodies as we developed our characters. Given my own background of growing up a black, gay, working-class man in Detroit, Michigan, among a predominantly black population, and living in the Bay Area at the time of the performance, I was able to draw from my own experiences in my portrayal of Félix. Despite the challenges of portraying an Afro-Cuban, I played Félix as a careful and streetwise black gay man who is attractive, flirtatious, and charming, and who uses these attributes to his advantage. He is smart and from "around the way," as we say in African American vernacular. He knows how to blend in with other black working-class people in Cuba. As I rehearsed the role, I watched documentary films and YouTube video clips to give me a sense of black men's style and comportment in Cuba. Although I would have the necessary theatrical convention of "a willing suspension of disbelief" on my side, I wanted my portrayal to serve as one means through which the audience members could at least get a glimpse of and imagine Félix as well as black queerness in Cuba, even though they would experience both primarily mediated by the Narrator's descriptions. Ultimately, Brown emphasized the importance of the audience members' recognition of and identification with the characters in the play, especially with the Narrator and Félix, so they could connect to and see themselves in the characters and in the story.

Mutual Recognition

As rumba music plays, people laugh and talk in the background and the narrator walks downstage, describing La Rampa, the area of the city that is the hub of social activity. As he walks casually across the stage, the Narrator gestures and responds to the imagined groups of people gathered in various spots before him. He talks about "rotating parties," the underground queer parties in La Habana.[15] He comes upon a celebration on the waterfront involving a crowd consisting of almost entirely Afro-Cubans. When the lights dim, I reenter through the audience, mingling with people as I make my way to the stage. As the Narrator continues to talk to the audience, he is interrupted. He sees me, Félix, as I get closer to the stage. Then the Narrator and I face each other and lock eyes. The audience responds to this moment with anticipation and sounds of affection as we smile and gaze at each other, clearly acknowledging our mutual attraction. Moments later the music changes from rumba to Cuban House, and we dance and dance and dance, until we stop and solidify our connection with long sensual, passionate kisses. The embrace and kissing are a prelude to the mutual black diasporic desire and romance yet to come. As we kiss, I can feel the longing and excitement in the entire room and the black queer audience members getting caught up in this ephemeral moment of black-on-black desire.

What factors play a role in this connection of desire and romance that the Narrator and Félix forge that, albeit temporary, transcends national boundaries, and the similar but not identical socioeconomic locations that each occupies in their respective societies of origin? In addition, how does the relationship between these men resonate with the experiences of audience members through the performance? First, upon arriving in Cuba, the Narrator immediately sensed the solidarity between himself and other Afro-Cubans. Set within the backdrop of a long history of cross-national relations between Afro-descended populations in Cuba and the United States, the solidarity between the Narrator and Félix is made possible at the point of their meeting.[16] This is in large part due to the characters' shared experiences as black gay men in a world of racism, white supremacy, and homophobia, experiences that many of the audience members share as well. As the African diaspora theorist Percy C. Hintzen notes, *mutual recognition* is the means through which black people recognize each other and have a sense of familiarity with each other wherever they are.[17] The basis of the connection between the Narrator and Félix is the recognition of shared experiences as black men in a largely white world, and as gay men in a largely heteronormative black world. Therefore, the mutual recognition of black queerness is part and parcel of the desire they feel for one another, among other factors.

Secondly, the mutual recognition between the audience and the performers, and the story being told, occurs in and through a revelatory process. In other words, through his writing and directing, Cedric Brown initiates the process of recognition between audience and the performers in the first scene of the show with the rumba dance and music. Since the Harlem Renaissance, music, dance, and other modes of cultural expression have served as a means through which Afro-Cubans and African Americans create transnational networks and linkages.[18] Shared cultural expressive forms like dance, music, theater, film, and visual arts are integral to historical forms of Afro-diasporic mutual recognition and cross-cultural linkages between blacks in Cuba and the United States. Therefore, at the Thick House, the live performance is the space and the occasion for black queer people to witness and co-create the revelations of the story and the particular moments that resonate with their lives in some way. According to the theater and performance scholar Jill Dolan, "Live performance provides a place where people come together, embodied and passionate, to share experiences of meaning making and imagination that can describe or capture fleeting intimations of a better world." The live performance presents the unique opportunity for audience members, the performers, the director, and the writer to engage in what Dolan calls a "theatrical communal practice." This theatrical communal practice brings people together to participate in expression and intervention, communication and fantasy, and reality and hope.[19]

The performance of *Cuban Hustle* draws from and reveals the shared identities and experiences of the mostly black queer audience members. The shared experiences and mutual recognition between the Narrator and Félix enable the black queer audience members in San Francisco to connect to the characters (the performers), the story, and the overall journey of the performance. Having an audience filled with black gay men in San Francisco contributes to this unique ephemeral transformative moment in ways only performance can do.[20] During the performance, black queer people are a part of the creation of an alternative queer public within which black gay men desire and love each other. For this performance event somehow made the practice of black queer desire and love more plausible and real, an experience that, in reality, seems implausible for most black gay men in San Francisco.[21]

Yet within this process of mutual recognition, audience members also bear witness to the complexity and messiness of black queer diasporic desire. While I suggest that one factor that constitutes Félix and the Narrator's mutual desire is the recognition of their shared experience and similar situatedness, still there are limitations that deserve some reflection. Félix and the Narrator refuse to take under advisement or be guided by all aspects of each other's situation. Both have a vision of the relationship that purposefully conceals the very factors that make clear the limits of their connection. For example, Félix does not take into consideration the fact that the Narrator is not wealthy even though he carries a United States passport.[22] Many black people are barely surviving in the United States. Félix's misrecognition of his and the Narrator's similar situatedness causes him to presume that the Narrator has more wealth than he actually does. But the Narrator's perceived wealth or financial comfort has to be viewed within the context of his social location in United States society, the country to which he returns. Nonetheless, the performance makes clear to the audience that Félix's expressed desire is constituted by a combination of physical and emotional attraction as well as aspirations of socioeconomic gain.

Love and Money

Some of the misgivings of the relationship for both the Narrator and Félix are made clear early on in the performance. Again, the socioeconomic differentiation between the Narrator and Félix is endemic to the relationship. For some, this socioeconomic differentiation makes the demise of the relationship inevitable. For example, after the hot dancing and sensuous kissing, the euphoria in the theater quickly diminishes as the Narrator soon after begins to read the letters from Félix. As he reads these letters requesting money and goods for his family, members of the audience begin to openly express dismay and skepticism. During the latter parts of the performance, audience members are reminded of the exploitation that is thought to typify relationships that occur across third and first world borders. Yet, I argue that the process of mutual recognition requires a nuanced means through which to understand the complexity of the characters' lives. The socioeconomic differentiation between the Narrator and Félix is only one aspect of the relationship despite the way that it ends.

Very soon in the relationship, the Narrator is made aware of a financial dimension to Félix's desire. On the first day of their meeting, Félix asks the Narrator to go to the dollar store to buy basic necessities for his family. And as the relationship increases in intensity, so do the requests for money and goods. In fact, out of the little money he has, the Narrator gives Félix and his family close to $3,000, in addition to assuming the costs of all the lodging, transportation, food, drink, and social activities during both of his visits with Félix in Cuba. Throughout this journey of desire and heat, longing and hope, romance and love held by the Narrator as well as the audience, by the relationship's end, he has given Félix and his mother a lot of money. As the Narrator faces the audience to read Félix's letters again and again, and as my voice is heard making these requests for money and goods, I can feel the audience becoming less and less in favor of the relationship between the two men. Sadly, Félix takes the money and disappears, and after several months of absolutely no communication, the Narrator faces the audience for the last time to read a letter from Félix, indicating that he has moved to Barcelona, Spain.

Palpably shaken, the Narrator pauses and looks up from the letter and out to the audience. Then, after this brief dramatic pause, delivering the most painful blow, Félix says, "I also now have a *novio* [a boyfriend]; we have been together for two months. It is going well." The

Narrator looks up, pauses again, looking away from the letter. Finally, we hear the closing words from Félix, "Mi querido amigo, I thank you for all that you have done for me. I hope to never forget you. Chao" (371). The sound of my voice slowly fades away.

In the performance, the Narrator acknowledges that he clearly understands the financial dimension of his relationship with Félix. Although he struggles with the tendency to see desire, love, and money as always already mutually exclusive, by the end of the performance, the Narrator concludes, "If I had to buy love, buy adventure, so be it. Félix—and Cuba—changed me, made me more confident and open to possibilities" (370). In the end, *Cuban Hustle* exposes what is obvious but too often denied about erotic or sexual relations throughout the diaspora. Just as in other sexual and romantic relationships, gay or straight, and no matter whether it occurs within or across geopolitical lines, or across class status, desires for socioeconomic advancement can be—often are—pursued through emotional and erotic attachments.[23] These are but a few examples of some of the less obvious facets of this relationship and the overall circumstances under which it occurred. The critical point brought to bear in this analysis of the performance is that diasporic desire is about recognition *and* misrecognition, love *and* money, fantasy *and* reality, loss *and* gain, all functioning simultaneously.

As the performance theorist David Román aptly explains, "Performance is a cultural practice that does more than illustrate the social and historical context in which it is embedded. At its best, it shapes and transforms the way we understand and experience our lives."[24] The audience experiences *Cuban Hustle* through the Narrator's memory, a reflection of a love affair he experiences across national boundaries with both Cuba and one of the country's black citizens, Félix. As one of the performers, I was heartened by the reception from the audience both during the performance and after. As typical of the collaboration between audience and performer in black theater/performance events, audience members testified and affirmed, and boisterously expressed dismay, as well as participated in and coproduced the action. Out of the four shows, all but one sold out; audience members laughed, cheered, sighed, and gasped with the performers. We held a question-and-answer period after one of the shows and many audience members communicated their desire to experience more moments such as this. Others shared their appreciation for the various perspectives on black gay lives that were engaged in the piece. Ultimately, the performance of *Cuban Hustle* proved to be a moment of intervention because it galvanized black queer people around our similar social positions and experiences to take part in the auspicious occasion to engage in the practice of black queer diasporic desire at the theater.

Notes

I thank the members of the Black Sexual Cultures Writing group—Mireille Miller Young, Xavier Livermon, and Matt Richardson—for their comments on earlier versions of this essay.

1 The Thick House is a contemporary venue for artistic projects that "reflects and engages the San Francisco Bay Area's racially and culturally diverse audience community." The Thick House functions similar to a community arts center that serves as a venue and host for professional theater as well as community and neighborhood projects. For more information, see the Thick House website, http://www.thickhouse.org/home.html.

2 Although I use this term mostly to refer to black gay men, "queer" is an umbrella term that includes LGBT people as well as all nonheteronormative gender and sexual identities, experiences, and desires.

3 Percy Hintzen and Jean Rahier, "Introduction: Theorizing the African Diaspora: Metaphor, Miscognition, and Self-Recognition," in *Global Circuits of Blackness: Interrogating the African Diaspora*, ed. Jean Muteba Rahier, Percy C. Hintzen, and Felipe Smith (Champaign: University of Illinois Press, 2010), xiv.

4 A good example of this is Hurricane Katrina, which created a diaspora because it forced mostly poor and low-income black residents of New Orleans out of their homes to be displaced in other parts of the country after their livelihoods were destroyed by the hurricane.

5 Marlon M. Bailey, "Rethinking the African Diaspora and HIV Prevention from the Perspective of Ballroom Culture," in *Global Circuits of Blackness: Interrogating the African Diaspora*, ed. Jean Muteba Rahier, Percy C. Hintzen, and Felipe Smith (Champaign: University of Illinois Press, 2010), 101–2.

6 Bailey, "Rethinking the African Diaspora," 99.

7 David L. Eng, Judith Halberstam, and José Esteban Muñoz, "What's Queer about Queer Studies Now?," *Social Text* 23, nos. 3–4, 84–85 (2005): 7.

8 According to the 2002 Cuban census, Afro-Cubans compose 10.08 percent of the Cuban population and those who identify as mulatto compose 24.86 percent.

9 Ian Lumsden, *Machos, Maricones, and Gays: Cuba and Homosexuality* (Philadelphia: Temple University Press, 1991), 146–47.

10 Jafari S. Allen, "Blackness, Sexuality, and Transnational Desire: Initial Notes toward a New Research Agenda," in *Black Sexualities: Probing Powers, Passions, Practices, and Policies*, ed. Juan Battle and Sandra L. Barnes (New Brunswick, NJ: Rutgers University Press), 93.

11 See Leslie Fulbright, "Black Population Deserting San Francisco, Study

Says," *San Francisco Chronicle*, August 8, 2010, http://articles.sfgate.com /2008-08-10/bay-area/17121007_1_african-americans-black-families-public -housing. San Francisco is known throughout the country—throughout the world even—as a queer mecca. Yet on the other hand, the city is simultaneously the site of race, ethnic, and class exclusion. It is the largest non-black city in the union. According to the most recent census data, of a total population of just above 800,000, African Americans make up a mere 6.5 percent. Moreover, San Francisco is one of the most expensive places in which to live, hardly a site of achievable good living for the many working-class black people, let alone black queer people, seeking such a life. As a result, the vast majority of the city's queer population is white and privileged.

12 Out of a sample of 1,142 MSM, 56 percent were white, 22 percent were Latino, 14 percent were Asian, and 9 percent were black. Raymond and McFarland's overall argument is that because black MSM are the least desirable as partners, their sexual networks are smaller and thus facilitate a more rapid spread of HIV among already very small black MSM communities. If chosen at all, black gay men and MSM were more likely to be chosen by other black gay men as romantic and sexual partners. It is worth noting that the authors in the study suggest that "the racial disparity in HIV observed for more than a decade will not disappear until the challenges posed by a legacy of racism towards Blacks in the U.S. are addressed" (630). H. Fisher Raymond and Willi McFarland, "Racial Mixing and HIV Risk among Men Who Have Sex with Men," *AIDS Behavior* 13, no. 4 (2009): 630–37.

13 In the performance, Félix does not openly identify as gay, but of course both of his intimate romantic relationships revealed to the audience in this story are with men. Thus, it is safe to say that he is at least queer, given the fact that not all men who love and/or have sex with men identify as gay.

14 Lumsden, *Machos, Maricones, and Gays*, 146–47.

15 Because there are no marked spaces for gay and lesbian Cubans, "rotating parties" serve as opportunities for gender and sexual minorities in Cuba to socialize at venues that are queer while being unmarked as such.

16 Frank Andre Guridy, *Forging Diaspora: Afro-Cubans and African Americans in the World of Empire and Jim Crow* (Chapel Hill: University of North Carolina Press, 2010), 5.

17 Marlon M. Bailey and Xavier Livermon, "An Interview with Percy Hintzen," in *40 and Counting: An Anthology Commemorating Four Decades of African American Studies at the University of California, Berkeley*, ed. Ronald Williams II (Berkeley, CA: African American Studies Department, University of California, 2010), 63.

18 Guridy, *Forging Diaspora*, 149.

19 Jill Dolan, *Utopia in Performance: Finding Hope at the Theater* (Ann Arbor: University of Michigan Press, 2005), 91.

20 David Román, *Performance in America: Contemporary U.S. Culture and the Performing Arts* (Durham, NC: Duke University Press, 2005), 57.

21 Dolan, *Utopia in Performance*, 2.

22 My own experiences in Ghana, West Africa, for example, suggest that some black people in the global South assume that a U.S. passport signifies wealth no matter who holds it. I suspect some would suggest that at the very least the person with a U.S. passport has more wealth than the average Ghanaian, black or not. Yet I often inform my Ghanaian friends about what it is like to be a black person in the United States, a country where the costs for basic sustenance in life are very high. In the United States the race and class stratification refracts socioeconomic progress for black people in specific ways.

23 Xavier Livermon, "Queer(y)ing Freedom: Black Queer Visibilities in Post-Apartheid South Africa," GLQ: A Journal of Gay and Lesbian Studies 18, nos. 2–3 (2012): 297–323.

24 Román, Performance in America, 57.

CHAPTER 12

Interview with Cedric Brown

D. Soyini Madison

D. Soyini Madison: Why did you write this play? What do you want your readers/audience to feel at the end of the play?

Cedric Brown: *Cuban Hustle* was originally a book manuscript, which I excerpted and used in a 2006 performance piece that I directed. A local theater professional I respect urged me to develop it further and more fully, resulting in this script. I originally wrote the manuscript because I needed to get the story off of my chest and wanted others to assist me in making sense of the dynamic between the Narrator and Félix.

I'm not invested in what audience members feel at the end, as long as they think that the story is interesting. Strike that—I do want people to have learned a little about the economic conditions facing contemporary Cubans. Other than those things, I'll let the work speak for itself.

DSM: Is this a story about sex or love? Do you worry that the play reinscribes the stereotype of gay relationships being more about sex than love?

CB: This is an interesting question—I'm actually not at all worried about reinforcing stereotypes of either gay men or black men being hypersexual. If anything, I've been more concerned about my treatment of Félix, and by implication, Cuban men. In earlier versions I tried to contextualize the piece by saying that it's "my story," as if that qualification would limit the generalizations that people might make about any of the characters. But then I realized that all of the characters are implicated—Félix, the Narrator, Señora Silvia, the policeman—so I decided to let the story speak for itself.

Back to the sex versus love question: I think the story is about a relationship—intimacy is the word I've used before—and sex is certainly a big part of that connection. Both the Narrator and Félix have access to sexual action in their respective home cities, so sex with each other wasn't the central focus of the relationship. Intimacy and trust were. The Narrator is looking for a partner (in spite of the lopsided power dynamic), and Félix is looking for a provider. These are things that they supposedly find in each other.

DSM: Is the Narrator naive? Is he desperate? What does the Narrator want?

CB: The Narrator is desperate to be in love. This isn't his overriding original intention, as he traveled to Cuba out of an initial sense of adventure and curiosity about a place that holds a good deal of intrigue and mystery for Americans. Yet, once he's in Havana, he discovers that relationships are a commodity and he decides to partake. He mentions that as a black gay man in San Francisco, he's out of vogue. San Francisco's gay social scene can be very isolating for black men. The Narrator wants to be in a relationship with another black man but isn't able to make a "domestic connection" for a host of reasons. He seizes this opportunity to engage in this relationship with Félix, even with the obvious pitfalls and barriers, because it comes about so easily. And perhaps because they share a mutual sense of need—emotional and economic.

DSM: And what about Félix, is he simply a hustler? How are we to understand Félix, or, how do you feel about Félix?

CB: I'm not sure. It's up to the audience to decide what constitutes a hustler. I don't believe that a mere street hustler would possess Félix's emotional commitment and staying power. One of the great difficulties about telling this story is trying to give a voice to Félix when the interpretation is strictly through the Narrator's eyes. I think the biggest clues about who Félix is come from his letters. But even those are subject to dual filters—the translation from Spanish to English and the Narrator's perspective. There may be cultural norms of which the Narrator isn't aware, which makes the reading of what is "truth" even more precarious. This is one of the reasons that my Cuban American husband has trouble with this piece—he says that too many stories about Cubans are told from non-Cuban perspectives, which don't capture the nuances of individual and collective Cuban frames of reference.

DSM: Who was being exploited in the relationship between Félix and the Narrator?

CB: Again, that's up to the reader/viewer to decide individually. Both are engaged in this relationship for things other than emotional intimacy. It's easy to say that the Narrator is being exploited, but he's pretty clearly complicit with everything he's asked—or decides—to do.

DSM: The moment of sexual violence was layered with desire and ambiguity. What is meaningful about this moment?

CB: That moment was an extreme example of the push-pull dynamic present in the relationship—Félix goes too far, and then atones and brings the Narrator along. Or, from another vantage point, the Narrator gets disillusioned, but can't let go of the relationship. In this scene, despite having sex against his will, this is the first time that the Narrator says, "I love you."

DSM: There was no mention of the U.S. embargo prohibiting U.S. citizens from traveling to Cuba. It seemed the Narrator could go back and forth with no problem, but there is a problem with traveling to Cuba. How do you feel about the politics of this being completely absent from the play? Why Cuba as a location for your play?

CB: Since this piece is based on a real experience, I included details of the round-trip travel in an earlier version, but couldn't figure out a way to mention it here without distracting from the flow of the story. I've assumed that viewers/readers would know that U.S. citizens have very limited and restricted travel opportunities to Cuba. Yet this story is proof that it is possible for an American to travel to and from Cuba (usually through a third country or with a licensed tour group). I know someone who went six times while trying to maintain a similar relationship.

Cuba is one of the few places in the world that U.S. citizens aren't permitted to visit as casual tourists. This, and the socialism that prompted the embargo, creates simultaneous feelings of intrigue and low-level fear. When people ask me about my travel experiences there, most want to know what Cuba is like, as it's largely portrayed in U.S. media as being stuck in the 1950s and isolated from the world (which it isn't). The Narrator even describes the images that were compelling for him about this "ominous paradise." So in this regard, it was the perfect backdrop for a performance piece. While the love-and-money relationship could be set in almost any developing nation, the Cuban locale adds a certain mystique because of its sense of inaccessibility—and even ideological hostility—to most Americans.

DSM: There is a line in the scene with the policeman where the Narrator expresses the freedom in the USA to contest police brutality (even wishing in that moment that he were home in the U.S.). This scene also suggests that racism in Cuba is more brutal and more a factor of inequality than racism in the USA. Are you concerned about how readers will respond to this moment in the play, [readers] who feel very sympathetic to Cuba, the revolution, and feel Cuba has much more progressive racial politics than the U.S.?

CB: I absolutely wanted to challenge notions of a Castro-inspired racial utopia in Cuba! While the generation of Afro-Cubans who witnessed the Revolución are firm believers in how it improved the status of blacks and women in Cuban society, the generations of Cubans of color who have lived under the current regime are chafing at its limitations. The lack of economic mobility and the ongoing racism—however subtle it can be—is quite present in their daily lives. Remember, the sense of African inferiority is a four-hundred-year-old institution and can't be easily eliminated in two generations. So while I think Cubans have a certain cross-racial ease that U.S. citizens don't share, antiblack attitudes are still strongly in play there.

As a "thoughtful observer" of Latin American racial dynamics—I certainly don't claim to be an expert—I believe that the racial intermingling and the complexion continuum (from "white" to "mixed" to shades of black to "black") belie a deeper rejection of a positive black self-identification. But that is now starting to shift with the growing Afro-identity consciousness driven in part by hip-hop culture!

Additionally, U.S.-based sympathizers of the Revolución tend to forget that Cuba is a police state! So while I'm down with the idea of a more equitable society, I'm uncomfortable with sacrificing one's freedom of speech and sense of self-actualization in order to achieve that equity. But of course it's easy for me to sit here and say that, surrounded by my American middle-class privileges.

DSM: Is it a play about desire or more about the politics of poverty in the so-called Third World . . . a political economy of love? Félix and the Narrator's sexual/material relationship seemed like an ironic and contrasting metaphor for the geographic/ideological relationship between the USA and Cuba. Could it be?

CB: Wow, "political economy of love" is a terrific way to describe the subtext of this piece; I think it does speak to the confluence of desire, intimacy, and politics (and I left out a section that dealt with immigration policies—that was a Pandora's box unto itself). The play is absolutely a metaphor for the relationship between the U.S. and Cuba—

we're enticed by one another yet we want power on our own terms. One is intrigued by cultural spiritedness and authenticity; the other is compelled by access to materials and a certain freedom. I didn't intentionally create this play as representative of anything other than [the characters] themselves (and true experience on which this is based), so it's most interesting that the characters are genuinely products of their respective national/cultural zeitgeists.

Part VII

Seens from the Unexpectedness of Love

Pamela Booker

CHARACTERS (IN ORDER OF APPEARANCE)
CHORUS—composed of the cast
TheEX
TheFACE
DIRECTOR
LEADINGLady

NOTES

▸ All actors should possess a strong sense of physical movement.

▸ Time shifts between present-time action and memory-invoked story-telling. The characters also alternate between speaking tenses that include interior/private voices and exterior/public voices within a given movement.

▸ Masks play an important role in the performance and should be interfaced at director's discretion.

▸ Setting kept to a minimum with greater emphasis on visual projections if used.

▸ Sound and lighting as determined.

MOVEMENT I
OF MARRIAGE, MEMORY, AND SUMMER CLOTHES

SEEN 1: "When I Fall in Love . . ."

[AT RISE:
All cast appears as chorus of voices as noted. All are masked. DIRECTOR and LEADINGLady carry silver trays with two pairs of rose-colored glasses and a long-stem rose on each.]

Fig. VII.1. *Seens from the Unexpectedness of Love.*
Photo by Julie Lemberger, courtesy of Pamela Booker.

CHORUS
We said we would be forever.
We said we would show each other the world
Filled with sacred/supple nights
And malleable/morning kisses.

TheEX
We said our lives and our choices
Were surmountable

TheFACE
That children and careers
The acquired demands
The unanticipated compromises

CHORUS
(**swift**) Of two who love each other who are trying to do this thing right
together of two who love each other who are trying to do this thing right
together . . .

TheEX
Would not sour
The buttery taste of our dreams
Nor dilute our red sky at dawn
Quartz rose love

TheFACE
Fueled by desire, imagination and trust
That played a love supreme
As if composed by Coltrane.

TheEX
We said our love would flourish
Because it must

TheFACE
Not because it had to
But that it must

TheEX
In the way that blood and oxygen must
Conspire with organs to keep life
Present in the body.
It will be forever . . .

Both
It will be forever . . .

[EXIT DIRECTOR and LEADINGLady. TheEX FREEZES IN THE SHADOWS.
MUSIC RISES: Violin or recording of "When I Fall in Love . . ."

LIGHTS crossfade to TheFACE who drags out an already filled large plastic trash bag. She reaches for a stack of clothes and begins stuffing them
into another bag. Each piece of clothing is painstakingly studied. Her
body and facial expressions recall the events that wore the clothing;
emotions reveal anger, sadness and the satisfaction of completing her
task.

MUSIC and LIGHTS FADE TO BLACK.]

[The outer and inner lobbies and staircase of a walkup apartment build-
ing. TheEX is seen in the outer-lobby carrying an empty garment bag.
An array of masks of many colors dangle precariously from the bag and
TheEX tries on several "faces."]

TheEX
You chastised me for not remembering what dress you wore to Steve and
Edie's wedding.

CHORUS
She may again forget the color of your dress, but she knows the color of
your eyes that float like almonds set upon pearl disks. She knows the
thickness of your eyelashes which send forth cool, tender breezes on
nights that are hot and intoxicating. She knows the lower east-side of
your strong, elegant back, and the collard-green birthmark that dances
across your calf. In times of longing—

TheEX
—and there is always longing

CHORUS
She sips hungrily from the pools of Egyptian musk and salt that dwell
in the arc of your neck and moisten the insides of your armpits and in-
between your thighs—

TheEX
—thighs that wear me . . . Wear me . . . Wear me. . . . Why then, would
I need to remember a dress worn to someone else's wedding? (beat) My
face. My face.

[TheEX selects the black & white mask and places it on her face, then
rings the doorbell. TheFACE's voice screeches expectantly, crackling in
tune with the intercom.]

TheFACE
Who is it?

TheEX
Me.

TheFACE
Just a minute, I'll be right there.

[TheFACE runs quickly to a rack of masks, tries on several, then swiftly pulls out one that is blue and the other black & white. The black & white mask is placed on her face, in a ritualistic fashion; as if arming herself for the encounter. The blue mask is concealed on the body. There is the rhapsodic, echoing sound of an apartment door opening/closing and footsteps descending the stairs. This sound is repeated several times, each level softer than the last. Simultaneously, TheFACE mimes a fluid, gentle, but steady movement down two flights of stairs as TheEX speaks.]

TheEX
I enter the building's entryway with the air of a trespasser. Stay calm. Be charming. I wonder, is my face on properly? My face, my face.

[TheFACE gestures reaching the landing, then opens the door.]

TheEX
Two flights later, I am greeted by TheFACE that once made me laugh, once a muse, once a life-mate, once a muse. Today, clichés relax us.

TheFACE
Come in.

[TheEX enters as TheFACE moves to close the lobby door.]

TheEX
Hello.

TheFACE
How are you?

TheEX
Hello.

TheFACE
How are you?

Seens from the Unexpectedness of Love **399**

TheEX
Hello.

TheFACE
You look well.

TheEX
You look well.

TheFACE
Well, okay. Let's get your clothes. **(strolls eagerly toward the upper staircase as TheEX hovers near the entrance.)**

TheEX
(with masked alarm) Aren't the clothes in the basement?

TheFACE
No, as a matter of fact, I brought them up earlier. I needed to . . . SEPARATE mine from yours. Let's go up. **(TheFACE moves as if ascending stairs.)**

TheEX
(shakes head in mock agreement, then speaks to TheFACE with beats) Mmmm . . .Yes. *Separate.* That makes sense. You *separated* our clothes upstairs? **(to audience)** Now that's strange. But stay calm, don't say anything stupid. Smile. Be charming. Yes, charming. Charming. **(repeats twice)** I—am—charming. **(suspicious)** Hauling boxes of clothes all the way from the basement to the third floor? Why, when she could just as easily have handed them to me in the lobby? What should I be thinking right now? Think. THINK. What's she up to? It's, it's already late, I'm leaving next week and I need my summer clothes!

TheFACE
Did you say something?

CHORUS
I said, I'm leaving next week
I'm leaving next week
I'm leaving and I need my summer clothes!

TheEX

(startled) Who . . . me? I . . . I said I'm following you. After you! (They begin to mime climbing stairs.) (reflective w/beats) I used to call this building home, and shared a life with this strangely distilled face that's greeted me as if I'm picking up hand-me-downs for the Salvation Army. (to TheFACE w/ strained gaiety) I see the neighbors still haven't set out their recycling!? (resumes interior voice) Innocuous small talk is all I can manage as we scale the stairs to the third floor apartment that TheFACE and I shared for the decade. Yet, after ten years, each of my hairs stand on end and bad vibes are swing-dancing about my head. (TheFACE pauses as TheEX continues.)

TheFACE

(beats) We fell in love while working in the theater. Me and TheEX. Virginia Woolf captures in a sentence our life together when she said, "I don't think two people could have been happier." A rather ironic declaration on married life, don't you think, (slight chuckle) considering it's borrowed from the suicide note that Woolf left her husband—

TheEX

—her husband Leonard! Yes. TheFACE and I, we died slow, painful deaths like Virginia—

TheFACE

—and her husband Leonard.

TheEX

Drowned. Yet for years we were both "happy."

TheFACE

We were filled with a genuine purpose, wouldn't you say?!

TheEX

Yes! Oh yes, absolutely.

TheFACE

Building a life together, buying things, paying off credit cards.

TheEX

Vacationing. Serving as role-models for our high-maintenance friends, you know—"deconstructing" other people's dysfunction.

TheFACE
We did! Playing leading roles one day, supporting roles the next. Damn good characters we were—fully dimensional, believable and passionate about our craft.

TheEX
Yes, *passionate.*

Both
We fell in love while working in the theater.

[Actors remove their masks.]
MUSIC PLAYS.

LIGHTS TO BLACK.

MOVEMENT II—FLASHBACK

SEEN 3: The Theeeeatre!

[Space arranged to give the impression of a theater, front of house and backstage. TheEX should carry a clipboard and the DIRECTOR is pretentious-looking and grand sounding.]

CHORUS
(speaks in the round with a sense of revery)
She walked effortlessly into the vacancy of MY life.
She walked effortlessly into the vacancy of MY life.
She walked effortlessly into the vacancy of MY life.
She walked effortlessly into the vacancy of MY life.

TheEX
I believe it was Picasso who said, "painting is stronger than I am, it makes me do what it wishes . . ."

[ENTER DIRECTOR]

DIRECTOR
This turned out to be the last day of the final moment of callbacks.

TheEX

The DIRECTOR and I, the stage manager, shaking our heads, sighed collectively, **(both sigh)** wishing that she'd appeared at least one week sooner.

DIRECTOR

You see, the leading role was already cast. It would have been . . . Irrational . . . No, mad, to audition the practically, almost cast, LeadingLady
for yet a third time! Then again this was the "theeeatre" and sometimes
that's the way life happens, isn't it? Mad and irrationally.

TheEX

Where was she all this time?

DIRECTOR

Exactmo! I've been looking for her type for months now!

TheEX

(reflective) I've been looking for her type for a lifetime.

DIRECTOR

We shall call her *SupportingCharacter*! It's the only remaining role. Yes, her
role shall be small, but smart, and full of and full of—

TheEX

—of verve, pizzazz!

DIRECTOR

Yes! Yes! Verve, pizzazz! And her presence, though brief, shall be everlasting!

TheEX

Little did I fathom that she would steal the show and my sense of reason
before the final curtain call.

CHORUS

All actors to the stage please.
To the stage please.
All actors to the stage.

Seens from the Unexpectedness of Love **403**

TheFACE
Fasten me, pin my hair.

TheEX
Her lines intoxicated me.

TheFACE
Backstage was best. Oh what charades and acts of foreplay were contained in the dressing room, between, around and through our unscripted, unspoken lines.

TheEX
She asks me to replace a fallen light-bulb from her mirror. I do, with the only bulb available—an impotent one of not more than 60 watts. Tonight, it glowed 100 times its capacity.

Both
Backstage was best.

[ENTER LEADINGLady. She is dressed extravagantly and takes up space with her presence.]

LEADINGLady
(mumbling the lines) Out damn! Out damn, spot! Out damn! Out damn, spot!

TheFACE
The leading lady strutted about despondently like Macbeth's wife asking all who were brave enough to respond—

LEADINGLady
How now! What news of my reviews and delivery and such? Director, oh director! I'm ready for my close-up. And don't NOBODY bring me no bad news. Bad news gives me wrinkles . . .

TheFACE
Sensing treachery, ME in the wings, she brayed—

LEADINGLady
Where was I? That's right—Out damn! Out damn—line?!

TheEX & TheFACE
Spot!

LEADINGLady
Yes, spot! Thank you my dears. **(to TheFACE)** You must be the new girl? Welcome dahling. Oh my, must'nt dally. I have sooo many lines to remember. I'm the star you know. Yes, carry on then . . . Out, out, out! **(EXITS mumbling lines.)**

TheEX
She observed that you, the mere SupportingCharacter delighted them nightly **(points to audience)** with the magnanimity of being small. While they applauded politely for the LeadingLady at curtain call, they howled like wolves and unabashedly stomped their feet for you. I was charmed. The LeadingLady was pissed!

TheFACE
She wanted "off with my head!"

TheEX
What she wanted was your cute ass off the stage! **(They both chuckle as they EXIT.)**

[**LEADINGLady ENTERS struggling with her lines. DIRECTOR also ENTERS coaching her. Theirs becomes a sexually charged exchange.**]

DIRECTOR
I need more! Give me more. Come now LeadingLady—feel the textures. See the colors. Imagine your lines a finely drawn set of bodily demarcations.

LEADINGLady
Deee-Mark what?!

DIRECTOR
(screams to audience) Learn your lines cow! Okay, okay, center Director, center. **(to LL)** Let's take it from the top—again. Slowly, delicately, piannisimo. Make love to those syllables. And 1, 2 and 3—
(He mouths the phrases with her.)

LEADINGLady

(to audience) I'll show him who knows how to "make love" and who knows how talk about it! **(mocks Director with heightened sexy voice/ gestures)** Uuuuut! Oowwwwttt! Deeeeemn. Daaaaammmm!

DIRECTOR

Yes, yes, that's it. Feel it—feeel it! I mean feel it baby.

LEADINGLady

Uuuuut! Oowwwwttt! Deeeeemn. Daaaaammmm!

DIRECTOR

Good. Again. **(begins self-flagellating)** Give it to me baby.

LEADINGLady

Uuuuut! Oowwwwttt! Deeeeemn. Daaaaammmm!

DIRECTOR

Oh, yes . . . I'm feeling you. Right there. Don't stop. Don't stop.

LEADINGLady

(moans) Oh, Mr. Director, you're exhausting meeee. . . .

DIRECTOR

Only to make it as good for you. AGAIN. This time without interruption. For . . . for . . . peak effect.

LEADINGLady

Daddy wants it rough? **(slutty tone/gestures/grunts)** Uuuuut! Oowwwwttt! Deeeeemn. Daaaaammmm!

DIRECTOR

FREAK me baby, yes baby. Oh don't stop. Don't stop. . . . .

DIRECTOR and LEADINGLady together

Uuuuut! Oowwwwttt! Deeeeemn. Daaaaammmm! **(repeat)**

DIRECTOR

Oh GOD, you are breathtaking! **(falls from exhaustion, then crawls on all fours, EXITING behind LEADINGLady.)**

[ENTER TheEX & TheFACE chuckling at the pair.]

TheEX

Over the weeks, the bard Will's musings on how we are all merely **(points to departed Director+LeadingLady)** players on the ever so bizarre stage of life competed with my thoughts. What was my role in this odd affair and why so much adieu **(points to TheFACE)** with this player?

TheFACE

I dreamt that I had entered into the abyss of some actor's nightmare.

TheEX

Here I was a simple stage manager, standing by as the familiarity of our town and my station in it was conspicuously altered by a landscape whose scenes were filled with strange, enticing cues.

Director and LEADINGLady

(holler from OFFSTAGE) Familiarity breeds contempt!

TheEX

I was not cued for the affection of a woman, yet I knew that I would not be able to exit without her.

TheFACE

A host of friends, family, wannabees and well-wishers, joined us for the closing performance. I was restless, unfocused, glad to see this run over with and in a quandary about our impending good-bye. Portia was wrong, the "quality of mercy" is strained and so too is the unexpectedness of falling in love as the house lights slowly dissolve to black.

TheEX

I watched from the shadows your movements, the roll of your eager shoulders, the extension of your welcoming arms, the confidence of your stroll. You greeted fans awaiting you at house right. I crossed to meet you down center. Time stopped. I was eclipsed by a force—making me do what it wanted. I thrusted my lips upon your startled but approving mouth **(they kiss)**. In the sanctity of our private world, we consummated a public intimacy that would linger.

TheFACE
And then linger. **(they kiss again)**

TheEX
I love you.

TheFACE
I love you. **(beat)** This was no longer rehearsal. Neither of us dared to question the deed—

TheEX
—nor repeat it. We were trapped willingly in a sound barrier of compressed, limitless time, joy, time.

[Both are giddy as they dance with each other.]

TheFACE
How did we withstand the reverberations humming through us? We had surpassed human weightiness, elevated to a vastness preserved only for the goddesses.

TheEX
Venus herself smiled sumptuously upon us bearing witness . . . Bearing witness.

TheEX & TheFACE
(together) I love you.

[The LEADINGLady releases a piercing laugh/scream as she ENTERS with the DIRECTOR. He is carrying her bouquets of flowers. TheEX and TheFACE are startled by the shrill.]

TheEX
The LEADINGLady was exiting, her entourage, within arm's reach, gazed wantonly like captivated pedestrians—

TheFACE
—or sitting ducks!

DIRECTOR
(to LEADINGLady as he hands her the flowers) You were faaabulous
daaahling.

LEADINGLady
Yeeeesss, I was. (then to TheFACE) But you were fabulous too lovely.

DIRECTOR
She was, indeed!

LEADINGLady
Hope we can do it again.

TheFACE
We will. (to audience) In another lifetime.

LEADINGLady
Smooches daaahlings! Smooches! (EXITS on arm of DIRECTOR.)

V/O
Eve
Eve

TheEX
Where . . . do we go? What do we do with this?

V/O
Confesses
Confesses

TheFACE
Tomorrow and tomorrow—

CHORUS
To Eve.

TheEX
And tomorrow?

[ENTER DIRECTOR]

DIRECTOR
(to TheEX) Duty calls stage manager. I say, duty calls.

TheEX
I bid you a rigorous adieu—

TheFACE
But not good-bye, my lady.

[TheEX EXITS with DIRECTOR AS MUSIC SWELLS ON TheFACE.]

LIGHTS TO BLACK.

SEEN 5: THE "L" WORD

[The setting is a pastoral/Elysian field. ENTER DIRECTOR and LEADING-Lady carrying silver platters with two pairs of rose colored glasses on each. They speak while dressing TheFACE. ENTER TheEX carrying pink roses. They turn to dress TheEX in her glasses. All actors move to a choreographed movement and exchange partners throughout, configuring in the shape of "L" at the end.]

CHORUS
Locks fall upon you resolutely.

TheFACE
A terrific downpour.

TheEX
Rainfall.

CHORUS
Steady determined wetness.

TheEX & TheFACE
Longing.

CHORUS
Caressing the shoulder
They arc like fluid streams of

TheEX   TheFACE
Licorice
Smooth/slender Languid
Often they   Lounge
Being of a   Lofty nature

CHORUS
Sigh gently when stroked
By familiar fingertips
Or lie placidly across

TheEX
Landscapes
Written on the body
Licking limbs

TheFACE
Flanking
Rounds and mounds
Breasts and chests
Loitering.

CHORUS
Eagerly they rise
Eagerly they rise to meet
To meet
Eagerly

TheFACE
Yes, eagerly to meet
The ebbs and flows of the back

TheEX
Looping
Lustily
Around our chocolaty necks

CHORUS
Spilling
spooning
spiraling

Seens from the Unexpectedness of Love **411**

TheFACE
Lingering
as if jewels

TheEX
Pearls
Lodged

CHORUS
Between thick thighs/torsos
& ample waists
Seeking hidden crevices
Among graceful hips

TheEX & TheFACE
Intertwined. Locked.

TheEX
Each strand magnificent carriers
Of independent secrets
And faint scents

TheFACE
Woven/threaded/kneaded
Palmed in oils
Coconut frankincense
Sandalwood
myrrh

CHORUS
Love.

TheEX
At dawn locks dance among themselves
Spray across pillows

TheFACE
Form inverted pyramids or crowns
Divined for majestic heads of
Goddesses and warriors.

CHORUS
This is where
Laughter
Lurks
Within dreams
And reams of
Locks.

[DIRECTOR + LEADINGLady collect glasses from the lovers then EXIT. The entire tone of their world turns to a stark reality. Thunder and lightning crackle. An uneasiness preoccupies them.]

TheEX
We discovered the sameness of gender, afraid to call it the "L" word, yet enchanted by the strangeness of this new fruit.

TheFACE
The smell, the taste, the touch of woman. We consumed each other with epicurean delight.

TheEX
In gregarious portions.

TheFACE
Convinced that our lives depended on it.

TheEX
It did. The hunger, the hunger. We sipped, nibbled, gnawed, chomped and suckled the "L" word.

TheFACE
For more than a decade we lived and danced on the emotional fringes of the "L" word. Instead, it was simpler to choose the "S" word—to say we loved the "sameness" of each other. We learned not to limit ourselves to categories or placards or the politics. We thought we could avoid the politics. We didn't expect to *become* our own cause! In reality, we were terrorized by the intolerance and the hatred . . .

TheEX
The self hatred and the legislated . . .

Seens from the Unexpectedness of Love **413**

V/O
Recording of an antigay platform.

[ENTER LEADINGLady and DIRECTOR, MARCH IN CARRYING LARGE CROSSES AND BIBLES.]

CHORUS
(whispers, then shouts) Bible thumpers, Bible thumpers, we are the bible thumpers . . . **(repeat)**

TheFACE
Like scum-carrying creatures from the bottom of a dead pond, they crawled up and coated us with the residue of their stinking disapproval.

TheEX
It was pervasive. Who am I kidding? It was ugly. **(points)** It's still ugly!

TheFACE
It was noxious. Mean.

TheEX
It hurt, damnit. And it was all so unexpected.

CHORUS
(taunts) Love is always unexpected. How you respond to it is choice! Man should choose woman! Woman should choose man! It's just not right!

TheFACE
You're all so smug and so fucking righteous!

TheEX
You reduced our "marriage" to sound-bite and curtsey.

TheFACE
No . . . in all fairness WE did that . . .

TheEX
You're too polite! We didn't have help or role-models. And all they said over and over again—

[HOUSE LIGHTS UP. Lovers + Chorus move to confront audience.]

CHORUS
(stern) It's just not right!

TheFACE
Our parents, Our friends said it. Well, ex-friends.

CHORUS
It's just not right!

TheEX
Every religious doctrine said it.

CHORUS
It's just not right!

TheFACE
The television said it.

CHORUS
(all actors—builds into frenzied sermon-like voice) Gods says, it's just not right. Therefore WE are your God. And we are RIGHT. But you're NOT. RIGHT. WE say YOU'RE just not right! Move to the right. Buy right. Live right. Speak right. Pee right. Right shoe? Right fit. Alright. Rite Aid. Aids? Ohhhh . . . my . . . No. That's not right. Get right . . . we know . . . with Jessssssuuuus. (clap) He'll fix everything. Like Mikey, he's eats from a bowl of cereal and the world is made RIGHT. Make it all right. Make ME all right. If you eat right with Jessssssuuuus. (clap) It'll be all right. RIGHT! Get to know Jessssssuuuus. (clap) Get to know, ha, get to know, yes, get to know, get to know, I said, get to know (clap) Jessssssuuuus and it will be alright. RIGHT? RIGHT? RIGHT . . .

TheEX
No, it's not right! Not what Our friends said. Our families.

TheFACE
YOU, you moderates, liberals, FUCKa—I mean . . . FUNDamentalists!

TheEX
Our families. My family . . . and ever so politely, our heterosexual friends, questioning . . . are you sure? Or remaining silent.

[ACTORS RETURN TO STAGE. HOUSE LIGHTS OUT.]

TheEX
Have you said it? Or thought it?

TheFACE
What?

TheEX
You know . . .

TheFACE
Maybe I have said it.

TheEX
(confessional) I even knew a sister who told her father about the yearn-ings that her sister had for girls.

TheFACE
Oh, you mean the "G" word.

TheEX
She discovered it in her journal you know. A sacred, private sanctuary.

TheFACE
Mmm . . . What was *your* sister doing reading *your* journal anyway?

TheEX
It . . . it wasn't my sister. You're right. It was my sister. The one place in this entire schizophrenic world that allows you to confess all of your truths, your fears, joy, that you love . . . that you love . . . women.

TheFACE
That you love is all that matters.

TheEX
Like Pandora and that damn box—she succumbed to the temptations of seeking evidence of her sister's tainted ways.

TheFACE
Now you know—some treasures are better left unexplored.

Pamela Booker

TheEX

Mmm-hum, I do. Yet she remained silent with her sister—ME—about her discovery as if terminal illness or sin had been detected and could only be discussed in the most hushed of tones or preferably not at all.

TheFACE

What is it about the "L" word that makes them crazy?

TheEX

Or righteous?

TheFACE

Or silent and shoutin'—this is a man and woman's world—

TheEX

With the Saviour's word

TheFACE

Ye who love same have no place in this world.

[SOUND of lightning flares as the Chorus chants.]

CHORUS

(whispers to shouts) Bible thumpers, Bible thumpers, we are the bible thumpers . . . (repeat until EXIT.)

TheEX

It's better to speak, we learned, for we were never meant to survive. We were never meant to survive. Anyway.

TheFACE

This love, this love is stronger than we are.

TheEX

How do you choose such a thing?

TheFACE

How do you deny it?

LIGHTS TO BLACK.

[ENTER CHORUS WITH BLACK & WHITE MASKS. THEY BEGIN CHANT AS TheEX and TheFACE change into their masks.]

CHORUS
All actors to the stage please.
Standing by.
House to half.
Standing by. Standing by.

MOVEMENT III
ALL ACTORS TO THE STAGE PLEASE.

SEEN 6: "Your friends exhausted me . . ."

[TheEX and TheFACE place Black & White masks on their faces. Together they speak opening chant with Chorus.]

CHORUS
Your friends exhausted me
Exhausted me
Your family wore on my nerves
on my nerves
Your friends exhausted me
Exhaustion!
Your family wore on my nerves
The very last nerve
Your damn friends exhausted me!
Exhaustion!
And lordy, your family wore on my nerves!

TheFACE
Your problem where our friends and even our family were concerned was that you took them all too seriously—at least as seriously as they mis-took themselves. You were resented for that. They didn't really want "truth" from us. Collusion, certainly. Obedience, always. They wouldn't know the elements of "truth" if it was choking any of them by the throat. Yet you insisted on it—confusing your truth with their delusions. In the end, you were resented for pointing out their flaws. Who could possibly live up to your standards? I simply stopped trying.

TheEX

It was too hard for me to keep up with appearances, wearing other people's expectations of my life. It was exhausting. Family, friends . . . Family . . .

TheFACE

Hmmm . . . Maybe it was the "we" that exhausted you?

TheEX

Maybe. For a long time we loved . . . Didn't we . . . ?

TheFACE

(pause) We did.

TheEX

But . . . But then . . . We started gasping for breath

TheFACE

Fighting off death, lingering. I . . . I . . .

TheEX

I couldn't breathe in your company anymore. We loved until we bled. I have bite marks to prove it.

TheFACE

Oh, baby, I have bite marks too. And then you left.

TheEX

Over time, our plot, though intricately staged, revealed a weak, sometimes forced structure, incomplete arcs and loose links. We climaxed until we ached—then simply lost the ability to sustain our momentum.

TheFACE

Will you come back?

TheEX

I don't think I can.

TheFACE

We . . . just unraveled didn't we?

TheEX

In a matter of scenes. Eventually we started dropping cues in mid-
sentence or cut whole pages, just got sloppy. Foreplay became fore-
shadowing and overbearing. Drama became comedy became tragedy.
Clearly, *you* are directing.

TheFACE

But I asked you to come back!

TheEX

Yes, but only as I stood by in stage-left unpreparedness. Reduced to
understudy and lingering. Waiting in the wings for a cue from you. Some
sign that you were also prepared to help us save us. But you were too
busy directing other people's scenes.

CHORUS

All actors to the stage please.
Standing by.
House to half.
Standing by. Standing by.

TheFACE

But I asked you to come back!

TheEX

I—couldn't—breathe. I was drowning . . . like Virginia. Stones weighing
me down in my pockets, and you—

TheFACE

No, YOU, were some place holding auditions or "humoring" confessions
out of people. (beat) I asked YOU to come back!

TheEX

But first—You asked me to LEAVE.

CHORUS

(Repeat then echo out.)
All actors to the stage please.
Standing by.
House to half.

Standing by. Standing by.
House out. House out. House out.

[TheEX and TheFACE resume the climbing stairs mime in unison as the sound of their ascendancy echoes their movement. They freeze with the increased volume of the Chorus as Chorus EXITS.]

LIGHTS SLOWLY FADE ON THEIR TABLEAU.

SEEN 7: SUMMER CLOTHES–PRESENT TIME

[Both actors arrive at the apartment door; it squeaks when opened. A red "couch" dominates the room. Both also switch to their blue face masks, but each hides the change from the other while tossing the Black & White masks aside.]

TheEX

HI kitties! Miss Daisy! Miss Ross! Miss me? (The sound of cats meowing lovingly as TheEX stoops to nuzzle them, then hiss and scamper away.) (nervous chuckle) This door is still noisy. So, how are things between you and Mr. Scrooge? Has he raised the rent yet? I remember he was threatening to before . . . before—

TheFACE

(snaps then regains composure)—before you left!? Yeah, he's still threatening, but I'm resisting him. (breathes) I'm doing yoga now and meditating. (breathes) Learning to breathe. And learning to resist all things and people included, who in any way disrupt the (breathes again) mindfulness that I've reclaimed for myself—since you left.

TheEX

How "zen" of you . . .

TheFACE

Well, like I said, I needed to . . . to separate our clothing. We both agreed it would be best to separate.

TheEX

I thrust my elbow back sharply, a feeble attempt to diffuse the awkwardness and at the same time deliver a fresh supply of blood to my neck

Seens from the Unexpectedness of Love **421**

muscles. **(gingerly)** So, where are the clothes? You know, you really didn't have to trouble yourself . . . Bringing them all the way up here.

TheFACE
(points offstage) They're in your old study. **(Gestures to the red couch)** Have a seat.

[TheFACE CROSSES OFFSTAGE BUT CONTINUES EXCHANGE WITH TheEX.]

TheEX
I sit. Guarded banter preoccupies us again the way lint does when you're wearing black clothing.

TheEX
(shouts) How's your Health?

TheFACE
Fine.

TheEX
How's the new book coming along?

TheFACE
Fine. School? Teaching this semester?

TheEX
Fine. Two classes.

TheFACE
Fine.

TheEX
Your family?

TheFACE
Fine. Your family?

TheEX
Fine.

BOTH
Fine.

[TheFACE returns dragging two bulging trash bags. TheEX rises from the couch to offer assistance. TheFACE's body language suggests otherwise.]

TheEX
What the hell? I mean . . . what happened to the boxes that I packed?

TheFACE
Oh, um . . . when I brought them up, it was just easier to put all of the clothes into plastic bags. (TheFACE freezes as TheEX speaks.)

TheEX
(Moves to survey TheFACE up close then mimicks.) "It was just easier to put all of the clothes into plastic bags." (screams) That's really fucked up! (sighs) Doesn't matter, I have a garment bag with me. (beat) Look at her, with those blue-blank features, scrutinizing me with the vigor of a computer screen—cyberspace blue. The flatness of the eyes and the glare are compelling. (TheEX falls back onto the couch.) Ahhh. The couch. (rubs it) Yes . . . We spent months searching for this defining beauty.

[TheFACE resumes action.]

TheFACE
I desperately wanted southwest themes and colors since our first visit to Santa Fe, the summer of 1995 wasn't it?

TheEX
Yes, the summer of 1995 and the start of my restlessness.

TheFACE
(mocking) Oh, was that the "official" year?

TheEX
Let's be nice. (points) The red couch.

TheFACE
Yes of course, the red couch. (with beats) Once a symbol of our passion, it now strikes me as blood-soaked and splattered, patterned after our lives—suppressed dreams and scarlet trespasses. Our unscripted

entries, our exits, and the accumulated squalor of superficial friends, left red spreading between us like we used to spread between each other's thighs. In love. Now, I just feel soiled. We exhausted ourselves, running from Macy's to Bloomingdales, in search of a perfect motif. Santa Fe red. Commitment demands lengthy rehearsals and pink. How could two people invest more energy in their decor than they do the dressings of their everyday desires?

TheEX
If I knew, I wouldn't be collecting my summer wardrobe in garbage bags like somebody's motherless child.

TheFACE
Would you like some water? Juice?

TheEX
Yes, water, thanks. (Picks up a magazine.)

[TheFACE crosses to the kitchen. We see her survey a set of masks of assorted colors and designs. She inspects/rejects several as one would wine glasses for smudges or knives for sharpness. She then quickly grabs a bottle of water that she offers to TheEX.]

TheFACE
I'm sorry but I only have bottled water. I seem to have broken all my glasses . . .

TheEX
(nervous) Really? I . . . I love bottles. (gestures to bag of clothes) Well, I should get started.

[TheEX places garment bag on the floor and begins to pull clothing from a plastic bag. TheFACE moves quickly again to the "kitchen" and quietly slips on a red mask. She returns to stand behind the couch where she catches TheEX off-guard.]

TheFACE
(circles TheEX) Who knew that summer clothing could be so high maintenance considering how flimsy the material is, really. Oh the shallow people and materialities we spend our time with. Linens, muslins, cottons, khaki . . . (chuckles coldly) LIGHTWEIGHT. CHEAP.

[TheEX is visibly startled. She swigs from the bottle of water and continues to frantically pack.]

TheFACE (cont'd.)
(pacing) You know . . .

TheEX
(panicked) I knew it! There's a monologue coming and I still have another bag to sort. (Looks up and fully registers the RED mask.)

TheFACE
(seething) You and I need to have closure.

TheEX
Closure? Fair enough. (to audience) Yes, we deserve a stirring last scene. A heartfelt final curtain. I felt it coming, percolating beneath that terribly enlightened statement. (mocks) We need closure. I'm meditating and resisting all negativity. I'm enlightened and so superior to you because I'm doing yoga, yadda, yadda, yadda.

[As TheFACE continues pacing her expletives turn into a series of sharp "wahs," "wahs," "wahs," similar to the Charlie Brown classroom teacher's voice. The rant continues as TheEX speaks to audience.]

TheFACE
What a deceitful, shallow, thoughtless, insensitive, spineless, heartless, sorry-ass COWARD you are. If you were so unhappy with me, with us . . . Wah-wah-wah-wah-wah-wah-wah. . . .

TheEX
(Falls onto the floor in a prostrate position while folding clothes into garment bag.)

TheFACE
(Voice rises and falls) Wah-wah-wah-wah-wah-wah-wah. You haven't even accepted how deeply you've violated the trust that I thought we lived by . . . Wah-wah-wah-wah-wah-wah-wah. . . .

TheEX
Just keep packing. Efficiency and a fast escape is all that motivates me.

Seens from the Unexpectedness of Love **425**

[Nina Simone's version of "You Put a Spell on Me" plays as TheFACE continues mouthing rants.]

TheFACE

I thought . . . I thought . . . she must have put a spell on you. That's it isn't it?! SHE—PUT—A—GODDAMN SPELL ON YOU! What happened? Did you lose your mind? That's it—you lost your mind . . . lost YOU . . . I thought your were MINE!

TheEX

TheFACE-is-ugly, contorted, spittle hanging from the corners of the mouth, or is that blood?

TheFACE

I thought we were special. Ten years! Ten years! Turns out I'm as dispos-able as those flimsy clothes you're arbitrarily packing. This skirt goes—these shorts get tossed! Trash. It's all trash to you isn't it? (TheFACE FREEZES.)

TheEX

(quickly surveys TheFACE) Puss colors the eyeballs. Just a half bag more. This other stuff is crap. Couples clothes. Matching colors and themes. Identity meshed in the folds and blends of the fabric. Wounded threads. She's right, some of it is trash now. But none of it was arbitrary. (beat) Our life together was never arbitrary. Family reunion tee-shirts, faded. And the hideous "ethnic" wear! We were like anthropologists collecting useless fashion artifacts—African kente cloths, Native American vests, East Indian tunics and these ghastly multi-colored Japanese kimonos. My only fashion rule is, if you haven't worn it for more than two seasons, toss it. (holds up the shorts as if inspecting them) plaid shorts? What was I thinking? (surveys TheFACE closely) The voice rests, as do the jowls, although I notice the twitching of an ear. The hands are fisted. The veins bulging, expanding and rising as rage must.

[TheFACE UNFREEZES.]

TheFACE

(seething/pacing) Do you have anything to say for yourself?

[TheEX stares at TheFACE as she searches for her misplaced RED mask.]

TheEX

(evenly) I suppose it really doesn't matter what I have to say since obviously, you need to say more. I didn't come to argue. (LOCATES MASK AND SLIPS IT ON.)

TheFACE

(growls) What did you come for then?

TheEX

To pick up my summer clothes! I didn't come to defend my behavior. Just to pick up my summer clothes. (TheEX coughs, then cups mouth, then pulls a long string of RED from the mouth.) Red floods my mouth. I feel some of it splatter onto the garment bag. Stay calm, but charming has fled my mind. I spot my shirts, squashed like cloth accordions, raking the bottom of the last bag. There they lie, more obedient than myself between a doubled-over, seersucker jacket. Squatting on numb limbs I brace myself against the wall, only to disturb the cats, (sound of hissing cats) feverishly licking at each other's private parts. Trying not to spill any more red, I gingerly release the words cramming my mouth. (Turns to TheFACE) If my behavior was so depraved, why did it take this long for me to get your attention?

[TheFACE coughs up then spits out red.]

TheFACE

(exhausted) Of course. It's always about you!

LIGHTS TO BLACK.
MUSIC UP.

[ENTER DIRECTOR and LEADINGLady MARCHING IN RHYTHM TRANSPORTING LOVERS TO ANOTHER MEMORY. THEY ARE DRESSED COLORFULLY AND MOVE IN THE SPIRIT OF A BACCHANAL.]

MOVEMENT IV
4 BEATS OF BETRAYAL

[This movement involves a call and response exchange that plays like a club/party scene that overlaps with different musics. Each "SEEN" represents a different beat or sensation. Movement changes from hard marches to "couples dances"—soft hustles, swing, waltz, etc., given the emotional landscape.]

BEAT #1: Thud, Thud. Boom, boom: HOUSE MARCH

CHORUS—ALL
I hear your heavy-footed Noise.
I hear you. Your Noise.
No, I hear you.
Heavy-footed Noise.
Thud, thud. Boom boom.
Thud, thud. Boom boom.
I hear you. Your noise.
What does it sound like?
BETRAYAL.
HEART-BREAKER.
BOOTYSHAKER.
NOISE. I hear you.
Bouncing/pouncing/grinding through your consciousness
It disturbs me.
Wears me OUT.
What?
Your NOISE.
Thud, thud. Boom boom.
Thud, thud. Boom boom.
The bashing of blunt objects shunted upon soft things.
But is this love, love, love? Mixed cuts
Cutting confessions, thrashing, spinning
Searing amplified house
deep deep house
Bone-breaking
Inner-ear-shattering
Heart-breaking
Deep deephousehearthouseheart
House-breaking
BETRAYAL.
HEART-BREAKER.
BOOTYSHAKER.
NOISE. I hear you.
I HEAR YOUR NOISE.
But is this love, love, love? Remixed.

Still you are too immobilized to move away from
MOVE AWAY!
MOVE AWAY FROM THE SPEAKER.
MOVE AWAY!
HEART-BREAKER.
BOOTYSHAKER.
I hear you.
HEART-BREAKER.
BOOTYSHAKER.

DIRECTOR and LEADINGLady (**continue softly repeating refrain while moving through the Lovers until directed to exit.**)
HEART-BREAKER.
BOOTYSHAKER.
I hear you.

TheFACE
My heart lies impaled as certain reality leaps
Through windows of opportunity not danced to
Promises made then left to melt
Like old 45s in hot pools of sun.

TheEX
Dull pain pumps its way into my third eye
Stalks my fourth wall
But is unable or unwilling to push, push through. Move on.

TheFACE
(**cries**) You broke my heart.

TheEX
(**moves to embrace TheFACE who pushes her away.**) I loved you.

TheFACE
I saw her finger, saw her finger running down your back. Scratchin, scratchin, tracing the delicate notches of your spine. Casually scratching away the confidential layers of me as though I was never there. Scratchin me! Scratchin, scratchin. Me. Soon, that finger will discover you have no backbone and it will stab you!

LIGHTS TO BLACK. MUSIC UP. EXIT DIRECTOR AND LEADINGLady.

Seens from the Unexpectedness of Love **429**

[TheEX is seated at a desk writing with a feather quill pen. TheFACE is seated writing from inside a bathtub. They struggle to capture the words.]

TheFACE

We are writing all the things we should have said. Betrayal leaves my psyche blank, like unmarked pages in books without themes, margins, no words.

TheEX

Words escape us. Empty overtures flutter aimlessly, loosely, and un-harnessed. In moments, strange inquiries are composed and recanted. (scribbles) I don't dream of you anymore. Do you dream of me? We don't exchange dreams anymore—Only sullen post-scripts left hanging or dangling from torn shirt-sleeves or scribbled onto steamy bathroom mirrors with masked indignation.

TheFACE

(scribbles) By the way why did you leave? Why did you leave me?
Are you seeing someone? Else? Are you? Are you seeing someone?
Seeing someone? Else? Are you seeing some one? Else?
Are you? I am weeping.
Signed, *feeling betrayed.*

TheEX

(scribbles) *Dear feeling betrayed:*
Seeing someone? Else? What does that mean when we see too much and so many? Be certain of your questions. (I want to scream!)
I caution you to Be certain. (cries) OH GOD, I want to purge myself flush myself of these lies and foreign odors that do not smell of you.
(I want to scream!) I said—BE certain! Listen to me and BE CERTAIN (whispers/haunted) I said—BE certain of what you ask. BE certain! Then listen.
But first, BE certain!
Signed, Your devoted lover.
p.s.—Sorry that I have made you weep—but if I had stayed, I would only have pulled out your heart and battered you with it. Of course—
I have done that anyway. Please forgive me.

LIGHTS FADE AS SOUND OF A HUNGRY CROWD RISES.

BEAT #3: SUCKER-PUNCHED! TECHNO/ELECTRONIC

[Slowly TheEX and TheFACE put on a pair of boxing gloves and begin to simulate boxers sparring. At directed intervals DIRECTOR moves about them as referee, pulling them apart, etc. The LEADINGLady is dressed as the sexy ringside "babe" and parades with a score card denoting ROUNDS 1-2-3. Bell rings at start of end and start of each round.]

ROUND 1: BELL RINGS.

TheFACE
Betrayal is finding oneself drawn to the center of a boxing ring without preparation, training or a coach—

DIRECTOR
Look out! There's an upper-cut, a sucker's punch!
About to knock you on your artless ASSumptions.

TheFACE
How could a person called "friend" whisper in the ear of my lover, my

Fig. VII.2. *Seens from the Unexpectedness of Love.*
Photo by Julie Lemberger, courtesy of Pamela Booker.

spouse, my Soulmate when my back was turned and still be rewarded with something virtuous—my lover and her devotion.

TheEX
(swipes) Take that!

[TheFACE FALLS. TheEX STANDS OVER HER. DIRECTOR INTERVENES.]

TheEX (cont'd.)
You didn't know 'cause you didn't want to know!

DIRECTOR
(stands over TheFACE, who remains down) And 5-4-3 . . .

LEADINGLady
(shouts) Get up honey or you'll look like you want more! (to TheEX) Bully!

TheEX
(helps TheFACE stand) I need you to get up! (gently) 'Cause I know it's too hard to know.

BELL RINGS.

ROUND 2: BELL RINGS. LEADINGLady PARADES WITH SIGN.

TheFACE
(recomposes/swipes back) I know you better than you know yourself. All your insecurities, your lies. Your high threshold for inflicting pain. I know you!

TheEX
Familiarity breeds contempt!

TheFACE
You played at love, all the while concealing fragments of a deceitful personality, a wayward, dismembered spirit manifesting a thousand selves. Shiva goddess with a snake in her mouth. You wouldn't know the truth unless it crawled up on you during Halloween or a lunar eclipse.

BELL RINGS.

DIRECTOR

To your corners ladies. Final round.

[LEADINGLady parades with sign ROUND 3. EACH LOVER PREPARES FOR FINAL
EXCHANGE. BELL RINGS AGAIN. SOUND OF CROWD SHOUTING MADLY.]

TheEX

Your betrayer matches a rapist's profile. Bam!

TheFACE

Someone you know. Zap!

TheEX

Ouch! Someone you love blindly. Kapowee!

TheFACE

Someone you have tossed open doors for. Boom!

TheEX

And allowed them access to the forests of your personal domain.

TheFACE

Only to witness yourself ravaged

TheEX

Violated.

TheFACE

(stumbles) Cut down. (BOTH SHOW SIGNS OF FATIGUE.)

TheEX

Ambushed like . . . like lush tropical forests at nighttime.

BOTH

As the moon watches in meek terror, beaming impotent rays upon a
nasty perpetrator who steals away into the dark, dusty bush

TheEX

(strikes then falls) Their fingerprints and savage breath written across
your private parts.

Seens from the Unexpectedness of Love   **433**

TheFACE
(strikes at air then falls) And what of your heart? My heart?

BELL RINGS. CROWD ROARS. DIRECTOR and LEADINGLady move to stop the
fight.

DIRECTOR
And 5-4-3-2-1 (continues counting out until end of scene.)

LEADINGLady
Your heart you say? (Holds up sign with picture of a heart) Yes, well
. . . It'll be found discarded along unmarked pathways on the following
morning. In bits and teeny, weeny pieces. But go—you must try to re-
trieve it, otherwise, be assured—your betrayer stands poised to eat the
remains . . .

[MUSIC CHANGES. WHILE LEADINGLady SPEAKS LOVERS RECOMPOSE THEM-
SELVES. SHE AND DIRECTOR HELP THEM DISROBE AND REMOVE GLOVES.]

BEAT #4: "BUT! I NEVER MEANT TO HURT YOU!"—JAZZY
_____

LEADINGLady
Betrayal of this magnitude is maddening really. I for one don't understand how any of us survives it. Ask Hamlet, Caesar, any president's wife.
How else, you ask bewildered, sucker-punched!, could a once inviting,
reliable, trustworthy figure, so methodically strip you of your dignity, bits
of your sanity, and then ever so eloquently exclaim: "But! I never meant
to hurt you!" with a perfectly cited exclamation mark looped coolly at
the close of that pitiful confession? Sometimes it's better that you don't
explain. . . .
(laughs uncontrollably) But! I never meant to hurt you
To spill open your gut. But! I never meant to hurt you!

TheFACE
(reaches for picture of heart from LEADINGLady) Nor did you plan to dis-
lodge a life sustaining organ, the heart. Ordinarily a robust muscle now
reduced to fatty tissue and listlessness—mangled from triple, by-pass
deceit.

TheEX
But! Never meant to hurt you

To spill open your gut
But! I never meant to hurt you.

LEADINGLady

Well, sweetie, what was it then that you aspired to? You two were good together. You really were. (**EXITS.**)

TheFACE

(**chuckles**) Yes, what was it that you aspired to? Shopping?

TheEX

Reading.

TheFACE

Playing solitaire?

TheEX

Praying or dreaming. Resting on clouds hoisted upon old world spires at dawn.

TheFACE

Maybe . . . maybe you should have taken a long walk with me and confessed—

TheEX

What? How confused, sad, or pissed off I was at you—

TheFACE

Not me—at the disembodiments of YOUR life. The mediocrity you imagined in YOUR life and held me responsible for.

TheEX

You're right. I should have confessed. Instead—

TheFACE

Instead, one day you cocked your head, betrayal rushed into your bloodstream, poisoned your system and distracted you the way dogs are distracted by flies as they buzz around their shit.

TheEX

I, I was distracted.

TheFACE
You learn, flies demand attention.

TheEX
(clears throat) Yes, well, whether you're the offender or the offended, betrayal thrives on atonal vibrations.

TheFACE
There's nothing innocuous about this distinctly human cadence.

TheEX
Brutal.

TheFACE
Deadly.

TheEX
A virulent strain will permanently scar you.

TheFACE
You learn—other species kill when offspring become intolerable—
Humans simply betray.

[TheFACE and TheEX pause. Slowly they place red masks on their faces.]

MOVEMENT V
EPILOGUE

SEEN 8: THE MASQUERADE IS OVER

[SOUNDS OF OVATIONS PIERCE THE ROOM; the audience is heard wildly shouting "bravo! Bravo!" Red roses are tossed to TheEX and TheFACE from offstage. Awash in clamors and screams they move about the stage as if matadors who have just slained a bull. They bow to the heightened cheers of their audience. Action returns to apartment as TheEX finishes packing.]

TheFACE
Our audience can't get enough. It really is all about the "performance," isn't it dear? (They both take a final bow.)

TheEX

I stand, immobilized, thinking myself plunging through a series of
French absurdist plays. Watching in horror, the monstrous transformation of an unexpected love.

[TheFACE resumes ranting as the SOUND OF A VIOLIN SURGES. Suddenly a
spectacular force of light appears and spills onto her.]

TheFACE

Wah-wah-wah-wah-wah-wah-wah . . . (She freezes. TheEX resumes a
prostrated position as she completes packing clothes.)

TheEX

TheFACE is chanting ancient invectives. I can tell from the way her body
flails—possessed by Chango, the Yoruba deity, at once male and female,
hurling its body through red forests. There, the bag is full. The zipper,
closed. Closure. Apparently, so is the past decade of my life, though not
as neatly. (TheEX raises up off knees.) The bag is heavier than I expected.
I should have called a car.

[TheFACE doesn't respond, but moves toward the door where the light is
even brighter and bursts through the crevices. She opens the door to an
explosion of light and music.]

TheFACE

It's time for you to leave.

TheEX

(dry chuckle) Exit stage right.

TheFACE

Leave.

[TheEX moves to cross the threshold with garment bag, then stops as
the TheFACE noticeably relents.]

TheFACE

Wait—I . . . For a long time we loved, didn't we?

TheEX

(pause) We . . . We did.

TheFACE
For a long time we loved, didn't we?

TheEX
We did.

[TheFACE then walks over to the cabinet and grabs the rack of masks.
One by one, she begins discarding hers and TheEX does the same. As
the sound of their closing sentences are repeated, lights slowly fade on
both actors ridding themselves of their masks.]

MUSIC AND LIGHTS FADE OUT.

FINIS

"Public Intimacy"

WOMEN-LOVING-WOMEN AS DRAMATURGICAL TRANSGRESSIONS

Omi Osun Joni L. Jones

When *The Color Purple: The Musical* opened on Broadway in 2005, Black women-loving-women moved front and center in the U.S. theatrical landscape.[1] Due in part to the critical and popular success of Alice Walker's Pulitzer Prize–winning epistolary novel, the musical made an impressive showing at the box office by recouping its $11 million investment in its first year on Broadway and grossing more than $103 million by January 2008. While Black theatergoers typically account for approximately 4 percent of Broadway audiences, this group composed an unprecedented 50 percent of the audiences for *The Color Purple: The Musical*.[2] Black lesbians, whom the Combahee River Collective considered to be the ultimate challenge to patriarchy and the clearest evidence of social and political emancipation, were appearing in the most commercial and commodified of all theatrical forms.[3] Notably, Black audiences were responding in record numbers. Pamela Booker's *Seens from the Unexpectedness of Love* gives me an opportunity to examine Black woman-to-woman theatrical love and its ability to map a road to personal and dramaturgical freedom. As theatrical works examine transgressive personal truths, their structure, style, and tone must likewise forge new forms. This essay, then, notes the ways in which Booker's piece offers both love and dramatic form as strategies of resistance to repressive conventions.

"Black Is, Black Ain't"

Marlon Riggs's last film, *Black Is, Black Ain't*, opens with Black men and women of many hues proclaiming the varied possibilities of Blackness.[4] They shout, sing, moan, and whisper, "Black will get you, and Black will leave you alone. Black can let you move forward, and Black will make you stumble around. Black can be your best friend, cozy as the night; Black can do you in, make you cuss and fuss and fight." These pronouncements do not have to include "Black is Queer and Black ain't Queer" because the film itself does this work through a powerful sequence of spiritual leaders who denounce homosexuality alongside Riggs's poignant narrative about being a Black gay male artist and activist. In the visual and verbal texts of the film, Black Queerness is both embraced and interrogated as a given of Black life on the one hand, and a threat to it on the other.[5] *Seens from the Unexpectedness of Love* offers a similarly paradoxical understanding of Black Queerness.

Seens is a highly theatricalized play of five movements and eight "seens" (rather than scenes) in which characters don masks, directly address the audience, compete in a physical and verbal boxing match, interact with a chorus, and sometimes perform scenes shaped by specific musical genres. The understood public conventions of theatrical scenes are played against the personal perception of seeing and being seen. The play charts the dissolution of an intimate relationship between two Black women discovering woman-to-woman love for the first time. The play is both Queer and Black, not only because of the identities of the characters, but because of the world Booker creates around them. In so doing, Booker challenges the disremembering in which Black Queer people are omitted from Black history and Black life generally.

In identifying the practice of disremembering, Matt Richardson notes, "Black queers are, in many respects, dead to Black memory" and are "the anxiety-producing mnemonic that signals to the unconscious that it must protect itself from remembering."[6] TheEx and TheFace, the former lovers and main characters of *Seens*, are Black women who operate within a Black cultural context thereby requiring audiences to acknowledge the reality of Black Queer lives. They speak of collard greens, Egyptian musk, Coltrane, and Chango. These are not women whose sexuality distances them from the particulars of Black life; rather, their very lovemaking is rich in its Black references. As the women make love, the other characters join them in verbal and physical interplay noting, "Locks fall upon you resolutely," "Licorice Smooth/slender," "Around our chocolaty necks," "between thick thighs," "Intertwined. Locked," "Palmed in oils/Coconut frankincense/Sandalwood/myrrh," "At dawn locks dance among themselves/Spray across pillows . . . Form inverted pyramids or crowns/Divined for majestic heads of Goddesses and Warriors" (411–12). TheEx and TheFace understand their loving through a Black lens, a critical frame of cultural and political specificity. Indeed, when TheEx says they were "afraid to call it the 'L' word," her fear could be as much about limiting her sexuality with the label lesbian as it is about being associated with the very white lesbian world of the popular television series of the same name (413). Understanding *Seens* as conceived through a Black lens parallels the play's emphasis on *seeing*, or perspective—Black perspectives, the perspectives of the lovers themselves, and the perspectives of the society in which they attempt to live and love.

Importantly, Booker also seems to assume her audience is Black. As LEADINGLady struggles to learn her lines repeatedly mumbling, "Out damn! Out damn, spot! Out damn! Out damn, spot!," TheFace clarifies the line by saying, "The leading lady strutted about despondently like Macbeth's wife." Immediately after this, LEADINGLady responds, "How now! What news of my reviews and delivery and such? Director, oh director! I'm ready for my close-up. And don't NOBODY bring me no bad news" (404). Booker explains the well-known line of *Macbeth* but doesn't feel the need to identify Evilene's now classic line from *The Wiz*.[7] Similarly, an assumed familiarity with Black references occurs as TheEx packs her clothes to leave the apartment she once shared with TheFace. TheFace screams, "I thought . . . I thought . . . she must have put a spell on you. That's it isn't it?! SHE-PUT-A-GODDAMN SPELL ON YOU! What happened? Did you lose your mind? That's it—you lost your mind . . . lost YOU . . . I thought you were MINE!" (426). The stage directions indicate that Nina Simone's version of "I Put a Spell on You" plays under the scene. Many Black audience members would have gotten the Simone reference even without the music.[8] Other Black musical allusions include Nat King Cole's "When I Fall in Love" as the ironic romantic background to the play's prologue, and the use of House music and jazz in the scenes of betrayal.

Blackness is once again the understood foundation for the women's world as the social penalties for Queer desire are laid out. As the Chorus assumes the role of a homophobic minister delivering a sermon, it declares: "Get right . . . we know . . . with Jessssssuuuus. (clap) He'll fix everything. Like Mikey, he eats from a bowl of cereal and the world is made RIGHT. Make it all right. Make ME all right. If you're all right with Jessssssuuuus. (clap) It'll be all right. RIGHT! Get to know Jessssssuuuus. (clap) Get to know, ha, get to know, yes, get to know, get to know, I said, get to know (clap) Jessssssuuuus and it will be all right" (415). Although the stage directions simply state "all actors—builds into frenzied sermon-like voice," Booker's use of the clap and the guttural "ha" strongly suggests that this is specifically a Black preacher in the Baptist or AME traditions. Black people are also referenced when TheEx acknowledges the legislated hatred that terrorized her and TheFace as well as the self-hatred of those who condemned them. The idea of self-hatred likely suggests those Black people who refuse to admit to the complexity of their own sexual desire and practices. Booker seems to be speaking directly to Black people even as her play operates outside some of the unstated conventions of Black theater.

Seens does not fit the Black theater of Amiri Baraka, who declared in 1965 that "white men will cower before this theatre because it hates them."[9] Rather than exploring the contours of Blackness and racism, Seens focuses on the challenges of sexuality and homophobia. Race is never an explicit theme in the play; instead sexuality is literally and figuratively central. The juxtaposed scenes of lovemaking and public condemnation are pivotally positioned in the play. The first innocent yet transgressive kiss occurs immediately prior to these scenes and the unraveling of the relationship occurs immediately after them. Even though the audience learns that the women have been together for ten years, in stage time, the beginning, censure, and unraveling of the re-lationship are adjacent to each other and occur right in the middle of work. This play is an exploration of Black Queer love in which Queer-ness is foregrounded. Booker's interest lies in how eros operates rather than how race functions, and she explores her interest in sexuality without muting the Blackness of TheEx and TheFace.

In an important way, for TheEx and TheFace, Blackness is a fact of life rather than the sum total of it. Seens represents an expression of Black theater in which Blackness itself is not the subject, but is the understood given circumstance. Situating Seens as Black theater pushes the boundaries of what Black theater has been and might be. While this work surely fits W. E. B. Du Bois's 1920s dictum that Black theater be for, by, about, and near Black people, it does not do the social uplift work that is also associated with the productions Du Bois created through his KRIGWA Players.[10] Black Queer subjects challenge the very middle-class respectability that characterizes theater as high culture, and reflect the dominant political history of Black struggle in the United States. When Queer is added to the formula of Blackness the social respectability that some have fought to attain is simply impossible.

Prisons and Closets

Patricia Hill Collins likens Black sexuality to the mutually influencing locations of a prison and a closet, as Blackness itself has been criminal-ized and locked down, and Black Queerness has had to remain tenaciously hidden to avoid the fatal taint of disrepute. When one is not free, secrets are required for survival. Collins explains how the prison in which Blackness has become incarcerated requires closeted sexuality: "Women, lesbian, gay, bisexual, and transgendered people, children, people living with HIV, drug addicts, prostitutes, and others deemed to be an embarrassment to the broader African American community or a drain upon its progress or simply in the wrong place at the wrong time become targets of silencing, persecution, and/or abuse. This is what prisons do—they breed intolerance."[11]

Black lesbian characters have found a home in the working-class settings of some theatrical productions but are less well represented in middle-class contexts. In discussing the relationship of sexuality and class in plays with lesbian characters by Ed Bullins, Sharon Bridgforth, Shirlene Holmes, and Cheryl West, Lisa M. Anderson suggests that lesbian characters are more likely to be found in "strong black working-class cultures."[12] This is also true of August Wilson's *Ma Rainey's Black Bottom*, with Ma Rainey's publicly transgressive behavior—as blues singer, as a loud and aggressive Black woman, as Dussie Mae's lover—keeping her well outside the world of the Black middle class in spite of her money and fame. This working-class location for Black lesbian characters keeps the middle class protected and may account for the apparent acceptability of *The Color Purple: The Musical*, as Celie and Shug live outside the sanctions imposed by the controlling glare of the Black middle class. TheEx and TheFace, however, are solidly middle class as demonstrated by their professions and their language. The women are theater artists. They met during auditions for *Macbeth* in which TheEx was the stage manager and TheFace was favored for the role of Lady Macbeth. They quote Shakespeare, Picasso, and Virginia Woolf, and comfortably use phrases like "unanticipated compromises," "sacred/ supple nights," "the buttery taste of our dreams," "I bid you a rigorous adieu," "our love would flourish," and "clichés relax us." These are women whose education and literary linguistic gestures root them in middle-class realities.

The Black middle class's deep investment in disavowing any threat to its tenuous status results in Black Queer theatrical characters rarely making their way into middle-class theatrical settings. Booker achieves a radical move when *Seens* breaks with the tradition of presenting Black lesbian characters in protective working-class environments—and indeed, TheEx and TheFace are soundly punished for their love. Audre Lorde notes that Black women are terrified of being named lesbian because lesbians challenge the very patriarchal structure that defines the role of woman and keeps women beholden to patriarchy for their existence, albeit a subservient one.[13] The unknown terrain and responsibility that freedom brings can be so frightening that such freedom creates a defense of even a stultifying status quo. TheEx and TheFace are not afraid to openly love each other but by doing so they become enmeshed in public political sanctions that serve to maintain patriarchy. TheEx prophetically says, "In the sanctity of our private world, we consummated a public intimacy that would linger" (408). The privacy of eros dangerously seeps into public view and disrupts the carefully closeted Black sexual identities. Love and eros are never solely personal and private. They are always laced with the very public politics of national and individual identities, and the attendant claims of these identities.

Immediately after a richly erotic scene of lovemaking between TheEx and TheFace, the Chorus, acting as the disapproving and regulating society, declares, "Love is always unexpected. How you respond to it is choice! Man should choose woman! Woman should choose man! It's just not right!" (414). Queer is sexualized in the way that Blackness is racialized, and like race for Black people, sex for Queer people becomes public through what literary scholar Omise'eke Natasha Tinsley calls the "violence of normative order," which necessitates extinguishing Queer realities.[14] It is the *visible* fact of Queerness, of public sexual intimacy between TheEx and TheFace—both the *scene* it makes as display of Queerness, and the act of Queerness being *seen* by a policing public—that must be immediately punished by society. Equally important, the characters are rejected by their friends and family as staunchly as they are denigrated by the society at large. These middle-class women-loving-women find no haven in their middle-class community.

In considering community, it is important to note that TheEx and TheFace are not surrounded by a Queer community. They seem to have no Queer support for their love. In a risky dramaturgical move, they attempt to shame the audience through the Chorus for their homophobia, thereby making them complicit in the tensions of their relationship.

> TheFACE: You're all so smug and so fucking righteous!
> TheEX: You reduced our "marriage" to sound-bite and curtsey.
> TheFACE: No . . . in all fairness WE did that . . .
> TheEX: You're too polite! We didn't have help or role-models. And
>   all they said over and over again—
> [HOUSE LIGHTS UP. Lovers + Chorus move to confront audience.]
> CHORUS: (stern) It's just not right!

TheFACE: Our parents, Our friends said it. Well, ex-friends.
CHORUS: It's just not right! (414–15)

These Black women are working to understand their sexuality through their direct address to the audience, which allows them to demonstrate that they are not licentious sexual monsters. They give voice to the questions the audience may be asking—"TheEX: How do you choose such a thing? TheFACE: How do you deny it?" Booker devotes substantial stage time to exposing their inner struggles, which opens a space for experiencing their humanity, for dissolving judgment. The characters share their innocence:

TheEX: We discovered the sameness of gender, afraid to call it the "L" word, yet enchanted by the strangeness of this new fruit.
TheFACE: The smell, the taste, the touch of woman. We consumed each other with epicurean delight.
TheEX: In gregarious portions.
TheFACE: Convinced that our lives depended on it.
TheEX: It did. The hunger, the hunger. We sipped, nibbled, gnawed, chomped and suckled the "L" word.
TheFACE: For more than a decade we lived and danced on the emotional fringes of the "L" word. Instead, it was simpler to choose the "S" word—to say we loved the "sameness" of each other. We learned not to limit ourselves to categories or placards or the politics. We thought we could avoid the politics. We didn't expect to *become* our own cause! In reality we were terrorized by the intolerance and the hatred . . .
TheEX: The self hatred and the legislated . . . (413)

In stage time, the collapse of the relationship pointedly titled "Your friends exhausted me" occurs immediately after the public censure and the private reflection on how the characters navigated their Queer identities. In spite of the fact that the women were together for ten years, what the audience sees is a swift progression from the first rush of desire to the termination of the relationship. This quickness and this juxtaposition suggest that community—"We didn't have help or rolemodels"—is important to the maintenance of Queer relationships. Because Queerness is a publicly private reality for many, a supportive community becomes essential for safety and self-understanding.

Fig. 13.1. *Seens from the Unexpectedness of Love.*
Photo by Julie Lemberger, courtesy of Pamela Booker.

"It Really Is All about the 'Performance,' Isn't It Dear?"

Performance is a governing principle in *Seens*. In the play's epilogue, after reviewing how their relationship began and unraveled, TheFace says to TheEx, "Our audience can't get enough. It really is all about the 'performance,' isn't it dear?" (436). The performers then bow and offer their closing understanding about "the monstrous transformation of an unexpected love."

Theatrical performance confounds an easy dichotomy between public and private truths, between real and pretend, between individual and communal responsibilities. Because theater is public and communal, it makes the politics of sexuality visceral for everyone present. The women find each other in the theatrical space of possibility, where their transgressive love can be, where masks, clothes/costumes, and furnishings/sets are chosen and discarded as needed for each moment of seeing and being seen, each acknowledgment of corporeality. In an important way, the play asks what it takes to be seen—by one another, by the world at large, and by one's self. The play's intriguing use of the homophonic "seens" and "scenes" positions theater (scenes) as the site of knowing (seens). Theater, with all the paradoxes of truth and artifice, becomes an apt way of examining a relationship. The play uses theater as a place where audiences and characters come to collaboratively pretend in a world of make-believe *and* to know themselves more keenly through the distinctive experience of communal public embodiment.

Because TheFace and TheEx work in the theater and because *Seens* is a work of theater, the performative nature of the play's core themes of gender and sexuality are foregrounded. These women love and make love without apparent attention to the traditional performances of masculinity and femininity. Their bodies are female bodies, their gaze appreciates the femaleness of their identities, and their femaleness is not in dialogue with maleness. In fact, TheFace and TheEx are so similar that it is difficult to distinguish them by what they say or do. By making the women almost indistinguishable, Booker eschews butch-femme stereotypes and allows for a more expansive expression of their Queer identities. The choice not to sharply differentiate the women also transforms their public intimacy into social spectacle as erotic affection between two women undermines the accepted necessity for men in sexual life. Being seen—as in, freely revealing their erotic selves *and* being viewed by society—creates the spectacle.

There is very little evidence in the play regarding the gender performance of either woman. Booker creates a productive gendered ambiguity that challenges the audience members to relinquish what they may believe to be true about Queer people, and about intimate relationships in general. Importantly, the absence of these gendered codes can also extend an understanding of what Black Queer theater might be. In discussing Black lesbian and gay films, Kara Keeling challenges the requirement of specific cues to ensure recognizability. She explains, "I am arguing here that the appearance of black lesbian and gay images is made possible through a regime of visibility that has conceded to currently hegemonic notions of 'lesbian and gay sexuality' and to the primacy of binary and exclusive gender categories in the articulation of sexuality."[15] In several other theatrical works with Black women-loving-women characters—Shay Youngblood's *Shakin' the Mess Outta Misery*, the musical adaptation of Alice Walker's *The Color Purple*, Sharon Bridgforth's *no mo blues*, August Wilson's *Ma Rainey's Black Bottom*—the Queer relationships are characterized by butch-femme gender performances. By avoiding marked gender performances and the butch-femme binary, *Seens* discards a necessary feature of patriarchal frames and resists creating recognizable and therefore tolerable Black Queer women. This choice amplifies the spectacle of Queerness as women-loving-women publicly enact intimate relationships without regard to expected gender binaries.

Making TheEx and TheFace almost interchangeable serves another important function. The similarity of their characterizations and the theatricality of their names place focus on the ideas they present rather than encourage empathy for one or the other. As their scenes of betrayal are revealed, neither seems clearly right or wrong, neither operates as an obvious heroine or villainess. In *Seens*, the attention is on the density of relationships rather than the specifics of character.

Performance is sensory and visceral and felt. The fact of Blackness, as Frantz Fanon came to learn while walking the streets of Paris, is an always already marked everyday life performance.[16] The fact of Queerness, for some, is a private performance that dangerously spills into the public domain through acts of intimacy—a held hand, a lingering gaze, a wet kiss, a knowing laugh. Because TheEx and TheFace have made love, are they now lesbians? Did their private actions change their public identities? How much public/private fluidity is there in loving? Must all loving be named, and have all possible names for loving already been identified? Does a shift in one's private performance ethically necessitate a shift in one's public self-performance? *Seens* does not attempt to answer these questions but instead provocatively and persistently raises them.

Theater encourages a confrontation with embodiment, an embodiment that resists stereotype or predictability. The audience members must contend with the human beings in the performance as well as those seated next to them. In an essay about her work, Booker writes, "Plays also allow for the *realness* that affirms black female representation. You know, the kind of *realness* that makes audiences squirm uncomfortably in their seats."[17] It is inside this squirming that growth can take place.

Perhaps it is this interest in "realness" that causes Booker to have TheFace and TheEx speak in first person major character narration as they describe their actions to the audience. They break the fourth wall theatrical convention and have "real" conversations with the audience. Early in the play, TheEx says to the audience, "I enter the building's entryway with the air of a trespasser. Stay calm. Be charming. I wonder, is my face on properly? My face. My face" (399). Although the characters do not speak of themselves in the third person, this self-narrating is reminiscent of Chamber Theatre, which provides language for the psychological workings of a character and a scene.[18] These choices root the play in very particular theatrical traditions in which the audience is brought into the action and the act of being in the theater is part of the production.

Seens' awareness of the importance of performance or constructed realities is also present in the use of masks, clothes, and furnishings, which relate directly to the theatrical elements of character, costume, and set. Each character selects a mask for several of the scenes. When the women agree to meet for the first time since their separation, they each choose a black-and-white mask, suggesting that their current positions allows for no gray area, only the definitive irresolvable division of opposites. As black and white are the colors of separation, red is the color of their eros and their passion. TheFace shifts to a red mask before leveling accusations at TheEx, who loses her composure, telling the audience, "Red floods my mouth" as she coughs up red string and declares that their carefully selected red couch was "once a symbol of our passion" (423). TheEx and TheFace are ever aware of their lives as a series of staged events. The theater is their work and their primary life metaphor. They describe their relationship as if it were a play: "Playing leading roles one day, supporting roles the next. Damn good characters we were—fully dimensional, believable and passionate about our craft." Then, punctuating the metaphor, they declare jointly, "We fell in love while working in the theatre" (402). The masks are their way of interacting with one another, until the end of the play when they discard their many masks one by one.

TheEx's clothes serve a similar function as the masks: they reveal emotional dimensions of the relationship and underscore the constructedness of life. There are several clothing references in the play: "summer clothes," "dressings," "We were like anthropologists collecting useless fashion artifacts," "wearing other people's expectations," "Who knew that summer clothing could be so high maintenance," "linens, muslins, cottons, khaki . . . LIGHTWEIGHT. CHEAP." In the present time of the play, TheEx comes to collect her summer clothes from TheFace in the apartment building where they once lived. Since the breakup, TheEx's clothes have been stored in the basement, a kind of closet where secrets are kept and potentially forgotten. TheFace brings the boxes of clothes up to the third-floor apartment and sorts through them, placing TheEx's clothes in a trash bag. In the apartment, each item is examined for the stories it carries. Although placing the clothes in a trash bag might seem like a way to destroy the memories, bringing them into the apartment can also reanimate them. As soon as TheEx arrives in the apartment, the women begin to recall the events of their relationship, and the play is set in motion. Just after the central sequence of flashbacks in which the women meet, fall in love, then end the relationship, we return to the apartment and the sorting of clothes. During the scene, TheFace begins to rant and TheEx kneels over the bag of clothes while packing. The ritual-like elements of this moment are more specific in the final scene of the play. In the epilogue, TheEx packs the summer items she needs into the garment bag she brought for this purpose. While TheFace is "chanting ancient invectives" and "her body flails—possessed by Chango," TheEx states, "There, the bag is full. The zipper, closed. Closure. Apparently, so is the past decade of my life, though not as neatly. [TheEx raises up off knees.] The bag is heavier than I expected" (437). Just as the carefully sorted clothes are about to cross the threshold of the apartment with TheEx's departure, TheFace yields with, "For a long time we loved, didn't we?" TheEx responds, "We did" (437). They repeat these lines as the blinding light from the opened door and the raging violin music envelop the space. This final scene is tellingly entitled "The Masquerade Is Over."

Through the ritual-like elements of TheFace's chants and TheEx's kneeling, the women rid themselves of the masks that kept them concealed from each other. They let go of the posturing that required specific clothes and color schemes. Compelled by both the ritual and the glaring light of the outside world, they simply affirm the love they shared. Those carefully sorted clothes never go outside the door, as if their separated lives cannot go any further. Ultimately, they were more committed to artifice, to the disposable elements of performance than to the abiding intimacies it can provide. As TheFace asks, "How could two people invest more energy in their decor than they do the dressings of their everyday desires?" (424). *Seens* offers performances of gender and sexuality that are nonnormative and in so doing sheds light on the complex performances of intimacy.

Finis

Seens sits squarely in a Black theater tradition even as it may remain, for some, in the shameful shadows. It is Black theater because it resists external definitions of Blackness. Black theater is the action of our humanity. Here, our bodies *are*. Here, the contradictions and layers of who we all diversely are cannot be erased or ignored. Black theater that includes Queer identities—particularly women-loving-women identities, given the way such loving has the unique potential for dismantling patriarchy—can become a true "hollering place" as Pearl Cleage describes her vision of theater that allows the voices of Black women—

all Black women—to be heard.[19] Perhaps to let out the next whoop and holler in such a theater is to achieve erotic autonomy, the ultimate freedom for a people whose sexuality was used as evidence of our nonhumanity. M. Jacqui Alexander notes that "erotic autonomy has always been troublesome for the state," and *Seens* suggests that this troublesomeness can herald in moments of personal exposure and truth.[20] By the end of the play, the women have discarded their material and emotional masks, and acknowledged that they did indeed love. As a powerful final statement *Seens* offers love as the space where closets are abandoned, prisons are empty, and Black is everything we create it to be.

Notes

1 Throughout this essay I capitalize Black as a way to consciously acknowledge the cultural and political weight of this dense concept. Capitalizing also discourages the tendency to reduce Black to a color, thereby minimizing the historical complexity of race.

2 The January 24, 2008, issue of Playbill.com provides box office figures for *The Color Purple: The Musical*. In the November 10, 2009, issue of HamptonRoads .com, Scott Sanders, the show's original producer, describes focusing on Black women, Black churches, and ads in the *New York Post* rather than the *New York Times* as strategies for ensuring a healthy Black turnout for the production. Patrick Healy of the *New York Times* notes that the audience-development strategies launched for *The Color Purple: The Musical* were later used for the musical *Memphis* and David Mamet's *Race*. Among the fluctuating cast members for *The Color Purple: The Musical* were *American Idol* winner Fantasia Barrino, legendary R&B/soul singer Chaka Khan, gospel music icon BeBe Winans, and LaKisha Jones, an *American Idol* finalist. Having these well-known artists in the production was another important way to attract Black audiences.

3 Combahee River Collective, *Words of Fire*, edited by Beverly Guy-Sheftall (New York: New Press, 1995), 231.

4 Marlon Riggs, *Black Is, Black Ain't* (California Newsreel, Signifyin' Works, 2004).

5 By capitalizing Queer, I intend to foreground the specificity and expansiveness of gender and sexual expression. Queer, then, becomes an adjective (describing a thing), a noun (a thing itself), and a verb (the action generated by the concept). Capitalizing also encourages engagement with the reader, rather than lowercase, which almost renders this potent term innocuous.

6 Matt Richardson, "The Queer Limit of Black Memory," in *Listening to Archives: Black Lesbian Literature and Queer Memory*, manuscript, 4–5.

7 *The Wiz: The Super Soul Musical of "The Wizard of Oz,"* first performed in 1975, is the seven-time Tony Award–winning retelling of L. Frank Baum's *The*

Wonderful Wizard of Oz from a Black cultural reference point. It was made into a film starring Michael Jackson and Diana Ross in 1978. Evilene, *The Wiz*'s Wicked Witch of the West, opens Act II by belting out the warning song "Don't Nobody Bring Me No Bad News." It opens with the ominous lyrics "When I wake up in the afternoon/Which it pleases me to do/Don't nobody bring me no bad news/'Cause I wake up already negative/And I've wired up my fuse/So don't nobody bring me no bad news." The catchy repeated chorus has made the phrase readily identifiable among many Black theatergoers.

8 Some audience members might have associated the lines of the play with "Screamin'" Jay Hawkins, a blues singer who became popular in 1956 when he wrote the original version of "I Put a Spell on You." With either Simone or Hawkins as reference points, Booker's line calls forth a Black musical history.

9 Amiri Baraka, "Revolutionary Theatre," in *Selected Plays and Prose of Amiri Baraka/LeRoi Jones* (New York: William Morrow, 1979), 130.

10 W. E. B. Du Bois's attempts to generate social uplift for Black people are discussed in his influential essay "The Talented Tenth," which first appeared in *The Negro Problem: A Series of Articles by Representative Negroes of To-day* (New York: James Pott and Company, 1903). Du Bois was committed to higher education, political action, and the arts as tools for improving Black life in the United States. An analysis of his work on social uplift can be found in Jacqueline M. Moore's *Booker T. Washington, W. E. B. DuBois and the Struggle for Racial Uplift* (Wilmington, DE: Scholarly Resources, 2003). In 1925, Du Bois founded the KRIGWA Players, the theatrical branch of the NAACP's Crisis magazine. KRIGWA is an acronym that stands for the Crisis (spelled with a "K" to "Africanize" the word) Guild of Writers and Artists. Though begun in New York, the KRIGWA Players also had venues in Cleveland, New Haven, Baltimore, and Denver. For more information on this significant development in Black theater history, see Ethel Pitts Walker, "Krigwa: A Theatre by, for, and about Black People," *Theatre Journal* 40, no. 3 (October 1988): 347–56.

11 Patricia Hill Collins, *Black Sexual Politics: African Americans, Gender, and the New Racism* (New York: Routledge, 2005), 91.

12 Lisa M. Anderson, *Black Feminism in Contemporary Drama* (Urbana: University of Illinois Press, 2008), 99.

13 Audre Lorde, "Scratching the Surface: Some Notes on Barriers to Women and Loving," in *Sister Outsider* (Freedom, CA: Crossing Press, 1984).

14 Omise'eke Natasha Tinsley, "Black Atlantic, Queer Atlantic: Queer Imaginings of the Middle Passage," GLQ 14, nos. 2–3 (2008): 199.

15 Kara Keeling, "'Joining the Lesbians': Cinematic Regimes of Black Lesbian Visibility," in *Black Queer Studies: A Critical Anthology*, ed. E. Patrick Johnson and Mae Henderson (Durham, NC: Duke University Press, 2005), 218.

16 Fanon's encounter led to his famous poetic exegesis of the exclamation leveled at him—"Look, a Negro!" See "The Fact of Blackness" in Frantz Fanon's *Black Skins, White Masks* (New York: Grove, 1952).

17 Pamela Booker, *Dust: Murmurs and a Play* (Rochester, NY: Evolutionary Girls, 2008), 43.

18 Developed by Robert Breen while he was a professor of oral interpretation at Northwestern University, Chamber Theatre is a method of adapting prose fiction for ensemble performance. It retains the narration, embodies the narrator singly or through multiple performers, and emphasizes the psychology of the characters and the consciousness of the story itself. Characters often speak narrative passages about themselves, which necessitates speaking about themselves in the third person, thereby allowing for multiple perspectives to exist simultaneously.

19 Pearl Cleage, "Hollering Place," *Dramatists Guild Quarterly* (Summer 1994).

20 M. Jacqui Alexander, *Pedagogies of Crossing: Meditations on Feminism, Sexual Politics, Memory, and the Sacred* (Durham, NC: Duke University Press, 2005), 22.

CHAPTER 14

Interview with Pamela Booker

Tavia Nyong'o

Tavia Nyong'o: I saw *Seens from the Unexpectedness of Love* on the stage here in New York in 2005, but I reread it this week and thinking back to the performance I saw that was directed by . . .

Pamela Booker: Anita Gonzalez.

TN: I realized that I had no recollection, or sharp recollection of the gender of the protagonists.

PB: Which is good.

TN: And then as I began to read it I was looking for the clues in the written text. Of course, it becomes and feels like a theme: the question of gender and sameness. It's not presented in this very direct fashion as a kind of problem drama. So, given that same-sex love is always—not always, but in American politics and in culture these days so frequently—dealt with as a problem, how did you come to this particular approach?

PB: Well, you know, I first wanted to acknowledge your comment in recognition of not having an awareness of gender in the characters. That was part of my impulse when I first started writing this. Originally, and this is just an aside, I wanted to write something that would have male and female characters represented in characterization and, in fact, hopefully when it [the play] gets done again at some point I would still love to see that particular device have more play. Now, how does one get to that place? You're asking almost for a releasing of what could be seen as problematic by an audience. And in some regards, I don't know. It certainly was not written from a place of intentionality in that regard. I think that one's knowing or a person's knowledge can oftentimes influence it. I guess the narrative that grows between these two characters grows between distinctly rooted places of familiarity, and within that familiarity I think there are some larger global features or universal themes that are necessarily implicit in how people love regardless of gender, and I think that that was really the point of entry for me. How can I tell a story about how people, these two people in this case, as it's revealed happen to be women who shared a journey through love together. And what was that journey about? And ultimately what was the outcome?

TN: That's really interesting to hear because one of the theatrical devices that the play uses that speaks to the common experience of love, and also the experience of falling in and out of love, is the device of the rose-colored lens. People start the play wearing rose-colored lenses and it's kind of a motif: pink and rose and red as the colors of love and as the colors of possibly maybe delusion. I got connotations of the *Wizard of Oz* and I know that that is a different color, but I wondered if that was somewhere in your mind when you are thinking about Dorothy on her journey to Oz . . .

PB: It's funny that you would mention Dorothy, because I have to tell you that the *Wizard of Oz* is one of my top three favorite films . . .

TN: I'm not surprised.

PB: I can't say, though, that the *Wizard of Oz* was necessarily a direct or deliberate metaphor, but certainly I can see how you could get that sort of juxtaposition. Certainly how we—what is it?—our expectations or that which we anticipate around the condition of love is almost always going to be beyond what the love can provide us. And I don't at all say that from a place of being cynical because I really believe in a holistic love, but I think that oftentimes people do have expectations of love beyond what it can provide for us, especially romantic love—and we see how that translates in relationships, friendships, expectations that parents have of their children of sometimes having to shift to a hard love. And I think that when the rose-colored lens[es] are removed from the eyes, in terms of how we expect this person to behave and to react to us and provide for us, is oftentimes really very imbalanced.

TN: The characters mentioned early on in the play about serving as role models for our high maintenance friends. [laughs] Does that add to the pressure of love with or without illusions, the expectation that you be a role model—that your love be a kind of role model for others in some ways?

PB: Does it add to the expectation?

TN: Does it add to the difficulty of sustaining?

PB: I think it does only if you take that on, and I think part of what this narrative is attempting to say is if I were to personalize it in some way, that we have all in different moments taken on being a role model. Oftentimes we slip into it without even knowing. And I think oftentimes, too, that will happen to us when we allow other people's projections to shape what we imagined behavior should be or, again, what kind of reaction and response to what is being experienced in a relationship. An example of that for me is my first long-term partnership. And particularly in looking at some of the variances and imbalances that have existed around same-sex couples. On the one hand, we can say that historically because they were not role models, they could not provide. I really do in every way reject whatever this sort of heterosexual model of behavior in coupling [is]. Who is to say that those [models] are necessarily right? So I think on some level there needs to be an invention and there have been inventions of what same-sex relationships can be and are. But I think the danger in that is that people then become these types, and within that they are expected to behave a certain way—and then to critique how you are behaving. And if you are not behaving according to their standard or according to their model, it becomes really difficult for you to be able to be seen as a socialized relationship. I look for where we can locate ourselves around human behavior. And if something lends itself to how you practice it. If something is ethical, if something is just right, if something is operating from a place of high vibration, it doesn't matter whether it is same-sex or some other combination, it's good. It's good love. At the same time, if it is not working, then it's just not good love.

TN: I wanted to ask you about the metatheatricality of the play. I guess I should ask, do you see it as a metatheatrical work?

PB: Do you mean in terms of layering or echoes or . . .

TN: . . . well, for an example in that opening scene TheEX says that "we fell in love while working in the theater" and that becomes a recurring motif. And what you were saying just now about role playing and about coming to believe certain roles in your interpersonal life—in the play *Seens from the Unexpectedness of Love* the theater becomes a metaphor for both the possibility in those mechanics, but also maybe some of the limitations, the constrictedness of that.

PB: And the spectacle. The spectacle is very active in it as well. Definitely. Love is oftentimes staged, right? So we have people who platform where they are going to have movement and how they are going to interact with one another on the stage and I think whether or not the staging is realized, it happens in the same way that we talk about the inherent performative video of all relationships. Alright? Now, if you step outside of that and have the opportunity to look at that in a pan-optical way—the way these characters do—they are also critiquing that kind of voyeurism. I'm sort of all over the place with this, but I remember this discussion that Hortense Spillers had. She was talking about black folk being able to exercise what she called "interlogues" around those issues that are particularly pernicious to community behavior. And there is a lot of fear and potential detriment in that in terms of how it can be misinterpreted or miscast by this audience, who is constantly watching what you are doing on this stage. So, in this play I wanted to have fun and give these characters, who are their own players, the opportunity to exercise that privilege and not be concerned with who's listening to their interior monologues as well as to the exterior ones; to be their own critics and to be their own witnesses, and, yes, at the heart of that they are also critiquing the play that goes on within the theater and oftentimes the incestuous nature of it, the hyperreality of it.

I, as someone who has been a theater artist since adolescence, have come to understand that you are part of these many communities for this period of time—for however long it's going to run. I've worked in the past on Broadway and you're in a show for a year and these people become extended family. You take on roles and there are scripts that are assigned and that you assume and that you write for yourself around identity and authority and this is an opportunity to be able to watch. You tend to be able to act it out and just to watch it again. And I think what is the through line, what is the emotional reality of it all? And what does it say about who these people really are when they go home at the end of the day from the theater and remove their masks?

TN: Picking up on that, do you have any particular reflections or reminiscences about being in a particular theater family that produced that kind of staging of things?

PB: There was a festival that we did and I don't remember the full name, but festivals are, by their very nature, frenetic, because everything is kind of limited: time and money and resources. It is this group of people that we know as actors who are willing to step in to this place with you for a period of time and say I find this script that you have written compelling and it engages me in some way and yes I will be a part of it. And so there is this embracing by a very small community of actors, and they were extraordinary actors and they were all equity. I've been very, very fortunate the times I have been produced to get really good professional actors who were literally between jobs and who really wanted to do my work. And so that has always just been really affirming for me. And I was working with Anita Gonzalez, who is an extraordinary performance artist-practitioner, who is now transitioning to becoming a teacher, scholar, dance historian, and director on her own terms, and Anita and I go back some years to when she was dancing with Urban Bush Women. And we were watching each other grow up and move into these places where we could be impactful in our work, on other people's work, and we had always wanted to collaborate on a project. And that, to me, is like firmament when you can come back to a new situation, but with someone who has familiarity and who is now informed with whatever your aesthetic is, and the qualities of production that are important to you as the writer, and the original expression in this work and having someone who can capture that makes all the difference in having the support and the continuity with the group of artistic practitioners. And that's been really wonderful for me to experience, especially on this production.

TB: Are there any final thoughts or anything you want to put on the record?

PB: One closing thought that I hope is conveyed to whoever gets to see the play or read the play is that one of the comments or offerings if you will that the characters put out there is: *we did love, didn't we?* And I see this as a question that is illuminating not only for this couple, but for any isolated couple that is sometimes forced to question: *is the love still there?* And also, for us to look at that as a larger humanity: we *did* love. So I am really very interested as someone who is moving through this path of [the] early twenty-first century in a time that is in the midst of some really deep chaos that we get back to this question of we did love and finding our way around to perhaps actualizing it.

Part VIII

Berserker

Paul Outlaw

Text by Paul Outlaw, Essex Hemphill, and Samuel R. Delany, with excerpts from *The Confessions of Nat Turner* and from transcripts of interviews with and statements made by Jeffrey Dahmer.

NAT TURNER was born into slavery in 1800 in Southampton County, Virginia. In August 1831 he led a small army of slaves on a thirty-six-hour rampage through the county, in which they axed or beat to death fifty-nine white men, women, and children. Turner, after being tried, convicted, and sentenced to execution, was hanged and then skinned in November 1831. The texts here consist of excerpts from a statement he allegedly made while awaiting trial that was published in a pamphlet as *The Confessions of Nat Turner*.

JEFFREY DAHMER was born in 1960 in Milwaukee, Wisconsin. In July 1991, he admitted having killed seventeen young men, primarily of African American descent, whom he had photographed, strangled, dismembered, sexually abused, and, in some cases, cannibalized over the course of thirteen years. Dahmer was found guilty of the murders and sentenced to life in prison, where he was killed by a fellow inmate in 1994.

The texts here consist of statements he made to lawyers, to psychologists and, at his trial, to the court.

OTHER TEXTS BY:

PAUL OUTLAW (2003).

ESSEX HEMPHILL—excerpts from "Balloons" and "Ceremonies," both
    included in *Ceremonies: Prose and Poetry* (Plume Books, 1992).

SAMUEL R. DELANY—excerpt from "The Tale of Fog and Granite" (1985)
    from *Flight from Nevèrÿon* (Wesleyan University Press, 1994).

THE CONFESSIONS OF NAT TURNER, THE LEADER OF THE LATE INSURRECTION
    IN SOUTHAMPTON, VIRGINIA, AS FULLY AND VOLUNTARILY MADE TO
    THOMAS R. GRAY (1831).
LEE SANDLIN—excerpt from "Losing the War," published in *The Chicago
    Reader* (1997).
DEATH HAVE MERCY (Traditional song).

BLACK.

SOUND: *three knocks, like metal striking wood followed by rumbling
guitars and bass mixed with ambient noises.*

*Lights reveal, one at a time, six large black plastic trash bags placed
about the stage. They are full or semi-full. The floor of the stage is
covered by a 20-foot square translucent plastic tarp. A seventh bag is
revealed on a long table upstage.*

"PAUL"   (*voice-over as the bags are revealed*)
                In black plastic bags tied at the top they were buried. Their
                faces swollen with death rise in my dreams. I read of them:
                young boys, young men lured to a house. Their penises were
                filled with excited blood: first hard then soft they became as
                Death with its blistered lips kissed them one by one. They
                were grapes on Death's parched tongue.
                    In plastic bags tied at the top they were buried. Twenty-
                five of them and more unclaimed young boys, young men.

                SOUND: *more upbeat, rock/funk guitars and percussion. Lights reveal
                an eighth black trash bag beneath the table, from which a figure begins
                to emerge.*

"PAUL"   (*onstage*)
                For three days I have walked by a dark gray house at the end
                of my street where lives a man out of whose home I have
                seen young boys, young men coming and going, coming and
                going. And for three days from the second-floor windows,
                music from dusk to dusk has fallen like petals of black roses
                softly to the ground.
                    But tonight, evening of the third day, I call the police and
                tell them not about faces rising like balloons. I tell them
                instead about music, about petals from black roses falling

Fig. VIII.1. *Berserker*. Photo by Ray Busmann, courtesy of Paul Outlaw.

softly to the ground. Perhaps they will understand. Maybe they will come to my street and knock at the door of the gray house where lives this man I have not seen for three days, whose face is beginning to rise in my dreams like balloons.

SOUND OUT.

He strikes the table three times and begins to dance a series of gestures and movements, as . . .

SOUND: *. . . the funky guitar track continues and finally fades out as the following text is heard.*

MALE VOICE   *(voice-over)*
Oh yes, the Vikings knew: prolonged exposure to combat can goad some men into a state of uncontrolled psychic fury. On the battlefield they begin to exhibit the most inexplicable and gratuitous cruelty.

Berserker **463**

> They become convinced that they're invincible, above all rules
> and restraints, literally transformed into supermen or werewolves.
> The Vikings called such men "berserkers."

SOUND OUT.

"PAUL"   These were not hate crimes, they said.

SOUND: AMBIENT NOISES.

He again strikes the table, smashing three tomatoes. He begins to re-
move objects from the trash bag on the table.

"TURNER"   Having murdered Mrs. Waller and ten children, we started
              for Mr. Williams', killed him and two little boys. Mrs. Wil-
              liams fled, but she was pursued, brought back, shown the
              mangled body of her lifeless husband and told to get down
              and lay by his side, where she was shot dead.

He drinks from a glass on the table.

"DAHMER"   I put sleeping pills, about seven pills, in his drink. The next
              morning he was lying there, his chest had been crushed.
              Sometime during the night I had been beating him in the
              chest with both fists—my fists were bruised. I just remem-
              ber waking up lying on top of him. And the complete shock.
              That afternoon I got a large suitcase with wheels, put him in
              a cab and drove home. When my grandma went to church I
              took the body out. Using a sharp knife that I got somewhere
              I stripped the flesh off the bones and put it in three plastic
              hefty bags and kept the skull and the scalp.

"TURNER"   In my childhood my elders strengthened me, saying I was
              intended for some great purpose, and my master noticed
              my uncommon intelligence. He remarked that I had too
              much sense to be raised as a slave or ever be of any use to
              any one as a slave.

SOUND OUT.

He leaves the table, moves through the space.

"PAUL"　　My sister and I are worried about the future. We're afraid our family is going to fade away. Fade to white. Now, we don't usually see eye to eye about race. I like white people, she doesn't. I'm idealistic, she's pragmatic. But we both are uncomfortable about what's happening. Let me run it by you.

My parents had six kids: five boys and a girl. Now, my mother's real light-skinned, like this . . . (*showing his palm and stroking it*) . . . and my father was darker . . . like this . . . (*slapping his stomach*)

We kids are anywhere from here to here . . . (*slapping his wrist, pointing to his stomach*)
Okay: my oldest brother (*slapping wrist*) and his wife have got three kids: the oldest, my niece Sharon (*pointing to back of hand*) was married to a guy whose father was Puerto Rican and whose mother was Irish-American. He looks Italian. (*showing palm*)

He and Sharon have two young children, my grandniece Katherine and my grandnephew Kansas. Cute kids, very pale . . . (*showing palms*)

My next oldest brother (*stroking his stomach*) died of a broken immune system. He and his wife, who is half-Puerto Rican, half-Pacific Islander (*stroking the sole of one foot*) didn't have any kids.

Okay: then comes my sister herself (*slapping his chest*) who has one son, my favorite nephew—(*stroking his forearm*) and she had high hopes for him until he started dating (*exposing his teeth and tapping them*) a white girl. As far as offspring is concerned, he's a question mark for now.

Then we got my middle brother (*slapping his neck*) who went through a mysterious and messy divorce after less than a year of marriage. I've never seen the kid and I don't believe that it's his, no matter what story she's telling the court now all of a sudden. Another question mark.

And then there's me. (*patting his face cheeks*)

SOUND: AMBIENT NOISES.

"DAHMER"　　(*back at table*)
When I was a little kid I was just like anybody else. Once I found a dog, and cut it open just to see what the insides

looked like, and for some reason I thought it would be a
fun prank to stick the head on a stake and set it out in the
woods. I brought one of my friends back to look at it and
said I'd stumbled upon it in the woods.

"TURNER"   I had a revelation, which fully confirmed to me that I
was ordained for some great purpose in the hands of the
Almighty. I had a vision, and I saw white spirits and black
spirits engaged in battle. I had a vision that the sun was
darkened. I had a vision that the thunder rolled in the
Heavens, and blood flowed in streams. I had a vision . . .

"DAHMER"   *(methodically cleaning table)*
Is it possible to be influenced by spirit beings? I know that
sounds like a cop out, but from all that the Bible says there
are forces that have a direct or indirect influence on people's
behavior. The Bible calls him Satan. I suppose it's possible
because it sure seems like some of the thoughts aren't my
own, they just come blasting into my head.

*One of the trash bags seems almost to jump at him from the floor, as he
stoops to put something inside. As the contents fly out, he springs back
and falls to the floor.*

They're not the kind of thoughts that you can just shake off
and they're gone. They do not leave.

"TURNER"   While laboring in the field, I discovered drops of blood on
the corn as though it were dew from heaven.

*He opens a bag, begins removing contents and smearing them over
himself.*

Then on the leaves I found numbers and shapes of men
in different attitudes, portrayed in blood. For the blood of
Christ that had been shed on this earth and had ascended
to heaven for the salvation of sinners was now returning
to earth as dew. So it was plain to me that the Saviour was
about to lay down the yoke he had borne for the sins of
men, and the great day of judgment was at hand. I heard a
voice: "Such is your luck, such you are called to see, and let
it come rough or smooth, you must surely bear it."

466 Paul Outlaw

Fig. VIII.2. *Berserker*. Photo by Ray Busmann, courtesy of Paul Outlaw.

Fig. VIII.3. Paul Outlaw surrounded by "entrails" and drenched in red light in a scene from *Berserker*. Photo by Ray Busmann, courtesy of Paul Outlaw.

He begins a sliding step across the stage, pushing a bag across with his feet.

"DAHMER"   There was a hitchhiker along the road. He wasn't wearing a shirt. He was attractive; I was attracted to him. I passed him and stopped: "Well, should I pick him up or not?" I asked him if he wanted to go back and smoke some pot, and he said, "Oh, yeah."

SOUND: AMBIENT NOISES *fade out as the rumbling guitars and bass from the opening are heard again.*

He runs to the upstage wall and, during the following text, slowly edges across the wall, from stage left to the right.

"PAUL"   "Yeah, you're ready."
      I was a skinny little fourteen-year-old Black boy.
      I stood before George grinning, my undershorts and pants were down around my knees.

George was at least thirty years older than I, tall, and slightly muscular beneath his oversized work clothes: khakis, a cotton short-sleeved shirt, and a white apron. He wore black work boots.

George was a white man. For weeks he had whispered he wanted to suck my dick. Catching me alone in the store, he would quickly serve me, seizing the opportunity to whisper in my ear.

After weeks of being coaxed and teased to come by, I finally succumbed. I sneaked up to the store very early that morning, before it opened.

I was a skinny little fourteen-year-old Black boy.

"Ahh! Ahh!"

I trembled and panted as he stroked me.

George liberated his equally swollen cock from his pants. It sprang out engorged with blood and fire. The head of it was deep pink in color. I was startled to see that the hair surrounding it was as red as the hair on his head.

George drew me into his mouth. It was hard to tell which of us was enjoying the cock sucking more. Suddenly he hurried to the front of the store and promptly returned with a short stack of grocery bags, newspapers, and a small jar of Vaseline.

"You're gonna fuck me."

After spreading the newspaper and bags on the floor behind the deli counter, George opened the Vaseline, scooped out some with his index finger, and pushed it up into his asshole. In and out, in and out. My dick was so hard I thought it would break into a thousand pieces of stone around our feet. After thoroughly greasing his asshole, George then scooped out more Vaseline and smeared it all over my dick. He had now laid down and beckoned me to climb on. Led by his hand, my cock entered his ass in one smooth penetration.

I would mount him and pour my adolescence into him, from the spring through the late summer, night and day. I would lie to get away from home and friends to be with him before the store opened, fucking him at the back of the store and at his house at the end of his work day while his mongrel dog sat and watched us.

If we had been caught, the law would have charged him

with molesting a minor, but I wanted him to suck my dick. I wanted him to touch me. I wanted to fuck his ass. I wanted him.

I didn't think I would be punished in hell. My dick did not fall off in his mouth. I did not turn green from kissing him. I didn't burst into flames during our orgasms. In fact, during orgasm, I often called out: Jesus.

SOUND OUT.

He moves away from the wall and walks downstage.

I didn't know that George had initiated most of the boys I knew, and some of their older brothers, one by one. After their orgasms they were cruel and nasty to him, but what they really resented was the recognition of their own *homo* sexual desire.

SOUND: AMBIENT NOISES.

On all fours, he moves backward toward and under the table.

"DAHMER"   We had some beer, and I could tell he wasn't gay. I didn't know how else to keep him there so I got the barbell and hit him over the head then strangled him with it. To have complete control. I was very frightened.

He moves around the table.

Paced the house for a while. Couldn't get any sleep. I did masturbate. Figure out a way to dispose of the evidence.

He goes to one of the bags, slashes it, then gets in and does a kind of sack race across the stage.

Buy a hunting knife. Slit the belly open, masturbate again. Cut the arm off. Cut each piece. Bag each piece. Triple-bag it. Then drive to drop the evidence off a ravine. Halfway there, get pulled over by the police.

"TURNER"   *(emptying another bag . . .)*

470 Paul Outlaw

The eclipse of the sun was the sign that I should slay my
enemies with their own weapons. Then I communicated
the great work to the men in whom I had the greatest confidence. I asked Will if he thought to obtain his liberty.
(*. . . and putting it on, like a shirt*)
He said he would or lose his life. It was agreed we should
commence at home. They all went to the cider press and
drank, except myself.

"DAHMER"   (*sitting on edge of table, bags on torso and legs*)
The police pulled me over for driving left of center. Do the
drunk test. I pass. Shine the flashlight on the backseat, ask
me what the bags are. I tell 'em it's garbage. And they believe it, even though there's a smell, and give me a ticket for
driving left of center.

He kicks bag off feet.

SOUND: *Deconstructed '50s country western tune.*

"PAUL"   My adolescent desire drove me to the parking lot of a nearby
country bar one night—and one night only—discreetly asking the white patrons: "Can I suck your dick—for free?" My
request was never fulfilled because I believe the men were
shocked that I would so boldly solicit them. "Can I?" I was
lucky no one summoned the police to come for me. I was
lucky I wasn't dragged off to some nearby wooded area and
killed.

SOUND: AMBIENT NOISES.

"TURNER"   (*on the floor, approaching one of the bags with a utensil*)
We entered the house secretly to murder them whilst
sleeping. It was then said that I must spill the first blood. I
entered my master's chamber, armed with a hatchet. Since
it was dark, I was not able to give a death blow. The hatchet
glanced from his head, he sprang from the bed and called
his wife. It was his last word. Will struck him dead.

"DAHMER"   I took the drill while he was asleep: I didn't want to keep
killing people and have nothing left except the skull.

He grabs the bottom of the bag that had been on his feet and embraces it as it empties out.

If I could have kept him longer, all of him, I would have.

He grabs a bag, beats it several times against table, pushes it across the table, then climbs after it onto the table.

"TURNER"   Will nearly severed her head from her body with his broad ax.

He begins ripping the bag off his torso.

"DAHMER"   It's a lot like a festering sore, it doesn't get better, it gets worse until one day . . .

SOUND: *'70s funky R&B instrumental.*

"PAUL"   *(lying on his side on the table)*
. . . the night is so clear to me—it was mid-August, sultry, humid, and the anticipation of returning to school was in the air. My buddies and I were all out talking with some of the older boys—including Leon's brother, Crip—talking about everything from sports to girls.

Lulled by stories of pussy conquests, petty scams, and recent ass-kickings, I had become intoxicated on the blossoming masculinity surrounding me. I might as well have been shooting semen from wet dreams straight into my veins for the high I was on in this gathering.

Crip was standing. From where I sat I could eye his crotch with a slight upward shift of my eyes. Well, one of the times that I peeked, Crip caught me.

"I see you looking at my dick!"

Immediately, all conversation ceased and all eyes focused on me and Crip.

"Do you wanna suck my big, Black dick, muthafucka? Do you, nigga?"

Thank God my instincts told me to stand up: "No."

"Well, why are you looking at my dick? Is you a freak? You must wanna suck it. Are you a faggot? You can suck it, baby."

The fellas were laughing and slapping palms all around by this time. The sexual tension in the air was palpable enough to be slapped around.

"You shouldn't be looking at a muthafucka's dick unless you plan to suck it. Are you funny, nigga?"—more raucous laughter from the fellas.

"No."

Crip was but an inch or two taller than me, and a pretty Black male. He carried beauty as agilely as some Black men carry footballs and basketballs and pride. I was surely attracted to him, but to even have hinted at that . . .

SOUND OUT.

So there we stood . . . The conversation resumed its boisterous, brash bravado.

He climbs onto table and curls up in a ball.

I excused myself from the fellas, crossed the street, locked the door behind me, and cried myself to sleep in my bed. It would not be the last time. It would not be the last time I would lock the door behind me and go to my bed alone, frightened of desires and dangers.

SOUND: AMBIENT NOISES.

He jumps up and stands on table.

"TURNER"   All forty men shouted and hurrahed as I rode up. I formed them in a line as soldiers and paraded them through all the maneuvers I knew. It was my object to carry terror and devastation wherever we went.

"DAHMER"   I boiled the upper portion of the body for about two hours and then the lower portion for another two. Soilex removes all the flesh, turns it into a jelly-like substance and it just rinses off.

"TURNER"   Sometimes I got to the houses in time to see the work of death completed.

"PAUL"   Okay: there's my oldest brother; niece; grandniece, grandnephew;
Next oldest brother; sister; middle brother;
And then there's me.
Me and my husband, who was born in Germany, aren't
thinking about kids at this point.
Finally, my little brother got one Puerto Rican girl pregnant. The result: Christopher, aged fifteen. The woman my
brother in fact married, also Puerto Rican, gave birth about
fourteen years ago to Joseph.
Are you still with me? Let's review: there's Christopher
. . . Joseph . . . Katherine . . . Kansas . . . some of my family's
contribution to Generation Z . . . so far.
I, for one, am fine with it; I say, mix it all up, create
dozens of new human breeds until "race" becomes mean-
ingless. These babies are all children of color, certainly, and
will at various points along the line know what it means to
be a nigger, but—our society is still so color-conscious that
lighter skin still guarantees privilege: if you have the choice,
it's easier to be white . . . (*pointing to white shredded paper*)
. . . than black . . .

He looks at a trash bag, then runs to grab it.

That's what makes me and my sister want to go berserk
sometimes. We're afraid our family is going to fade away. It's
like when you clean your black clothes: with every washing
the color fades, and if some bleach gets in there, well, that
fabric can lose all its color, and a lot of times, it gets eaten
away. They're always talking about getting your whites
whiter, but how often do you hear anyone talking about
something to get your blacks blacker?

SOUND: AMBIENT NOISES.

He takes two large bones from the bag.

"DAHMER"   I laid the clean bones in a light bleach solution, left them there for a day and let them dry for about a week in the bedroom on newspaper.

"TURNER"   I would view the bodies in silent satisfaction and immediately start in quest of other victims.

He jumps onto one of the bags as if to crush it.

"DAHMER"   My consuming lust was to experience their bodies.

He jumps on another bag, stomps it with one foot.

"TURNER"   My consuming lust was to experience their bodies.

SOUND OUT.

"PAUL"   My consuming lust was to experience their bodies. The first time I saw a photo of Jeffrey Dahmer I thought: "He's hot. I'd do him in a minute." That face, so simple and all-American. Those eyes, so soulful and troubled. Those lips, so . . . then I read about what he'd done and saw those other photos and I was horrified, of course. Of course. But to this day, whenever I see an image of his face, that face, the first reaction is in my balls. I'm not gonna lie to you. And I've seen photos of the guys he brought home . . . I mean, before he made them his own. Chances are, I would have ended up in Jeffrey's refrigerator, if I'd been living in Milwaukee in the late '70s and '80s.
I was a tall, skinny, twenty-something black man.

SOUND: *'80s electro-funk song (and live microphone).*

He grabs a mike and mike stand and begins to prowl the stage and audience as if performing at a comedy club or a rock concert.

That's when I was going berserk, first in New York and then in Germany, in West-Berlin. Running wild in the streets of the East Village and Kreuzberg, in the West Village and along the Motzstraße. Dancing through the nights at Metropol, Pyramid, Dschungel, Studio 54! Cri du Chat, Better Days, Risiko, the Cockring! Querelle, Buttermilk Bottom, SchwuZ, the Crisco Disco!

Like the song says: "Dance . . . music . . . sex . . . romance."

Sex in the 80s. Before I moved to Berlin, sex was something that I usually did in the dark. I wanted romance, but
the guys I'd fall for were not biting. For the black guys, I
wasn't big enough or bad enough or . . . black enough. And
for the white guys who would look at a black man, I wasn't
big enough or bad enough or . . . black enough. But I was
getting a lot of sex. After about a dozen drinks or a couple of
'ludes or a hit of acid, I would land in somebody's bedroom
or the nearest bathhouse . . . somewhere in the dark. 'Cause
you know what they say: if no one sees it, then it didn't happen.

But then I moved to West Berlin and hmmm . . . I noticed,
with delight, that German men were so much *nicer* to me
than most white men back home had ever been—I felt like
flavor of the week, the month. And suddenly alcohol and
drugs were that much more fun when you didn't *have* to do
them to get laid. One spring Sunday in Berlin, I found myself making out with a tall German guy with blond dreadlocks on a crowded elevated subway train at six o'clock in
the morning, sun streaming through all the windows. In the
light. I realized that I felt, for one of those rare moments in
life, completely safe: I didn't expect anyone to beat me up or
kill me for being who I was. And I wouldn't have stood for it
if they'd tried. I felt invincible and I was . . .

SOUND: *the funk is interrupted by Bavarian biergarten music.*

. . . in Germany.

You know, I'd been living in Berlin for about a year before
it hit me that Germans were white people. I'm not kidding.
Look, the first months I was so excited about how *European*
everybody was and how undeniably cool Berliners could be,
you know, so I hadn't been thinking of Germans as white,
per se. "White folks" had always been an American notion
for me, and, let's face it, I wasn't in the States. I was there.
I preferred to think of these people as just, well, German
(although my Jewish friends back home did have a problem
with *that*).

But—after the first year, little things were starting to get on my nerves. Just a few little things. Like I'm at this party and this guy Gerhard starts on me: "Tell me, Powl, are your perrents Afro-Amerikaner? Boce of dem? Det is nawt pawssible! You are not rilly bleck!" It gets better. "Please don't understend me fahlse, but your color, na ja, well, your fahter is white, yes? You are, you know, uh, Mischling?"

According to the Nuremberg Laws of the Third Reich, *Mischling* described a German resident of impure ancestry; nowadays it's just the word used for mulatto, and, also, by the way, for a mongrel dog.

See, although in the U.S. I'd always been considered your run-of-the-mill, garden-variety . . . nigger, for many Germans only dark-skinned Africans are *really* black.

Oh, then this guy I was dating, we'll call him Wolfgang, invited me to visit him at his parents' house outside of the city of Saarbrücken. Sure! Well, it turned out that Wolfgang's village was more a *suburb* of Saarbrücken, so this was to be my introduction to the suburbs of Germany. Well, surprise, surprise, surprise! The suburb of St. Ingbert looked, smelled and *felt* like any suburban community in middle America! Same houses, same lawns, same cars, same garages, same neighborhoods, same people, oh my God what was this colored city boy doing with these suburban white people?!!!

It was slowly dawning on me that all Northern Europeans had something scary in common . . . they could resemble a variety of white people I thought I had left back home . . . the big, unsophisticated, homophobic, racist, suburban variety . . .

SOUND OUT.

But things took a turn for the worse in Greece of all places. That summer I traveled by ferryboat from the mainland to Zakynthos, one of those beautiful Greek islands, and it was the first time I'd been out of Germany since becoming a freshman expatriate. On the ferry: lots of Italians, lots of Greeks, lots of Southern Europeans, who I noticed looked different from the Germans I'd spent most of that year with. They were . . . well, they were less *white*. Which was OK.

I was lying on deck, covering myself with baby oil like
I used to do every summer, 'cause I liked to get good and
dark. I was on board for about a day, the sun was incredibly
bright, and I got my deep chocolate brown summer coat.

But you know what? Within a week I was seeing the skin
on my hands and my shoulders and even in my face start
to come off in flakes and fall down like snow! I was totally
freaking until Sabine, one of the German girls I knew on the
island, burst out laughing and told me I was peeling.

I *knew* that! "Nein, Paul, you hev bean sunburnt!"

That was a first for me! I'd never seen a black person with
a sunburn before. Damn! First the Germans went all white
on me and now it looked like I was turning white, too . . .

SOUND: *microphone off, then ambient noises.*

He returns to table, as if drawn by an irresistible force to the bones.

"DAHMER"   I just felt like that all day long. It was a craving, a hunger, an
             incessant, never-ending desire to have someone at whatever
             cost, someone really nice-looking and I just kept doing it,
             doing it and doing it. These were not hate crimes.

"TURNER"   We were about to be attacked. All deserted me but two,
             whom I sent to rally anyone they could. But when I discov-
             ered white men riding around, I scratched a hole in a field
             and concealed myself for six weeks.

*He begins crawling around, gathering bags, debris and piling them
around himself as he takes refuge under the table.*

             I only left in the dead of night to get water; I was afraid of
             speaking to any human being, and returned every morning
             to my cave before the dawn of day.

"DAHMER"   If I hadn't been caught, I'd still be doing it, I'm quite sure
             of that. I was very careful for years and years, making sure
             that nothing incriminating remained. But it just seemed like
             it finally went into a frenzy. Everything really came crash-
             ing down. The whole thing started falling down around my
             head.

Fig. VIII.4. *Berserker.* Photo courtesy of Paul Outlaw.

"TURNER"   A dog was attracted by some meat I had, and crawled in my
             cave to steal it. It discovered me and barked. I begged the
             two Negro men who came after the dog for concealment.
             They fled from me.

        SOUND OUT.

"PAUL"   *(sings)*
             (gradually emerging from beneath the table)
                  O death have mercy
                  O death have mercy
                  O death
                  Just spare me over another year

                  If I was a flower in my bloom
                  Make death coming down so soon

                  O death have mercy
                  O death be easy
                  O death
                  Just spare me over another year

What is this that I can't see?
Cold icy hands all over me
Stretch my eyes, want to stretch my limbs
This is the way that death begins

O death have mercy
O death be easy
O death
Just spare me over another year

Humming the song, he moves upstage away from the table.

"PAUL"   **(spoken)**
I've seen old barracks where slaves were once housed.
I've seen rows of stone benches with the iron rings sunk
along their tops, out in the sun at the edge of an overgrown field, where five hundred were once chained while
they ate their gruel in the rain . . . a line of fifteen or twenty
scrawny wretches passing on the road, chained to a plank
they carried on their shoulders by day, that they dropped
between them to eat off at the evening meal, the bunch of
them led along by some leather-aproned men, one with red
eyes, one with a harelip, and one with a cough worse than
any of his charges.
    You've never ridden through some clutch of huts and
yam fields, off in the forest where the slavers have been by
only a night before. And you watch the fathers wandering
about, crying for their stolen sons and daughters, stopping
now and again to beat their faces bloody against sharp-
barked palms or on the slant rocks, while the tearful and
silent women throw handfuls of sand into the evening's
cooking pot for the grieving meals they'll eat for a week
after such a raid.
    I may be tuned into a white world, but I don't want my
nephews and niece to forget their black heritage: they probably won't learn about it in school, it rarely makes it on to
primetime TV, and, frankly, my sister and I are convinced
they won't get enough of it at home. Their parents are from
Generations W and X, folks not always known for their
sense of history . . . history.

SOUND: *"Death Have Mercy" is heard again, this time sung by a woman.*

Our African fore-mothers, about whom *we* can only guess and fantasize, were abducted and in bondage produced generations of American children, black, brown, yellow . . . with every change in hue, with every son and daughter stolen, sold, lost, we moved further away from the connection to our Generation A until today . . . as my sister holds one of these fading babies (perhaps one day her own grandchild), the expression on her face is tinged with horror, delight, berserker rage and love.

He rocks the table like a cradle. The song becomes louder and then fades out as lights fade to black.

Appendix

The following details the preexisting copyrighted, non–public domain material incorporated into *Berserker*.

Excerpts from "Balloons," from *Ceremonies* by Essex Hemphill:

In black plastic bags tied at the top they were buried. Their faces swollen with death rise in my dreams. I read of them: young boys, young men lured to a house. Their penises were filled with excited blood: first hard then soft they became as Death with its blistered lips kissed them one by one. They were grapes on Death's parched tongue.

In plastic bags tied at the top they were buried. Twenty-five of them and more unclaimed young boys, young men.

For three days I have walked by a dark gray house at the end of my street where lives a man out of whose home I have seen young boys, young men coming and going, coming and going. And for three days from the second-floor windows, music from dusk to dusk has fallen like petals of black roses softly to the ground.

But tonight, evening of the third day, I call the police and tell them not about faces rising like balloons. I tell them instead about music, about petals from black roses falling softly to the ground. Perhaps they will understand. Maybe they will come to my street and knock at the door of the gray house where lives this man I have not seen for three days, whose face is beginning to rise in my dreams like balloons.

Excerpts from "Ceremonies," from *Ceremonies* by Essex Hemphill:

"Yeah, you're ready."

I was a skinny little fourteen-year-old Black boy.

I stood before George grinning, my undershorts and pants were down around my knees.

George was at least thirty years older than I, tall, and slightly muscular beneath his oversized work clothes: khakis, a cotton short-sleeved shirt, and a white apron. He wore black work boots.

George was a white man. For weeks he had whispered he wanted to suck my dick. Catching me alone in the store, he would quickly serve me, seizing the opportunity to whisper in my ear.

After weeks of being coaxed and teased to come by, I finally succumbed. I sneaked up to the store very early that morning, before it opened.

I was a skinny little fourteen-year-old Black boy.

"Ahh! Ahh!"

I trembled and panted as he stroked me.

George liberated his equally swollen cock from his pants. It sprang out engorged with blood and fire. The head of it was deep pink in color. I was startled to see that the hair surrounding it was as red as the hair on his head.

George drew me into his mouth. It was hard to tell which of us was enjoying the cock sucking more. Suddenly he hurried to the front of the store and promptly returned with a short stack of grocery bags, newspapers, and a small jar of Vaseline.

"You're gonna fuck me."

After spreading the newspaper and bags on the floor behind the deli counter, George opened the Vaseline, scooped out some with his index finger, and pushed it up into his asshole. In and out, in and out. My dick was so hard I thought it would break into a thousand pieces of stone around our feet. After thoroughly greasing his asshole, George then scooped out more Vaseline and smeared it all over my dick. He had now laid down and beckoned me to climb on. Led by his hand, my cock entered his ass in one smooth penetration.

I would mount him and pour my adolescence into him, from the spring through the late summer, night and day. I would lie to get away from home and friends to be with him before the store opened, fucking him at the back of the store and at his house at the end of his work day while his mongrel dog sat and watched us.

If we had been caught, the law would have charged him with molesting a minor, but I wanted him to suck my dick. I wanted him to touch me. I wanted to fuck his ass. I wanted him.

I didn't think I would be punished in hell. My dick did not fall off in his mouth. I did not turn green from kissing him. I didn't burst into flames during our orgasms. In fact, during orgasm, I often called out: Jesus.

I didn't know that George had initiated most of the boys I knew, and some of their older brothers, one by one. After their orgasms they were cruel and nasty to him, but what they really resented was the recognition of their own *homo* sexual desire.

My adolescent desire drove me to the parking lot of a nearby country bar one night—and one night only—discreetly asking the white patrons: "Can I suck your dick—for free?" My request was never fulfilled because I believe the men were shocked that I would so boldly solicit them. I was lucky no one summoned the police to come for me. I was lucky I wasn't dragged off to some nearby wooded area and killed.

. . . the night is so clear to me—it was mid-August, sultry, humid, and the anticipation of returning to school was in the air. My buddies and I were all out talking with some of the older boys—including Leon's brother, Crip—talking about everything from sports to girls.

Berserker **483**

Lulled by stories of pussy conquests, petty scams, and recent ass-kickings, I had become intoxicated on the blossoming masculinity surrounding me. I might as well have been shooting semen from wet dreams straight into my veins for the high I was on in this gathering.

Crip was standing. From where I sat I could eye his crotch with a slight upward shift of my eyes. Well, one of the times that I peeked, Crip caught me.

"I see you looking at my dick!"

Immediately, all conversation ceased and all eyes focused on me and Crip.

"Do you wanna suck my big, Black dick, muthafucka? Do you, nigga?"

Thank God my instincts told me to stand up: "No."

"Well, why are you looking at my dick? Is you a freak? You must wanna suck it. Are you a faggot? You can suck it, baby."

The fellas were laughing and slapping palms all around by this time. The sexual tension in the air was palpable enough to be slapped around.

"You shouldn't be looking at a muthafucka's dick unless you plan to suck it. Are you funny, nigga?"—more raucous laughter from the fellas.

"No."

Crip was but an inch or two taller than me, and a pretty Black male. He carried beauty as agilely as some Black men carry footballs and basketballs and pride. I was surely attracted to him, but to even have hinted at that . . .

So there we stood . . . The conversation resumed its boisterous, brash bravado.

I excused myself from the fellas, crossed the street, locked the door behind me, and cried myself to sleep in my bed. It would not be the last time. It would not be the last time I would lock the door behind me and go to my bed alone, frightened of desires and dangers.

Excerpt from "The Tale of Fog and Granite," from
Flight from Nevèrÿon by Samuel R. Delany:

I've seen old barracks where slaves were once housed. I've seen rows of stone benches with the iron rings sunk along their tops, out in the sun at the edge of an overgrown field, where five hundred were once chained while they ate their gruel in the rain . . . a line of fifteen or twenty scrawny wretches passing on the road, chained to a plank they carried on their shoulders by day, that they dropped between them to eat off at the evening meal, the bunch of them led along by some leather-aproned men, one with red eyes, one with a harelip, and one with a cough worse than any of his charges.

You've never ridden through some clutch of huts and yam fields, off in the forest where the slavers have been by only a night before. And you watch the fathers wandering about, crying for their stolen sons and daughters, stopping now and again to beat their faces bloody against sharp-barked palms or on the slant rocks, while the tearful and silent women throw handfuls of sand into the evening's cooking pot for the grieving meals they'll eat for a week after such a raid.

Excerpt from "Losing the War" (*Chicago Reader*) by Lee Sandlin:
The Vikings knew: prolonged exposure to combat can goad some men into a state of uncontrolled psychic fury. On the battlefield they begin to exhibit the most inexplicable and gratuitous cruelty. They become convinced that they're invincible, above all rules and restraints, literally transformed into supermen or werewolves. The Vikings called such men "berserkers."

CHAPTER 15

What's Nat Turner Doing Up in Here with All These Queers?

PAUL OUTLAW'S *BERSERKER*; A BLACK GAY MEDITATION ON

INTERRACIAL DESIRE AND DISAPPEARING BLACKNESS

Charles I. Nero

Nat Turner and Jeffrey Dahmer are the two central figures in Paul Outlaw's "one-person, one-act play" *Berserker*. The odd and unexpected pairing of Turner and Dahmer can provoke gallows humor as when a colleague of mine said I should call the essay "What's Cooking?" Nat Turner was a slave whose rebellion against his enslavers in Southhampton, Virginia, in 1831 unleashed a torrent of racial violence. Turner's rebels killed sixty white men, women, and children. The white retaliation against blacks was even more ferocious as whites executed more than two hundred African Americans and tortured many more in a rampage that extended far beyond Virginia. In her narrative *Incidents in the Life of a Slave Girl*, Harriet Jacobs recalled how in the neighboring state of North Carolina every black person, free and enslaved, became a target as poor whites ransacked homes looking for evidence that might indicate support for Turner.[1]

Jeffery Dahmer cannot be connected to any literal, life-and-death freedom struggle. He was a white serial killer convicted of murdering seventeen boys and men between 1978 and 1991. Dahmer's victims were African- or Asian-descended men whose only crime was their willingness to become his sexual partner. Dahmer's gruesome crimes involving rape, drugs, torture, dismemberment, cannibalism, and necrophilia were those of an insane, brutal psychopath.

Why place these two men together in one work? What do they say about each other: the freedom fighter and the psychopath? What could possibly be learned from a juxtaposition of Dahmer and Turner? Why include in the performance autobiographical reflections and works by other black gay male writers Essex Hemphill and Samuel Delany? Is Outlaw exhuming the hoary claim that sexual disturbance fueled Turner's insurrection as William Styron had infamously implied in his

1967 Pulitzer Prize–winning novel?[2] What is Nat Turner doing up in here with all these queers? I struggled with these questions as I prepared this essay. I believe that the answer is a complex one. Dahmer and Turner embody a quintessential American masculinity for Outlaw. They are berserk warriors, enacting their violence on a landscape that is a battlefield between black and white nations. I view Outlaw's *Berserker* as a black gay meditation on interracial desire and blackness disappearing on this battlefield.

The Berserker

The berserker, a figure in European mythology, represents the rapaciousness and brutality that have governed sex and desire across racial lines in Outlaw's drama. In the most thorough study Michael P. Speidel observes that berserkers were warriors with two defining characteristics: they "scorned [body] armor" and they "raged uncontrollably in a trance of fury."[3] Outlaw calls attention directly to this figure at the outset of his performance when he appears nude onstage, seemingly possessed, sometimes dancing, and describing the contents of garbage bags full of the entrails of murdered people. A recorded male voice then proceeds to tell us about the berserker figure: "Oh yes, the Vikings knew: prolonged exposure to combat can goad some men into a state of uncontrolled psychic fury. On the battlefield they begin to exhibit the most inexplicable and gratuitous cruelty. They become convinced that they're invincible, above rules and restraints, literally transformed into supermen or werewolves. The Vikings called such men 'Berserkers.'" By choosing the figure of the berserker for his performance work, Outlaw draws attention to a neglected mythological figure that was important for the cultural unity of Europe. Speidel finds attestations of berserker warriors from 1300 BC to AD 1300—a period that includes the Bronze, Iron, and Middle Ages—and from a geographic region that spans as far north as Scandinavia, westward to Ireland, and southeastward along the Mediterranean into Turkey and India. In fact, Speidel conjectures that the berserker warrior may have been important for the spread of Christianity beyond southern Europe and the Mediterranean. He notes that Frankish warriors attributed to Christ the image of a berserker as in a "sixth-century terracotta plaque found . . . depicting Christ as an elite warrior, hair bound up, wearing a necklace and strutting naked" and in Nordic sagas that depicted Christ as "God's berserker."[4] From Speidel's perspective the berserker warrior was an important figure in the production of a cultural identity among the tribes and nations in what is presently Europe. The mythology about the berserker warrior was crucial for establishing Europe's identity as the center of Christendom.

Disappearing Blackness

In a direct address to the audience, Outlaw states, "My sister and I are worried about the future. We're afraid our family is going to fade away. Fade to white." Pointing to the different skin colors of his own nude body, Outlaw draws attention to his observation that his family is both a result of interracial unions and a contemporary desire to cross boundaries of race and ethnicity. His mother is the color of the palms on his hand, while his father was the color of the skin on his caramel-colored stomach. His youngest brother has had children with and without marriage to lighter-skinned Puerto Rican women. His niece married a man who looks Italian but is actually the son of a Puerto Rican father and an Irish American mother; they have two "very pale" children. One of his nephews has lost favored status having decided to marry a white woman.

Paul Outlaw gives particular attention to the desire among blacks to embrace whiteness. Historically, there have been genocidal impulses and practices to eradicate blacks, but it is no less true that blacks as well as other racial minorities may desire and even long to embrace whiteness or an ethnicity perceived as closer to it than is blackness, as Outlaw suggests is happening in his family. This longed-for embrace is particularly acute in the Americas, where blackness has been the basis for systematic and categorical exclusion from citizenship and humanity. One result of this exclusion is shame associated with dark skin color. In order to resolve this shame it has not been unusual for people of African, Spanish, and Caribbean descent throughout the Americas to engage in "whitening" practices that run the gamut from skin bleaching to choosing to reproduce with lighter-skinned people.[5]

The film scholar Richard Dyer astutely made remarks that are particularly relevant to the issue about skin color that Outlaw raises in *Berserker*. In his classic study *White*, Dyer states, "If race is always about bodies, it is also about the reproduction of those bodies through heterosexuality."[6] Thus, a central concern for race is its conservation through the control of reproduction, that is, by regulating the specific types of bodies that must engage in heterosexuality to produce new generations of a race. Racial conservation discourses are inherently oppressive because they imply a control of women's reproductive capacities as well as an enforcement of compulsory heterosexuality. It seems, then, that Outlaw is at the center of a contradiction upholding practices that are directly related to his own oppression. He appears to be a gay man upholding racial conservation, a practice that is complicit with a homophobic heterosexuality. I argue against this conclusion. I believe that what Outlaw is doing is acknowledging a legitimate concern about blackness. However, as a gay man he is also acknowledging the complexity of desire. These two realities—blackness and gayness—are sometimes contradictory, which is what his performance work *Berserker* presents.

The Battlefield

The sparse mise-en-scène on which the play is set alludes to a mythological American battlefield. Other than a table, everything onstage is black, white, or red. The table is set in the center of the stage, surrounded by nine or ten large black plastic garbage bags. The black garbage bags contain either white popcorn, mounds of spaghetti dyed fiery red, or shredded white paper. The contents of the bags stand for entrails, body parts, and fluids. It is on this symbolic setting of a battlefield that Outlaw places his American berserkers.

American masculinity continually imagines itself as innocent, even as the most violent acts of rapaciousness and brutality have been committed for its sake. Outlaw uses the table and the plastic bags to represent this innocence. The table is a long rectangle that is sometimes a hiding place and sometimes a workstation. As a hiding place the table recalls a child's site for play during mealtimes. Indeed, as the stage lights come on for the first time, Outlaw evokes this image of childhood innocence when he emerges from under the table completely nude. What is even more striking is that Outlaw crawls out from under the table from inside one of the black garbage bags, suggesting either a discarded child or a child emerging from a black womb. This child, tossed in the garbage or emerging from the black womb, performs the monologues of Dahmer and Turner, the former the psychopath who reasons that he can only be close to the nonwhite males he desires by killing and devouring them, and the latter the slave who reasons that he can gain his freedom only by destroying the white people who stole his labor to build America.

The table is also a worksite indicating that innocent boys grow up to be men. Outlaw suggests this point when he conceals his nudity, first with tight red running pants, suggesting perhaps masculine blood and desire, and then a see-through vinyl butcher's apron. Outlaw stands behind the table, facing the audience, and uses it for a significant part of the play as a chopping block where Dahmer and Turner demonstrate how they killed and decapitated their victims. In one provocative instance, Outlaw uses a large mallet to whack red tomatoes as he recites in gruesome detail the murders that each of the berserk warriors has committed. Outlaw appears to be a butcher, doing his work, dismembering parts of carcasses, human ones.

This allusion to the butcher-as-berserker continues as Outlaw incorporates into his performance a prose selection by the late black gay poet Essex Hemphill. In the essay "Ceremonies" Hemphill recalls his teenage initiation into homosexual sex with the local butcher, the redheaded George. In what was for me the most erotically charged moment of the play, Outlaw pantomimes the redheaded George showing the young Hemphill how to have hot, masculine, man-on-man sex. It is worth noting that at this point in the play, Outlaw's attire, his translucent vinyl apron and red shorts, has a spectral resemblance to George's uniform. The fact of sex in the butcher shop raises several issues. The first points to the battlefield allusion as George and the young Hemphill have sex amid the entrails and carcasses of meats that are destined to be sold to humans for food. Second is the use of the camp trope of homosexuality as cannibalism that appears so frequently in writings by gay males.[7] In the case of Outlaw's performance, though, the placement of Hemphill's text in the butcher shop that is the site for Dahmer's and Turner's grisly acts conjures another image, this one, from James Baldwin.

Here Be Dragons

James Baldwin titled one of his last published essays "Here Be Dragons." The title was a reference to the unknown area in ancient maps that later became the Americas, but for Baldwin it also referred to a structure of "violence" that is "not merely literal and actual but appears to be admired and lusted after."[8] Outlaw, an astute reader of Baldwin, suggests that Dahmer and Turner are emblematic of this structure.[9] What I want to explore in this section is a hypothesis that I believe Outlaw suggests by his use of Dahmer and that the selection of Hemphill's "Ceremonies" reinforces. Namely, it is the desire or lust that blacks, as Americans, have for the masculinity that the berserker implies. Of course, this lust sits at the site of a contradiction: historically the berserker is the same destroyer of blackness that produced the various hues and shades in Paul's family that he and his sister rant against.

Outlaw explores African Americans' attraction to the white berserker through an interpolation of Hemphill's texts as mediators between the narratives of Turner and Dahmer. In his memoir essay "Ceremonies," Hemphill writes about how his desire for sex led him to the racial battlefield that eventually culminated in his relationship with the butcher, George. As an adolescent and before meeting George, the sexually charged Hemphill found himself soliciting sex with white men in the parking lot of a country and western bar. This is incredibly frightening when one considers that a popular African American view is that country and western bars are havens for both macho and white supremacists types.[10] Hemphill recalls the dangers of his venture when he writes, "I was lucky I wasn't dragged off to some nearby wooded area and killed." When Hemphill finally finds sex with George, Hemphill, although only fourteen at the time, makes it clear in his narrative that he understands that he was in a dangerous situation. Had they been caught, George could have been convicted of a crime and sent to jail. Further, Hemphill makes it clear that George was violating not only the law, but the codes of masculinity, too. Other boys had had sex with George, however: "After their orgasms they were cruel and nasty to him, but what they really resented was the recognition of their own *homo* sexual desire." Here Hemphill is presenting George, the berserker, as a sexual outlaw. Fully thirty years older than the young Hemphill, George was willing to risk jail and the condemnation of fellow males for the sake of pleasure. "Here be dragons," as Baldwin so astutely observed, for George is not only a sexual outlaw; he is an enemy to the neighborhood as a white man earning his living off of black people. It is worth noting as well that George's profession is a butcher, someone who cuts and carves dead meat to sell to the public, a fact that also suggests his connection to a berserker. George is part of the conquering force of whiteness that in this country created public policies that allowed whites to enter into commercial enterprises but denied those opportunities to blacks. George is part of the racial war battlefield in America, and Hemphill desired him.

One of the interesting aspects of this desire that I would like to comment upon further is George's hair color. Outlaw keeps in his performance this erotic description that refers to George's hair color: "George liberated his equally swollen cock from his pants. It sprang out engorged with blood and fire. The head of it was deep pink in color. I was startled to see that the hair surrounding it was as red as the hair on his head." This description of George's red hair is very similar to descriptions of berserkers in classical literature who are often described as warriors having a fire surrounding their heads or shoulders before they have an "aristeia," a moment of glory on the battlefield. *The Iliad*, book 5, lines 1–8, has the following reference:

> There to Tydeus' son Diomedes Pallas Athene
> granted strength and daring, that he might be conspicuous
> among all the Argives and win the glory of valour.
> She made weariless fire blaze from his shield and helmet
> like that star of the waning summer who beyond all stars
> rises bathed in the ocean stream to glitter in brilliance.
> Such as the fire she made blaze from his head and his shoulders
> and urged him into the middle fighting, where most were
>   struggling.[11]

The hero Achilles comes to be associated almost exclusively with fire by the end of the *Iliad*. Athena surrounds Achilles's head with fire (*Iliad* 18.205); his helmet gleams like a star (*Iliad* 19.378); and Hephaestus, a god associated with fire, begins to burn the plains and river to help Achilles in his battle with the river Scamander (*Iliad*, book 21).

It is important to note how Outlaw plays with the color red throughout the performance. Some of the black garbage bags on the stage are filled with spaghetti dyed red to suggest entrails. He pounds red tomatoes on the table chopping block to suggest crushed skulls. But the most profound signifier is the tight red pants that Outlaw wears throughout the production. Even the choice of the transparent butcher's apron seems to imply that we, as an audience, can never forget that Outlaw is wearing a red undergarment to gird his loins. What is Outlaw signifying through this spectacular garment?

James Baldwin's use of the redheaded berserker is helpful for understanding the desire that Outlaw expresses through his use of the color red, especially his red undergarment. The red-haired berserker initially appears as a menacing presence in Baldwin's 1968 novel *Tell Me How Long the Train's Been Gone*. In a flashback the successful African American stage actor Leo Proudhammer reveals how Caleb, his incarcerated brother, had been terrorized both sexually and violently by a guard named Martin Howell, "a big, dumb Irishman with red hair." "The first time I saw this red-haired mother-fucker," Caleb says, he rode up on a horse, looked down, and yelled out, "Nigger, if my balls was on your chin, where would my prick be?"[12] The next use of the red-haired berserker image was less menacing, supporting Emmanuel S. Nelson's claim that Baldwin's novels can be read in succession as a greater awareness and acceptance of homosexual and interracial desires.[13] In his final novel, *Just above My Head*, Baldwin uses the classical image of the berserker for the character Guy Lazar, the French lover of the novel's protagonist, the gospel singer Arthur Montana. Baldwin evokes the image of Guy as a berserker in ways that make use of his physique as well as his past. He is a physically imposing figure that Arthur describes as a "red-haired giant."[14] Guy's past also suggests racial warfare; he comes from Nantes, a city that was the largest slave trading port in France, a fact which surely Baldwin was aware of and found useful for his character's biography.

Guy's image as a berserker is cemented when we learn that he is a military veteran, having served for France in Algeria during Algeria's bloody War of Independence. The war had as many as one million casualties and other disastrous results: the devastation of the Algerian economy, the movement of hundreds of thousands into refugee camps, and the expulsion of the European settler community. Guy's experience on this bloody North African battlefield is compounded by the fact that the men he wants to love are of African descent. His previous lover, Mustapha, was an Algerian man who was deported. Guy complains that "his history is clinging to him" (427). When Guy tries to explain the dilemma that his history presents, Arthur forbids him because he is only too aware of Guy's history, and the kinship he, an African American, shares with colonized Algerians.

What is surprising about the relationship with Guy is that Arthur continually associates it with freedom. When they kiss and make love, Arthur finds himself "trembling in a kind of paroxysm of liberty" (410). In another instance Arthur claims that when alone with his lover Guy, he feels "a kind of thrill of freedom" (414).

Outlaw has a passage in *Berserker* that is remarkably similar to the sense of freedom that Baldwin ascribes to Arthur's encounter with Guy. Rather than France, though, it is Berlin where Outlaw found the freedom to pursue his berserker. Outlaw recalls "making out with a tall German guy with blond dreadlocks on a crowded elevated subway train at six o'clock in the morning, sun streaming through all the windows," and, he says, "I realized that I felt, for one of those rare moments in life, completely safe: I didn't expect anyone to beat me up or kill me for being who I was." Also, like Baldwin's Arthur, Outlaw feels that Germans are different from whites, or simply not "in his imagination" as Baldwin wrote. "You know, I'd been living in Berlin for about a year before it hit me that Germans were white people. I'm not kidding," states Outlaw. To Outlaw white people were in the United States, not Germany. After some time in Berlin Outlaw comes to realize, much as Baldwin's Arthur did, that the Germans share a kinship with white Americans. Nevertheless, Outlaw's time in Germany allowed him to experience something that he calls "freedom."

It seems that the freedom that Baldwin, Hemphill, and Outlaw describe is intrinsically connected with an erotic embrace of a white man, and more specifically, with one who evokes the image of the berserker. For Baldwin's Arthur it was the redheaded soldier Guy; for Hemphill, the butcher George; for Outlaw, the "tall German guy with blond dreadlocks." The freedom that Baldwin, Hemphill, and Outlaw are struggling with is the meaning of a black gay man's desire *for* the male racial other in a racist society. History imprisons as well as constructs desire. It is not easy to forget or evade history and its consequences for African Americans. It is all the more difficult for a member of a minority group within a minority, the gay black man like Outlaw, Hemphill, or Baldwin, to articulate that the male racial other is a figure of desire. To do so is to risk an accusation of self-hatred as when Eldridge Cleaver viciously attacked James Baldwin for daring to write about desiring white males. In his 1968 best seller *Soul on Ice*, Cleaver called Baldwin's homosexual and interracial desires "a racial death wish."[15] For Cleaver, Baldwin's desire was collusion with the racist practices that have been making blackness disappear since the beginning of the transatlantic slave trade.

Conclusion

The berserkers, Turner and Dahmer, reveal Outlaw's cognizance of racial histories and politics that have created, as Andrew Hacker so aptly put it in his book title, "two nations: black and white, separate, hostile, unequal."[16] Yet erotic desire for the racial other cannot be contained easily. I am reminded of Isaac Julien's brilliant *The Attendant*, a short video/film set in an art museum.[17] The visitors leave the museum, but a youngish white man in black leather remains. He and a middle-aged older black male museum attendant exchange knowing glances. A famous nineteenth-century antislavery painting by the French painter F.-A. Biard, titled *Scene on the Coast of Africa*, comes to life. The tableau, which Biard created to visually narrate the brutal history of slavery—the exchange of people for goods, whipping and branding, and concubinage—becomes a contemporary interracial, gay s/m *tableau vivant*. The ships and chains of slavery have been refashioned into the accoutrement associated with contemporary s/m: black leather with shiny metallic surfaces, rubber and latex, uniforms. Iconic gay s/m images by Robert Mapplethorpe and Tom of Finland replace the "high art" on the museum's walls. In some scenes black men whip whites, while in others, white men whip blacks. Here is Julien's quite brilliant discussion about the juxtaposition:

> Could not the fetish slave-band in the film, mimicking the metal collars worn by black slaves—which, for some readers, enacts this colonial memory—be read as something else: namely, the unspeakable masochistic desire for sexual domination? Surely in this post-colonial moment, black queers should have the choice of acting out the roles of "slaves" or "masters" in the realm of desire and sexual fantasy. For instance, if today a black gay man was to participate in such an act for sexual pleasure, could not the resulting "representation" of inter-racial s/m be read as a parody? Or would it be moralistically read into the cheap sociology of a pathological, black/self-hating discourse?[18]

The point that Julien makes is important. The enactment of a sexual fantasy about slavery is not slavery. The continuation of the race does not depend upon correct sexual practices, and to argue that it does involves using the logic of a totalizing heterosexuality that makes homosexuality as well as other nonprocreative sexualities always already in need of regulation by the law.

Outlaw, as himself, presents the point that Julien makes in *The Attendant* when he comes center stage, in front of the large table, and remarks that he was filled with desire the first time he saw a photo of Dahmer. "That face, so simple and all-American . . . whenever I see an image of his face, that face, the first reaction is in my balls. I'm not gonna lie to you. . . . Chances are, I would have ended up in Jeffrey's refrigerator, if I'd been living in Milwaukee in the late '70s and '80s." After the performance I overheard some of the black male audience members echoing Paul Outlaw's remarks about how "hot" and sexually attractive they found Dahmer. What was remarkable about Outlaw's remark and the conversation after the performance was that all of the men acknowledged that they, too, might have been dead, one of Dahmer's victims had they lived in Milwaukee in the 1980s. They were referring to the fact that Dahmer embodied a type of American masculinity to which they were attracted. The berserker's masculinity is its ordinariness, or what Outlaw calls a face "so simple and all-American." It is not surprising that Outlaw concludes the performance by turning over the table that has been his hiding place and butcher's station to show us its surface: an American flag. To live under this flag is to live with a history that shapes our desire and that is shaped by our desire. Outlaw's meditation reminds us that the desire for a man of a different race that lures us into danger is the outcome of, as Isaac Julien so aptly stated, living in a Western culture that "is in love with its own (white) image."[19] Indeed, "Here be dragons!"

Notes

1 Harriet A. Jacobs, *Incidents in the Life of a Slave Girl: Written by Herself*, edited and introduction by Jean Fagan Yellin (1861; Cambridge, MA: Belknap Press of Harvard University Press, 2009), 63–64.

2 William Styron included a homosexual encounter involving Turner in *The Confessions of Nat Turner*. The imagined homosexual encounter, and other so-called erotic disturbances like interracial yearnings, fueled the anger and animosity that was in the retort *William Styron's Nat Turner: Ten Black Writers Respond*, ed. John Henrik Clarke (Boston: Beacon Press, 1968).

3 Michael P. Speidel, "Berserks: A History of Indo-European 'Mad Warriors,'" *Journal of World History* 13, no. 2 (2002): 254.

4 Speidel, "Berserks," 269.

5 We think all too often that whitening in the black world occurs through informal practices of dating and mating in which some darker-skinned people choose lighter-skinned people. See Kathy Russell, Midge Wilson, and Ronald Hall, *The Color Complex: The Politics of Skin Color among African Americans* (New York: Anchor Books, 1992). However, Latin American studies scholars have called our attention to overt state policies and practices. Throughout the nineteenth century, Cuba, Argentina, and other Latin American states deliberately encouraged the in-migration of people from Europe to decrease the percentage of African-descended people. Increasing the white population was a method to control newly freed African-descended people. See William Luis, "Reading the Master Codes of Cuban Culture in Cristina Garcia's *Dreaming in Cuban*," *Cuban Studies* 26 (1996): 214; Kristin H. Ruggiero, "The Legacy of Sarmiento's Civilization and Barbarism in Modern Argentina," in *Sarmiento and His Argentina*, ed. Joseph T. Criscenti (Boulder, CO: Lynne Rienner, 1993), 183–93; Manuel de Paz and Manuel Hernández, *La esclavitud blanca: Contribución a la historia del inmigrante canario en América, Siglo XIX* (White slavery: Contribution to the history of immigration from the Canary Islands to the Americas in the nineteenth century) (Santa Cruz de Tenerife: Taller de Historia, 1992), 178. The work of Latin American scholars should lead us to reexamine the role that whitening has played in state policies, such as immigration, housing, or employment in the United States.

6 Richard Dyer, *White* (London: Routledge, 1997), 25.

7 See David Bergman, "Cannibals and Queers," in *Gaity Gransfigured: Gay*

Self-Representation in American Literature (Madison: University of Wisconsin Press, 1991), 139–62.

8 James Baldwin, "Here Be Dragons," in The Price of the Ticket: Collected Nonfiction, 1948-1985 (New York: St. Martin's Marek, 1985), 678.

9 Outlaw's first solo performance work was titled "Here Be Dragons" and deftly included excerpts from Baldwin's essay.

10 This viewpoint is expressed comically in the movie 48 Hours when Eddie Murphy masquerades as a cop doing an interrogation in a country and western bar.

11 All references to The Iliad are from The Iliad and the Odyssey of Homer, trans. Richard Lattimore (Chicago: University of Chicago Press, 1952). I thank Lisa Maurizio, my colleague in Classical and Medieval Studies at Bates College, for bringing these attestations to my attention.

12 James Baldwin, Tell Me How Long the Train's Been Gone (New York: Dell, 1968), 178–79.

13 Emmanuel S. Nelson, "The Novels of James Baldwin: Struggles of Self-Acceptance," Journal of American Culture 8, no. 4 (Winter 1985): 11–16.

14 James Baldwin, Just above My Head (New York: Dial Press, 1979), 404. Subsequent references to this book are given in parentheses in the text.

15 Eldridge Cleaver, Soul on Ice (New York: Dell, 1968), 127–28.

16 Andrew Hacker, Two Nations: Black and White, Separate, Hostile, Unequal (New York: Scribner, 1992).

17 Isaac Julien, dir., Mark Nash, prod., The Attendant (San Francisco: Frameline, 1993).

18 Isaac Julien, "Confessions of a Snow Queen: Notes on the Making of The Attendant," Critical Quarterly 36, no. 1 (Spring 1994): 123.

19 Julien, "Confessions," 125.

CHAPTER 16

Interview with Paul Outlaw

Vershawn Ashanti Young

Vershawn Ashanti Young: Why this show? Why now?

Paul Outlaw: That's a funny question to ask any artist. I think that, as an artist, you're driven to express something, it's something that needs to get out of you. I have been noticing, since the eighties, that the stories that I want to tell, or the messages that I want to put out there, have to do with history—American history, personal history—and when I say American history, the next thing that comes to my mind is race; and when I say personal history, the first thing that comes to mind is sex/gender/sexuality and race.

I can clothe it in any number of different ways. I can do a fictional piece, a play, a performance event, but it's always going to be this American story: the history of connection and clash between black folks and white folks.

VY: What's the relationship between Jeffrey Dahmer, Nat Turner, and 2008?

PO: When I was invited to do the festival, I was very excited about it, because this happens to be the year that a white woman and a black man were running for president, and one of them became the next president. And there wasn't a real discourse on race during the early stages of the campaign. There were a few flare-ups, but how could there be a discourse on race in the campaign when there hasn't been one for real, since 1865. [laughs] So I found that my piece was timely then, more than it had ever been.

VY: In what way?

PO: The first time I performed the piece, an audience member told me that when I was doing Nat Turner, I reminded her of George Bush—

that was at the beginning of the latest Iraq war. There was this martial quality that I had, especially when I was standing on the table. So take away the race, take away the sexuality issues, and what we're left with is the violence issue.

Another person told me that when I put the plastic bags on my body, I reminded him of the notorious Abu Ghraib image. I think that there are resonances beyond my main issues. Again, we're talking about American history.

VY: Is this a history project?

PO: Well, on the one level, it is a personal history project. I talk about my adolescence, about early sexual experiences, about coming out in the seventies, and then living in Germany in the eighties. I don't talk about my return to United States or my personal life now.

VY: Are you addressing a particular constituency?

PO: It's for anybody. It's fun when I do my piece in front of a gay audience or a racially mixed one. The ideal audience for this piece, I have to say, is probably young people between the ages of seventeen and thirty, with their parents.

VY: It does not take long in your show for the stage to get messy . . . and by the end it's a holy mess. What's that all about?

PO: I am working in a nonlinear, nontraditional form. I felt there had to be some kind of representation of blood, of gore. We are talking about Jeffrey Dahmer, who kept body parts and stored them in his house, which was a mess. And Nat Turner, after he was caught, was dismembered, he was skinned, his parts were missing.

There's also this level of "child at play": A child plays with food, makes a mess. These two men went berserk. I am not saying they were children, but they reached an animalistic, childlike stage, where one is free to follow one's body's impulses. And animals and children make messes.

And beyond the characters, as the actor I had the reaction: "This is the mess this country has made of itself." That's kind of what I am after, what I am going for in the piece.

VY: So you obviously are very political in some ways. What's the politics of the show?

PO: It has no politics. I don't think that a piece of art can have politics.

VY: You don't think aesthetics and politics can mix?

PO: They can. But I don't think you can set out to be political. If you do, what you're going to make is a piece of propaganda.

VY: I also mean the politics of representation. The plastic bags that you used on the stage, the American flag onstage—that's a politics of representing.

PO: I leave that to the viewer, to the audience, or to the critic to tell me what that is . . . is it desecration, is it blasphemy, is it political? I just create from my need to create.

VY: I see. Could you talk about the composition of the piece?

PO: My director, Tanya Kane-Parry, comes from a strong movement background—she has dance training. She studied for a while at the Experimental Theater Wing of New York University. My work has always been connected to some movement basis. I still work with a dance theater company where there are actors, musicians, and dancers. So when I started working on this piece, I came together with Tanya, whose interest was of course to make this a movement piece. Mine was, too. When I realized where the piece was going, that it was going to be about violence and historical figures, I saw that it already lent itself to being a choreographed movement piece.

VY: Can you vivify the movement in your piece—in other words, how does it look?

PO: There's several ways it looks—one way is sometimes that there's a certain abstraction to my movement. I might shake my head and point my finger and say no, but in the piece, I might turn completely away from you and stick my tongue out in that direction. It might seem bizarre, but you might look at it again and actually it does make some kind of human sense, or physical sense.

Another example of abstract movement is when Jeffrey Dahmer is talking about picking up a hitchhiker—the movement I'm doing there is really hard to describe on tape—and I'm moving across the stage sideways; but I'm keeping my feet on the ground. And basically my toes move to the side and then my heels. I'm pushing a bag [with my feet] as I'm doing it. And I'm holding a knife in my hand and raising the knife from my other hand in an image that could be described as a windshield wiper. If you get the image of a windshield wiper, it becomes specific that he's in a car talking about a hitchhiker. That's kind of an abstract movement.

And then there's pure movement—that would be the dance at the beginning of the piece.

VY: Would you describe it?

PO: I begin the piece with movement, for example, the symbolism of coming out of a bag. To me it suggested a birth, coming out of a womb of some sort. And I emerge nude. So that suggests that there's not a lot of baggage. Basically, I am representing birth and death at that moment. I am also one of the dead bodies in the bags. When the audience comes in, they see seven bags onstage, and it's very eerie and ominous: You see the bags and you don't know what's in them, you don't know what to anticipate. You just see seven bags, and then the lights go to black, and when those lights come up again, all of a sudden, there are eight bags. What comes out of the first bag? A naked human being. You've just been hearing [in the opening voice-over] about these boys whose bodies were found in bags, so I'm basically giving myself over to that as the opening image, and then the second part of it is this birth— it's an image of human birth but it's also the image of theatrical birth—I am starting the play.

VY: I was not prepared for the complete nudity. What function does that have for the audience?

PO: To start the play nude came out of the fact that I'm emerging out of death into this new life—i.e., the play. And also that I'm going to be playing three major characters. So when I play Jeffrey Dahmer or Nat Turner, in a literal sense, it's from a blank canvas. When I finally do put clothes on, the red biker shorts and the transparent apron, they symbolize several things—it's a mixture of a butcher, an undertaker, a priest, an exterminator, a surgeon.

That movement, the dance, is a prologue or an overture. You hear a recorded, distorted voice talking about how the Vikings would get themselves into a frenzied state of war. That is the meaning of the word "berserker": on the battlefield, they would lose control. And I do this dance, which is pure dance. There's music playing, there's no text, and I do a series of movements. The intent behind that, on the one hand, is this transformation into the berserker. This dance is a conjuration. I'm conjuring Jeffrey Dahmer and Nat Turner. Every movement in that dance is in the piece. Every single movement that happens occurs later in the piece.

The other kind of movement that I deal with is heightened movement, where what I'm doing actually does literally go with what I'm saying, but it's actually a little bit larger. And that would be, for example, when Nat Turner is imagining that he sees "blood on the leaves." First of all, it's just a very large gesture, extending the arms, smearing myself with the stuff that I find on the stage, turning 360 degrees in a circle, falling to the ground, you know, this moment with a knife, where the knife is "speaking" to me. I mean, all these things are normal but they're just larger than normal.

VY: You've talked somewhat about the symbolism, what do the bags symbolize?

PO: The bags are symbols for a lot of things. On a literal level, they represent the same plastic bags that Jeffrey Dahmer put his victims in. The plastic bags also simply represent garbage. I'm not talking about victims of violence but actual garbage: the trash, the mess, the garbage of this country—that's there, too. Also they're magic bags. Bags of tricks, because in many ways, not to go too far with this point, but the show is a kind of circus, and I'm doing all these little magic tricks. I have popcorn flying out of one bag, I have bones in another, I have pornography in yet another. I can put a bag on as an evening gown or as a shirt. They're all my trick bags.

VY: Would you call your piece experimental?

PO: The work that I do is not what I would call old-school traditional theater by any means but I'm very old-school about it—about things like sound and lighting choices, especially sound. Even if the audience doesn't know, on a conscious level, the meaning of all of the stuff on the soundtrack, on some subliminal level, it's going to affect them, and it's going to inform the piece. Of course, as a performer, you always pray for those moments where there's somebody sitting in the audience who gets everything that you are doing.

To me, an evening in the theater is a very sacred event. It's like going to church. When a play is scheduled to start at 8:00 PM, for example, there is an appointment that has been made between the actors, the audience, and the theater itself and there's an energetic thing that happens.

VY: What's the effect of the lighting in the show?

PO: We have one area of light that is cold, and that's the light for Jeffrey Dahmer and Nat Turner—cold, glaring light. For the scenes where it's me talking to the audience directly, we have a warmer light that is mostly only downstage. It looks almost like the light in a living room, like a normal domestic light. Then we have special light for [the text by] Essex Hemphill at age fourteen, losing his virginity. That's a red light, that kind of traditional sex light. For other scenes we have a bluish, lavender light, just to suggest the evening, the outdoors. And then we have the one special on the floor, and that light is basically just to create a corridor, in which I'm restricted, "caught in the headlights," and that's also used in the opening of the piece.

VY: What about the characters? What do Dahmer and Nat Turner's confessions have in common?

PO: Me—I am what they have in common.

VY: But you have texts from Essex Hemphill, Jeffrey Dahmer, and yourself. What's the relationship to Nat Turner? Is Nat Turner a queer presence?

PO: Only in the sense of what I say in the piece, that I want to inhabit his body . . . his rage. I want to make it my own, I want to channel that. Someone asked me if I was trying to make Nat Turner a queer. I said no, it's not supported by the text or anything that I'm doing with the text. He's not having any homoerotic experience. But gay men seem to have a thing with Nat Turner.

VY: What kind of thing?

PO: The thing is, most of them—well, I can't say in this day and age that it's true for everyone. But every gay black man from my generation has had an experience of being humiliated by [their] peers for appearing to be gay, and not only by [their] peers but by [their] family and by white people as well. I can't think of any black man I know who doesn't have a fantasy of beating someone up. Nat Turner is someone who said no, you know? I think, as much as some gay men relate to Judy Garland and divas, I think other ones relate to violence—going off on somebody—as a fantasy, from the place of "I have been put down."

VY: Could your representation of Nat Turner invite criticism?

PO: I'm going to be criticized for doing Nat Turner no matter what I do. I think the only way you can do Nat Turner without being criticized is to stand at a podium with a book in your hand and you read from the *Confessions* in a stentorian kind of way—you're not actually dramatizing him, you're doing oral interpretation. But, as soon as you give him a voice, a body, a shape, an emotional state, then you open yourself to the criticism. A black person might say, "He's not strong enough, powerful enough, mythical enough"; a white person might say, "He's not violent enough, psychotic enough, insane enough." Everyone's going to have something to say.

VY: What performance choices did you make to portray him?

PO: Several. He was thirty years old and had been living as a slave, so one of the images I had was of pain in his back, just from being a work-horse. I also put into his body the image I had of a wrestler, that he was low to the ground, always ready to spring forward, to grab someone and tackle them. For his voice, I found tapes of an old man, from decades ago, from Southampton County [Virginia], which was the same place that Nat Turner lived. I just listened to his inflection and his vowels, and I worked with a speech coach. For Jeffrey Dahmer I went with a Milwaukee accent, plus for him I had tapes of his actual voice.

VY: Talk about the difference between the two.

PO: For Dahmer, after looking at the photographs and from watching him in court, I wanted a very rigid body—I found that he had a certain stiffness, that he was not comfortable in his body. That stiff, square upper body contrasts with the slightly stooped, more smooth and flexible upper body of Nat Turner. And as "Paul" I let myself lean back. I was working for those contrasts.

VY: That's actually very helpful for me, because my racial lens made me read Dahmer as someone who had a kind of pride that Nat did not have, because of Nat's lowness to the ground.

PO: Not at all. Dahmer's stiff. He cannot move his upper body. Dahmer has a stick up his ass, his legs move from the hip, and Turner has more of an animal grace. That is a positive thing for me, I feel much more comfortable in that body as an actor.

VY: Did Dahmer ever actually experience sexual intimacy?

PO: Oh, yes, before, during, and after. His madness was that he could not accept that he was attracted to men, and further he could not accept that he was attracted to men of color. His way of dealing with that was to kill them and save them in jars in the refrigerator as a way of still possessing them. That word "possess"—possession, ownership, slavery—is like the other side of Nat Turner, who really was a slave. What's obvious to me is that these two are the flip sides of this coin, violence as a way of dealing with an impossible situation.

VY: Dahmer was not in an impossible situation.

PO: For him it was. If America had addressed its racial problem, he might not have been freaked out by his sexuality and by the fact that he was attracted to black men.

VY: Did Dahmer love his victims?

PO: I don't think he was capable of love. I don't think you can love until you love yourself, and he clearly did not love himself.

VY: I want to ask you to respond to something from Robert Hayden's poem, "The Ballad of Nat Turner." The poem's crescendo describes how Nat is becoming one with nature . . . how nature is spurring him on, encouraging him. He sees himself wrapped up with the animals and so forth. Hayden writes about that spiritual state: "I behold the conqueror's faces and lo, they were like mine, I saw they were like mine, and enjoyed in terror, wept, praising, praising Jehovah." In your piece, he doesn't have this heroic quality.

PO: I disagree completely. For me, when I'm discovering the "blood on the corn and the numbers on the leaves," that is the being one with nature that you're talking about. That total sense of power, and connecting to the heavens and the dew on the ground, that's a feeling of oneness and power. Also when I'm standing on the table, Nat is just completely reveling in this feeling of power with the other men, the soldiers, that he has marching. It just expands into this joy and feeling of power.

VY: And that's what comes through in Hayden's poem as well—that identification with other conquerors. It's not just a relationship with victims; Nat has a relationship with the victims and what Hayden calls the conquerors.

PO: The conquerors and also what he calls his soldiers and also the spirits that have told him, in this night of the eclipse, what must be done—he's connecting to them. It's about this one night of power.

VY: Can Dahmer be heroic? Perceived as heroic?

PO: He's a protagonist of this piece and people often confuse protagonist with hero. The hero of this piece is me. I am you, whether you are a white person in the audience or a black person in the audience. When I say "you," I am saying that my audience for this piece is America—this is our thing. This is our problem. This country is more willing to address the holocaust, which is not our story. It may be the story of some people in this country and their relatives, but it is not a sin that this country committed. But our own sin, our own holocaust? That we will not deal with.

VY: What do you make of James Baldwin's praise of William Styron's novel [*The Confessions of Nat Turner*] when he says that this is the beginning of our common history.

PO: No, the beginnings of our common history are the slave ships that brought us here. That is the beginning of this mess.

VY: *Berserker* is the second installment of a trilogy. How are you going to complete it?

PO: Well, the first piece was partly inspired by Anna Deavere Smith's work. I did twenty-five different characters. They were all real people who had lived from the early part of the twentieth century to the end of the twentieth century. This piece [*Berserker*] is nineteenth century and twentieth century. I used verbatim text and I also borrowed text from other authors to get my point across.

The next piece is going to be probably ninety-nine to [one] hundred percent original material. Without going into too much detail, it's going to be three scenes, one set in the 1850s, one in the 1950s, and one in the 2050s. So it is once again historical; but it's also a fantasy based in history, as opposed to the other two pieces, where I am taking history and making them into fantasy.

Part IX

I Just Love Andy Gibb
A Play in One Act

Charles Rice-González

CHARACTERS

Roy:	a 14-year-old, dark-skinned Puerto Rican gay kid/ spirit who grew up in the Soundview projects in the Bronx. He has a love for and obsession with the 1970s pop star Andy Gibb, younger brother of the famous Bee Gees.
Carlos Padró:	a 39-year-old, dark-skinned Puerto Rican gay man. Works as a features writer for a magazine and lives in Spanish Harlem with his roommate Pedro Ortega, whom he's known since college.
Pedro Ortega:	a 40-year-old (but looks 30 years old) Puerto Rican/Latino gay man who is light skinned, has light brown hair, almost blond. He often passes for white and in an American/Eurocentric way is gorgeously stunning.
Sharon:	a 12-year-old Latina girl/spirit who is overweight. She is Roy's best friend.
Voice of Roy's Aunt:	a Latina matriarch in her late 50s with whom Roy lives. We hear her voice from offstage.

Time: Present day, New York City.

Place: The bedroom of Carlos/Roy.

Staging: The play has a dreamy quality. Most of it takes place on a plane just beyond the edges of reality where two time periods are intersected. The main and only set is a bedroom that flips between the modern day bedroom of Carlos, and Roy's bedroom in 1978. Roy's bedroom walls are covered with teen pin-ups and there is a bed in the middle of it with a small desk stage left with a record player on it and a small stool in front of it. There is a night table beside the bed with an alarm clock. When it is Carlos's room the walls are plain white with a couple of art posters on the wall. But it is basically neat and sparse with a bed center stage, a desk with stool stage left and a night table with a clock radio on it.

Synopsis: Carlos, a dark-skinned Puerto Rican man who is about to turn 40, is visited by a spirit from 1978 in the form of Roy, a trigueño (dark-skinned), gay, 14-year-old Puerto Rican kid who is obsessed with Andy Gibb. Roy helps Carlos take a look at his life and his choices surrounding the issue of love in his life, particularly his unrequited love for Pedro, Carlos's roommate since college. All the while, Roy is blissfully trapped in his own obsession with Andy Gibb. They guide each other to places where they can examine how race affects desire and perceptions of beauty, their choices, and consider making a change.

SCENE 1

*The bedroom of Roy. The door to the bedroom is stage right. The stage is dark except for very dim blue light in which we can see Carlos asleep in his bed. Suddenly, Andy Gibb's "I Just Want to Be Your Everything" pops on. Carlos is startled by the music and blindly reaches out to hit the alarm clock next to the bed. He keeps hitting buttons on the alarm clock but nothing happens. He then lifts his head to see if he is hitting the right buttons. It doesn't seem to turn off. Stage left a light comes up on a 14-year-old Puerto Rican boy, Roy, who is sitting on a stool reading a **Teen Beat** magazine, groovin' along with the music and mouthing the words to the song. Carlos doesn't see the boy yet. He sits up to examine the clock. When he flips a switch on it, the radio begins to play National Public Radio. Carlos is puzzled because the Andy Gibb music continues to play. The kid is annoyed by the sound of the radio and reacts as if any interruption to Andy Gibb singing is akin to a sacrilegious act.*

ROY   Hey! Turn that off. I'm listening to Andy.

CARLOS   *(Carlos sees the boy, freaks out and lets out a yelp)*
             ¡Ooooo-Eeee!

He jumps out of bed and stumbles toward the door. It is locked. He turns around with his back to the door. Roy is staring at him.

ROY	Are you gonna turn it off or should I?

Carlos is paralyzed. Roy, a little exasperated, slips off the stool and walks over to the clock radio, examines it, finds the on/off button and turns it off.

ROY	*(sings whatever phrase is playing from the song)* I just love Andy Gibb and I'd do anything to be his every- thing. *(and he returns to the stool to continue reading his magazine)*

Carlos has been trying the door knob, still with his back to the door. He does not take his eyes off of Roy. He turns on the light switch, and we see that we are in Roy's bedroom which is covered with all kinds of posters of teen heartthrobs from the late 1970s: John Travolta, Erik Es-trada, Willie Aames, Parker Stevenson, Shaun Cassidy, the Bee Gees, Robbie Benson, Donny Osmond and one wall dedicated solely to Andy Gibb. There are a few women thrown in including a poster of Farrah Fawcett, Kristy McNichol, Marie Osmond (in some of the ones with Donny), and another of Charlie's Angels with Cheryl Ladd. Carlos looks around the room and back at Roy who is still grooving to the music.

CARLOS	Uh, excuse me.
ROY	Yes.
CARLOS	Where am I?
ROY	In my room.
CARLOS	How did I get here?
ROY	I don't know. Exactly.
CARLOS	Well, you don't seem bothered by my being here.
ROY	I am. I don't like being disturbed when I'm with Andy. Look, as long as you don't get between me and him things will be alright. *(He rolls his eyes, hops off the stool and walks* *toward Carlos extending his hand)* My name is Roy.
CARLOS	*(presses himself against the door)* Stay right there!
ROY	*(stops)*

What is your problem?

CARLOS   YOU! THIS!
(closes his eyes and breathes to relax)
OK, I'm dreaming. Time to wake up. (He opens his eyes)

Roy shakes his head in disbelief.

CARLOS   (to himself almost as if he were in a chant) OK, so if this is my dream . . . I am in control . . . I am in control . . . I am in . . . (He closes his eyes and opens them)

ROY   It's not a dream.

CARLOS   Shut up!

ROY   No way! I'm not shutting up, so I guess you are not in control, so this is not a dream. (He goes back to reading his magazine)

CARLOS   I went to sleep in my own bed in my own apartment and it would be impossible to wake up anywhere else unless this was a dream.

ROY   Stop wasting time and just accept that you're here with me and Andy. Let's get down to business so you can get out and I can go back to being alone with Andy. We are together forever.

The music is still playing and suddenly we hear someone on the other side of the door.

ROY'S AUNT   (offstage)
Roy, por Dios. Turn down esa música. Tu y ese jodío Andy Gibb me van a volver loca.

CARLOS   Who's that?

ROY   (rolling his eyes)
My aunt, she is not a fan of Andy Gibb . . . or even the Bee Gees. She says they sound like alley cats in heat.

Roy lowers the music.

CARLOS   So where's your room?

ROY	In the Soundview projects in the Bronx.
CARLOS	How did I get back to the Bronx?
ROY	It's still your room and it's mine. It's both at the same time.
CARLOS	That's impossible.
ROY	Well you're here and I'm here. Can't you see me?
CARLOS	Who are you?
ROY	Roy. I told you that.
CARLOS	Yes . . . but . . . are you a spirit or something?
ROY	In some ways yes, and in other ways, I'm very human. What I have is a memory of my past and the here and now. This moment. And the next one. And the next one. And I have my room and my posters and music . . . especially Andy Gibb. I could just listen to him forever.
CARLOS	You can? He's not all that great.
ROY	What?! Oh, you have to go.
CARLOS	Good! How do I get out of here?

Carlos tries the door.

ROY	You really don't like Andy Gibb . . . not even a little.
CARLOS	I hate him. His voice is too high and he whines.
ROY	(*gasps*) That's because you're old, like my aunt.
CARLOS	I am not old.
ROY	(**checks out Carlos**) You are and you have to go.
CARLOS	Unlock it and I'm gone.
ROY	I wish I could. But nobody comes in and nobody goes out of that door . . . ever.
CARLOS	Then how did I get here?
ROY	Forget that! How can you not like Andy? Even if you don't like his voice, which makes no sense to me, he's beautiful.
CARLOS	Well in a skinny white boy kind of way . . . yeah.

ROY	Skinny White-boy? *(looks to the heavens)* This visitor has to go.
CARLOS	*(looks up)* Who are you talking to?

Roy waves his hand up to the heavens.

CARLOS	So, assuming that this is real, how do I get back?
ROY	I don't know it's different . . . sometimes the visits are short.
CARLOS	Is this going to be a short visit?
ROY	That depends on you.
CARLOS	What do I have to do?
ROY	Talk.
CARLOS	We've been talking.
ROY	Not even. You've been asking a bunch of questions and insulting me and Andy.
CARLOS	That's talking. So we talk and then things go back to normal.
ROY	No! Things are never supposed to go back to normal. Normal is why we have met.
CARLOS	But I want things to go back to normal. I want to be in my apartment right now.
ROY	So what is your normal life like?
CARLOS	What?
ROY	That is the kind of talking we have to do so you can move on and I can get back to Andy.
CARLOS	So you are here to give me some kind of help?
ROY	Don't know if I can help.
CARLOS	How old are you?
ROY	Fourteen.
CARLOS	You don't talk like a 14-year-old.

ROY	I'm not normal. Isn't that great? You want to listen to Andy's other album. I just got his new one.

Roy gets up and stops the album.

CARLOS	Do I have a choice?

Roy shakes his head "no" as he puts on the second album. "Shadow Dancing" begins to play. Roy grooves and does a little dance. He sings along with Andy.

CARLOS	I had that album.
ROY	(still *grooving*) I thought you didn't like Andy Gibb.
CARLOS	I grew out of him.
ROY	Thought you weren't old?
CARLOS	You said you just got his new one? What year is this?
ROY	1978.
CARLOS	So I'm back in 1978 or did you come to 2007?
ROY	Both.
CARLOS	So, if I went out that door I could see myself as a kid.
ROY	You can't go out that door.
CARLOS	But what about your aunt? . . . I heard her. . . .
ROY	Just a voice in my head.
CARLOS	Are you dead? Am I dead?
ROY	No way and no way.
CARLOS	(thinks a bit) Roy, I don't need help with anything. I'm like you. I have everything I need . . . and . . . I just want to go back.
ROY	To what?
CARLOS	My life! I love it! I have no complaints. I have a good job and great friends and great family, I'm completely happy.
ROY	So I wonder why we met?

CARLOS	Do you think it was a mistake? (*He looks up*)
ROY	Doubt it. But if so, you'll probably fade away. (*Stops dancing. He looks around the room expecting something to happen. Since nothing does he switches gears.*) Wanna look at Teen Beat? It's a special Andy Gibb issue.
CARLOS	No. I want to go back to my room.
ROY	Well, if it's like mine. I understand. My aunt lets me put up any poster I want, I get to listen to Andy all day. When I listen to him I close my eyes and pretend he's singing to just me.

*Roy closes his eyes and holds the **Teen Beat** magazine to his chest.*

CARLOS	(*looking at the large Andy Gibb poster*) As much as I hate to admit this . . . I used to think that Andy Gibb was hot.
ROY	Well hands off, he's all mine. My best friend Sharon and I fight over him. One time he was playing at this amusement park in New Jersey . . .
CARLOS	Great Adventure?

Sharon appears and sits at the edge of the stage.

ROY	Yep!
SHARON	I begged my mother to take me . . .
CARLOS	Who's that?
ROY	Just a voice in my head.
SHARON	. . . So when my stepdad came home from work they took me and Roy. I'm asthmatic so she brought her pump. We listened to Andy's songs in the car on the way there, but that was all we got to hear. When we got there, they had closed the park because it was packed. Roy and I held on to each other and cried. We stuck our heads outside the window to see if we could hear anything . . . but nothing.

Sharon exits.

CARLOS	I remembered hearing about that concert on the radio. I wanted to go, but I was too scared to let anybody know that I did.
ROY	Why?
CARLOS	'cause boys are not supposed to . . .
ROY	Oh that. Yeah, I know. (*He lights up*) But we can't help it, right? I mean some kids make fun of me . . . not Sharon . . . she is the best. We read Stephen King's *The Shining* together. She is only 12, but she is smart . . . and she wants to be a nurse.
CARLOS	Where is Sharon?
ROY	Home, I guess.
CARLOS	(*Carlos goes to sit on the bed*) I wish I could've done this in my room. I was too scared.
ROY	Well, I gotta put up some girls, too. I don't think that if I had only boys my aunt would be OK with that. She keeps asking me why don't I put some pictures of the family on the walls.
CARLOS	Why not?
ROY	My family? For what? I'd rather have them up. (*referring to the teen boys*) I have so many magazines and posters! I just keep switching them around. And they are soooo cute! (*Carlos laughs*) You know what I mean, right?
CARLOS	Yes, they are cute, and they're all white.
ROY	So.
CARLOS	(*looking around the room*) They're kind of the same.
ROY	The same? You're nuts. They're different. Look at John Travolta. He has dark wavy hair, his eyes are sharp blue. They look right through to your soul. And the Hardy Boys look completely different from him and from each other. Parker Stevenson has green eyes and kind of sandy blond hair. His eyes are small and he has a nice smile and kind of a strong, muscle-like body, where Shaun Cassidy's hair is darker and

his eyes are brown. Robbie Benson has got black hair and his eyes are sooo blue they are like the sky in the morning right before the sun comes up. And Donny Osmond—

CARLOS   I got it.

ROY   (*ignores Carlos*) But Andy's my favorite. He looks like an angel. He has the best eyes, a beautiful smile and his hair is so beautiful. Look at him. And when he sings my heart can't take it. When I heard "I Just Want to Be Your Everything" he was singing to me about being completely together and being completely in love. He would *build his world around me, darlin'*. He would do anything for love and he would want me to do anything for love. And he says "*if you give a little more than you're asking for, your love will turn the key.*" Well, I'll do anything to be his everything.

CARLOS   Wow, you're convinced.

ROY   I just love Andy Gibb. I wrote him a bunch of letters, but I haven't sent them yet.

CARLOS   Why not?

ROY   I want to give them to him in person. I know that he doesn't open his mail. And my feelings are too private for anyone else to read. I just want him to read them, 'cause I know that if he did he would understand. That Great Adventure trip was a close call. If we had left earlier, you and I would be having a different conversation.

CARLOS   Well, uh . . . Never mind.

ROY   What?

CARLOS   Andy is singing to girls.

ROY   He has to. Just the same way I have to put up girls on my wall. Just so that everybody doesn't freak out completely. You know they can say, "Oh, he's OK."

CARLOS   Yeah, but you are OK . . . we are OK.

ROY   I know you are OK. You told me. Do you have someone you love the way I love Andy Gibb?

CARLOS   Well I had a ton of crushes like you. I mean Willie Aames over there did it for me. I was an *Eight Is Enough* freak just to see Willie.

ROY   He's pretty cute.

CARLOS   He looks a little like Andy Gibb.

ROY   No way!

Carlos walks around examining the posters.

CARLOS   I had forgotten about a lot of these people. I used to read *Teen Beat* and all those magazines, too. I kept them hidden 'cause, "only girls" read those magazines.

ROY   So you're into Willie Aames.

CARLOS   I was. That was a long time ago. Wait! I don't want to talk about old teen idols.

ROY   They are not old.

CARLOS   For me they are . . . I'm almost 40.

ROY   Wow, that's old. My mom is old and she is 36. I think Erik Estrada is that age.

Roy points to Erik Estrada's picture.

CARLOS   (*getting caught up in the images again*) Oh shit Erik Estrada.

ROY   I put him up on my wall because my mother loves him and I think he's Puerto Rican like me . . . what about you?

CARLOS   Me? . . . Yes, I'm Puerto Rican.

ROY   I speak a little Spanish but . . . anyway . . . so, who do you like now?

CARLOS   You mean like movie stars or someone like that?

ROY   Whatever.

CARLOS   Well there are some good looking men, but it's different now that I am older. And you probably wouldn't know who I was talking about anyway, right?

ROY   I guess. What year are you living in?

CARLOS	It's 2007. (*thinks out loud*) You would be about my age about now and I was your age back then.
ROY	Wow! So you are in the year 2007. Are there flying cars and stuff like that?
CARLOS	No, we haven't hit the flying car phase yet. Did I know you? I'm feeling like I knew you, or that you are me back then, but then you are not, right?
ROY	Well, I'm Roy and you're Carlos and do I look like you?
CARLOS	No, but you said you lived in Soundview, and I grew up there, too. Maybe we were friends?
ROY	I don't have any friends named Carlos. Ricky, yes and as I told you Sharon. And there is this 16-year-old boy who lives across the hall . . . he's so beautiful. Almost like Andy . . .
CARLOS	Wow, he must be cute for you to compare him to Andy. Is he a white boy?
ROY	No, you've got this thing with white boys.
CARLOS	I've got—?
ROY	Relax . . . he's Puerto Rican. Oh he's cute, like you have no idea. But I am just 14 and he is like this older teenager and he is in to different stuff like salsa music. He loves listening to this singer called Hector Lavoe.
CARLOS	I know who Hector Lavoe is.
ROY	You know him!
CARLOS	No, not personally, but I know who you are talking about.
ROY	Well I never listen to that kind of music. My mother and older people listen to salsa, but this guy, he has a portable 8-track player that he listens to his salsa with in front of our building and he sings along.
CARLOS	Wait! I remember that boy.
ROY	You do?
CARLOS	I didn't know him but I remember a young skinny guy with blondish tight curly hair listening to salsa music on a

portable 8-track player. I thought he was a white boy, but there weren't many white people living in the projects, much less ones who listened to salsa. I can see him sitting in front of the building . . .

CARLOS AND ROY (*both recalling the image of the Salsa boy*)
. . . wearing Pro-Keds . . . and a light blue T-shirt and red bell-bottom pants.

CARLOS He was cute. He lived in the first building on the top of the hill.

ROY That's where I live.

CARLOS I lived in the buildings down by the Big Park.

ROY The Big Park? I can't go down there. The Big Park is too far and my aunt says she likes me to be where she can call out the window and I can hear her. And there are gangs that hang out near the hand ball courts there.

CARLOS Wow . . . I walked all around there. I can't believe we didn't see each other.

ROY Well *if* you are here, I don't see you either.

CARLOS It would've been great to have been friends.

ROY It would have been a snap. I don't know any kids like me. Maybe Ricky . . . he likes Andy Gibb, too.

CARLOS So, maybe you were sent to remind me of my past, and I am here to show you your future.

ROY So what is the future like?

CARLOS I have a great job and good friends.

ROY Are you in love?

CARLOS Not at the moment.

ROY Were you ever in love?

CARLOS Not like . . . well . . . I have not really had a big great love.

ROY That sounds horrible.

CARLOS It's not like I haven't tried.

ROY	How can you talk about being so happy when you don't have love?
CARLOS	I have lots of love . . . family . . . friends and . . .
ROY	And who?
CARLOS	My best friend, Pedro. He's my roommate.
ROY	You guys share a room?
CARLOS	We share an apartment.
ROY	Do you love him?
CARLOS	Yes, we love each other, not the way that you love Andy Gibb.
ROY	Then how?
CARLOS	We've known each other for a long time and we take care of each other.
ROY	But you don't love him?
CARLOS	Well (*pause*) . . . I do . . . but sometimes people don't love you back in the way that you want them to. Almost like you and Andy.
ROY	Oh, but he'll love me. Once I get him my letters, and I probably have to be a little older, too.
CARLOS	Definitely.
ROY	So you just have to let that person know exactly how you feel and then they will understand.
CARLOS	I've told him, and he doesn't feel the same way.
ROY	That doesn't sound good. I don't know what I would do if I was in your place.
CARLOS	Well Roy, you seem pretty convinced that if you get your letters to Andy, you two will be together. It's a lot more complicated than that. For instance, you haven't figured in Victoria Principal . . . Andy's girlfriend.
ROY	(*puts his hands to his ears*) What?! Why are you telling me that?

CARLOS	Because . . . it is OK to have a crush on Andy, but—
ROY	It's not a crush. I just love Andy Gibb! And if she is his girl-friend, which is news to me, then I can't let her get in the way.
CARLOS	Well maybe they got together after 1978, but Roy . . . to everyone's knowledge, Andy's not into men, he's great to look at and his music touches you, but the reality of you two being together is pretty impossible. He's just not into boys.
ROY	(angrily) So what about your friend Pedro? Is he not into "boys"? What excuse do you make up for him not loving you back?
CARLOS	There's no excuse. It's just the way it is. He doesn't love me.

Silence. When Carlos says those words it is as if he was making a confession.

ROY	Why not?
CARLOS	I don't know why not.
ROY	So, what are you waiting for?
CARLOS	I'm not waiting . . .
ROY	No?
CARLOS	No.

Roy shrugs his shoulders and looks at the magazine. Carlos watches him.

ROY	So what is Pedro like?

Black out

SCENE 2

The stage is dark except for two pools of light. In one pool of light, up-stage right sits Pedro, an attractive, white-looking Puerto Rican man. In the other pool of light Carlos places a stool and sits on it. He is wearing a sweatshirt with "Adelphi University" on it. Roy sits on the bed and watches.

CARLOS   *(to the audience)*
           Go ahead. Check him out. Go on, everybody does it. I'm used
           to it by now.
           (Carlos looks at Pedro)
           I used to stare at him. At his face. His hands. His neck. His
           feet, just trying to find a flaw, but he's just about perfect . . .
           like those golden boys in ads selling men's underwear. Some
           people might say, "I don't like his hair," or "He's too pale."
           But most agree he's beautiful. So, go on and look at him.
           (Roy gets up from the bed, circles Pedro and checks him out)
           My eyes have had the pleasure of seeing him almost every
           day for the last twenty years . . . They've seen him smile and
           cry. After all we have lived together since the first day we
           met. It was . . . well, it wasn't love at first sight. I would've
           liked that. We met my first day in college.

Light on Pedro fades to black.

           I remember leaving my apartment in the Soundview sec-
           tion of the Bronx. It was a big deal that I was going away to
           college, so everybody was out to see me off, my neighbors,
           my aunts and my grandmother. My parents had to work so
           Lucita, a dear friend of the family, loaded up her cab, and
           whoosh we were off. I arrived to my dorm room with my big
           maleta and about 500 shopping bags. I was wearing a sweat-
           shirt . . .

Lights up on Pedro who is still sitting on the stool, then lights up on stage.

PEDRO   *(to Carlos)*
           . . . with the school's name and emblem on it. Do you know
           that you're not supposed to wear your own college stuff on
           campus? We all know where we're at. You can wear it when
           you go off campus . . . if you actually want other people to
           know where you go. Or you can wear other school's shirts
           while you are on campus. But not any rival schools or if you

want to be snobby you can wear Columbia or NYU, as long as it doesn't remind you that you didn't get in. So they stuck me with a freshman. Last semester that could have been a good thing. (*He gets up, circles Carlos and checks him out*) Maybe it would not have made much of a difference.

CARLOS   Woah, pa, calm down. Let's make sure this ain't a mistake before you keep going . . . this is 402, right?

PEDRO   Yeah.

CARLOS   So I guess we're roommates. My name is Carlos Padró.

Carlos offers his hand to Pedro to shake his hand.

PEDRO   Pedro Ortega.

CARLOS   You're Latino, too? Damn, bro. I couldn't tell. But that's great. I thought they were gonna stick me with some blanquito. Pero. I'm with a bro. Where you from?

PEDRO   The Bronx.

CARLOS   Holy shit, me too! I can't believe it another Latino from the Bronx.

PEDRO   And you think it was a coincidence?

CARLOS   I don't care. It's cool. Tu sabe, two homies, chillin'. Studying together, luchando junto, helping out one another. Tu sabe . . .

PEDRO   I don't really talk Spanish. I understand it but, I prefer English.

CARLOS   Look, I don't care. I can talk English, too. So, where do you live in the Bronx?

PEDRO   Near Montefiore Hospital.

CARLOS   I live in Soundview. Do you know Soundview? Well, I live in the projects there. Right down Randall Avenue—

PEDRO   No, I don't know Soundview.

CARLOS   That's OK, maybe on a break or something you can come over to my—

PEDRO	Your side of the room is over there. I had a really fucked up semester last year, and I have a lot of work ahead of me if I'm gonna stay in this school. I don't want to get started on the wrong foot with you, so what I need is peace and quiet. I hope you're not noisy and I hope you can keep to yourself and mind your own business. But keep in mind that room changes can be requested until the end of the week. *(pause)* In case . . . you want to . . . go. Now, I'm gonna work out, so don't touch any of my stuff without my permission, and you probably don't know anybody yet, but nobody comes into my room without my permission.

Turns away. Light fades out. Pedro exits. Lights up on Carlos on the stool.

CARLOS	How was I supposed to know that he was last semester's biggest pato slut on campus, and he fucked every Juan, Dick and Harry . . . and professor . . . and faculty advisor . . . and a dean or two? His first roommate was this white guy from Rhode Island who flunked two classes their first semester together because they had sex every day, and would miss class, exams or anything that interfered with their fucking. The swimmer switched rooms so he could get away from Pedro's ass and graduate. His next roommate was a tough Italian kid from Brooklyn with dark curly hair and bright green eyes, who was an avowed heterosexual up until the first few moments after moving in with Pedro. Within moments Pedro was on his knees and the Brooklyn kid's cock was slamming Pedro's tonsils. His next roommate was a blond born-again Christian from Florida . . . well you get the picture.

Roy moves to the stool where Pedro had sat. Pedro is on the bed, naked with his back to the audience, and he is resting on his side. At first we do not see Pedro, but the lights fade up as Carlos speaks.

CARLOS	Pedro ultimately got put on academic probation for fucking just about anyone instead of going to class. But, to give you a sense of the kind of luck I have, we became roommates just as he'd entered his celibate phase so he could focus and graduate. So, sleeping three feet away from me would be

the most beautiful guy my eyes had ever seen. A guy who had even fucked a couple of charity cases, for which I think I automatically qualify. I just arrived a semester too late. That first week I stayed up late thinking crazy thoughts like "why couldn't I have been born a year earlier, anything to have known him pre-celibacy." He loved being naked in our room reading or taking a nap, so it was torture. I tried making my-self look good to him. I worked out and read the right books, just to be desired by him. He lasted about two months be-fore he nabbed the star lacrosse player—a big, broad guy from New England whose family owned some syrup com-pany in Vermont. Pedro graduated, and I helped him every step of the way. But he never fucked me, celibacy was the first reason, but ultimately . . . I just wasn't his preferred fla-vor.

(Carlos looks behind him to see Pedro still lying across the bed with clothes strewn all around him)

It'd be so much easier if I were beautiful, like him. And I am not talking inner beauty, but the kind that draws attention when you step into a train car and everyone looks at you . . . repeatedly. The kind that causes strangers to send you anonymous notes. The kind where I don't have to make the first step in order to get to know someone when I go to a party. The kind that lies before me. I try to imagine what it would be like to be beautiful like Pedro. To be desired.

PEDRO	*(begins to get dressed)* I am desired.
CARLOS	To be wanted.
PEDRO	I am wanted.
CARLOS	To be caressed.
PEDRO	I'm caressed.
CARLOS	To be kissed.
PEDRO	I am kissed.
CARLOS	To be licked.
PEDRO	I am licked.
CARLOS	To be longed for.

PEDRO	I am longed for.
CARLOS	But what I've known is longing.
PEDRO	To be longed for.

Pedro begins to exit the stage. Roy watches and follows Pedro offstage. Carlos slowly goes back to the bed and gets under the covers.

CARLOS	Desire.
PEDRO	To be desired.
CARLOS	To search.
PEDRO	To be sought after.
CARLOS	To always be reaching out, and never touching.
PEDRO	To be touched over, and over, and over, and over, and over . . .
CARLOS	To be loved.
PEDRO	. . . over and over and over, again.

Black out.

SCENE 3

Carlos's room. Carlos is sleeping in his bed. There is a knock on the door. Pedro enters. He is buttoning his shirt, tucking it in his pants.

PEDRO	Carlos? Dude, are you OK?
CARLOS	*(waking up and taking in his room)* I was having a wild dream.
PEDRO	What was with that Andy Gibb music you were playing in the middle of the night?
CARLOS	You heard it?
PEDRO	I think the whole fucking building heard it. I banged on the wall and yelled at you to lower it.
CARLOS	I was having this dream about a 14-year-old kid who was in love with Andy Gibb.

PEDRO	Every 14-year-old faggot was in love with Andy Gibb. Anyway, could you do me a big favor?
CARLOS	(sits up in bed) Sure.
PEDRO	Could you pick up my laundry?
CARLOS	Sure.
PEDRO	I hate to ask but they'll be closed by the time I get home from work and there is a shirt that I need tonight.
CARLOS	Sure.
PEDRO	Thanks (and he blows him a kiss). It's seven thirty, you better get up.
CARLOS	Pedro?
PEDRO	What?
CARLOS	The Andy Gibb dream felt real.
PEDRO	Well music gets mixed in to my dreams, too. I've set my clock radio to a light music, and I dream I am on a romantic date. I set it to rock and boom I'm at a concert.
CARLOS	Well I was in this kid's room and he was listening to Andy Gibb.
PEDRO	Listen, I'm gonna be late for work. So pick up my laundry. I left the ticket and some money on the table. I was a little short, so if you could put in the difference I will pay you tonight.
CARLOS	Sure.
PEDRO	You are the best. I couldn't be more lucky to have you in my life.
CARLOS	Thanks. I'm lucky to—
PEDRO	There is a shirt that I want to wear later for my big date. And it would be perfect with these black pants that hug everything in the right places.
CARLOS	Another date?
PEDRO	Carlos, this is a big one. It's with the guy who looks like a

40-year-old Antonio Sabato, Jr. How old is Antonio Sabato, Jr.?

CARLOS   Thirtysomething.

PEDRO   Really! Hmmmm. Do I look . . . thirtysomething?

CARLOS   You . . . are beautiful Pedro . . . you have nothing to worry about.

PEDRO   You're the best Carlos. I gotta run. Thanks.

Pedro closes the door.

CARLOS   Pedro!

PEDRO   What? (*Carlos says nothing*) What's going on Carlos?

CARLOS   I don't know.

PEDRO   I'll see you later.

Carlos stares at the door as he leaves. Then he plops down on the bed and covers his face with the bedsheet.

Fade to Black

SCENE 4

Carlos is in his bed with his sheet over his head, but he is back in Roy's room. Andy Gibb's "Love Is (Thicker than Water)" is playing. Roy is tearing out posters from his teen magazines and singing along. Roy is dressed in a neat button-down short-sleeved shirt and bell-bottom slacks.

CARLOS   Roy?

ROY   Hey! Get out of that bed!

CARLOS   So you're still here?

ROY   Yes, you are still here.

CARLOS   Did you see Pedro?

ROY   I can see why you are so hooked on him. For an old guy, he is seeeexy. I have never seen anything . . . uhhhhh . . . I mean anyone like that! But it hurts you a lot that he doesn't love you back.

CARLOS   I say to myself that it doesn't matter. That he and I could be just friends . . . but *(pause)* it does matter.

Roy carefully selects images and presses them into a self-stick photo album.

CARLOS   And he is going on a date with some guy that looks like Antonio Sabat—forget it. You wouldn't know who he is . . . but he says like it doesn't matter.

ROY   Not to him. But . . . *(and he stops and thinks a moment)* . . . why do you keep wanting something from him that he won't give you?

CARLOS   You are definitely not 14.

ROY   *(chuckles)*
          You're funny Carlos, but really. Wouldn't it be cool if you could love someone who wants to give you love right back?

CARLOS   *(sarcastically)*
          Right.

Roy finishes putting together the scrapbook, walks over to Carlos, sits at the edge of the bed with him and looks him in the eye.

CARLOS   You look nice.

ROY   Thanks, but I'm serious. People fall in love with *each other* all the time. *(Carlos continues to look at Roy. Roy chuckles.)* You're a snap. I like talking to you . . . even though you say the craziest things about Andy Gibb.

CARLOS   Thanks Roy . . . now if you were about 25 years older . . .

ROY   Ill, my heart belongs to Andy. *(He says jokingly)*

CARLOS   I'm joking. *(Feeling a little uncomfortable with their proximity, he stands and walks away from Roy)* So, what were you doing?

ROY   It's Sharon's birthday *(and he shows off his outfit)* . . . and I am making her a scrapbook with some newly released photos of Andy Gibb. I even sent away to get a signed autographed photo of Andy for her. I waited three whole months for it to arrive and then I saved it for this special day. Check it out.

CARLOS   Wow! She is going to love it.

Roy takes the scrapbook from Carlos and wraps it in tissue paper and ties it up with a ribbon.

ROY   I put her favorite pictures in it . . . and the words to all the songs . . . not that we don't already know them all . . . but you know . . . so that she can have them forever. There are even some baby pictures I found of Andy.

CARLOS   You thought of everything.

ROY   Oh! And I got her an Andy Gibb T-shirt and . . .
              (He pulls out a small shopping bag) . . . a special gift.

A young overweight girl in a big fluffy dress walks in through the door that "never" opens. She and Roy interact with each other as if Carlos is not in the room.

SHARON   Hey Roy! Your aunt said I could come into your room.

ROY   *(genuinely surprised)* Sharon! Oh my goodness. What are you doing here?
              Your party is gonna start soon.

SHARON   I wish I wasn't having a party.

ROY   Why not? We are gonna have fun and your mom said you could play all the Andy music you want right?

SHARON   Yeah, but . . .

ROY   But what . . .

SHARON   Nobody is going to come . . . and there is just going to be a bunch of grown-ups and some of my cousins who I hate.

ROY   I'm going to be there.

SHARON   Thanks Roy. You are my best friend. I would rather just bring my cake and ice cream here to your room and we could eat the whole thing and just listen to Andy.

ROY	That would be "on the money."

And they slap five.

SHARON	But instead I have to wear this dress.
ROY	It's OK.

Sharon flashes him a "give me a break" look.

ROY	It's ugly.
SHARON	Thank you. But my mother said, "Sha-Sha, you look like an angel." So, I told her that she should wear it and she started to cry. So, I had to say that I liked it, and now I have to wear it on my birthday. It's tight and itchy.
ROY	That sucks.
SHARON	So, I was just waiting for my party to start and I wanted to see you, so I came over.
ROY	Well, happy birthday, Sharon. I got you presents.
SHARON	Alright. *(and she puts her hand out and Roy slaps it "five.")* But you didn't have to get me a present.
ROY	Oh I didn't get you a present, I got you presentssss.
SHARON	More than one?
ROY	Yep! I was going to bring them over, but you can have them now.
SHARON	I'm not supposed to open any of my presents until later.
ROY	So what! Nobody will see you. You can open them now. Then I'll wrap them again and you can open them later and act all surprised.
SHARON	I like that.
ROY	C'mon . . . here they go.

He hands her the wrapped scrapbook and the small shopping bag.
Sharon sits on the bed and opens the shopping bag and pulls out the
Andy Gibb T-shirt. She holds it up over her dress.

SHARON	(*squeals*) I love it. And it fits me! I wish I could wear it today.
ROY	It looks great.
SHARON	Thank you, Roy. (*and she hugs him*)
ROY	Take it easy. There's more . . . look in the bag.

Sharon pulls out a box.

SHARON	A disco-dancing Andy Gibb doll! You must have spent a lot on this.
ROY	Only the best for my best friend.
SHARON	I love it. Now Andy can dance with us when we listen to him. *Do it light . . .*
ROY AND SHARON	*Takin' me through the night . . . Shadow dancin', baby you do it right . . . Uh huh.*

They laugh.

ROY	Open your other present.

Sharon tears through the tissue paper and opens the scrapbook. She squeals when she sees the autographed photo.

SHARON	Is it real?
ROY	Yep! I got a certificate saying that it is officially Andy's signature.

Sharon peels back the protective plastic covering and gently touches Andy's signature.

SHARON	Andy's hand was here. I'm gonna need my asthma pump.
ROY	Calm down! You don't have to get all sick on your birthday,
SHARON	Touch it, Roy.

Roy touches it.

ROY	Thank you! To be honest I got it for me and I was going to

show off, but then I wanted you to have it. I could always send for another one.

SHARON   Thanks for giving it to me.

ROY   OK, enough. I gotta wrap it up so that I can take it over. And remember to act surprised.

SHARON   I will! I will!

ROY   You better. So did you invite Robinson?

SHARON   He's not coming.

ROY   Why not?

SHARON   Please. He just makes fun of me.

ROY   But you still like him.

SHARON   Not as much as I like Andy, but Andy's not going to like me.

ROY   Well it doesn't matter . . . 'cause he's all mine.

SHARON   Not if I meet him first.

They laugh.

SHARON   Anyway, I don't want Robinson or anyone to see me in this dress.

ROY   You're right. Maybe I should stand outside your apartment and tell people that the party is cancelled, so they could go away, then we could come back here and disco dance with Andy.

SHARON   I wish. Maybe we'll get to do that anyway . . . I don't think anybody is coming.

ROY   I'm coming to your party.

They look at each other for a moment. Sharon smiles.

SHARON   Thanks for my presents. I can't wait to get them.

ROY   I'm glad you like them.

SHARON   Please . . . it's Andy.

She starts to exit.

ROY   Wait! Where are you going?

SHARON   I'll see you in a little bit, right?

ROY   *(He hesitates for a moment and then perks up)* Yep!

SHARON   OK . . . Hurry up, alright.

ROY   I will be there . . . definitely . . . Happy Birthday, Sharon.

Sharon smiles and hugs Carlos. He hesitates a moment and then hugs her and holds her tightly.

SHARON   *(Sharon gently pulls away)*
                 So, hurry up already. My cousin Cuca was already there and she makes me sick.

Sharon exits. Roy goes to the door, tries the knob and it doesn't open. He sits on the floor in front of the door looking exhausted. Carlos comes from upstage over to him. Roy is silent.

CARLOS   What's the matter?

ROY   That is what I want to know. Whenever I have a visitor . . . one of you . . . nobody ever comes through that door. It's just me, this room and Andy. How did Sharon get here?

Roy tries the door again. It doesn't budge. He places his hand on the door.

ROY   I can't remember the last time I saw Sharon . . . I mean really see her, touch her. My life now is just memories and sounds from the other side of this door . . . and the visitors. That's it. I miss her, Carlos. I love her . . . way more . . . than I love Andy.

Roy sinks into his words and cries softly. Carlos sits next to Roy and hugs him.

ROY   What's happening Carlos? I'm supposed to help you. And now . . . I don't know what's happening. Other people that

I have helped don't know my neighborhood or me or anything. But you come from my neighborhood. And now
Sharon shows up out of the blue. I was happy. But I am not
so sure . . . I don't want you to leave, Carlos.

CARLOS   Maybe I can keep visiting you. Maybe we missed our chance
            to be friends back in 1978 and now we are having that
            chance?

ROY   Then what? You will go away and I'll be alone.

CARLOS   You have helped me a great—

ROY   (covers Carlos's mouth)
            Don't 'cause then you will have to leave.

CARLOS   I don't want you to be alone.

ROY   So, we have to keep on talking . . .

CARLOS   About what . . .

ROY   I don't know. I don't have answers. After you told me about
            Pedro, I thought, "That's it!" You are stuck on him and we
            just gotta unstick you and then you can move on. Are you
            still stuck on him?

CARLOS   Well, I realize that I have to look somewhere else to find
            love.

ROY   Stop! No, wait! If what you just said is true . . . you should
            be going away. (He stops and looks around the room expecting
            something to happen) But you're still here . . . so keep talking
            . . . 'cause there's gotta be something else going on with you.

CARLOS   Maybe it's not just about Pedro, BUT it is about Pedro. Now I
            am sounding like you.

Roy laughs.

ROY   What else could it be about?

CARLOS   I've been thinking about you and your room and how I was
            just like you. I fell in "love" with Pedro the first time I laid
            eyes on him. And falling for him was easy since he was so
            beautiful . . . in the way that Andy and all these boys are
            beautiful.

ROY	They are.
CARLOS	And they're everywhere. (*He paces around the room looking at the images*) It would take some work to see more than just their beauty. Why do we even think they're beautiful?
ROY	I don't think about it. They just are.
CARLOS	How do you know that?
ROY	I don't know. They just are. I can't help it.
CARLOS	Everywhere we look we're shown how beautiful they are. Even in my time when there are Black and Latino people who are supermodels and leading actors and actresses. But they (*and he points to Andy and the boys on the wall*) are the ultimate.
ROY	What's wrong with that?
CARLOS	Nothing. Except if they're all we see then you and I don't see each other. How can we see our beauty unless we make a conscious effort to look from there (*and he looks at the posters on the wall*) to there (*and he looks at Roy and pauses*) . . . and you . . . you're beautiful. Your face . . . your skin . . .

Roy examines the skin on the back of his hands. He looks at his fore-arms and then lifts his shirt and looks at the skin on his stomach.

ROY	I am not! You don't see me in any pictures.
CARLOS	That doesn't mean you're not beautiful. Let's take a look in the mirror?
ROY	You're not so bad looking yourself.
CARLOS	Gracias.
ROY	De nada. See I know a little Spanish.
CARLOS	Beautiful. Outside and in.
ROY	Wanna listen to Andy?
CARLOS	Whatever you want.

Roy runs to the record player and picks up an Andy Gibb album.

ROY	We could listen to something else.
CARLOS	Have any salsa?
ROY	No.
ROY	Let's see. Leif Garrett? Bay City Rollers?
CARLOS	Pedro loved the Bay City Rollers?
ROY	Pedro? Pedro's an asshole.
CARLOS	(laughs) Yes. It would be easier for me to just go with the idea that Pedro is just an asshole than it would be to consider that—

Andy Gibb's "Everlasting Love" plays in the background.

ROY	You're dark skinned and Pedro's a blanquito.
CARLOS	I thought that didn't matter, because Pedro's Latino, but I put up with the way he treated me just as long as he stayed with me.
ROY	He's not with you.
CARLOS	Not in the way I'm thinking. (thinks to himself) Let's make a deal.
ROY	What?
CARLOS	Let's not buy into the world's negative view of us negritos.
ROY	(laughs and extends his hand) Deal.

They shake.

CARLOS	(holds on to Roy's hand) This isn't a done deal. You and I will have to make it, again and again. And I can see you, beautiful Roy . . . back then you and I walked the same streets, played in the same parks and I couldn't see you.
ROY	I don't look like that salsa boy.
CARLOS	No, you don't look like the salsa boy. I don't look like the

salsa boy or like Andy Gibb. And you will grow to be . . . (*he stops himself*) Will you grow up?

ROY I guess so.

CARLOS You have been 14 since 1978. In a way, so have I.

ROY I don't want you to go, Carlos. I don't want to be alone . . . anymore.

CARLOS Can you leave this room? Maybe I can go and still visit with you.

ROY It hasn't happened before. But everything is different.

CARLOS Imagine if I had seen you back then and we had been friends.

ROY That would have been a snap . . . what did you look like?

CARLOS Maybe about your height . . . I used to have an afro.

ROY Like Michael Jackson . . .

CARLOS He did have a 'fro once, I suppose.

ROY He doesn't have an afro?

CARLOS A lot has changed with Michael.

Andy Gibb's "Without You" plays. The images of the teen idols fall off the walls or disappear. Andy's image is last. Music fades out.

ROY Andy's dead, right?

CARLOS Yes. He died on March 10, 1988. Five days after his 30th birthday.
I don't know how I know that.

ROY Part of me wants to think that I won't be with him because he's dead. But if I give up Andy what do I have?

Carlos walks to Roy to embrace him but begins to fade before he reaches him.

ROY Carlos! You're fading. Wait. Don't go.

Andy Gibb's "Time Goes On" plays. Roy reacts to it as if it was a haunting sound instead of the voice of his idol.

CARLOS   What if I hold on to you? Maybe you could come with me?

They embrace.

ROY   It's not working. You're slipping away. Don't go. *(looks to the heavens)*
Don't take him away. Carlos, don't leave me alone.

Carlos continues to disappear. Roy calls out and reaches out to him.

ROY   We walk the same streets. Ride the same subways. We still live in the same neighborhood. I'm already there. I have been all along.

CARLOS   I can see you, Roy.

ROY   I can see you!

They reach out to each other.

ROY   I will see you, Carlos.

CARLOS   I'll look for you, Roy.

Andy Gibb's "I Just Want to Be Your Everything" comes on and Carlos and Roy remain in an embrace. The lights fade slowly out on them as the music fades. There is a spot on Erik Estrada. Spot fades out on Erik Estrada and stage goes to black.

CHAPTER 17

Learning to Unlove Andy Gibb

RACE, BEAUTY, AND THE EROTICS OF PUERTO RICAN

BLACK QUEER PEDAGOGY

Lawrence La Fountain-Stokes

Puerto Rican black men loving one another in the Bronx: a radical proposal? In his groundbreaking 1989 film *Tongues Untied*, Marlon Riggs proposed that "Black men loving black men is *the* revolutionary act." In his 2004 play *I Just Love Andy Gibb* (first staged in 2007 at the Pregones Theater in the Bronx),[1] Charles Rice-González gives Riggs's proposal a queer Puerto Rican twist by exploring the ways in which Puerto Rican black gay men internalize dominant paradigms of beauty that favor white or light-skinned individuals (epitomized in the play through the figure of the white Anglo-Australian singer Andy Gibb) and discriminate against black or dark-skinned Latino men like themselves. Rice-González offers a therapeutic dream play where two Puerto Ricans, one an adolescent and the other an adult man, can come to terms with their internalized racism, particularly with the ways in which it contributes toward a low sense of self-esteem; the play advocates something closer to the "Black Is Beautiful" motto of the 1970s but in a diasporic Puerto Rican queer context.[2] The playwright does not go as far as Riggs in his advocacy for homoraciality, as the Puerto Rican sociologist Manolo Guzmán has termed the practice of same-race sexual and affective relations;[3] his impetus seems more self-contained, that of loving oneself, or one's image and kind: seeing oneself as beautiful, not as a narcissistic gesture, but in terms of recognizing blackness as beautiful. At the same time, the playwright's toying with the erotics of Puerto Rican black queer pedagogy queers Riggs's proposal in quite an unlikely way, as it proposes a potentially transgressive intergenerational relationship as a possible way to heal the wounds of racism.

I Just Love Andy Gibb is a deceptively light piece set in New York, mostly in a bedroom in the Soundview projects of the Bronx. The play is divided into four scenes and focuses on the interactions between Roy, a dark-skinned or "trigueño" fourteen-year-old "gay kid/spirit" obsessed with Andy Gibb, and the older Carlos Padró, who is also dark skinned and thirty-nine, and has an unrequited love attraction to his best friend and housemate Pedro Ortega.[4] As the play develops, we learn that Roy is an extrasensory presence with human attributes, possibly a dream character in Carlos's imagination, and that Roy visits Carlos with a special mission. This visit is staged as a therapeutic intervention: Carlos has an unacknowledged problem, and it is Roy's job to help Carlos figure out what it is and how to address it.[5] The play ultimately proposes an intergenerational model of erotic pedagogy in which Roy and Carlos can learn from each other, partly as a result of their age differential; Roy can also be seen as a younger iteration of Carlos, as a mechanism that allows Carlos to see himself in the past and leads to introspective reflection and change.

The therapeutic and pedagogical scenario of I Just Love Andy Gibb does not occur in a realist setting, but rather in the realm of the fantastic or as dream work. Most of the play's action (scenes 1 and 4) takes place in this otherworld, perhaps in Carlos's mind (during sleep) or as a surrealist landscape. The events portrayed entail the nonrealistic confluence of two distinct times and spaces (Roy's 1978 Bronx bedroom and Carlos's 2004 Spanish Harlem bedroom); the characters are unable to leave this space during their interactions, adding a claustrophobic dimension reminiscent of Jean-Paul Sartre's play No Exit (1944) and of Luis Buñuel's film The Exterminating Angel (1962).

Roy and Carlos's conversations in their shared room are complemented by "waking moments" of reality, which include a flashback that locates Carlos and Pedro back in the early to mid-1980s at Adelphi University on Long Island (scene 2) and a scene in which Carlos talks to Pedro in the apartment they share in Spanish Harlem (scene 3). Roy and Carlos's exchanges will also be interrupted by the offstage voice of Roy's aunt, who complains in scene 1 about the loud Andy Gibb music, as well as by two very important appearances in scenes 1 and 4 by Sharon, "a 12-year-old Latina girl/spirit" who is Roy's best friend and comrade-in-arms in their shared fan admiration of Andy Gibb.

The tensions at the heart of I Just Love Andy Gibb concern Roy and Carlos's shared experience of loving or idealizing someone who does not reciprocate their love. In both cases, that nonresponsive person is white or light skinned. Roy and Carlos's idealized, platonic love is contrasted with their meaningful exchanges onstage; the platonic relationships are portrayed as ultimately detrimental and undesirable. There is an additional figure of desire that is introduced in their conversations: a handsome light-skinned Puerto Rican "Salsa boy" (a sixteen-year-old neigh-

Fig. 17.1. *I Just Love Andy Gibb*. Photo courtesy of Charles Rice-González.

bor who liked listening to salsa music in the Bronx in 1978), whom both Roy and Carlos remember. Rice-González portrays Andy Gibb, Pedro, and the white "Salsa boy" as extremely desirable and then deconstructs them: Andy Gibb is unattainable; Pedro is a narcissistic, self-centered, manipulative individual who takes advantage of Carlos and does not love him; and the white Puerto Rican Salsa boy is likewise inaccessible. Furthermore, Carlos insists that liking only white men is actually damaging to one's sense of self, even if these men are Puerto Rican.

The idealization of Andy Gibb in this play operates through the structure of fan adoration and approximates some elements of religious hagiographic worship, specifically the reification of the saint's image and of objects associated with his figure.[6] Rice-González's play is simultaneously a tribute to Andy Gibb and a critique of his adoration, specifically of the ideologies and mechanisms that led to this adoration. The play is a nostalgic recuperation of his person (as an extremely handsome man) and of his work (as a key exponent of late 1970s pop music), highlighted in numerous ways, including through the very title of the play, in its dialogue, and through Roy and Sharon's particular fanlike behavior. Gibb's visual and sonic presence onstage, particularly through posters in Roy's room and through the musical score, also contributes to this tribute. Roy and Sharon's adoration is particularly noticeable as it entails memorizing and singing Gibbs's songs, collecting memorabilia such as signed photographs and a dancing doll, purchasing a T-shirt with his image, keeping a scrapbook, and attempting to go to his concert at an amusement park in New Jersey. Most notably, Roy will continuously affirm his attraction throughout the play, repeatedly saying, "I just love Andy Gibb" and enumerating Andy Gibb's appeal: "I just love Andy Gibb and I'd do anything to be his everything"; "I have my room and my posters and music . . . especially Andy Gibb. I could just listen to him forever"; "Even if you don't like his voice, which makes no sense to me, he's beautiful"; "I get to listen to Andy all day. When I listen to him I close my eyes and pretend he's singing to just me"; "But Andy's my favorite. He looks like an angel. He has the best eyes, a beautiful smile and his hair is so beautiful." Carlos relentlessly criticizes Roy for his fascination but at a certain moment acknowledges his complicity in this behavior ("As much as I hate to admit this . . . I used to think that Andy Gibb was hot"), and also says that he did not publicly articulate his desire to go to an Andy Gibb concert due to gender constraints and fear of censure: "'cause boys are not supposed to." This declaration posits Roy as more liberated and in some ways freer and happier than Carlos was at the same age.

Carlos's obsession with Pedro Ortega marks a significant part of the play, and Pedro's seductive ability is highlighted in diverse ways. Scene 2 begins with a speech directed to the audience, in which Carlos literally invites us to appreciate Pedro's beauty:

> CARLOS: (to the audience) Go ahead. Check him out. Go on, everybody does it. I'm used to it by now. (Carlos looks at Pedro) I used to stare at him. At his face. His hands. His neck. His feet, just trying to find a flaw, but he's just about perfect . . . like those golden boys in ads selling men's underwear. Some people might say, "I don't like his hair," or "He's too pale." But most agree he's beautiful. So, go on and look at him. (Roy gets up from the bed, circles Pedro and checks him out) My eyes have had the pleasure of seeing him almost every day for the last twenty years.

As scene 2 develops, Pedro actually appears naked, lying on his bed. Carlos complains about Pedro's unavailability (his unwillingness or lack of interest in dating or having sex with him) and states: "So, sleeping three feet away from me would be the most beautiful guy my eyes had ever seen." Carlos then remarks on how Pedro "loved being naked in our room reading or taking a nap, so it was torture."

The most dramatic exemplification of Pedro's attractiveness occurs immediately after this pronouncement, when Pedro stands up (still naked) and starts to get dressed. Carlos proceeds to articulate a fantasy desire, that of being as beautiful as Pedro, followed by a double or parallel monologue:

> CARLOS: It'd be so much easier if I were beautiful, like him. And I am not talking inner beauty, but the kind that draws attention when you step into a train car and everyone looks at you . . . repeatedly. The kind that causes strangers to send you anonymous notes. The kind where I don't have to make the first step in order to get to know someone when I go to a party. The kind that lies before me. I try to imagine what it would be like to be beautiful like Pedro. To be desired.
> PEDRO: (*begins to get dressed*) I am desired.
> CARLOS: To be wanted.
> PEDRO: I am wanted.
> CARLOS: To be caressed.
> PEDRO: I'm caressed.
> CARLOS: To be kissed.
> PEDRO: I am kissed.
> CARLOS: To be licked.
> PEDRO: I am licked.
> CARLOS: To be longed for.
> PEDRO: I am longed for.

In this scene, Carlos points out a structural problem or challenge: the social bias that exists in American society favoring certain individuals with particular appearances, especially young, attractive, white-looking ones such as Pedro (even if they are Latino), and that discriminates against those judged to be less attractive.[7] Carlos's unrequited attraction becomes entangled in longing and envy, and leads him to fantasize about an ideal world. Pedro, being the narcissist that he is, fully takes advantage of his good looks. It is not clear if Carlos's speculative exercise is particularly beneficial to his own sense of self-esteem, but it does generate an extremely sexy moment in the play.

Rice-González's incorporation of the white Puerto Rican Salsa boy disrupts the alienating patina of whiteness created around Andy Gibb and Pedro Ortega. *I Just Love Andy Gibb* is slightly less Manichean in its rejection of beautiful male whiteness than Marlon Riggs's film, where the handsome and kind white friend of the filmmaker is portrayed as a curse; this quite possibly has to do with Rice-González's acknowledgment of the racial heterogeneity of Puerto Ricans, a diversity that he does not want to negate or criticize. In a certain way, we could argue that the playwright is proposing a critical form of whiteness (more a type of brownness) that is consonant with Salvador Vidal-Ortiz's self-reflexive theorization about what it means to be a "white person of color": an individual who can be described as white but who is nevertheless racialized and marked as Other due to certain cultural or linguistic features or self-identifications.[8]

Roy and Carlos's shared admiration of the white Salsa boy gives them a common memory and allows them to envision a more positive, autochthonous or vernacular image for white male Puerto Ricans, particularly by emphasizing his similar class status and his redemptive, antiassimilationist cultural traits: loving salsa, the premier manifestation of Afro-diasporic Puerto Rican culture in New York in the 1970s.[9] As the script indicates:

ROY: There is this 16-year-old boy who lives across the hall . . . he's so beautiful. Almost like Andy . . .
CARLOS: Wow, he must be cute for you to compare him to Andy. Is he a white boy?
ROY: No, you've got this thing with white boys.
CARLOS: I've got—?
ROY: Relax . . . he's Puerto Rican. Oh he's cute, like you have no idea. But I am just 14 and he is like this older teenager and he is into different stuff like salsa music. He loves listening to this singer called Hector Lavoe.

As the conversation progresses, Carlos also remembers the salsa boy:

CARLOS: Wait! I remember that boy.
ROY: You do?
CARLOS: I didn't know him but I remember a young skinny guy with blondish tight curly hair listening to salsa music on a portable 8-track player. I thought he was a white boy, but there weren't many white people living in the projects, much less ones who listened to salsa. I can see him sitting in front of the building . . .
CARLOS AND ROY: (both recalling the image of the Salsa boy) . . . wearing Pro-Keds . . . and a light blue T-shirt and red bell-bottom pants.
CARLOS: He was cute.

This reinscription of salsa and of one of its leading exponents, the light-skinned Puerto Rican singer Héctor Lavoe (who died of AIDS complications in 1993), serves to "creolize" whiteness and locate the dominant mainstream Anglo pop music that marks the play (the music of Andy Gibb) in contiguity with Afro-diasporic Puerto Rican sounds. The mention of an eight-track player, a nowadays completely outdated technology of musical reproduction, serves as a nostalgic wink to audiences old enough to remember what this is.

While inaccessible, the Salsa boy is not a spiteful, assimilated character such as Pedro (who rejects Carlos, the Spanish language, and even the Bronx) or a mediated, commercial mass media figure like Andy Gibb. However, his idealization clearly demonstrates how complex and overwhelming the aesthetic privileging of whiteness is. The uncritical embrace of such figures, accompanied by a rejection of blackness, ultimately entails an internalization of hegemonic racism. How, then, do Puerto Rican black gay men overcome this situation? Rice-González proposes three strategies: talk therapy, dream therapy, and role model or icon substitution.

As I noted earlier, *I Just Love Andy Gibb* stages a therapeutic exchange based on conversations between Roy and Carlos. These conversations are clearly identified as the necessary step to reach a solution:

CARLOS: What do I have to do?
ROY: Talk.
CARLOS: We've been talking.
ROY: Not even. You've been asking a bunch of questions and insulting me and Andy.
CARLOS: That's talking. So we talk and then things go back to normal.
ROY: No! Things are never supposed to go back to normal. Normal is why we have met.
. . .
CARLOS: So you are here to give me some kind of help?
ROY: Don't know if I can help.

Here, the fourteen-year-old Roy is posited in the role of the therapist or psychoanalyst while Carlos becomes the patient or analysand. Roy goes on to ask a series of key questions and make key observations that allow Carlos to gain consciousness of his personal life. Roy's questions and observations focus mostly on Carlos's relationship with Pedro: "Are you in love?"; "Were you ever in love?"; "How can you talk about being so happy when you don't have love?"; "Why do you keep wanting something from him that he won't give you?"; and finally, "Wouldn't it be cool if you could love someone who wants to give you love right back?" Roy also sympathizes with Carlos's situation in recognizing that Pedro is, in fact, quite handsome: "I can see why you are so hooked on him. For an old guy, he is seeeexy. I have never seen anything . . . uhhhhh . . . I mean anyone like that! But it hurts you a lot that he doesn't love you back." In turn, Carlos's responses constitute key revelations to himself: "I have not really had a big great love"; "Sometimes people don't love you back in the way that you want them to"; and finally, "I realize that I have to look somewhere else to find love."

Once Carlos has achieved this moment of clarity, Roy is relieved from his responsibilities as therapist. To Roy's surprise, the roles are reversed, and now Carlos acts as Roy's therapist or psychoanalyst, posing questions and making observations that follow up on the numerous critiques of Andy Gibb that Carlos has made throughout the play. Carlos's consciousness-raising discourse includes commenting on the prevalence of white beauty ideals in mass media and the lack of appreciation for black and brown standards of beauty.[10] As the script indicates:

CARLOS: Everywhere we look we're shown how beautiful they are. Even in my time when there are Black and Latino people who are supermodels and leading actors and actresses. But they (and he points to Andy and the boys on the wall) are the ultimate.
ROY: What's wrong with that?
CARLOS: Nothing. Except if they're all we see then you and I don't see each other. How can we see our beauty unless we make a conscious effort to look from there (and he looks at the posters on the wall) to there (and he looks at Roy and pauses) . . . and you . . . you're beautiful. Your face . . . your skin . . .

This fascinating exchange incorporates didactic analysis as part of the therapeutic intervention, but also includes an exercise in praise that can be seen as an act of flirtation. Roy immediately denies that he is beautiful with the argument that "you don't see me in any pictures," to which Carlos responds:

CARLOS: That doesn't mean you're not beautiful. Let's take a look in the mirror?
ROY: You're not so bad looking yourself.
CARLOS: Gracias.
ROY: De nada. See I know a little Spanish.
CARLOS: Beautiful. Outside and in.

The conversation is clearly an act of flattery. Roy and Carlos complement their mutual physical admiration by affirming linguistic knowledge of Spanish (speaking Spanish to each other as a sign that they are beautiful "outside and in"), a gesture of cultural and ethnic affirmation as Puerto Ricans. This act of empowerment also potentially crosses the line of the therapeutic and pedagogical into that of the erotic.

A key moment in the play's talk therapy occurs through the linguistic disavowal of whiteness or more specifically of white people, signaled as "blanquitos" (using a disparaging Puerto Rican vernacular diminutive), and their substitution through the embrace and resignification of another vernacular diminutive, that of "negritos." The term "blanquito" comes up in reference to Pedro, who is also described as an "asshole," a fascinating term given that the play is about homosexual men and that Pedro is in fact the only avowedly sexually active character in the play:

> ROY: Pedro? Pedro's an asshole.
> CARLOS: (laughs) Yes. It would be easier for me to just go with the idea that Pedro is just an asshole than it would be to consider that—
> Andy Gibb's "Everlasting Love" plays in the background.
> ROY: You're dark skinned and Pedro's a blanquito.
> CARLOS: I thought that didn't matter, because Pedro's Latino, but I put up with the way he treated me just as long as he stayed with me.
> ROY: He's not with you.
> . . .
> CARLOS: Let's make a deal . . . Let's not buy into the world's negative view of us negritos.

This conversation serves to demythify overarching assumptions of Puerto Rican ethnic solidarity and signals possible intragroup racism or a differential in power based on race. Carlos's expectation that Pedro would like him because of their shared ancestry turns out to be incorrect. Likewise, Roy feels empowered to insult Pedro through lexical choice, using vernacular terms such as the Puerto Rican "blanquito" and the American "asshole." Blanquito, as the anthropologist Jorge Duany states, is a disparaging term used to mark class differences and, I would add, to disqualify white Puerto Ricans from belonging to the national community, what Benedict Anderson has termed the imagined nation.[11] The term "negrito" used by Carlos can also be a disparaging word for black people in Puerto Rico and at times serves as a means of infantilizing and belittling. Yet it is often used as a transracial term of endearment and has been reclaimed and promoted by Nuyorican poets such as Pedro Pietri and Sandra María Esteves.[12] The fact that Roy and Carlos's conversation is followed by Roy's laughter perhaps suggests that they are trying to defuse the charged tenor of these terms, even as they clearly favor the latter.

The "realist" representation of a series of therapeutic conversations that I have just outlined operates in parallel with the conceit that these are all part of a dream or fantasy scenario. While there are explicit declarations in the play that Roy and Carlos's interactions are not a dream (as Roy states, "It's not a dream"), these are belied by other moments in which Carlos tells Pedro about what happened: "I was having a wild dream . . . this dream about a 14-year-old kid who was in love with Andy Gibb." Pedro even confirms hearing the loud music: "What was it with that Andy Gibb music you were playing in the middle of the night? . . . I think the whole fucking building heard it. I banged on the wall and yelled at you to lower it."

As a counterpoint to daily, lived experience, Carlos's dreams can be seen as a form of restorative therapy—in other words, an unconscious nighttime sleep practice through which the mind seeks to heal a fractured subjectivity.[13] In the traditional Freudian model of psychoanalysis, the analysand narrates her dreams to the psychoanalyst, who helps in their interpretation, looking for hidden signs that link the dreams to family life and childhood trauma.[14] Rice-González's model differs in that the therapeutic activity occurs *within* the dream itself: the dream consists of a dialogue that is meant to generate self-awareness and does not seek to establish childhood family causality but rather to assess and revert adult behavior influenced by social norms, inequalities, and prejudices. Both models (Freud's and Rice-González's) see the working of the unconscious as a space to negotiate tensions and contradictions in individuals' lives. Rice-González dispenses with the professional therapist and substitutes him with an inner child that can be accessed by distancing oneself from the realm of consciousness. The model entails reciprocity (a hallmark of a Paulo Freire–inspired pedagogy of the oppressed in which learning and teaching are bidirectional), which is why Carlos also teaches Roy.[15]

The play's third strategy for the reversal of racist preconceptions is role model or icon substitution. As I have shown, I Just Love Andy Gibb highlights the attractiveness of certain representations of white masculinity, be they Anglo-American or Puerto Rican, and even celebrates some of these: the pleasure of being a fan of a heartthrob musician such as Andy Gibb; the physical beauty of a handsome man such as Pedro, who even appears naked onstage; and the cultural identification with the heterosexual white Puerto Rican Salsa boy. However, the play also illustrates the limitation of dwelling in this pleasure in terms of crafting a positive sense of self, and as such proposes a necessary distancing from those individuals and their substitution with black Puerto Rican models, particularly through a revalorization of Roy and Carlos's own beauty and the celebration of an alternative 1970s heartthrob, the Puerto Rican actor Erik Estrada, whose iconic image appears at the very end of the play in center stage illuminated by a spotlight.

How do Roy and Carlos go from being stigmatized, marginalized, emotionally vulnerable figures to become something closer to self-confident role models? Roy acknowledges Andy Gibb's death; Carlos gains the tools to take control of his affective life and hopefully move forward (we do not know that he will be successful at this endeavor but at least there is hope); and loving Erik Estrada is proposed as potentially more beneficial to one's sense of self than loving a white man, as it is a recognition that a dark-skinned Puerto Rican actor can be handsome and successful. Alas, this particular shift encourages displacement from a very androgynous, soft masculinity—that of Andy Gibb, a singer marked by his long hair and falsetto voice—to a much harder, working-class, macho one: that of Estrada, best known for portraying hot-headed Latino cops and truck drivers.

Perhaps one of the most interesting aspects of *I Just Love Andy Gibb* is its engagement with perversion: with the thin, shifting, blurry line between a completely innocent or fantastic notion of an adult's (Carlos's) dream dialogue with his inner child (Roy), and the very suggestive potential for a queer "misreading" of this exchange as an erotic intergenerational dynamic between a young adolescent and an adult man, particularly in the context of a therapeutic interaction in which it is quite common for the patient or client to feel affective or erotic attraction to the therapist or counselor (in other words, to cathect). The first sign of this occurs during a conversation between Roy and Carlos, when Carlos states, "Thanks Roy . . . now if you were about 25 years older . . ." Roy reacts with feigned disgust at this sexual innuendo and jokingly states his unequivocal preference for Andy Gibb, which leads Carlos to apologize. As the stage notes indicate, the exchange produces discomfort and leads Carlos to establish physical distance and to change the topic of the conversation:

> CARLOS: I'm joking. (*Feeling a little uncomfortable with their proximity, he stands and walks away from Roy*) So, what were you doing?

This dynamic changes later when Roy and Carlos admire each other and perform a mutual seduction through compliments, as I discussed previously. By the end, Roy begs Carlos not to leave him: "I don't want you to go, Carlos. I don't want to be alone . . . anymore." Carlos imagines what being teenage friends would have been like, and vows to look for Roy in his daily life.

I Just Love Andy Gibb mixes pedagogical impulses with erotic ones, as the implicit lesson ("You, as a Puerto Rican black gay man, are beautiful and attractive") is not one that can easily or simply be transmitted through the sphere of the rational. There are multiple reasons for this, perhaps principally because the basic formulation that "black is beautiful" runs counter to centuries of racist Western philosophical meditations on aesthetics and racist Puerto Rican discourses that favor white ideals, as well as to the modern-day practices of Hollywood, the mass media, and the advertising industry. In this play, the pedagogical concept of the erotic comes closer to that envisioned by Audre Lorde in her essay "Uses of the Erotic," which is to say as a pedagogy of social transformation predicated on love and not hatred, on inclusion and not racism, but also as an antipatriarchal, feminist gesture (perhaps this is the key reason why the episodes with Sharon are so central to the play). The erotic becomes "that joy which we know ourselves to be capable of," an all-encompassing happiness. It is also a source of liberation: "I find the erotic such a kernel within myself. When released from its intense and constrained pellet, it flows through and colors my life with a kind of energy that heightens and sensitizes and strengthens all my experience."[16]

Ultimately, I Just Love Andy Gibb proposes "seeing each other" and "looking for each other" as the solution: it will take black Latino queer men looking for one another to change the current regime of visibility and invisibility which only privileges certain kinds of representations and aesthetics. This position echoes and expands Marlon Riggs's initial assertion. Rice-González offers audiences a theatrical interruption of our quotidian activities and allows us to envision alternative, more progressive realities. The play is our collective dream therapy, a communal social experience that invites us to reflect upon the effects of racism on Puerto Rican black gay men in the darkness of the theater, as we accompany Roy and Carlos on their voyage of self-discovery and self-realization.

Notes

1 Rice-González's play won first prize in the Pregones Theater Asunción Playwrights Project in 2005 and received a workshop production at Pregones in 2007.

2 For numerous scholarly explorations of Puerto Rican black identity in the diaspora, see Miriam Jiménez Román and Juan Flores, eds., *The Afro-Latin@ Reader: History and Culture in the United States* (Durham, NC: Duke University Press, 2010).

3 On homoraciality, see Manolo Guzmán, *Gay Hegemony/Latino Homosexualities* (New York: Routledge, 2006).

4 *Trigueño*, literally, "wheat-colored," is an intermediate racial category in Puerto Rico, indicating the person is of mixed European and African ancestry.

5 On unrequited Latino gay love, see Daniel T. Contreras, *Unrequited Love and Gay Latino Culture: What Have You Done to My Heart?* (New York: Palgrave Macmillan, 2005).

6 See Lisa A. Lewis, ed., *The Adoring Audience: Fan Culture and Popular Media* (London: Routledge, 1992).

7 See Bonnie Berry, *Beauty Bias: Discrimination and Social Power* (Westport, CT: Praeger, 2007); Deborah L. Rhode, *The Beauty Bias: The Injustice of Appearance in Life and Law* (Oxford: Oxford University Press, 2010).

8 Salvador Vidal-Ortiz, "On Being a White Person of Color: Using Autoethnography to Understand Puerto Ricans' Racialization," *Qualitative Sociology* 27, no. 2 (2004): 179–203.

9 See Frances Aparicio, *Listening to Salsa: Gender, Latin Popular Music, and Puerto Rican Culture* (Hanover, NH: Wesleyan University Press; University Press of New England, 1998).

10 See Clara E. Rodríguez, ed., *Latin Looks: Images of Latinas and Latinos in the U.S. Media* (Boulder, CO: Westview Press, 1997); Charles Ramírez Berg, *Latino Images in Film: Stereotypes, Subversion, and Resistance* (Austin: University of Texas Press, 2002); Hiram Perez, *A Taste for Brown Bodies: Gay Modernity and Cosmopolitan Desire* (New York: New York University Press, 2015).

11 See Jorge Duany, "Blanquitos," *El Nuevo Día*, December 9, 2009; Benedict Anderson, *Imagined Communities: Reflections on the Origin and Spread of Nationalism* (London: Verso, 1983).

12 Pedro Pietri, *Puerto Rican Obituary* (New York: Monthly Review Press, 1973); Sandra María Esteves, "A la mujer borrinqueña," *Yerba Buena* (Greenfield Center, NY: Greenfield Review Press, 1980), 63.

13 On dreams, see David Schulman and Guy G. Stroumsa, "Introduction," in *Dream Cultures: Explorations in the Comparative History of Dreaming* (New York: Oxford University Press, 1999), 3–13.

14 Sigmund Freud, *The Interpretation of Dreams* (Oxford: Oxford University Press, 2008).

15 Paulo Freire, *Pedagogy of the Oppressed* (New York: Continuum, 1993).

16 Audre Lorde, "Uses of the Erotic: The Erotic as Power," in *Sister Outsider: Essays and Speeches* (Freedom, CA: Crossing Press, 1984), 57.

CHAPTER 18

Interview with Charles Rice-González

Ramón H. Rivera-Servera

Ramón H. Rivera-Servera: Your work purposefully holds multiple identities in tension. How do these tensions and intersections define you as an artist?

Charles Rice-González: I think it's poetic that we're sitting in the lobby of Pregones Theater in the Bronx where *I Just Love Andy Gibb* was developed and where it had its premiere. In terms of definitions, I start with Audre Lorde. One of the things I take from her is her being able to embrace all of her selves. You know, being for her, being black, being a lesbian, being a mother, being a poet. You know, being a feminist, being a warrior. She always wanted to be introduced with all of her selves because I feel a lot of times I feel compartmentalized. And so in a way the compartmentalization comes from the outside for me. I'm not Latino *or* black *or* gay *or* this *or* that. I am Latino *and* black *and* gay, and, and, and. So I think that's the position or the place that I come from. In creating art I try to speak from where I am at, both in terms of my location and my identity.

Physically, the Bronx is very much in a lot of my work. I don't know if I'll be doing that forever but at this point in my life that's my place and my perspective. And the Bronx, much like myself, is about all those *ands*: black and Latino and gay. *I Just Love Andy Gibb* is grounded in all of these *ands*. I think one of the most difficult things about it was actually trying to keep those things together; trying to keep the blackness, and the queerness, and the Latino-ness together. You either deal with the queer issue, like it's about the kid coming out and embracing his queerness, or you deal with his color, his race. How do you integrate these two issues? Because it is not just one issue in the kid's life, and in developing the play, I was at times told that I needed to focus on one issue because the audience has enough trouble dealing with one issue. I tried to produce a single-focus script but as I continued developing the piece I realized I could not separate one aspect of his identity from the others.

RRS: You are better known as a narrative fiction writer. Did the form of the play facilitate your engagement with the multiplicities of a black-tino queer character?

CRG: I feel like with a play I was able to bring a lot together in a bigger way. It was about dealing with a lot of these issues straight on and with the tension provided by the audience. One of the things I love about theater in particular is the relationship to the audience. In theater there are physical people sitting there experiencing art and as a group. It's not like a novel where it's really an individual experience. If you are a playwright and you have the opportunity to actually be in the room, it's amazing to see an audience experiencing it.

In terms of the arc of my work as a writer, I feel that this play is really one of the pieces that best brings together the issues that I hold dear: race, sexuality, identity. For Latinos, for black Latinos especially, and for queer people, I feel that whole idea of development, of possibilities, of examining ourselves in a way that we could move forward is not always readily assumed. And I think that's one of the things I tried to achieve with I Just Love Andy Gibb. I try to have these characters both feel very grounded in their lives, but then when they come together the questions get raised or their lives get questioned and then they get into these really uncomfortable places. And then, I try to offer a place they can move towards.

For the younger character it's really that there's a certain naivety that he is stuck in, because he is fourteen years old forever. And he feels like or he understands that he is a spirit and that his job is to help people. He is this special little kid that comes into the lives of others and he helps them move on. But he doesn't realize that he is stuck and that he actually needs help himself. And then the other guy is thinking, "I'm an adult, I've got my shit together and what is this little spirit thing in my life trying to tell me what to do?" But then he listens to him and sees a reflection of himself and feels, "Oh yeah, he is raising shit that I'm not even aware of."

In a sense they help each other. And then, I don't know if everybody gets this, but, in a sense, they fall in love. That's near the end when he's doing the "look for me, you know, I'm there." The kid has this realization that they do not exist in the world together, but because they were stuck, they can see each other. So then he'll look for him in the world. So when he disappears that's the last time they meet, but if we were going to do the next chapter or the next thing, you would see them or if in the movie or some other version of the story you would do an epilogue, you would see them walking on the street and you would see the little boy as an adult and these guys, having that experience and at least beginning a conversation about seeing each other as beautiful and desirable and then, you know, wondering what it would be like to be together.

RRS: It is great to hear you talk about that because it is a moment of tension Larry La Fountain-Stoke dealt with in writing his essay [included in this collection]. He is trying to get to the uncomfortable aspects of that love because it can seem to border on pedophilia. But I think you see those erotics in a different, longer time line. It seems to me that that realization is erotic but in a temporal horizon that is deferred, which can introduce trouble because desire happens nonetheless.

CRG: I got similar feedback when touring around with the piece. I heard from audiences, at Q&As, but I also conducted a little survey. I asked people, "Do you want to share something with me privately about the piece?" I did it to say that I am here in the lobby and here is another opportunity for conversation. And some people filled out the piece of paper and gave it to me. It was interesting. Some of the comments pointed to the ambiguity of the relationship between the boy and the man. I felt uncomfortable. But I was thinking, as you said, that there's a certain amount of intimacy that the two characters share and they become emotionally very close. Sometimes they understand the boundaries they can't cross and they don't cross them. But it's like it's there and it's tangible. And I think we need to understand that. We need to not negate that, that there it is, that it exists in a lot of levels. That we have to understand because of society and laws and all that, that there are certain lines that we can't cross, but not to negate that those feelings do exist. So that's one part of it and why I decided that I wanted to keep it. And then the other part was exactly what you said. For me it was like the seed of their love is being planted in this interaction. And then, yeah, I want to look for you; I want to see what you look like as an adult.

And then there is this other story. The "I'm so fixated on this guy I've been in love with forever who really doesn't love me, doesn't care for me, and I really can't see that because in a sense I'm blinded by the fact that he's not really treating me so well and maybe it has something to do with the color of our skins. And because he's Latino, I'm excusing him." But now he's able to say, "Oh, I could . . . I could finally say I love you and if you were different and treated me differently and loved me back, then maybe, but I have to start expanding my view so that I could see more, see Roy as an adult. What would it be like to have coffee with him and would this intimacy continue when we, you know, when we see each other as adults."

And for the kid, he has been fourteen forever. So he has been fourteen for decades. He has been in this state of arrested development and locked in his room, worshipping his idols. For him this character comes in here and shakes that up and questions the why of everything, of being stuck.

RRS: It seems like each time he has an exchange with another character there is a new kind of wonderment, a fourteen-year-old wonderment. And in this wonderment perhaps lies the possibility for change that you speak about?

CRG: It's just like in life. When things get questioned, you have an opportunity for change or growth. And that's the problem with religion: you're not supposed to question it because it is what it is. You don't question it because if you do, then you start saying, I don't know, maybe that doesn't sound right, that doesn't work. It's not really resonating. And then your faith gets questioned.

RRS: The relationship itself, the possibility of assuming it, animates a similar nervousness about questioning things as they are, about recognizing the potential risk. You do the same thing in terms of the racial erotics of the play. Why Andy Gibb? What about his difference, racial and national?

CRG: I was drawn to Andy Gibb because he possessed that magnetism. During that time period he was the quintessential teen sex idol: white, cute, blond. He was marketed in a hypersexualized way: low-cut shirts and supertight pants that showcased his bulge. And with his soft, feathery hair he was also feminine and he sang about love and desire. Both characters are in a sense "blinded" by his mainstream beauty. Roy, the young man, is in the time period, riding the wave of what is offered as the norm for male beauty. Carlos connects to Roy's obsession because he, too, was obsessed with Andy Gibb when he was a teen. As far as Andy Gibb being an outsider, that is true, and yet he doesn't look like an outsider, which is why he was so easily accepted into American pop culture. The two black Latino characters feel more like outsiders than Andy Gibb would. And besides, being Australian was hot with the popularity of his brothers, the Bee Gees, and Olivia Newton-John.

RRS: Blacktino and the tensions this term continues to evoke seem productive for your artistic practice. But you have also been a curator and organizer of a key festival of performance and arts organized around the term, because your work, including the play we are discussing, engages with black Puerto Rican and more broadly race relations. How do you see this term working as an organizing concept for your practice? What does it do for you? What trouble does it create?

CRG: When we are acknowledging the black Latino we are going to the base, the root of race relations in America and Latino America. When I make the distinction of Latino America I am including Latinos in the USA and all the Latin American countries and the Caribbean. Growing up I was frequently asked to make the distinction between being black or Latino. Several Latino, specifically Puerto Rican, friends would say to me, "You're not black, you're Puerto Rican," as if there was something bad about being black. Then my African American friends would say, "You are black, but not really. You are a Spanish black." In a sense, they were devaluing me as a black person, but in another way acknowledging the mix. So, for black Latinos and Latinas it is about asserting our identity, owning our blackness as a "matter-of-fact" aspect of our identity, about shedding shame that is placed upon us by Latino cultures and by American culture, too. We can be invisible visibles. It is also about embracing blackness and offering up a diverse experience of living life as black and Latino, which includes dealing with a sense of value when in my own culture, the Puerto Rican one, there is a spoken and unspoken rule that the lighter you are, the better you are, the more *lindo* or beautiful you are. That you are not a *negro bruto* [dumb black person] and even if I were *bruto* it has nothing to do with being *negro*.

I like to deal with this head on, as I do with the play *I Just Love Andy Gibb*, but also I like to deal with it matter-of-factly in that I write about Latino characters who are various shades of brown/black. I like to have dark Latinos cast in a variety of roles that may be nondescript in terms of their shade of blackness. I remember when we were casting for the reading and for the workshop production of *Andy Gibb* it was a wild feeling to be seeing dark Latinos. An actor who auditioned for the role shared that it was wild to feel wanted because he was a black Latino. Usually, in terms of casting, he finds it difficult to get roles, because when they are seeing Latinos they are usually looking for light-skinned actors.

As far as trouble goes, I think some of the usual obstacles, the racist ones, still exist, because Latino or not, we are still black and have to combat the racism that exists in terms of interest in our projects or in our perspectives. That is one of the reasons creating our own spaces and our own works is vital to keep an expansive view of the Latino experience vibrant.

RRS: We began talking some about theater and live performance as a medium and you brought up specifically the role of the audience. Who do you imagine as your ideal audience for this play? Who are you trying to reach? How are you hoping to touch this audience?

CRG: I would love to reach black Latinos. That is the primary target. For us to come together and experience the work and even debate it. I am always so uplifted when I see myself, or an experience of my life, onstage, in literature, and in the world. I remember feeling prouder after we elected a black president and recently when gay marriage passed in New York City. Even though I was active in the fight, my personal view of marriage is that it is problematic. But still, the day after that law passed I walked the streets a little taller and feeling more validated. So, I think whether it's in a book or movie or play or work of art, when black Latinos are presented the black Latinos in the audience have an opportunity to feel valued and validated in who they/we are.

With the play I wanted black Latinos to include ourselves in the pantheon of beauty. Those ideas *que somos feos* or brutos or less than get ingrained into how we see ourselves. We internalize those ideas despite the fact that we know them not to be true and are all "grown up" and have had the chance to get educated and had our consciousness raised around race and other issues. Still elements of that backwards and false thinking remain within us. I wanted to challenge those ideas from a "naive" perspective of a child or young teen, a time when our identity, who we are, is front and center, but also from an adult who thinks he has worked through all of that. I specifically wanted Latinos to look at this issue. For us to not only look at the racism or the "prizing the white skin or lighter skin" from the perspective of *blancos* [whites] in America, but also from within our own cultures and how the "white is prized" by Latinos. Then I bring in the question of desire and how race, specifically blackness, may play a role in what we desire and how or whether we are desired. *Then* you add the queer perspective and the forest has grown so thick that we need an extra sharp machete to carve our paths.

I hope black Latinos come out of the play with a sense of value in who they are and also with the idea that the issue of being a black Latino or blacktino is not a done deal and it is something that we need to assert, embrace, and love every day. For everyone else, I hope they can see their role in perpetuating racist ideas.

RRS: I would love to hear you speak a bit more about the parallelisms between the young fourteen-year-old and his visitor. Can you say more about the at times ambivalent sense of them being one and the same person but also being representative of collective experiences for Latinos more broadly? I am interested here in the slippage between the particularities of the single encounter you stage in the piece and the broader implications of your work.

CRG: Exactly! In many ways they are the same person the same way that I was very similar to them and that there were other gay, black, Latino kids growing up in the Bronx or around the city in the 1970s who could similarly identify. Not that all of our experiences are the same—each person has their own particular circumstances, but there is also a universal experience that is shared by a group of people who are alive at a particular time and live in a particular region. It is a flashback for Carlos and a flash forward for Roy. Sticking to the locale of the play, there is a shared experience with Roy as a gay, black Latino kid growing up in the projects of the Bronx and Carlos who was the same age at that time. They both know and love/loved Andy Gibb and other pop stars. When Roy uses language like, "You are a snap," it is like an echo from the past for Carlos.

So what I was doing was several things. I showed that Carlos came from the same place, literally. I wanted to argue that our past can sometimes serve as a mirror to our future and by that I mean that the Carlos character thought he had a good handle on the issue of race in his life but was filtering it through a black-white paradigm and not acknowledging the connection to his own *latinidad*. Seeing Roy blinded by whiteness helps Carlos see how he was being similarly blind to his lighter-skinned Latino obsession. Lastly, by aligning them so closely I set up a conversation amongst the negritos, us talking to one another from a common place and experience. I know the conversation would have been different if Carlos was light skinned. They are connected by their color and the experiences of being black, Latino, and gay.

I also do this "seeing" thing. Toward the beginning of the play, Roy asks a confused and dumbfounded Carlos, "Can't you see me?" I was playing with the fact that Roy was there in the room and Carlos was so freaked out about waking up in the room that he in a sense didn't see or didn't want to see Roy. Then the dialogue at the end of the play returns to this dynamic of seeing:

CARLOS: I can see you, Roy.
ROY: I can see you!
They reach out to each other.
ROY: I will see you, Carlos.
CARLOS: I'll look for you, Roy.

With this ending, the characters have come together, acknowledged one another's beauty, and are prepared to see one another in their contemporary time, Carlos's present. And my hope is that when they meet, when they can see one another, they will continue their connection. They have in a sense already fallen in love throughout the play.

RRS: How do you see the intersection between black Latinos and African Americans figuring into the imagination of race in this play? Is there an intentional distancing from that dynamic in order to isolate a Latino issue from the inside or are there ways we might think of that historic and important intimacy and friction, especially in places of proximity like the Bronx?

CRG: There was most certainly a distancing. I think that pull in my life between African Americans and Latinos in general caused me to focus on the Latinos. Partly because we know how racist Latinos can be even to the point to prefer to deny my skin's blackness and group me with Latinos and separate me from African Americans. *Tu eres negrito pero no eres negro* [You are a little bit black but not black]. But their encounters with oppression are similar.

It can get confusing or disorienting, just like Carlos in the play. He just thought his roommate was being a jerk. Yes, and his roommate was being racist, too. But in a sense, he was buying into the "somos latinos" idea that we are all the same. We're not. Just imagine if the roommate was white? That would have been too easy, too obvious. I think the race issue amongst Latinos is a dialogue that needs to continue happening and go beyond *¿y tú abuela, adonde está?* Then we add the queer element and we shake up the discussion even more.

Contributors

Jossianna Arroyo is Professor of Latin American and Caribbean Literatures and Cultures in the Department of Spanish and Portuguese and the Warfield Center for African and African American Studies at the University of Texas at Austin. She is author of *Travestismos culturales: Literatura y etnografía en Cuba y Brasil* and *Writing Secrecy in Caribbean Freemasonry*.

Marlon M. Bailey is Associate Professor of Women's and Gender Studies in the School of Social Transformation at Arizona State University. He is author of *Butch Queen Up in Pumps: Gender, Performance, and Ballroom Culture in Detroit*.

Pamela Booker (www.pamelabooker.com) is an interdisciplinary writer/artist/educator and urban growing and sustainability enthusiast. Her literary, performance, and visual works have been published, staged, and exhibited in the United States and internationally in Malaysia, Singapore, England, France, and Germany. She is the recipient of several writing fellowships from Provincetown Fine Arts Work Center, the Norman Mailer Writers Colony, and VCCA (Virginia Center for the Creative Arts), among other places. An excerpt from her forthcoming novel, *Fierce! Remains*, which explores the early years of the AIDS crises through the fictional biography of a legendary drag queen, is featured in the collection *Black Gay Genius: Answering Joseph Beam's Call*. Pamela is also pleased to serve as community board member for the Open Meadows Foundation.

Sharon Bridgforth is a resident playwright at New Dramatists. Bridgforth is the spring 2014 Playwright in Residence in the University of Iowa's Playwrights Program. She is a recipient of the MAP Fund Award and the National Performance Network Creation Fund Award. She is author of *love conjure/blues* and the Lambda Literary Award–winning *the bull-jean stories*.

Jennifer DeVere Brody is Professor in the Department of Theater and Performance Studies at Stanford University. She is author of *Impossible Purities:*

Blackness, Femininity, and Victorian Culture and *Punctuation: Art, Politics and Play.*

Cedric Brown is a community investor and artist. For the past twenty years, his varied creative work has been shown in numerous venues in the San Francisco Bay Area. Cedric is the author of *Eyes of Water and Stone: From Havana with Love* and *Tar Heel Born: A Native Son Speaks on Race, Religion, and Reconciliation*; his shorter pieces have appeared in several anthologies and collections. Cedric lives in Oakland, California, with his spouse. His online archives are Oaktownbrown.com.

Bernadette Marie Calafell is Professor in the Department of Communication Studies at the University of Denver. She is author of *Latina/o Communication Studies: Theorizing Performance, Monstrosity, Performance, and Race in Contemporary Culture* and coeditor of *Latina/o Discourse in Vernacular Spaces: Somos de Una Voz?*

Javier Cardona is a performance artist and educator originally from Puerto Rico. He began his dance, theater, and arts in education career with *Los Teatreros Ambulantes de Cayey*, directed by Rosa Luisa Márquez and the visual artist Antonio Martorell. He has studied and worked with contemporary theater and dance masters such as Peter Schumann of the Bread and Puppet Theater, Osvaldo Dragún of the Escuela Internacional de Teatro de América Latina y el Caribe, Augusto Boal of the Theater of the Oppressed, Miguel Rubio of Yuyachkani, Viveca Vázquez of Taller de Otra Cosa, and Sally Silvers and Jennifer Monson of Bird Brain.

E. Patrick Johnson is Carlos Montezuma Professor of Performance Studies and African American Studies at Northwestern University. He is author of *Appropriating Blackness: Performance and the Politics of Authenticity* and *Sweet Tea: Black Gay Men of the South—An Oral History*. He is editor of *Cultural Struggles: Performance, Ethnography, Praxis* by Dwight Conquergood and coeditor of *Black Queer Studies: A Critical Anthology* (with Mae Henderson) and *solo/black/woman: scripts, interviews, and essays* (with Ramón H. Rivera-Servera).

Omi Osun Joni L. Jones is Professor of African and African American Studies at the University of Texas at Austin. She is author of *Theatrical Jazz: Performance, Ase, and the Power of the Present Movement* and coeditor of *Experiments in the Jazz Aesthetic: Art, Activists, Academia, and the Austin Project* (with Lisa L. Moore and Sharon Bridgforth).

John Keene is Associate Professor of African American and African Studies and English, and a core faculty member in the MFA in Creative Writing Program, at Rutgers University–Newark. He has published his poetry, fiction, nonfiction, criticism, and translations widely and is the author or coauthor of three books: *Annotations* (1995), *Seismosis* (with artist Christopher Stackhouse, 2006), and *Counternarratives* (2015). His translation of Brazilian writer Hilda Hilst's novel *Letters from a Seducer* appeared in 2014. He has exhibited his conceptual projects in Brooklyn and Berlin and blogs at jstheater .blogspot.com.

Lawrence La Fountain-Stokes is Associate Professor and Director of Latina/o Studies at the University of Michigan. He is author of *Queer Ricans: Cultures and Sexualities in the Diaspora*, *Abolición del pato*, and *Uñas pintadas de azul/Blue Fingernails*.

D. Soyini Madison is Professor of Performance Studies, Anthropology, and African Studies at Northwestern University. She is author of *Acts of Activism: Human Rights as Radical Performance* and *Critical Ethnography: Methods, Ethics, and Performance*. She is editor of *The Woman That I Am: The Literature and Culture of Contemporary Women of Color* and coeditor of *The Sage Handbook of Performance Studies* (with Judith Hamera) and *African Dress: Fashion, Agency, Performance* (with Karen Tranberg Hansen).

Jeffrey Q. McCune Jr. is Associate Professor of Performing Arts and Women, Gender, and Sexuality Studies at Washington University. He is author of *Sexual Discretion: Black Masculinity and the Politics of Passing*.

Andreea Micu is a doctoral candidate in the Department of Performance Studies at Northwestern University. Her research attends to indignation as a performance strategy and political affect during the current economic crisis in Europe.

Charles I. Nero is Professor of Rhetoric and American Studies at Bates College. He has published widely in the areas of race, gender, and sexuality.

Tavia Nyong'o is Associate Professor of Performance Studies at New York University. He is author of *The Amalgamation Waltz: Race, Performance, and the Ruses of Memory* and coeditor of the journal *Social Text*.

Paul Outlaw, born in New York City in Bellevue Hospital and raised on Avenue D in the Jacob Riis Projects, is a Los Angeles–based experimental theater artist and vocalist whose award-winning solo projects have been presented across the United States and in Europe. His work's recurring themes are race, sexual identity, violence, and American history. Paul was the recipient of one of the 2012 COLA (City of Los Angeles) Individual Artist Fellowships.

Coya Paz is Assistant Professor of Theater at DePaul University in Chicago. A cofounding artistic director of Teatro Luna, she is currently Artistic Director of Free Street Theater, a politically engaged youth theater company founded in 1969.

Charles Rice-González, born in Puerto Rico and reared in the Bronx, is a writer, longtime community and LGBT activist, and cofounder and Executive Director of BAAD! (The Bronx Academy of Arts and Dance). He is also Distinguished Lecturer at Hostos Community College—CUNY. His debut novel, *Chulito*, has received awards and recognitions from the American Library Association (ALA) and the National Book Critics Circle. He coedited *From Macho to Mariposa: New Gay Latino Fiction* (with Charlie Vázquez). He is also an award-winning playwright and serves on the boards of the Bronx Council on the Arts and the National Association of Latino Art and Cultures.

Sandra L. Richards is Professor in Residence and Director of the Liberal Arts program at Northwestern University in Qatar and Professor of African American Studies, Theater, and Performance Studies at Northwestern University. She is author of *Ancient Songs Set Ablaze: The Theatre of Femi Osofisan*.

Matt Richardson is Associate Professor of African and African American Studies at the University of Texas at Austin. He is author of *The Queer Limit of Black Memory: Black Lesbian Literature and Irresolution*.

Ramón H. Rivera-Servera is Associate Professor and Chair in the Department of Performance Studies at Northwestern University. He is author of *Performing Queer Latinidad: Dance, Sexuality, Politics* and coeditor of *Performance in the Borderlands* (with Harvey Young), *solo/black/woman: scripts, interviews, and essays* (with E. Patrick Johnson), and *The Goodman's Theatre Festival Latino: Six Plays* (with Henry Godinez).

Celiany Rivera-Velázquez holds a doctorate from the Institute of Communications Research at the University of Illinois at Urbana-Champaign. Originally from Puerto Rico, she has explored a broad range of LGBT/queer aesthetics and politics across the Spanish-speaking Caribbean and the United States.

Tamara Roberts is Assistant Professor of Music at the University of California at Berkeley, where she teaches courses on popular and folk music of the Americas. She is author of *Resounding Afro Asia: Interracial Music and the Performance of Collaboration* and coeditor of *Yellow Power, Yellow Soul: The Radical Art of Fred Ho* (with Roger Buckley). Tamara has worked nationally and internationally as a composer, sound designer, and performer in theater, dance, and film.

Teatro Luna was founded in June 2000 by Coya Paz and Tanya Saracho, with an original ensemble of ten women from diverse Latina/Hispana backgrounds. It is and continues to be Chicago's first and only all-Latina theater, with over a dozen ensemble-developed pieces.

Lisa B. Thompson is Associate Professor of African and African Diaspora Studies at the University of Texas at Austin. She is author of *Beyond the Black Lady: Sexuality and the New African American Middle Class.*

Beliza Torres Narváez is Assistant Professor of Theater at Augsburg College in Minneapolis, Minnesota. She is also a member of the Teatro Camagua theater group.

Patricia Ybarra is Associate Professor and Chair in the Department of Theatre Arts and Performance Studies at Brown University. She is author of *Performing Conquest: Theatre, History and Identity in Tlaxcala, Mexico* and coeditor of *Neoliberalism and Global Theatres* (with Lara D. Nielsen).

Vershawn Ashanti Young is Associate Professor in the Department of Communication, Performance, and Design at the University of Waterloo, Ontario, Canada. His recent publications include *Other People's English: Code-Meshing, Code-Switching, and African American Literacy* (2014); *From Uncle Tom's Cabin to The Help: Critical Perspectives on White-Authored Narratives of Black Life* (2014); and *The Routledge Reader of African American Rhetoric: The Longue Duree of Black Voices* (2015). In his new book project, *Straight Black Queer: Gender Anxiety and the American Dream,* he uses queer theory to examine such figures as Barack Obama, August Wilson, Dave Chappelle, and Tyler Perry.

Index